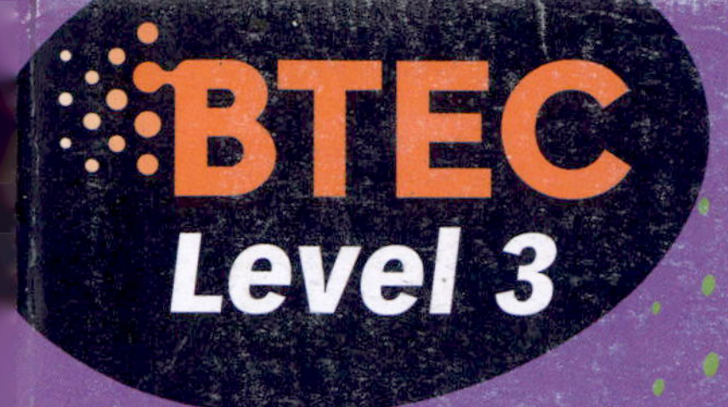

TRAVEL & TOURISM LEVEL 3

Book 1 BTEC National

Gillian Dale

A PEARSON COMPANY

Published by Pearson Education Limited, a company incorporated in England and Wales, having its registered office at Edinburgh Gate, Harlow, Essex, CM20 2JE. Registered company number: 872828

www.pearsonschoolsandfecolleges.co.uk

Edexcel is a registered trademark of Edexcel Limited

First published 2010

14
10 9 8 7 6

British Library Cataloguing in Publication Data
A catalogue record for this book is available from the British Library.

ISBN 978 1 846907 27 2

Typeset by HL Studios
Original illustrations © Pearson Education Limited 2010
Illustrated by HL Studios, Long Hanborough, Oxford
Cover design by Visual Philosophy, created by eMC Design
Cover photo © 2010 Masterfile
Back cover photos © Natasha Bratslavsky/Shutterstock; Paul Clarke/Shutterstock; Jules Selmes/Pearson Education Ltd.
Printed in Malaysia (CTP-PPSB)

Acknowledgements
Every effort has been made to contact copyright holders of material reproduced in this book. Any omissions will be rectified in subsequent printings if notice is given to the publishers.

Websites and Hotlinks
The websites used in this book were correct and up to date at the time of publication. It is essential for tutors to preview each website before using it in class so as to ensure that the URL is still accurate, relevant and appropriate. We suggest that tutors bookmark useful websites and consider enabling students to access them through the school/college intranet.

Acknowledgments

This book is for Elizabeth and Nick for their love, enthusiasm and support.

Gillian Dale would like to thank the following:

For sharing their work stories
Bruce Martin at Online Travel Training
Doug Garrett at ReBlackpool
Jo Quincey at Flight centre
Ed – an anonymous analyst
Elizabeth Dale at Siblu
Nick Dale – for his multiple experiences

For Customer Service expertise for Unit 4
Helen Oliver

For help with cashflow activities in Unit 2
Chris Fidler

For contributing job descriptions and recruitment processes for Unit 6
Simon Allen and Lindsey Brunton from Canvas Holidays

For efficient and speedy editing
Sarah Ware

And of course the team at Pearson Education Ltd especially
Elizabeth Kingston, Kate Davy and Jilly Hunt

About the author

Gillian Dale has many years experience teaching travel and tourism and running BTEC programmes. She has written several travel and tourism text books for various courses as well as units and materials for various qualifications.

She is a member of the Air Transport User's Council, an organisation which represents airline passengers' interests. She also works as an additional inspector for Ofsted and as an educational consultant and coach. Her main focus is curriculum design and programme development and her recent projects include developing courses in customer service for front line personnel who will encounter Olympic visitors, coaching programmes and e -learning seminars in project implementation and writing project proposals.

She has a Masters degree, PGCE, assessor awards and has held a fellowship at Cambridge University.

Photo credits

The author and publisher would like to thank the following individuals and organisations for permission to reproduce photographs:
Unit 1 p.**1** Jeremy Reddington/Shutterstock; p.**3** Pearson Education Ltd. Jules Selmes; p.**6** Chris Laurens/Alamy; p.**18** Pearson Education Ltd. Naki Kouyioumtzis; p.**20** Jeremy Reddington/Shutterstock; p**.29** Yuri Arcurs /Shutterstock; **Unit 2** p.**31** Shutterstock / Paul Banton; p.**33** Pearson Education Ltd. Jules Selmes; p.**35** City of Derry Council; p.**55** Rena Schild/Shutterstock; **Unit 3** p.**57** Andreas Kraze/Shutterstock; p.59 Pearson Education Ltd. Jules Selmes; p.**76** Andreas Kraze/Shutterstock; p.**77** Qing Ding/Shutterstock; p.**79** Paul Brennan/Shutterstock; p.**80** Pearson Education Ltd. Naki Kouyioumtzis; p.87 Shutterstock / Len Green; p.**89** ImageryMajestic/Shutterstock; **Unit 4** p.**91** Pearson Education Ltd / Jules Selmes; p.**93** Shutterstock/Flashon Studio; p.**107** Shutterstock; p.**107** Strakovskaya/shutterstock; p.**107** Shutterstock/Four Oaks; p.**107** Shutterstock/De Visu; p.**117** Gillian Dale, author supplied; **Unit 5** p.**119** Lonely Planet Images / David Wall; p. **121** michaeljung/Shutterstock; p.**133** Alamy; p.**136** Jeff Morgan tourism and leisure/Alamy; p.**147** Yuri Arcurs/Shutterstock; **Unit 6** p.**149** Alamy / PCL; p.**151** Pearson Education Ltd. MindStudio; p.**179** ©Online Travel Training; **Unit 7** p.**181** paradoks_blizanaca/ShutterStock; p.**183** Suzanne Tucker /Shutterstock; p.**187** Nikos Economopoulos / Magnum; p.**197** Photononstop/Christian Arnal/Photolibrary.com; p.**200** Sailorr/Shutterstock; p.**205** paradoks_blizanaca/ShutterStock; p.**209** Valua Vitaly/Shutterstock; **Unit 8** p.**211** Natalia Bratslavsky/ShutterStock; p.**213** Pearson Education Ltd. Jules Selmes; p.**217** Natalia Bratslavsky/ShutterStock; p.**222** Cut2White; p.**223** Pichugin Dmitry/Shutterstock; p.**232** DUSAN ZIDAR/Shutterstock; p.**241** Yuri Arcurs/Shutterstock; **Unit 9** p. **243** Alamy / Jack Sullivan; p.**245** Shutterstock/lev dolgachov; p. **251** Cindy Miller Hopkins / Danita Delimont, Agent/Alamy; p.**254** Debra James/Shutterstock; p.**259** © Joanna Quincey; **Unit 10** p.**261** leungchopan/Shutterstock; p.**263** Pearson Education Ltd. Jules Selmes; p.**265** northwestfocus / Alamy; p.**275** Sean Prior/Shutterstock; **Unit 12** p.**277** Liem Bahneman/Shutterstock; p.**279** michaeljung/Shutterstock; p.**284** imagebroker.net/Jochen Tack/PhotoLibrary.com; p.**285** Paul Clarke/Shutterstock; p.**288** Liem Bahneman/Shutterstock; p.**295** Robert Harding Travel/Christian Kober/Photolibrary.com; p.**299** age fotostock/Nacho Moro/Photolibrary.com; p.**305** ReBlackpool; **Unit 22** p.**307** Getty Images / PhotoDisc; p.**309** eyedear /Shutterstock; p.**312** Marcin Balcerzak/Shutterstock; p.**321** Monkey Business Images/ShutterStock; **Unit 23** p.**323** Mario Savoia/Shutterstock; p.**325** Photos.com; p.**327** Mario Savoia/Shutterstock; p**.329** Santiago Bara Juncal/Shutterstock; p.**339** Pearson Education Ltd. MindStudio

Acknowledgements

We are grateful to the following for permission to reproduce copyright material:

ABTA – The Travel Association for 'definition of retail travel business' and company details about ABTA, reproduced with permission; Office for National Statistics for data about 'jobs in tourism in the UK', Figure 3.3 "Top 20 UK towns visited", Figure 3.4 "Who visits Britain – Visits to the UK", *Travel Trends 2008*; and Figure 7.2 "UK residents' visits abroad by mode: 1980 to 2007, United Kingdom" from *Transport Trends 2008*, www.statistics.gov.uk © Crown copyright 2009. Crown Copyright material is reproduced with permission of the controller of the HMSO; Harvard Business School Publishing for an excerpt from figure "Consumer Segments Changing Behavior" from "How to Market in a Downturn" by John A. Quelch and Katherine E. Jocz in *Harvard Business Review* April 2009 http://hbr.org/2009/04/how-to-market-in-a-downturn/ar/1 copyright © Harvard Business School Publishing; VisitEngland for Figure 1.6 "Factors contributing to tourism trends in Britain, May 2010" from *Trends Update*, Issue 129, 13 May 2010, http://www.visitbritain.org/insightsandstatistics/publications/trendsupdate/tu129.aspx; "France market snapshot", from *France Market & Trade Profile*, p.2, November 2009, http://www.visitbritain.org/Images/France%202009_tcm139-167266.pdf; Figure 3.6 "8 segments in the Arkleisure model" from *Market Segmentation* p.2, 2004 http://www.enjoyengland.com/Images/Market%20Segementation%202005_tcm21-172137.pdf; Table 3.2 "Case Study Marketing England" adapted from *Enjoy England: International and Domestic market profiles* www.enjoyengland.com; Table 3.2 "Purpose of domestic trips in the UK", p.5 *UK Tourist 2008*, http://www.visitbritain.org/Images/TheUKTourist2008_tcm139-168477.pdf; Figure 3.7 "Almost 2/3 go for a "day-out" at least 3-4 times a year –and almost as many visit a specific tourist / visitor attraction" from *England Fact Book Key Statistics about English Tourism* p.48 http://www.enjoyengland.com/Images/Factbook_tcm21-170495.pdf; Extract from "International and domestic market profiles, 2007", http://www.enjoyengland.com/Images/England%20Domestic%20and%20International%20Market%20Profiles_tcm21-172146.pdf; Table 3.3 "Sources of Information when choosing a holiday destination in England from International and domestic market profiles, 2007" http://www.enjoyengland.com/Images/England%20Domestic%20and%20International%20Market%20Profiles_tcm21-172146.pdf; Case Study "Enjoy England quality rose" www.enjoyengland.com; Extracts from www.visitbritain.org; and Table 3.4 "Tourism trips taken in the UK 2007/08" from *The UK Tourist* from *The United Kingdom Tourism Survey 2008*, VisitBritain, copyright © VisitEngland; Holidaybreak plc for extracts from Holidaybreak plc Annual Report and Financial Statements 2008, Corporate factsheet 2009 copyright © Holidaybreak plc; Northwest Regional Development Agency for material in 'Case Study: Grants for tourism' from NWDA – The Northwest Regional Development Agency, press release 8 April 2009, reproduced with permission of NWDA www.nwtourism.net; Heritage Lottery Fund the 'Heritage Lottery Fund aims' www.lotteryfunding.org.uk/uk/heritage-lottery-fund, copyright © Heritage Lottery Fund. Using money raised through the National Lottery, the Heritage Lottery Fund sustains and transforms a wide range of heritage for present and future generations to take part in, learn from and enjoy. From museums, parks and historic places to archaeology, natural environment and cultural traditions, it invests in every part of our diverse heritage. www.hlf.org.uk; The British Association of Leisure Parks for BALPPA's aims, copyright © The British Association of Leisure Parks, Piers and Attractions; Grand Central Railway Company Ltd for material in 'Case Study Grand Central' copyright © Grand Central Railway Company Ltd www.grandcentralrail.com; International Travel Connections Ltd for the advert 'Christmas Getaway', ITC Classics, as published in *The Times*, 18th October 2009, copyright © International Travel Connections Ltd; Eurotunnel for 'More than Ever' poster from 'Eurotunnel on Track' Letter to Groupe Eurotunnel SA Shareholders, February 2009 www.eurotunnel.com, copyright © Eurotunnel; LEGO UK for details about Lego from www.lego.com, reproduced with permission; YHA (England & Wales) Ltd for details about YHA from www.yha.org.uk, reproduced with permission; Civil Aviation Authority for Table 3.1 "Top ten UK airports by passenger numbers, 2009" from Civil Aviation Authority - UK Airport Statistics, copyright © Civil Aviation Authority; Regional Tourist Board Partnership Limited for details about Welcome to Excellence, Tourism South East reproduced with permission on behalf of Regional Tourist Board Partnerships; Transport Direct, Department for Transport for text and Figure 3.8 "Journey(s) found for London Gatwick Airport to Manchester Piccadilly Rail Station" www.transportdirect.info/ copyright © Transport Direct, Department for Transport; VisitScotland for an extract from VisitScotland Press release, published in "Survey reveals that dolphin watching is top Scottish holiday" by Alison Chiesa, 28 July 2008, *Herald Scotland*, copyright © VisitScotland; Travelmole for extracts from "Ferry firms promote value with new ads" by Phil Davies, www.travelmole.com, 16 March, 2009; "What is the most popular UK attraction for overseas visitors?" by Bev Fearis, www.travelmole.com, 2 September, 2009; "APD hikes create discontent amongst public and airlines" by Dinah Hatch, http://www.travelmole.com/stories/1139124.php, 30th Oct 2009; and "Rain and cash caution prompt last-minute bookings" by Dinah Hatch, 15 July, 2009 www.travelmole.com/printable.php?news_id=1130028 copyright © Travelmole; British Waterways for extract in 'Case Study: Bow Back Rivers' from British Waterways, http://www.britishwaterways.co.uk/olympics/three-mills-lock/faqs, reproduced with permission; Visit York for details in "Case Study: The appeal of York", reproduced with permission; Metropolitan Police Authority for advice for tourists from http://www.met.police.uk copyright © Metropolitan Police Authority; Welsh Assembly Government for details about VisitWales in 'Case Study: Marketing Campaigns' and 'Case Study: sustainable tourism development in Wales' http://new.wales.gov.uk/topics/tourism/. Reproduced by kind permission of Visit Wales, the Tourism Arm of the Welsh Assembly Government – Crown Copyright © 2009; UNWTO for Table 3.5 "International Tourism Receipts" 2007 and 2008 from *Tourism Highlights 2009* UNWTO http://www.unwto.org/index.php; copyright © UNWTO, 9284400910; TUI Travel plc for material from 'Case Study Thomson's moneyback guarantee' www.agent-travel.co.uk/thomson.php; details about Menorca from http://www.thomson.co.uk/destinations/europe/spain/menorca/guide-to-menorca.html; Extract from http://flights.thomson.co.uk/en/flywithus_premium_service.html; and The First Choice 'Greener Holidays' brochure cover, reproduced with permission of TUI Group 2009; Virgin Atlantic Airways for details in 'Case Study Virgin' from http://www.virgin.com/travel/inside-virgin-travel/business-class, and an extract about Training Cabin Crew in Customer Service at Virgin from *Virgin Service Training Manual*, copyright Virgin Atlantic Airways; Chartered Institute of Marketing for their 'Definition of marketing' copyright © The Chartered Institute of Marketing. www.cim.co.uk; Advertising Standards Authority for the general principles from The British Code of Advertising, Sales Promotion and Direct Marketing, http://www.cap.org.uk/The-Codes.aspx copyright © Advertising Standards Authority; Canvas Holidays for extracts and Figures 6.3, 6.4 about Canvas Holidays www.canvasholidays.co.uk, reproduced with permission; Concord Hotels for material within 'Case Study: Concord Hotel Management Trainee Scheme', from http://www.concord-hotels.org.uk/management_scheme.php, reproduced with permission; ACI Europe for Table 7.2 "Top 30 ACI airports" from '2009 ACI-Europe Airport Traffic Statistics, Passengers' copyright © ACI Europe 2009; Mintel for Table 7.3 "Types of holiday to France taken, 2007 and 2008", figure 39 from 'Holidays to France - UK - February 2009' copyright © Mintel; Eurostar Group for details in 'Case Study Eurostar train services' and Figure 7.3 'Eurostar destinations and connecting rail routes' www.eurostar.com, copyright © Eurostar; Blue Water Holidays for the table 'Example of a Danube River Cruise' from www.cruisingholidays.co.uk, copyright © Blue Water Holidays; Canadian Association of Geographers for Figure 7.4 'The concept of a tourist area cycle of Evolution: Implications for Management of resources', by Butler, R.W., *Canadian Geographer*, Vol. 24(1), 1980, pp.5–12, John Wiley and Sons, copyright © 2008, 1980 Canadian Association of Geographers; Greek Island Postcards for details in the "Faliraki Case Study", www.greekisland.co.uk, copyright © Greek Island Postcards; UNWTO for Figure 8.1 "World Inbound Tourism" from *International Arrivals 2008* copyright © UNWTO, 9284400410; Kuoni Travel Ltd for Table 8.1 'Kuoni's top 20 destinations for 2009' from http://www.visitbritain.org/Images/Trends%20Update%20112_tcm139-173681.pdf; 'Reethi Beach Resort' from *Kuoni Worldwide, 2nd ed* Jan 2010 – Mar 2011, p.39; material in 'Case Study: 'Explorism is the new tourism' from http://www.kuoni.co.uk/information/news/long_haul_report_2009.html; and extract from *Kuoni Worldwide*, Sept 2009 – Dec 2010, p.121; copyright © 2009 Kuoni Brochures and Longhaul Report, Kuoni Travel Ltd; Wayfarers World Travel for an extract about Long-haul holiday destination from www.justtheflight.co.uk, reproduced with permission; Her Majesty's Stationery Office and the UK Hydrographic Office for Figure 8.8 'Time zone maps' HM Nautical Almanac Office, Council for the Central Laboratory of the Research Councils, © Crown copyright. Reproduced by permission of the Controller of Her Majesty's Stationery Office and the UK

Hydrographic Office www.ukho.gov.uk; Intrepid Travel for the travel pages 'Land beneath the wind' and 'Great Western Safari' included in 'Case Study: Mount Kinablu', 'Case Study: Tour Itinerary' and Figure 8.13. Copyright © Intrepid Travel *Holiday Brochure* 2010; Manchester Airport for Figure 9.1, "Airport of the Year" advertisement for Manchester Airport, published in Trade Travel Gazette 9 October 2009 copyright © Manchester Airport; Experian Hitwise for Figure 9.2 "UK travel searches by type, August 2009" from "How do people search for travel in the UK?" by Robin Goad, 7 October 2009, http://weblogs.hitwise.com/robin-goad/2009/10/how_do_people_search_for_trave.html copyright © Experian Hitwise; GTMC Euston Fitzrovia for an extract from Guild of Travel Management Companies 'Company Aims', http://www.gtmc.org/mission.aspx, reproduced by permission; Department of Health for an extract from "Pandemic flu - frequently asked questions" http://www.dh.gov.uk/en/Publichealth/Flu/PandemicFlu/FAQonly/DH_065088 © Crown copyright 2010; TWgroup Ltd for an extract from "Business travel: How TMCs are fighting the downturn" by Nick Easen, *Travel Weekly* 6 May 2009, www.travelweekly.co.uk copyright © TWgroup Ltd; Northumberland County Council for an extract about Tynedale Council Core Strategy, reproduced with permission; NI Syndication for an extract from "Valley of the Kings at risk from bad breath" *The Times*, 19th August 2009 copyright © The Times, 2009 www.nisyndication.com; Harlequin Hotels and Resorts in the Caribbean for an extract from the Harlequin Hotels and Resorts in the Caribbean policy, www.harlequinproperty.co.uk. Reproduced with permission; The Department for Culture, Media and Sport (DCMS), for their 'What we do-Tourism', www.culture.gov.uk © Crown copyright 2010; English Heritage for details about the English Heritage role from http://www.english-heritage.org.uk, copyright © English Heritage; Tourism Concern for material in 'Case study: Tourism Concern', reproduced with permission; Netherlands Board of Tourism & Conventions for the Holland website banner www.Holland.com, reproduced with permission; Wanderlust Magazine for material in 'Case Study: Kashgar, China' from "Threatened Wonders 2009" *Wanderlust,* Issue 101, February 2009 http://www.wanderlust.co.uk/article.php?page_id=2693, copyright © Wanderlust Magazine; Reef Relief for material in 'Case Study: Discover Coral Reefs School Program' from http://www.reefrelief.org copyright © Reef Relief; Salford City Council for an extract from "Salford Quays, The Quays is Greater Manchester's unique waterfront", www.salford.gov.uk, reproduced with permission; i-to-i for an extract about a community tourism project in India published on www.responsibletravel.com, copyright © i-to-i; Hunter Hammersmith Advertising for an extract about Sandals from www.sandals.com, courtesy of Sandals Resorts; Friends of the Lake District for material in 'Case Study: Friends of the Lake District' copyright © Friends of the Lake District, www.fld.org.uk; and The Travel Foundation for material in 'Case Study: Travel Foundation' from http://www.thetravelfoundation.org.uk reproduced by permission of The Travel Foundation.

Every effort has been made to contact copyright holders of material reproduced in this book. Any omissions will be rectified in subsequent printings if notice is given to the publishers.

About your BTEC Level 3 Travel and Tourism book

Choosing to study for a BTEC Level 3 National Travel and Tourism qualification is a great decision to make for lots of reasons. Studying Travel and Tourism will allow you to broaden your knowledge of the sector as well as deepening your skills.

Your BTEC Level 3 National Travel and Tourism is a vocational or work-related qualification. This doesn't mean that it will give you all the skills you need to do a job, but it does mean that you'll have the opportunity to gain specific knowledge, understanding and skills that are relevant to your chosen subject or area of work.

What will you be doing?

The qualification is structured into mandatory units (ones that you must do) and optional units (ones that you can choose to do). How many units you do and which ones you cover depend on the type of qualification you are working towards.

Qualifications	Credits from mandatory units	Credits from optional units	Total credits
Edexcel BTEC Level 3 Certificate	20	10	30
Edexcel BTEC Level 3 Subsidiary Diploma	40	20	60
Edexcel BTEC Level 3 Diploma	40	80	120
Edexcel BTEC Level 3 Extended Diploma	40	140	180

How to use this book

This book is designed to help you through your BTEC Level 3 National Travel and Tourism course. It contains many features that will help you develop and apply your skills and knowledge in work-related situations and assist you in getting the most from your course.

Credit value: 10

7 European destinations

This unit will provide you with the opportunity to study the European travel market. Many sectors in travel and tourism require a sound knowledge of tourism in Europe in terms of locational geography, key destinations and which markets are expanding or declining.

You will use resources to practise locating different countries, gateways and key leisure destinations within Europe. You should be able to locate key destinations and features on a map.

There are many different types of holidays available in Europe, ranging from traditional beach holidays to walking, skiing and city breaks. The choice depends on the motivation of the customer, so we will investigate different motivations and how they can be met.

You will find out what features and factors contribute to the appeal of destinations and appreciate the diversity of tourism products on offer in Europe.

Developing and declining destinations will be studied along with the factors that affect development. Tourists' tastes change and what was once a major destination can easily go into decline. You will find out that some destinations become less popular and why others are increasing in popularity.

Learning outcomes

After completing this unit you should:

1 be able to locate gateways and leisure destinations within the European travel market
2 know the types of holidays available in Europe to meet differing motivations
3 know the factors and features determining the appeal of leisure destinations in the European travel market for UK visitors
4 understand how factors affect the development and decline of the European travel market.

181

Introduction

These introductions give you a snapshot of what to expect from each unit – and what you should be aiming for by the time you finish it!

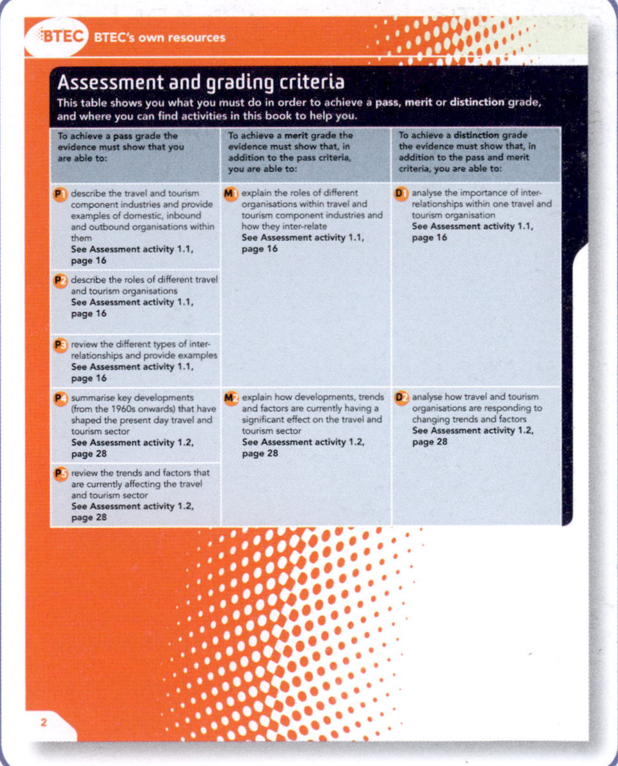

BTEC BTEC's own resources

Assessment and grading criteria

This table shows you what you must do in order to achieve a pass, merit or distinction grade, and where you can find activities in this book to help you.

To achieve a **pass** grade the evidence must show that you are able to:	To achieve a **merit** grade the evidence must show that, in addition to the pass criteria, you are able to:	To achieve a **distinction** grade the evidence must show that, in addition to the pass and merit criteria, you are able to:
P1 describe the travel and tourism component industries and provide examples of domestic, inbound and outbound organisations within them **See Assessment activity 1.1, page 16**	M1 explain the roles of different organisations within travel and tourism component industries and how they inter-relate **See Assessment activity 1.1, page 16**	D1 analyse the importance of inter-relationships within one travel and tourism organisation **See Assessment activity 1.1, page 16**
P2 describe the roles of different travel and tourism organisations **See Assessment activity 1.1, page 16**		
P3 review the different types of inter-relationships and provide examples **See Assessment activity 1.1, page 16**		
P4 summarise key developments (from the 1960s onwards) that have shaped the present day travel and tourism sector **See Assessment activity 1.2, page 28**	M2 explain how developments, trends and factors are currently having a significant effect on the travel and tourism sector **See Assessment activity 1.2, page 28**	D2 analyse how travel and tourism organisations are responding to changing trends and factors **See Assessment activity 1.2, page 28**
P5 review the trends and factors that are currently affecting the travel and tourism sector **See Assessment activity 1.2, page 28**		

2

Assessment and grading criteria

This table explains what you must do to achieve each of the assessment criteria for each of the mandatory and optional units. For each assessment criterion, shown by the grade buttons **P1**, **M1**, **D1**, etc. there is an assessment activity.

Assessment

Your tutor will set **assignments** throughout your course for you to complete. These may take a variety of forms including business reports, presentations, case studies. The important thing is that you evidence your skills and knowledge to date.

How you will be assessed

This unit will be assessed by one or more internal assignments that will be designed and marked by your tutor. Your assignments will be subject to sampling internally and externally as part of Edexcel's quality assurance procedures. The assignments are designed to allow you to show your knowledge and understanding related to the unit. The unit outcomes indicate what you should know, understand or be able to do after completing the unit.

Learner experience

Stuck for ideas? Daunted by your first assignment? These learners have all been through it before…

Mario, 18-year old BTEC National learner

This was the first unit we studied and it made me realise how many different organisations and industries there are in travel and tourism.

I had to get used to working with my group at the same time as all this new information was coming at me, but I found it easier when we started our assessment and we began to work together.

I spent a whole afternoon working out what was on the VisitBritain website, but I found lots of useful information. I had to go elsewhere for the developments so I used textbooks for these. I also found that the Thomas Cook website had historic milestones.

We had to present our information in a lively way, as we were going to take it on the road to three schools. I am quite good at drawing so I drew a timeline for developments with illustrations of planes, cruise ships and so on. Everything was beautifully labelled and we had little presentations that we shared to go with the timeline.

Our tutor had a reading area in our base room with trade papers and all the Sunday papers, so that we got used to looking at the press to see what had happened to affect travel and tourism.

Over to you!

1 What resources do you think you will be able to use for your assessments?
2 What newspapers do you regularly access?
3 Think about the kind of presentation you would like to do.

Activities

There are different types of activities for you to do: **Assessment activities** are suggestions for tasks that you might do as part of your assignment and will help you develop your knowledge, skills and understanding. **Grading tips** clearly explain what you need to do in order to achieve a pass, merit or distinction grade.

Assessment activity 1.1

P1 P2 P3 M1 D1 BTEC

Your tutor thinks it would be a good idea to 'spread the word' about travel and tourism and proposes a road show for local secondary schools.

The purpose is to spend half a day in each school mounting an exhibition or information session for Year 10 pupils. This will differ from the usual careers evening sessions in that it will be organised by students for students and it will be about the travel and tourism sector, not just the course, in order to create interest in travel and tourism.

For the tasks below, you could produce a display with illustrations and explanatory notes. You could design an information sheet to be distributed to students.

1 To give students an overview of the sector, describe the component industries. Include examples of different organisations for each of those industries. Make sure you give at least one example from each component industry. Also, make sure that your examples overall include organisations representing inbound, outbound and domestic tourism. Provide definitions of inbound, outbound and domestic tourism. P1
2 Describe the roles of three of the different organisations you have given as examples. These should be three different organisations from different component industries. Make sure at least one is a medium to large organisation. P2
3 Review, with examples, the different types of interrelationships in travel and tourism. P3
4 Explain the roles of different organisations within the travel and tourism component industries, including an explanation of how they interrelate. M1
5 Choose one travel and tourism organisation. Analyse the importance of its interrelationships with other travel and tourism organisations. D1

Grading tips

P1 You need to describe each of the component industries and identify the organisations with them to achieve. This means you must include accommodation (serviced and non-serviced); transport provision (road, rail, sea and air); attractions (natural, heritage, purpose-built, events); tour operations (mass market, specialist); travel agents (retail, business, call centre, web-based); tourism development and promotion; trade associations and regulatory bodies; and ancilliary services.

P2 Ensure you provide full descriptions and cover all the key roles of the organisations in your own words. State the role of the company in terms of its organisational aims and the products and services it provides.

P3 The types of interrelationships you should review are the chain of distribution, integration and how organisations rely on each other. Diagrams will help you illustrate interrelationships and interdependencies and make sure all your examples are up-to-date.

M1 You will need a detailed explanation for at least two of your interdependency examples, making sure at least one of the organisations is a medium/large company. If you select a multi-national company make sure you focus on the UK part of the company.

D1 You will need to explore all aspects of interrelationship and analyse their importance to the selected organisation and to the other organisations involved. Make sure that you choose an organisation that provides sufficient coverage of all aspects of interrelationships in your analysis.

There are also suggestions for activities that will give you a broader grasp of travel and tourism, stretch your understanding and develop your skills.

Activity: Capital cities

1 Choose one of the capital cities and find a guide for that city.
2 Describe three main features of the destination that would appeal to inbound visitors.
3 Consider whether these features would also appeal to domestic visitors and say why.

Personal, learning and thinking skills

Throughout your BTEC Level 3 National Travel and Tourism course there are lots of opportunities to develop your personal, learning and thinking skills. These will help you work in a team, manage yourself effectively and develop your all-important interpersonal skills. Look out for these as you progress.

PLTS

When you plan and carry out your research you will be practising your skills as an **independent enquirer**.

Functional skills

It's important that you have good English, maths and ICT skills – you never know when you'll need them, and employers will be looking for evidence that you've got these skills too.

Functional skills

As you read and summarise information from different sources you will gain functional skills in **English**.

Key terms

Technical words and phrases are easy to spot. The terms and definitions are also in the glossary at the back of the book.

Key term

Gross Domestic Product (GDP) – a measure of the value of goods and services produced in an economy in a year. GDP indicates the wealth and economic development of a country. Countries with developed economies usually have high GDPs and countries with developing economies usually have low GDPs.

WorkSpace

WorkSpace provides snapshots of real-world business issues and shows you how the knowledge and skills you are developing through your course can be applied in your future career.

There are also mini-case studies throughout the book to help you focus on your own projects.

WorkSpace

James Turner

PR Manager

I work for a Scottish tourist company that promotes Scotland to visitors and it is my job to ensure that the right message about Scotland, and everything we offer, gets out to the media. My job carries a lot of responsibility, but it is fascinating and I am always happy to go to work in the morning.

I manage a team of people who will be working on individual campaigns. I have to monitor them and know exactly what is going on at any time with any campaign. If something is late or overspent, ultimately it is my fault. I am given a budget for public relations each year and then I plan campaigns within that budget. The budget might be as much as £100,000. Of course, the campaigns must be related to our strategic objectives.

This year a major campaign has been our Homecoming Scotland celebration. We have had about 100 events celebrating the 250th birthday of Robbie Burns. My team handles press enquiries about the events, organises press releases and press launches for events. I spend a lot of time networking with media contacts. It is important to have good relationships with the media so that we can get events covered in the way we would like.

Members of the team attend exhibitions to promote Scotland, so recently we were in London at the World Travel Market.

I had to be a graduate to get this job and I also have a postgraduate Diploma in Public Relations. I had been working in PR in London before I took this job, but I am Scottish and I needed to show that I had a very extensive knowledge of Scotland and its tourism products to get this job. My bosses were looking for initiative and at my interview I was asked lots of questions about how I had developed previous campaigns. Creative thinking is very important too, as in PR we have to try to find new approaches to campaigns and events to catch the attention of the media.

Think about it!

1. How would you begin to organise a press launch?
2. How would you know whom to contact?
3. What other skills do you think are needed for this job?

89

Just checking

When you see this sort of activity, take stock! These quick activities and questions are there to check your knowledge. You can use them to see how much progress you've made and to identify any areas where you need to refresh your knowledge.

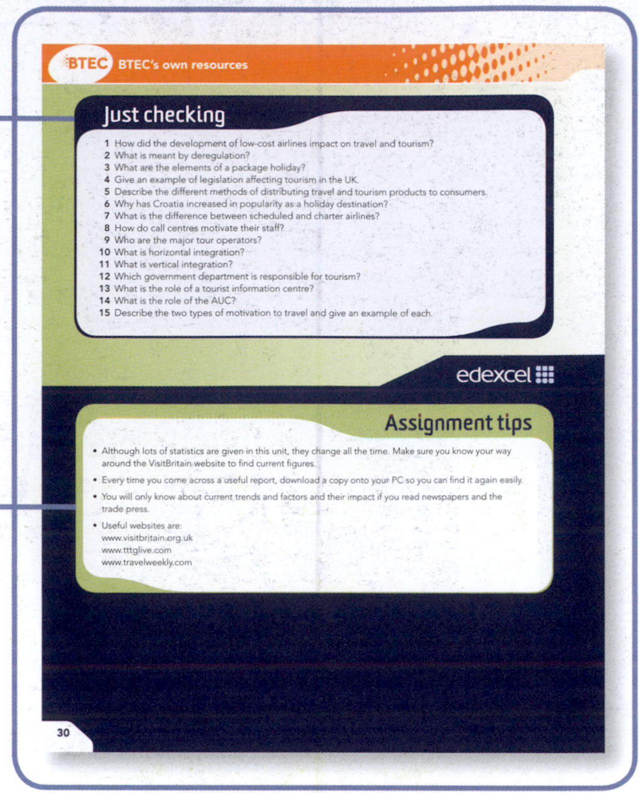

BTEC BTEC's own resources

Just checking

1 How did the development of low-cost airlines impact on travel and tourism?
2 What is meant by deregulation?
3 What are the elements of a package holiday?
4 Give an example of legislation affecting tourism in the UK.
5 Describe the different methods of distributing travel and tourism products to consumers.
6 Why has Croatia increased in popularity as a holiday destination?
7 What is the difference between scheduled and charter airlines?
8 How do call centres motivate their staff?
9 Who are the major tour operators?
10 What is horizontal integration?
11 What is vertical integration?
12 Which government department is responsible for tourism?
13 What is the role of a tourist information centre?
14 What is the role of the AUC?
15 Describe the two types of motivation to travel and give an example of each.

edexcel

Assignment tips

- Although lots of statistics are given in this unit, they change all the time. Make sure you know your way around the VisitBritain website to find current figures.
- Every time you come across a useful report, download a copy onto your PC so you can find it again easily.
- You will only know about current trends and factors and their impact if you read newspapers and the trade press.
- Useful websites are:
  www.visitbritain.org.uk
  www.tttglive.com
  www.travelweekly.com

30

Edexcel's assignment tips

At the end of each unit, you'll find hints and tips to help you get the best mark you can, such as the best websites to go to, checklists to help you remember processes and useful reminders to avoid common mistakes. You might want to read this information before starting your assignment...

Don't miss out on these resources to help you!

Have you read your BTEC Level 3 National Study Skills Guide? It's full of advice on study skills, putting your assignments together and making the most of being a BTEC Travel and Tourism student.

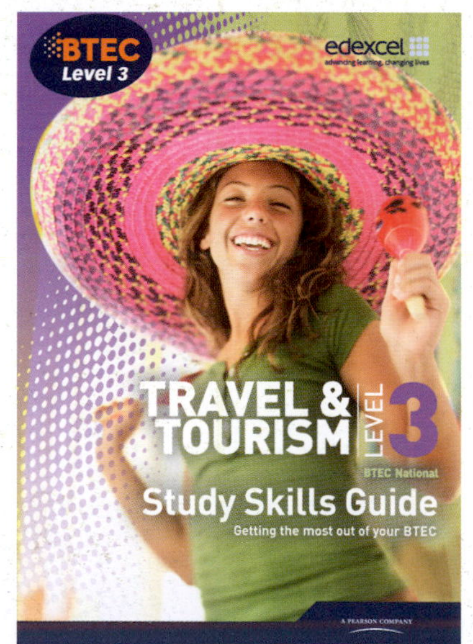

Ask your tutor about extra materials to help you through your course. You'll find interesting videos, activities, presentations and information about the world of business.

Your book is just part of the exciting resources from Edexcel to help you succeed in your BTEC course.

Visit: www.edexcel.com/btec or www.pearsonfe.co.uk/btec2010

Credit value: 10

1 Investigating the travel and tourism sector

The travel and tourism sector is dynamic, exciting and provides a challenging working environment. If you are reading this book, it is likely that you are considering a career in travel and tourism and that you are beginning your studies of the sector.

This unit aims to give you a sound introduction to travel and tourism so that you gain an overview of the various components and how they link together. You will also study the roles and responsibilities of travel and tourism organisations within the sector.

You will learn about the development of travel and tourism, particularly from the 1960s to the present day. You will find out how changes in demand, new travel and tourism products and changes in the distribution of products have affected the sector.

You will also look at the factors which currently affect the travel and tourism sector and the effects on development.

Learning outcomes

After completing this unit you should:

1 know the travel and tourism component industries and their organisations
2 understand the role of travel and tourism organisations and their interrelationships
3 know the developments that have shaped the present day travel and tourism sector
4 understand how trends and factors are currently affecting the travel and tourism sector.

Assessment and grading criteria

This table shows you what you must do in order to achieve a **pass**, **merit** or **distinction** grade, and where you can find activities in this book to help you.

To achieve a **pass** grade the evidence must show that you are able to:	To achieve a **merit** grade the evidence must show that, in addition to the pass criteria, you are able to:	To achieve a **distinction** grade the evidence must show that, in addition to the pass and merit criteria, you are able to:
P1 describe the travel and tourism component industries and provide examples of domestic, inbound and outbound organisations within them **See Assessment activity 1.1, page 16**	**M1** explain the roles of different organisations within travel and tourism component industries and how they inter-relate **See Assessment activity 1.1, page 16**	**D1** analyse the importance of inter-relationships within one travel and tourism organisation **See Assessment activity 1.1, page 16**
P2 describe the roles of different travel and tourism organisations **See Assessment activity 1.1, page 16**		
P3 review the different types of inter-relationships and provide examples **See Assessment activity 1.1, page 16**		
P4 summarise key developments (from the 1960s onwards) that have shaped the present day travel and tourism sector **See Assessment activity 1.2, page 28**	**M2** explain how developments, trends and factors are currently having a significant effect on the travel and tourism sector **See Assessment activity 1.2, page 28**	**D2** analyse how travel and tourism organisations are responding to changing trends and factors **See Assessment activity 1.2, page 28**
P5 review the trends and factors that are currently affecting the travel and tourism sector **See Assessment activity 1.2, page 28**		

How you will be assessed

This unit will be assessed by one or more internal assignments that will be designed and marked by your tutor. Your assignments will be subject to sampling internally and externally as part of Edexcel's quality assurance procedures. The assignments are designed to allow you to show your knowledge and understanding related to the unit. The unit outcomes indicate what you should know, understand or be able to do after completing the unit.

Mario, 18-year old BTEC National learner

This was the first unit we studied and it made me realise how many different organisations and industries there are in travel and tourism.

I had to get used to working with my group at the same time as all this new information was coming at me, but I found it easier when we started our assessment and we began to work together.

I spent a whole afternoon working out what was on the VisitBritain website, but I found lots of useful information. I had to go elsewhere for the developments so I used textbooks for these. I also found that the Thomas Cook website had historic milestones.

We had to present our information in a lively way, as we were going to take it on the road to three schools. I am quite good at drawing so I drew a timeline for developments with illustrations of planes, cruise ships and so on. Everything was beautifully labelled and we had little presentations that we shared to go with the timeline.

Our tutor had a reading area in our base room with trade papers and all the Sunday papers, so that we got used to looking at the press to see what had happened to affect travel and tourism.

Over to you!

1 What resources do you think you will be able to use for your assessments?

2 What newspapers do you regularly access?

3 Think about the kind of presentation you would like to do.

1 Travel and tourism component industries and their organisations

Set off

Tourism is big business!

Tourism is the provision of services to tourists. Everything that tourists do while they are on holiday is considered part of the travel and tourism sector. Tourism is a significant contributor to the UK economy; many businesses depend on tourism, directly or indirectly.

When we think about travel and tourism, we tend to think of national organisations like Thomson and Thomas Cook or attractions such as major theme parks. However, many businesses in the sector are very small, such as bed and breakfast accommodation or small visitor attractions. The sector is a major source of employment and contributes greatly to the UK economy. Jobs are also created indirectly by travel and tourism, for example in construction when a new hotel is built.

- How many people do you know who work in travel and tourism?
- What kinds of jobs do they do?

1.1 Types of tourism

Before you start looking at the components of the sector, there are some important terms to understand.

Domestic tourism

Domestic tourism relates to people who are travelling within their own country for tourism purposes. People on day trips are not officially tourists as they are not staying away from home. Statistics consider tourists to be people who stay away for at least one night.

However, as day trippers spend a lot of money in the tourism sector, particularly on travel and in the visitor attractions sector, it is important to measure the value of their spending. According to a recent study carried out by Deloitte (*The Economic Contribution of the Visitor Economy – UK and the Nations*), domestic day trips accounted for £47.6 billion in 2009.

Inbound tourism

Inbound tourism measures those people coming in to visit a country which is not their country of residence, for the purposes of tourism. If a tourist comes from the USA to the UK, then they are inbound to the UK. This also means that they are an outbound tourist from their own country.

Outbound tourism

Generally, when we use the term outbound tourism in the UK we are referring to UK residents travelling out of the UK. For example, you are an outbound tourist from the UK if you go to Spain on holiday.

Types of tourist

There are many types of tourist, but for statistical purposes they are categorised according to their purpose of travel, broadly as follows:

- leisure
- business
- visiting friends and relatives (VFR).

Leisure travel includes travel for holidays, cultural events, recreation, sports, religion and study.

Business travel includes all travel for business reasons, such as meetings, conferences and exhibitions. Usually business travellers have their expenses paid by their company, which can make a difference to the services they choose or have chosen on their behalf. VFR accounts for many trips, particularly within the UK.

Activity: Types of tourist

Study each of the examples below. What kind of tourists are they? Note that some examples might fit into more than one category.

Example	Type of tourist
Marianne is taking a holiday in the UK. She lives in Austria.	
Raj is going on holiday to Bournemouth. He lives in Leicester.	
Year 11 at Chichester Village College are going to visit Leeds Castle for the day.	
Sheena and Donald are going to Madrid for a weekend break. They live in Glasgow.	
Mary is a sales director. She is going to a sales conference in Barcelona.	
The Patel family are going on holiday to Disneyland, Paris.	
Jerry goes to visit his father in Dublin every Christmas.	
Mario is visiting the UK from Spain to undertake a language course.	

1.2 Travel and tourism component industries

By components of travel and tourism we mean the different parts of the sector that provide travel and tourism products and services. None of these components are able to work in isolation. Each relies on one, or more, of the other component parts to be able to operate.

As you study each of the components you will meet some examples of organisations, their roles and the products and services they provide.

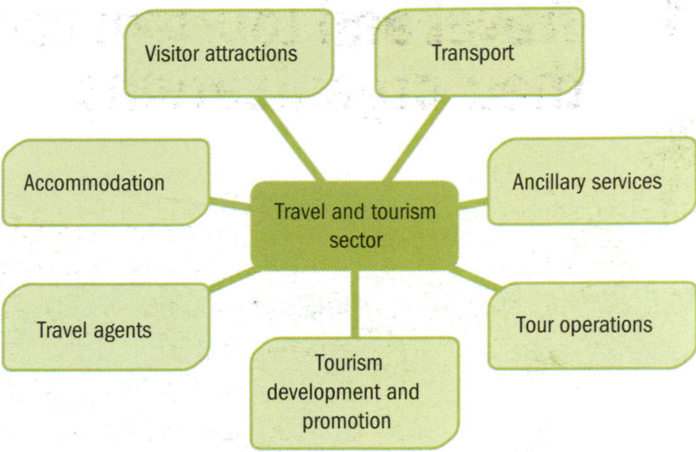

Figure 1.1: Components of the travel and tourism sector

Accommodation

There are many different types of accommodation available in the travel and tourism sector. Remember that accommodation can be serviced (which means that meals are on offer and your room will be cleaned for you) or it can be non-serviced (where you look after yourself and do your own cleaning, shopping and cooking).

Hotels

Hotels may be independently owned or part of large hotel chains. The chains tend to be more impersonal, but they do provide consistency of quality throughout the world. For example, if you were to stay in a Mercure Hotel in London or in Paris, the room would offer exactly the same facilities and often the layout is exactly the same.

Hotels offer many products and services, catering for different customers. The prestigious and more expensive hotels, like Sofitel, offer greater luxury. Budget hotels, such as Premier Inn and Travelodge, offer good value for money.

In addition, hotels cater for both business and leisure customers, so they need a range of products to suit each type. Conference customers may come for just a day and will need different services from the residents.

Activity: Local hotels

List the hotels in your town or local area. Find out which hotels belong to which group. Are there any independent hotels?

Choose one of the hotels in your area. Describe how the hotel appeals to different tourists.

Guest accommodation

This includes bed and breakfast accommodation, guesthouses and farmhouses. Homeowners who wish to capitalise on the extra space they might have available often run this type of accommodation. Many tourists consider it charming and an opportunity to experience local culture.

Scuttington Manor Guest House, Oast House, Tonge, near Faversham, Kent. Why are tourists attracted to guest accommodation such as this?

Self-catering accommodation may be in holiday parks or in rented apartments or holiday cottages. Cooking facilities will be provided. An example of this kind of accommodation in France is the popular *gîte*.

Transport – road

Cars

The private car dominates road travel. Car ownership is very high in the UK, and most domestic holidays and day trips are taken by car. In addition, many people choose to hire a car when abroad and this has led to the growth of the car hire sector.

Major car-hire groups in the UK include Hertz, Avis and Europcar. All have international operations. Their products and services have become very sophisticated, making car hire very easy and convenient for customers.

Car hire companies offer:

- on-line or telephone pre-booking
- airport pick-up or drop-off
- a wide range of choice of vehicles
- all insurances included in fixed prices
- one-way rentals – you don't have to return the car to the place where you picked it up.

Coaches

Coach operators have adapted their products to meet consumers' changing needs and coaches today are very luxurious. Fly-coach holidays are offered so that customers do not have a lengthy initial journey, but have the benefits of coach travel for touring, for example in California.

There are extensive coach networks operating in the UK, offering scheduled services between towns and also into Europe. Eurolines is a group of independent coach companies which claims to connect to over 500 destinations within Europe. Coach services are usually very comfortable with toilets, refreshments and DVD facilities available on board.

Transport – rail

Network Rail owns and operates the national rail network in the UK. Its role is to maintain the infrastructure and renew tracks as necessary.

The train-operating companies (TOCs) lease trains from rolling-stock companies. There are 29 TOCs in the UK and they compete for franchises to run each passenger service. There are similar companies for freight.

The Department for Transport issues the franchises. They also monitor the train-operating companies to make sure the interests of rail passengers are protected; they can fine the TOCs if they fail to meet agreed standards. The TOCs are commercial companies and aim to make a profit, but they do receive government grants. Examples of TOCs are Virgin Trains and South West Trains.

The TOCs are represented by the Association of Train Operating Companies (ATOC), an industry body that helps to promote their interests to stakeholders, government and the media.

Other important aspects of the rail system are the London Underground, Docklands Light Railway and, of course, Eurostar. Eurostar is the passenger train service through the Channel Tunnel. It operates from St Pancras International in London and Ashford in Kent to Paris, Lille and Brussels. Eurostar is owned by London and Continental Railways, and run by a management company.

Transport – sea

As residents of the UK we live on an island, so sea transport has always been an important part of the travel and tourism industry.

Ferries

Historically, the main mode of transport to the continent was by sea across the English Channel. When the Channel Tunnel opened, it was expected that ferry services across the Channel would be threatened. The tunnel did take about 50 per cent of the market, but passenger ferries have also been severely hit by low-cost airlines offering cheap fares to the continent. It is often cheaper to fly and hire a car rather than take your own vehicle.

In 1997, over 21 million passengers passed through Dover, which is the biggest port in the UK. By 2003, numbers had declined to fewer than 15 million and have not since risen above that. The first full year of Channel Tunnel operation was 1995.

Other operators in the Channel include Sea France and Brittany Ferries. Brittany Ferries operates on longer routes to France and Spain, for example Poole to Cherbourg, Plymouth to Santander and Portsmouth to Caen, St Malo or Cherbourg. Ferries also operate to the Channel Islands, for example Jersey and Guernsey.

The established ferry operator P&O is one of the main companies offering transport across the Channel, as some companies, such as Hoverspeed and Speedferries, have ceased operating.

Not all ferry travel is across the Channel. Here are some examples of other important routes:

- Stranraer – Belfast
- Fleetwood – Larne
- Fishguard – Rosslare
- Holyhead – Dun Laoghaire
- Hull – Zeebrugge
- Hull – Rotterdam
- Holyhead – Dublin
- Pembroke – Rosslare
- Douglas – Liverpool
- Ryde – Portsmouth.

Activity: Ports

1. Check the ports listed on this page on a map and make sure you know the location and the country of each.

   Choose one route and find out which ferry operators serve it. Produce an information sheet detailing the services provided and extra products, for example, a cabin, available on that route. A ferry brochure will help you.

2. The Scottish islands are accessible by ferry, both from the mainland and via inter-island services. Look for a map of the Scottish islands and identify some of the main routes.

Think about it

Irish Ferries advertises its ferries as 'cruise ferries'. Do you think this makes them more appealing?

Cruises

The cruise industry is enjoying steady growth. Companies are investing in new liners. New ships include the *Azura, Queen Elizabeth* and *Seabourn Odyssey* introduced in 2010. Major cruise companies you may have heard of are P&O Cruises, Cunard, Royal Caribbean and Princess.

The number of Europeans taking a cruise holiday reached an all-time high in 2008, with the UK topping the list with the greatest number of cruise passengers, reaching 1.5 million. Cruise companies are doing their utmost to reach new markets, such as families and younger people, rather than just the older age groups who traditionally take cruises.

River cruises are also growing in popularity. Popular destinations include the rivers Rhine, Moselle, Danube and Nile.

In the event of business failure, the Passenger Shipping Association (PSA) provides financial protection to the customers of tour operators who are bonded by the PSA (in the same way that travel agents are bonded by ABTA – The Travel Association).

Transport – air

Airports

The British Airports Authority (BAA) is the major organisation in airport ownership in the UK. BAA is owned by Airport Development and Investment (ADI) Limited, a consortium led by Grupo Ferrovial, a Spanish organisation. BAA owns the airports at:

- London Heathrow
- London Stansted
- Glasgow
- Edinburgh
- Aberdeen
- Southampton
- Naples (65 per cent stake)

BAA also has management contracts or stakes in other airports outside the UK, plus retail management contracts at two airports in the USA. Over 140 million passengers travel through the six BAA airports in the UK every year.

Other major UK airports are Birmingham, Manchester and London Luton, all owned by different consortia. Regional airports have grown in popularity with airports such as Leeds Bradford and East Midlands offering many short-haul routes.

Running an airport is a complex but profitable operation. The airport provides products and services to various groups of people and businesses:

- airlines are provided with the infrastructure and services to operate their flights
- customers are provided with facilities, such as restaurants and shops
- other businesses are provided with a location in which they can operate, for example car hire, retailing or ground handling.

The airport earns revenue from all these sources, but also has to work hard at keeping all its groups of customers happy.

Airlines

All UK airlines are privately owned. British Airways (BA) is one of the world's most famous airlines and one of the largest in terms of international scheduled services. It is the largest in the UK and flies to more than 200 destinations around the world. However, in 2009, its passenger numbers had fallen by 4.3 per cent due to the recession.

British Airways' main bases are at the London airports of Heathrow and Gatwick. The airline's products include four different types of cabin service ranging from Economy to Club World. It also fully owns subsidiaries such as British Airways CitiExpress.

Other major UK airlines include British Midland and Virgin Atlantic – these are **scheduled** airlines. The UK also has many **charter** airlines, such as Monarch and Thomson. Monarch also operates a scheduled service. Hundreds of other airlines from all over the world fly in and out of UK airports, paying for the services they use.

Key terms

Scheduled – these airlines run to a regular timetable that is changed only for the winter and summer seasons. The flights depart even if not all the seats have been booked.

Charter – these aircraft are usually contracted for a specific holiday season and run to a timetable set by the operator. For example, each major tour operator will need seats for its summer passengers flying to the Mediterranean. They fill every seat on the contracted aircraft and each seat forms part of the holiday package. The major tour operators own their own charter airlines, for example TUI owns Thomson airline.

Low-cost airlines

The principle behind the operation of a low-cost airline is to keep costs as low as possible, with few or no 'extras' offered to the customer without further charge. In this way the low-cost operators are able to offer very cheap fares. The low-cost airlines are scheduled airlines, for example easyJet and Ryanair.

Regulation of air travel

The Civil Aviation Authority (CAA) regulates the UK aviation sector. The CAA is an independent statutory body.

The Air Transport Users Council (AUC) is the UK's consumer council for air travellers. It receives its funding from the CAA. It acts as the independent representative of air passengers and aims to complement and assist the CAA in furthering the reasonable interests of passengers.

National Air Traffic Services (NATS) is the organisation responsible for air traffic control. It is a public/private partnership owned by the government, a consortium of seven airlines and NATS staff. It looks after UK airspace, but also the eastern part of the North Atlantic. NATS handles more than 2 million flights a year, carrying over 220 million passengers.

The major air traffic control centres are at Swanwick in Hampshire and Prestwick in Ayrshire. There are also air traffic control services at the country's major airports.

Attractions

The UK officially has 6500 visitor attractions. These UK attractions are important to both the domestic tourism market and the inbound tourism market. There are, of course, hundreds of different types of attraction, but they can be broadly divided as follows.

Natural attractions

These include beautiful beaches, lakes and landscapes. In order to protect them, some are designated Areas of Outstanding Natural Beauty (AONBs), National Parks or Heritage Coasts.

Heritage attractions

In the UK we have a wealth of historic houses, often cared for by the National Trust or English Heritage. We also have museums and galleries such as Tate Britain and Tate Modern, the Victoria and Albert Museum in London and the National Media Museum in Bradford.

Purpose-built attractions

Purpose-built attractions may be historic also, for example most museums are purpose-built. Favourite purpose-built attractions include theme parks, for example the theme park resort Alton Towers.

Events

Events such as the Edinburgh Festival or the Notting Hill Carnival attract many visitors. There are events in the business tourism sector too, such as the World Travel Market.

Associations

The British Association of Leisure Parks, Piers and Attractions (BALPPA) was founded in 1936. It is non-profit-making and its role is to represent the interests of owners, managers, suppliers and developers in the UK's commercial leisure parks, piers, zoos and static attractions sector. It has about 300 members.

The International Association of Amusement Parks and Attractions (IAAPA) is a similar organisation to BALPPA, but it is an international association and has members all over the world. The mission of the association is to promote safe operations, global development, professional growth and commercial success in the amusement industry.

Activity: UK attractions

To improve your knowledge of the UK visitor attractions sector, create a table similar to the one below. Use your local Tourist Information Centre (TIC) and the VisitBritain website (www.visitbritain.com) to help you complete it. Check your answers with your teacher or tutor.

Type of attraction	Two national examples	A local example
Historic house		
Garden		
Museum		
Art gallery		
Wildlife attraction		
Theme park		
Historic monument		
Religious building		

Tour operators

The role of tour operators is to put together all the different components that make up a holiday and sell them as packages to the consumer. They make contracts with hoteliers, airlines and other transport companies to put the package together. All the holiday details are described in a brochure, which is distributed either to travel agents or directly to customers.

Mass-market tour operators

These tour operators dominated the outbound market for years. The examples you will have heard of include Thomson, First Choice and Thomas Cook. Thomson and First Choice both belong to the parent company TUI.

Traditionally, these major tour operators were considered to be mass-market tour operators as they sold similar holidays in packages that appealed to the majority of holidaymakers. In contrast, specialist tour operators sold more individually tailored holidays or specialised in one destination or activity. Today, the large tour operators also offer many specialist products.

TUI AG is the largest travel group in the world. It does not just include tour operators. Thomson, for example, is also a travel agency brand and an airline. First Choice has a major travel agent in its portfolio and its own branded airline. First Choice offers holidays in destinations such as Majorca, Menorca, the Canaries, Spain, Turkey, Greece and the Caribbean. Winter sports destinations include France, Austria, Italy,

Andorra, Bulgaria and Switzerland, and there are some specialist brands such as Twentys, aimed at young people and Sunstart aimed at budget holidaymakers.

Thomas Cook also has travel agencies, airlines and hotels as well as tour operator brands, including Club 18–30.

Tour operators that offer air-inclusive packages are required by law to have an Air Travel Organisers' Licence (ATOL). This is a scheme that protects air travellers and package holiday makers from losing money or being stranded abroad if air travel firms go out of business. When a tourist books a holiday the cost of this financial protection is included in the price. Any package firm that includes a flight should by law hold a licence. ATOL is managed by the Civil Aviation Authority.

Specialist tour operators

There are many other tour operators in the market; some specialise in particular destinations, or in a product, for example diving holidays. Specialist tour operators are more prevalent as they respond well to the trend for tailor-made holidays with their specialist products and expertise in niche markets. Sometimes specialist tour operators focus on a particular destination, rather than a type of holiday. For example, Anatolian Sky specialises in holidays in Turkey.

Inbound tour operators cater for the needs of overseas visitors to the UK. An example is British Tours Ltd, which claims to be the longest-established inbound operator. It offers tours for different group sizes and has a wide variety of products, including a Harry Potter tour. The tours are available in many languages.

Domestic tour operators specialise in holidays within the UK for UK residents. They include coach companies which place advertisements in the local newspapers. Like outbound operators, they offer beach, city, touring and special-interest holidays.

Tour operators' associations

UKinbound is the trade body which represents tour operators and tourism suppliers to the UK. It was founded in 1977 to represent the commercial and political interests of incoming tour operators and suppliers to the British inbound tourism industry. It is a non-profit-making body governed by an elected council and funded by subscriptions from its members and from revenue-generating activities.

The Association of Independent Tour Operators (AITO) is an organisation which represents about 160 of the UK's specialist tour operators. AITO members are independent companies, most of them owner-managed, specialising in particular destinations or types of holiday.

The Federation of Tour Operators (FTO) is an organisation for outbound tour operators. It aims to ensure the long-term success of the air-inclusive holiday by influencing governments and opinion formers on the benefits to consumers of air-inclusive holidays compared with other types of holiday. Members pay an annual subscription based on the size of their organisation. The FTO produces health and safety guidelines for tour operators. The FTO has always worked very closely with ABTA and the two organisations merged in 2008 to become ABTA – The Travel Association.

Travel agents

The role of travel agents is to give advice and information and sell and administer bookings for a number of tour operators. They also sell flights, ferry bookings, car hire, insurance and accommodation as separate products. Thus, they are distributors of products.

Travel agents may operate through:

- retail shops
- business shops
- a call centre
- the internet.

Most travel agents are part of a multiple chain and these dominate the business. Examples you will be familiar with are Thomas Cook and Thomson. These particular chains are linked to tour operators and may try to prioritise their own company's products.

ABTA – The Travel Association is the body representing the sector. It also has tour operators as members. According to ABTA figures, in 2009 it had over 900 tour operator members and represented over 5000 travel agencies.

There has been a slight reduction in the number of agency branches in the past few years as customers choose to buy travel and tourism products through other means, particularly through travel websites.

Business travel agents

Business travel agents specialise in the business market. They aim to handle all the travel arrangements for large companies.

'Implants' are travel agents located within another business. They set up office within a company so that they are on hand to deal with the travel requirements of the company's personnel.

Call centres

Almost everyone has experience of speaking to staff in call centres – they are widely used by banks and insurance companies, as well as in the travel and tourism industry. Increasingly customers prefer to book travel by telephone or the internet, rather than by visiting a travel agent.

Call centres are often in out-of-town locations where rents, rates and labour are cheaper. Some banks and other companies have relocated their call centres to India to take advantage of lower costs. Some call centres are operator- or airline-owned and sell on behalf of that company exclusively. Others are specialist call centres and handle calls and bookings for many companies.

Call centres rely on high staff productivity to be successful. They motivate staff through incentives such as bonuses on sales targets reached. Call answering time, call durations, sales and complaints ratios are carefully monitored.

On-line travel agents

Websites are the most up-to-date means of distributing travel and tourism products and services. You will learn more about travel agents in Unit 9.

Tourism development and promotion

The development and promotion of tourism in the UK is mostly undertaken by organisations in the public sector such as VisitBritain and VisitWales. Within the public sector in the UK, the Department for Culture, Media and Sport (DCMS) is responsible for supporting the tourism industry at national level.

Other government departments have responsibilities for areas of tourism. The Department for Transport looks after aviation, railways, roads and the London Underground. The Department for Children, Schools and Families (DCSF) has responsibility for sector skills councils and training organisations. The Department for the Environment, Food and Rural Affairs (DEFRA) is responsible for issues affecting the countryside, wildlife and waterways, among others.

The structure of public sector tourism is shown in Figure 1.2.

The UK has four tourist boards: VisitBritain, VisitScotland, the Northern Ireland Tourist Board (NITB) and VisitWales. VisitBritain reports to the Department for Culture, Media and Sport (DCMS). VisitWales reports to the National Assembly for Wales and VisitScotland reports to the Scottish Executive. The NITB reports to the Northern Ireland Assembly

Activity: VisitBritain

You will use the VisitBritain website (www.VisitBritain.co.uk) a lot during your studies as it is an invaluable tourism resource. Use it now to find out:

- What are the objectives of VisitBritain?
- Who funds VisitBritain?
- What are the National Tourist Boards?
- What are Regional Development Agencies (RDAs)?
- Where are VisitBritain's overseas offices?

Functional skills

When you carry out your research, you will be finding and selecting information using **ICT** skills.

The overseas offices work closely with British diplomatic and cultural staff, the local travel trade and media, to stimulate interest in the UK.

Another example of the role of VisitBritain is its campaign to persuade high-spending tourists to come to the UK. It is important that inbound tourists spend money and boost the UK economy.

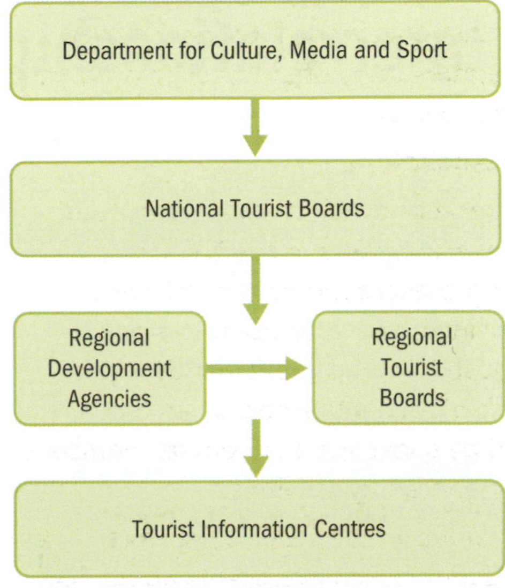

Figure 1.2: Public sector tourism

Regional Development Agencies (RDAs)

RDAs have responsibility for tourism in their regions and usually work closely with Regional Delivery Partners (RDPs).

There are nine RDAs in England. An RDA has a regional economic and a regional tourism strategy. RDPs are responsible for delivering the strategies. Sometimes the partners are tourist boards but adopt a different name to explain more precisely what they actually do. An example is Visit Manchester, an organisation which looks after tourism development, business tourism, leisure tourism and visitor services in Greater Manchester. The government is currently seeking to replace RDAs with Local Economic Partnerships (LEPs). It looks like this will happen by March 2012, with the LEPs set to cover smaller areas than the RDAs.

Local authority tourism departments

Local authorities play an important role in supporting the tourism industry because of their statutory duties and because tourism is a major contributor towards the economy. They have tourism departments and plans. Most towns also have a Tourist Information Centre (TIC) subsidised by the local council. They all rely heavily on generating income to ensure their financial viability.

The TIC provides a full information service for both residents and visitors. It gives information on visitor attractions and on accommodation. It usually provides a booking service for accommodation, and often incorporates a shop selling locally made crafts and gifts, as well as books of local interest. The shop is more than a service for visitors – it is an important means of generating funds.

Trade associations and regulatory bodies

The Association of Independent Tour Operators (AITO), and other trade associations and regulatory bodies, have a role to play in development and promotion. They represent the interests of their members and help them operate successfully in business.

The relevant trade associations for each component of the travel and tourism sector have been discussed as we have studied each one. In each area, we have seen that there are regulatory and trade bodies whose role it is to advise members and represent them, particularly to the government. Ensure you have understood the role of each of these associations or regulatory bodies.

Ancillary services

This term refers to organisations that do not have a direct role in travel and tourism, but play a supporting role, perhaps offering related products and services. Examples include insurance companies that offer travel insurance and car parks operators that provide parking facilities at airports as well as in other locations.

Think about it

Imagine you are going on holiday. From planning the holiday to returning home, think of all the ancilliary organisations that you might need the services of to support your holiday choice.

2 The role of travel and tourism organisations and their interrelationships

2.1 Roles of organisations

An organisation has a number of roles, many of which were discussed in the first part of this unit. These include:

- meeting key organisational aims
- providing products and services (e.g. accommodation, transport, selling products)
- being responsible to stakeholders
- being environmentally and ethically responsible
- contributing to international and UK economies.

In order to understand better the roles of organisations it is useful to look at specific examples (see page 13).

Aims

All organisations determine their aims as an organisation. These differ according to the type of business operation and structure of the organisation. You will explore this in detail in Unit 2. Aims will be written and you can find them on the websites of organisations or in their annual reports.

Most companies, especially those in private ownership, seek to make a profit. They can do this by making more sales (as long as they are at the right price) or by increasing their market share (taking sales from their competitors).

Thinking about the components of travel and tourism that have already been studied, you can identify those that are privately owned by individuals or by shareholders and that try to make a profit. This includes all of the accommodation, transport tour operations and travel agency industries. These organisations will fail to satisfy their shareholders if they do not make a profit, as shareholders invest in order to receive a return on their investment from company profits – known as a dividend (see page 36).

Examples of companies and their roles

British Airways

Here is an example of an airline, British Airways (BA), and its role. Remember that the airline aims to make a profit, but in 2009 it made a loss.

The role of BA is:

- to meet the needs of passengers by providing travel on the routes demanded and good in-flight service
- to meet the needs of freight customers
- to fulfil its responsibility to its shareholders, who expect British Airways to make a profit and provide a return on investment
- to provide sufficient remuneration and good working conditions to staff – the airline employs more than 40,000 people.

Activity: British Airways

Find out about the products and services available to British Airways customers. Compare Economy with Club World and make a table charting your comparison. This information is available on the BA website (www.ba.com).

Functional skills

Finding and selecting relevant information, then formatting and presenting it, will help to develop your skills in **ICT**.

VisitBritain

Other components of travel and tourism belong in public ownership – that is, they are run by the government or one of its departments. Their role is not to make a profit, but to provide a service to the community or to the electorate. VisitBritain is a good example.

The role of VisitBritain is to market the UK to the British and the rest of the world. Formed by the merger of the British Tourist Authority and the English Tourism Council, its mission is to build the value of tourism by creating world-class destination brands and marketing campaigns. It also aims to build partnerships with other organisations which have a stake in British tourism. These organisations include the British Council, UKinbound, the British Hospitality Association and the UK Border Agency.

Part of VisitBritain's role is to advise the government and other bodies on issues that might affect the British tourism industry. The aim is to provide advice that reflects the needs of both the tourism sector, and the tourist, and to recommend courses of action to the government.

- What is a leisure visitor?
- What is meant by impartial tourist information?

Passenger Focus

Another example of a government funded body is Passenger Focus.

It is an independent public body set up by the Government to protect the interests of rail passengers. The body campaigns for improvements in services for passengers by working with the government and the industry. The areas under scrutiny are fares and tickets, the level of service and investment. Passengers with complaints can have their complaint taken up by Passenger Focus. Find out more at www.passengerfocus.org.uk.

Passenger Focus doesn't have to make a profit and it doesn't have shareholders. It does have a responsibility to passengers to provide an appropriate service and it does have to account for its spending to the government.

Civil Aviation Authority (CAA)

All organisations have to comply with legislation and regulations that impact on their operations, for example health and safety at work. However, there are also organisations whose role is to ensure the compliance of others in the travel and tourism sector. A good example is the Civil Aviation Authority.

The responsibilities of the CAA are to:

- ensure that UK civil aviation standards are set and achieved

- regulate airlines, airports and National Air Traffic Services' economic activities and encourage a diverse and competitive industry
- manage the UK's principal travel protection scheme, the ATOL scheme, license UK airlines and manage consumer issues
- bring civil and military interests together to ensure that the airspace needs of all users are met as equitably as possible.

The CAA also advises the government on aviation issues. It receives no government funding, but is funded by the charges it makes for its services.

Other responsibilities

Most organisations have a published policy on 'corporate social responsibility' (CSR). This is where they explain how they aim to be environmentally and ethically responsible. This is particularly important in travel and tourism, as the sector has a great impact on communities and resources. This is explored in Unit 12 *Responsible Tourism*.

It is also the role of the travel and tourism sector to contribute to the economy. The sector does this by contributing to **gross domestic product (GDP)** and the **balance of payments**. It also creates employment.

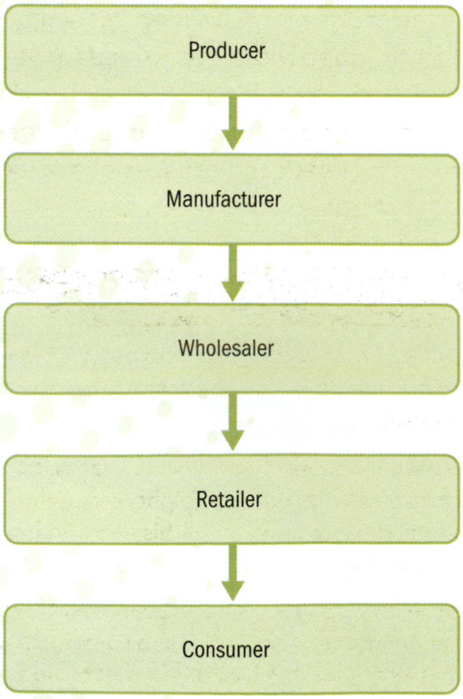

Key terms

Gross domestic product (GDP) – this is the value of all final goods and services produced within a country in a given period of time.

Balance of payments – one of the UK's key economic statistics. It measures the economic transactions between the UK and the rest of the world. It tells us the difference between spending on imports and exports.

2.2 Interrelationships

The different components of the travel and tourism sector cannot work in isolation. Each relies on others for its success. In this section you will examine how businesses work together and who needs whom.

The chain of distribution and integration

The chain of distribution (also known as the channel of distribution) is the means of getting the product to the consumer. It applies in any industry and traditionally takes the form shown in Figure 1.3.

In this traditional chain of distribution, businesses fit neatly into a category such as 'retailer' and perform the role of that business. However, the sector is much more complex than that and in many cases the traditional chain has been shortened. Figures 1.4 and 1.5 give some examples.

Producer
↓
Manufacturer
↓
Wholesaler
↓
Retailer
↓
Consumer

Figure 1.3: Chain of distribution

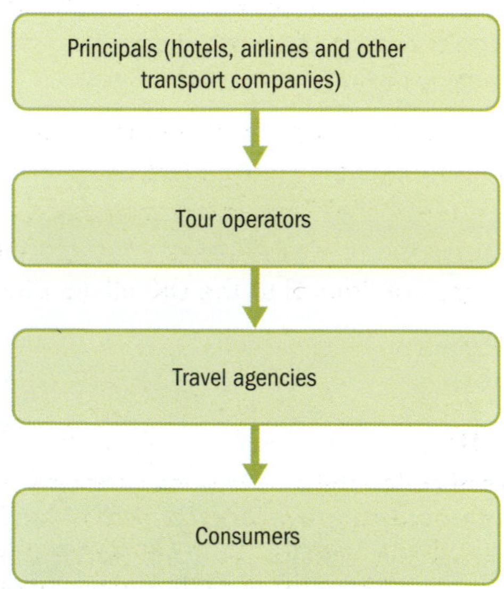

Figure 1.4: Simple chain of distribution in the travel and tourism sector

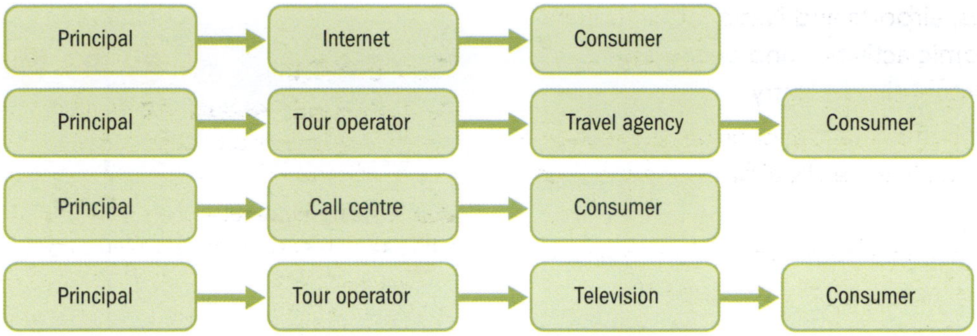

Principal → Internet → Consumer

Principal → Tour operator → Travel agency → Consumer

Principal → Call centre → Consumer

Principal → Tour operator → Television → Consumer

Figure 1.5: Channel/Chain of distribution in the travel and tourism sector

Vertical and horizontal integration

In addition, companies do not stick rigidly to one line of business. They tend to buy or merge with other businesses, always striving for greater commercial success and market dominance. When companies do this it is known as vertical or horizontal integration.

Vertical integration occurs when two companies at different levels in the chain of distribution merge or are bought. This may be backwards integration – for example, a tour operator buys a hotel – or forwards integration, for example a tour operator may buy a travel agency.

Tour operators have bought or created airlines, hotels and travel agencies. This means they own all the different components in the chain of distribution and are able to control the whole operation. They claim that this gives them **economies of scale** and allows them to offer better prices to customers. It can also mean that smaller operators are forced out of business.

If a tour operator buys another tour operator at the same level in the chain of distribution, this is known as horizontal integration.

Most of the major tour operators in the UK are vertically and horizontally integrated, owning their own travel agencies, airlines and often hotels, besides different tour-operating businesses. In fact, their operations are not limited to the UK; all are global operations.

Key term

Economies of scale – these occur when a company is able to spread its costs over mass-produced goods or services. Savings can be achieved through discounts for bulk purchasing, rationalisation of administration systems and management and lower production costs.

Thomas Cook Group

The Thomas Cook Group has companies in all parts of the chain of distribution: airlines, hotels, tour operators, travel and incoming agencies. Its UK operation, Thomas Cook UK & Ireland is described on its website www.thomascook.com.

The company owns about 800 travel agencies, a fleet of 45 aircraft and a workforce numbering some 19,000.

The UK's second largest vertically integrated leisure business comprises the tour operator brands Airtours, Club 18-30, Bridge, Cresta, CruiseThomasCook, Direct Holidays, Flexibletrips, flythomascook.com, Latitude, Manos, Neilson, Panorama, Style Holidays, Sunset, Sunworld Holidays, Thomas Cook, Thomas Cook Signature, Thomas Cook Sport and Tradewinds.

Interdependencies

No travel and tourism organisation can work in isolation. Each is dependent on others for its effective operation. For example, a visitor attraction depends on the transport industry to bring its customers to the attraction. It also needs the services of the local and regional tourist boards to promote it.

Activity: Airport

Study an airport of your choice. This might be one that you are able to visit or one that you can examine via its website.

- Describe the role of the airport in relation to its customer groups, airlines, freight companies and passengers. You could make this into a wall display with explanatory notes.
- Explain how an airport interrelates with other organisations from the travel and tourism industry, giving examples that include domestic, inbound and outbound tourism.

Assessment activity 1.1

Your tutor thinks it would be a good idea to 'spread the word' about travel and tourism and proposes a road show for local secondary schools.

The purpose is to spend half a day in each school mounting an exhibition or information session for Year 10 pupils. This will differ from the usual careers evening sessions in that it will be organised by students for students and it will be about the travel and tourism sector, not just the course, in order to create interest in travel and tourism.

For the tasks below, you could produce a display with illustrations and explanatory notes. You could design an information sheet to be distributed to students.

1. To give students an overview of the sector, describe the component industries. Include examples of different organisations for each of those industries. Make sure you give at least one example from each component industry. Also, make sure that your examples overall include organisations representing inbound, outbound and domestic tourism. Provide definitions of inbound, outbound and domestic tourism. **P1**
2. Describe the roles of three of the different organisations you have given as examples. These should be three different organisations from different component industries. Make sure at least one is a medium to large organisation. **P2**
3. Review, with examples, the different types of inter-relationships in travel and tourism. **P3**
4. Explain the roles of different organisations within the travel and tourism component industries, including an explanation of how they interrelate. **M1**
5. Choose one travel and tourism organisation. Analyse the importance of its interrelationships with other travel and tourism organisations. **D1**

Grading tips

P1 You need to describe each of the component industries and identify the organisations with them to achieve. This means you must include accommodation (serviced and non-serviced); transport provision (road, rail, sea and air); attractions (natural, heritage, purpose-built, events); tour operations (mass market, specialist); travel agents (retail, business, call centre, web-based); tourism development and promotion; trade associations and regulatory bodies; and ancilliary services.

P2 Ensure you provide full descriptions and cover all the key roles of the organisations in your own words. State the role of the company in terms of its organisational aims and the products and services it provides.

P3 The types of interrelationships you should review are the chain of distribution, integration and how organisations rely on each other. Diagrams will help you illustrate interrelationships and interdependencies and make sure all your examples are up-to-date.

M1 You will need a detailed explanation for at least two of your interdependency examples, making sure at least one of the organisations is a medium/large company. If you select a multi-national company make sure you focus on the UK part of the company.

D1 You will need to explore all aspects of interrelationship and analyse their importance to the selected organisation and to the other organisations involved. Make sure that you choose an organisation that provides sufficient coverage of all aspects of interrelationships in your analysis.

PLTS

When you plan and carry out your research you will be practising your skills as an **independent enquirer**.

Functional skills

As you read and summarise information from different sources you will gain functional skills in **English**.

3 Know the developments that have shaped the present-day travel and tourism sector

Since the 1960s, the travel and tourism sector has changed dramatically. It is unlikely that your grandparents had regular holidays abroad unless they were quite wealthy, but today foreign travel is within the reach of almost all segments of society. Certain key developments have made the possibility of travel open to almost all of us and continue to have an impact on present day travel and tourism.

Key term

Deregulation – this occurs when a government decides to remove restrictions on the operation of a business to allow greater competition and hopefully greater efficiency and reduced prices for customers.

Air passenger duty – a duty levied per passenger by the government. It is collected at the time of ticket purchase by the airline.

3.1 Key developments from the 1960s to the present day

Legislation

The UK government has always recognised the importance of tourism to the economy and has introduced new policies and laws over the years.

Development of Tourism Act 1969

The Development of Tourism Act established a British Tourist Authority and tourist boards for England, Scotland and Wales. The British Tourist Authority and the English Tourism Council have now been merged to form VisitBritain (see page 11). The Act's aim was to co-ordinate all the organisations that make up the tourism sector and provide it with a single voice.

Since this Act was passed the responsibility for tourism funding and development in Scotland and Wales has been devolved to the Scottish Parliament and the Welsh Assembly. Also, VisitScotland and VisitWales have been given the power to market overseas independently of VisitBritain. This has caused a lack of clarity in the role of VisitBritain, as its role is to market Scotland and Wales as well as England.

Transport Acts 1980 and 1985

The 1980 Transport Act ended licensing regulations affecting express coach routes and tours of over 30 miles. It led to competition between National Bus (then a public company) and private companies. The 1985 Transport Act brought about wholesale **deregulation**. This meant private companies could operate on any route.

Air passenger duty

In 1996, **air passenger duty** was reduced on economy flights, removing a barrier to the growth of inbound tourism. However, in 2006 it was greatly increased. Further increases have been planned from November 2010 causing controversy in the industry.

Tourism strategy

Tomorrow's Tourism – a growth industry for the new millenium, the government's tourism strategy, was published in 1999. It is still valid, although it has been reviewed.

Package Travel, Package Holidays and Package Tours Regulations 1992

As a result of an EC Directive, since 1992 all UK tour operators offering package holidays have been subject to the Package Travel Regulations. The regulations set out the tour operators' responsibilities to their customers and what those customers can do if the regulations are breached.

Product development

Holiday camps

Between 1945 and 1960, holiday camps were at their peak, catering for about 60 per cent of the holiday market. Warners, Butlins and Pontins were important names in the market. The holiday camp went into decline in the 1970s as demand for sunshine and package holidays abroad grew.

Now we have holiday parks such as Center Parcs. Its first village in the UK was opened in 1987 at Sherwood Forest. It offers short-break holidays, with mid-week or weekend breaks all year round, and longer stays if desired.

Butlins still exists and is owned by the Bourne Leisure Group.

Package holidays

Thomas Cook is credited with being the first person to organise a package holiday, in 1841. That was a trip from Leicester to Loughborough by train – not very far at all!

The first package as we know it today was in 1949 and was organised by Vladimir Raitz. He took 32 passengers to Corsica on a DC3 aeroplane. He charged them £32.50. The package included accommodation in tents, return flights, transfers and full board. He established Horizon Holidays in the same year, and by the end of the 1950s the company had grown to be one of the UK's major tour operators.

Other companies followed Horizon's example and package tours grew in popularity. The major growth came in the 1970s, as people became more prosperous and keen to see new places. Most of the package holidays were to Spain and its islands, where hotels were built rapidly to fulfil the demand from British and German tourists.

Currency restrictions were lifted in the 1970s. Before this, tourists were allowed to take only £50 in sterling out of the country. This led to an increase in the appeal of the package holiday as tourists could take more spending money with them.

Destination development

As the world realises the economic benefits tourism brings, more and more governments plough money into attracting tourists from overseas.

Dubai has constructed hotels, residential developments and shopping centres to attract tourists and added the infrastructure and transport links to bring the tourists in. There are few places in the world where tourists have yet to venture, but here are some more examples of developing destinations:

- China increased in popularity with the 2008 Olympic Games in Beijing. The authorities have allowed more tourists and developed facilities accordingly.
- The United Arab Emirates capital Abu Dhabi is described as the new Dubai with plans to add 25,000 hotel rooms in the next few years and a Guggenheim museum.
- According to ABTA – The Travel Association, the books and drama series about the No.1 Ladies' Detective Agency will attract visitors to Botswana.

Dubai has developed to become a modern destination. What other destinations have developed to meet modern needs?

Technological development

Reservations and bookings

One of the areas of greatest impact through new technology has been in the way bookings are made.

As demand for travel grew in the 1950s onwards, reservations departments were introduced. With the advent of computers, tour operators and airlines developed their own systems. Eventually these systems were linked to travel agencies via terminals and travel agents could make bookings in their offices. These are known as 'Viewdata' systems. Thomson decided to accept bookings only through Viewdata, which meant that the system was essential for any travel agent. By today's standards Viewdata is unsophisticated technology, although it is still used.

Meanwhile, airlines developed Computer Reservation Systems (CRS). Airlines started to use computers in the 1950s to store the huge amount of information they needed to access. The CRS was used internally by airlines and agents would use a publication called OAG (the Official Airline Guide) to look up flight times and details, then telephone the airline to make a booking. Today travel agencies have direct access to the CRS systems. Global Distribution Systems (GDS) link up several CRS systems and present them to the travel agent.

The internet has grown rapidly as a means of booking holidays and flights. With increased confidence and access to information, travellers happily book all aspects of their holiday on-line and in effect make their own packages.

Activity: Make your own package holiday

Use the internet to package your own imaginary holiday to Majorca. You will be travelling with a friend for a week. You will need to find information about a flight, a suitable hotel and car hire. Select the most suitable products for you. Do not use any resources other than the internet. Make notes on the products available, the web addresses and the costs. (Stop before you get to the final booking page!)

Self check-in at airports

Where this service is available, passengers can save time by checking in at a kiosk where they can choose their seat and print their own boarding pass. From there they can go to a 'fast bag drop' and leave their hold baggage. Passengers without baggage can go straight to the boarding gate.

On-line check-in for airlines

Using this system, passengers can check in without even being at the airport. From home or the office they go on-line and follow instructions to check-in, choosing their seats and printing their boarding passes. On-line check-in is used by most airlines and aims to reduce queues at check-in desks and subsequently the use of ground staff.

Transport development – air

The aviation industry in travel and tourism includes airlines and airports. The sector is heavily dependent on aviation for transporting passengers to their destinations.

In 1954 Boeing introduced its new passenger jet aircraft, the Boeing 707. It began commercial service in 1959 and dominated the market. The Boeing 727 was introduced in 1963 and has been one of the most successful series of passenger jetliners of the past 50 years.

In 1969 Boeing produced the 747 jumbo jet – a wide-bodied jet. The 747 can seat 500 passengers, though it usually holds 385. It cruises at about 965 kilometres per hour and has a non-stop range of just over 11,500 kilometres. It usually has a forward first class (or 'business class') section and a second level on which the cockpit and a lounge are located. This aircraft had the following impact on the package holiday market:

- it became possible to fly further in less time, making long-haul destinations more accessible
- increased capacity on the jet led to a decrease in the price per seat, bringing the price of holidays down
- as jumbo jets were used more, smaller aircraft were available for charter operations.

In 1976 British Airways, in collaboration with Air France, started the first supersonic airliner service, Concorde. Concorde ceased flying in 2003, but it had set the standard for luxury air travel.

Super planes

The Airbus A380 can seat between 555 and 800 passengers. Singapore Airlines was the first airline to fly the plane on an inaugural flight to Sydney in 2007. It was also the first airline to fly the superjumbo to Paris in 2009. However, airports which accept the aircraft have to make changes to infrastructure in order to accommodate the large plane and the large numbers of passengers boarding and disembarking. Some airports are reluctant to make such changes until major American airlines have committed themselves to these huge aircraft.

Another new aircraft is the 7E7 (787) Dreamliner introduced by Boeing. It has lower operating costs and fuel consumption than the current Boeing 767 and a greater flight range, so it is expected to be a popular choice for airline fleets. For example, this plane can fly from the UK to Hawaii non-stop. The plane is expected to be delivered in late 2010.

Introduction and growth of low-cost airlines

Deregulation of air travel in Europe led to the development of low-cost airlines. The European Union (EU) started the liberalisation process in 1987, when cost-related fares and certain types of discount fares were first allowed. The final stage of deregulation came in 1993.

Deregulation meant that EU airlines could establish themselves in any EU member state and obtain an operating licence. All routes within the EU are available to all EU carriers. Thus, an airline such as Ryanair can have a base in Frankfurt Hahn and fly to, and from, countries all over the EU. In 1995, easyJet launched a low-cost airline offering two routes from Luton to Glasgow and Edinburgh. Now there are many low-cost airlines flying travellers all over Europe.

In 2004 there was much expansion in routes as the EU grew to 25 states. It grew again in 2007, when Romania and Bulgaria joined the EU, to become 27 states. The new member states in Eastern Europe brought opportunities for travel to, and from, these countries. easyJet introduced flights to Budapest (Hungary), Ljubljana (Slovenia) and Bratislava (Slovakia). Ryanair flies to Riga in Latvia.

How and why have places in Eastern Europe, such as Ljubljana, grown in their appeal?

Low-cost airlines have encouraged people to travel more and gained new travellers when people who were not used to travelling abroad were attracted by the low prices. Many of the low-cost airlines operate from regional airports, so travel is even more convenient.

Transport development – sea

The traditional route across the Channel to our neighbours is the ferry. There are still regular services all round the British Isles, as we have seen (page 7). Other speedier forms of ferry were introduced in the 1960s, for example the hovercraft. However, the only hovercraft now operating is between the mainland and the Isle of Wight.

Channel Tunnel

For many years a tunnel between France and England was just an idea. In 1986, Foreign Affairs ministers of both countries signed the Franco-British Treaty in Canterbury. This was ratified in 1987, paving the way for the Channel Tunnel to become a reality. The tunnel would allow the British to leave their island without flying, and without risking seasickness, and encourage our continental neighbours to visit the UK.

Work on boring the tunnel began in the UK in 1987. The tunnel opened in 1994. Its original budget was £4.8 billion, but its final cost exceeded £10 billion. Ten major British and French construction companies were involved in the building of the tunnel, collectively known as the 'TransManche Link'.

Super ships

A new passenger ferry has been created by a French naval architect, Gilles Vaton. It is called a *Bateau à Grande Vitesse* (BGV), which means high-speed boat. Because of its high speed, the ferry could cut the journey from Portsmouth to Caen in France from six hours to under three, and the 20-hour journey from Marseilles to Algiers to nine hours.

High speed is not the boat's only advantage – there are already fast catamarans operating as ferries. The BGV can maintain its speed in all weathers, whereas the catamarans have to stay in port in rough weather. Boulogne was the first terminal to adopt the BGV in 2007.

Transport development – rail

Successive governments have cut rail services and closed railway stations since the 1960s. People had more cars and preferred to travel on an increasing road network than by train. However, the position is changing again with a great deal of investment in rail networks and new technology.

High-speed trains

High-speed train lines, such as France's extensive *Train à Grande Vitesse* (TGV) network, have helped maintain the success of the railways in some countries. The TGV is operated by the French nationally owned and subsidised rail company, the SNCF. The TGV travels at speeds of over 300 kilometres per hour.

The European high-speed rail network has been extended and TGV services now run direct from Paris, the Channel Tunnel and Brussels towards Germany. The Belgian high-speed trains are known as Thalys. It is important to note that such trains require new tracks to run on, which means substantial investment.

To keep abreast of our European neighbours and increase speed of transport to them, the track on the UK side of the tunnel has been renewed. New track has reduced the journey time of the UK leg from London by almost half.

A proposal has been made by Network Rail for a high-speed railway line linking Scotland and London. This would provide competition for airlines working routes between London and Scotland. It is estimated that the journey would take only two hours and sixteen minutes.

For the future, in order to compete with low-cost airlines, international train services in Europe will need to be overhauled. The European Commission wishes to open up competition in cross-border passenger rail links, including high-speed links like Eurostar and Thalys, to increase price competition between rival operators by 2010.

Lifestyle changes

Holiday patterns

There has been immense growth in the short-break market, both within the UK and with people travelling abroad. People take more holidays than ever before. Cities are very popular destinations, especially London, New York and Amsterdam.

Increased income and expectations

We are wealthier as a nation and have higher expectations than in the past. Most people have been abroad and most expect to take at least one holiday a year.

Improved education

The level of education achieved by people from all sectors of society has improved since the 1960s. More students go to university and more of the population achieve at least a Level 2 qualification, for example a GCSE.

The more educated we are, the more we are aware of the world and its possibilities. We are curious about different cultures and languages and keen to experience them. As we live in a multicultural society we are more familiar with different religions, foods and cultures and less anxious about the unfamiliarity involved in travelling to new places.

Age

One of the most important markets in travel and tourism is the 'grey' market. This refers to older people who have plenty of time and available funds and who want to travel. Older people these days are usually in good health due to the success of the National Health Service and the availability of good food.

Contributing to private pension schemes over their working years has led to a good income in retirement for many people. It has become common for people to retire earlier, even in their 50s, and take advantage of good pension arrangements. If the mortgage has been paid off and the children have left home, older people can party!

Saga is the most famous tour operator catering for older people, but many tour operators are aware of and market to this group.

Activity: Eastern Europe

ABTA – The Travel Association reports that eastern European destinations are seeing a surge in demand. Write a short informal report for a travel agent. Make sure you give examples of specific destinations. Describe the key trends and factors that have led to an increase in demand for eastern European destinations.

Functional skills

By communicating information in a suitable style and format, you will demonstrate your **English** skills in writing.

3.2 Present day travel and tourism sector

New products and services

There is a wealth of different products and services available catering for all tastes and markets.

Some of the latest products include:

- concierge travel – these services are targeted at the very wealthy and offer luxurious holidays customised to the tastes of the traveller
- more personalised services for mass tourists – examples of companies at the forefront of concierge travel for the masses are Virgin and Kuoni
- cultural tourism – for example roots tourism, where tourists take DNA tests and travel to countries like Africa seeking out their ancestral origin
- pop-up restaurants – this means people inviting guests into their private homes at a price, for example Jo Wood in London
- pop-up hotels – for example, modular hotels made from steel containers in China. Travelodge has one in Uxbridge.

Business operations

Following the severe recession of 2008/9 tour operators had to streamline operations, cutting capacity on holidays offered to customers. Forty tour operators failed between 2008 and 2009, showing what a difficult market it was. When the recession ends it seems likely that the travel and tourism market will improve and new companies may form.

Consumer demand

In 2009 consumers tended to book their holidays later hoping for reduced prices at the last minute. This, in turn, impacted on business operations as it made it difficult for tour operators and travel agents to forecast. This may have led to significantly reduced booking levels for tour operators outside the peak holiday periods.

The short-break market is still healthy with more cities and activities on offer. Many people are now choosing to stay in the UK for holidays due to the poor exchange rate of the pound to the euro

Types of organisations and competition

Remember that two major groups dominate the tour operating industry: TUI and Thomas Cook. In spite of their dominance, travel and tourism still includes hundreds of small businesses. Some are in tour operation, but most are in travel agency and hospitality businesses. You have seen how vertical and horizontal integration benefit businesses and there is no reason to expect this to change in the near future.

Numbers employed in travel and tourism

There are an estimated 1.4 million jobs in tourism in the UK, some 5 per cent of all people in employment. Approximately 130,400 of these jobs are in self-employment. If we add jobs indirectly related to tourism the figure is 2.8 million jobs.

Contribution to GDP

Tourism contributes to the economy and therefore to the GDP (see page 14) as visitors spend money on goods and services and also on transport to enter a country.

The impact on the economy of incoming and outbound tourism is recorded in the balance of payments (see page 14). Each sector of the economy is measured in terms of its imports and exports. **Travel services** have their own balance which contributes to the overall balance of payments. Transport is shown separately from travel services.

Tourism has a direct impact on the economy, contributing about 3.7 per cent of GDP (about £52 billion). There are also indirect impacts of tourism on the economy as tourism interacts with other businesses such as construction and retail. With indirect impact added, the contribution to GDP rises to about 8.2 per cent (2007). However, there is a £20.5 billion deficit between the amount UK holidaymakers spend abroad and how much foreign visitors spend here.

Key term

Travel services – these include the goods and services consumed by travellers, such as accommodation, meals and transport (within the economy visited).

Activity: Balance of payments

Find out what the current travel balance is. You can find this in *The Pink Book*, a government publication, in your library or online. Look at the transport balance also. Is there a deficit or a surplus? Discuss your findings with your teacher or tutor.

4 How trends and factors are currently affecting the travel and tourism sector

Many of the trends and factors currently affecting the travel and tourism sector were outlined in the last section. Here are some more.

4.1 Trends and their effects

Increased frequency of holidays

As people become more affluent they are able to take more frequent holidays. This had led to the popularity of the short break, often to a city.

The traditional pattern of holiday taking is a two-week summer break, often in a Mediterranean resort. Affluent families often add a winter ski break. According to a 2008 Mintel report, an estimated 7 million UK resident adults take two or more European holidays and an estimated 1.7 million take two or more long-haul trips annually.

The trend had turned in 2009 with UK residents making fewer outbound trips. According to the International Passenger Survey, trips abroad fell by 17 per cent, which has meant a decline in visitor numbers.

The effect of a decline in visitor numbers has included jobs in destinations being reduced and tour operators cutting capacity. Airlines have also cut capacity, which means they are operating fewer flights.

Holiday home ownership

There has been an upward trend in UK residents owning second homes, according to figures from the Office of National Statistics (ONS). Although some can be explained by higher divorce rates and people having second homes for work, it is acknowledged that about 50 per cent are holiday homes.

About 235,000 second homes are owned abroad by British citizens. Growth in these numbers can be attributed to the rapid growth of low-cost airlines, which allow cheaper access to holiday homes. Another factor is people from immigrant backgrounds, from countries such as India, Pakistan, South Africa and the Caribbean, wishing to own holiday properties back in their countries of origin.

Kent is predicted as an area of growth for second home ownership. Many second homeowners abroad have their home in Spain. There are many examples of people commuting from Spain during the week to work in the UK.

More recently, some of the developments of new holiday homes have been halted in order to allow for a reduction in the number of people buying holiday homes abroad during the recession. In some places, such as Dubai, buildings have been left half-finished until funding to continue the work can be found.

> **Think about it**
>
> What is the effect when people have bought a holiday home in a region that is served by a low-cost airline route and the airline decides to scrap the route due to recession?

Greater flexibility of booking

As people become more confident about travel and more used to travelling abroad and seeing different cultures, they are able to book the component parts of their holiday themselves rather than go to a travel agent. This is most likely to happen for more frequent lower-priced trips. When people are spending a lot of money, for example on a wedding or cruise, they are more likely to seek expert advice from a travel agent.

Many people now have access to the internet at home and are able to carry out research into travel and destinations and make their own bookings on-line. Websites, like Expedia, have profited from internet growth by providing the ability to make up holiday packages, selecting flights and accommodation as desired.

The effect of more people booking independently is that there is less demand for travel agency services. Web-based companies are able to compete more easily with large tour operators.

More independent travellers

Mintel reports a continuing rise in the number of independently booked holidays (see their report *British Holidays UK*). This is almost entirely due to the internet. It is not only young travellers who go independently, but also more upmarket customers who plan their own luxury trips and want value for money. However, it is not expected that the package holiday market will decline completely as it offers convenience and in some instances cheaper packages.

Opportunity for adventure

There is no one definition of adventure travel. Surveys have shown that some adventure holidays include activities such as bird watching and cultural activities. Others perceive adventure holidays to include extreme sports and risk-taking.

The effect of this is that, in spite of the difficulty of defining adventure travel, it is clear that organisations offering 'adventure travel' report increased interest and increased bookings. Tour operators are aware of the trend and have created, or acquired, activity or adventure holiday businesses. The travel group Holidaybreak is a good example, with many adventure holiday companies such as Explore and Regaldive.

Think about it

What is your idea of an adventurous holiday? Bird watching or extreme sport?

Short-term trends

Some trends are short-term, but have a serious impact on the sector. You need to look closely at these trends and assess the situation when you are reading the text. These trends include the following and relate to the recession of 2008–10.

Decline in incoming and outgoing passenger numbers

A decline in passenger numbers can be linked to a recession. An unusual way of looking at consumer behaviour in a recession was released by Harvard University psychologists. The suggestion is that rather than targeting customers according to age or lifestyle, the trade should look at customers' reaction to recession. Four groups were described:

- 'Slam the brakes on' – people at the lower end of earning, who stop spending as they are badly hit by the recession.
- 'Pained but patient' – can be persuaded to go on holiday as long as they think they are getting value for money.
- 'Live for the day' – mainly young and urban, who see little need to alter their spending habits.
- 'Comfortably well off' – in the top 5 per cent income bracket and not really affected by the recession, but may want to be more discreet in their spending.

Activity: Which category do you belong to?

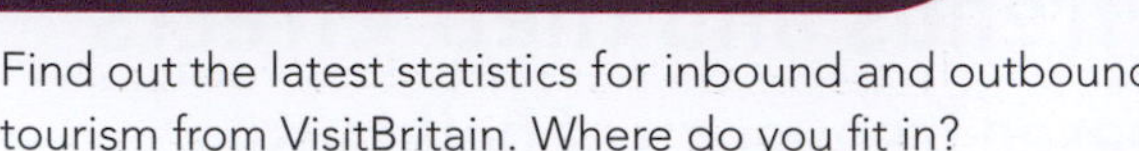

Find out the latest statistics for inbound and outbound tourism from VisitBritain. Where do you fit in?

Lower spending of UK tourists in Euro destinations

This trend is entirely due to the poor exchange rate (see factors below). In 2009 the pound (GBP) was weak against the euro; the exchange rate was around 1.1 euros to a pound. This was a significant drop from the 1.4 and even 1.5 of the previous few years. So UK holidaymakers found Europe very expensive.

The effect of this is that when people holiday under these circumstances they change their behaviour on holiday, spending less freely and eating in their accommodation rather than in restaurants. This means less revenue for businesses in the destination and leads to lower investment in improving or maintaining facilities.

Activity: Exchange rates

- Check the exchange rate of the pound (GBP) against the euro. What is the current trend? Check the US dollar as well.
- Work out the value of the following in euros at the current exchange rate: £10, £35, £150, £200.

Try to get into the habit of checking exchange rates at regular intervals.

Functional skills

As you calculate values using exchange rates you will need to identify mathematical methods. This will help to develop your skills in **Maths**.

Growth and expansion of regional airports

This has been a popular trend with passengers who like the convenience of travelling from a nearby airport. The trend is possible because it is government policy to expand regional airports laid out in their Aviation White Paper. However, airport expansion is also controversial due to environmental considerations, so a change of government might see a change to this policy. Low-cost airlines often use regional airports as they are cheaper, which means that the growth of low-cost airlines has contributed to the growth of these airports.

London City Airport increased capacity in 2009 from 80,000 to 120,000 flights per year. It is also launching a route to New York.

Withdrawal of some destinations by low-cost airlines

The 2008–10 recession has had a huge impact on aviation. Many airlines made a loss in 2009 and cut staff. Low-cost airlines consolidated their routes and withdrew some unprofitable routes.

Low-cost airlines continually review their routes at all times as their business model depends on having

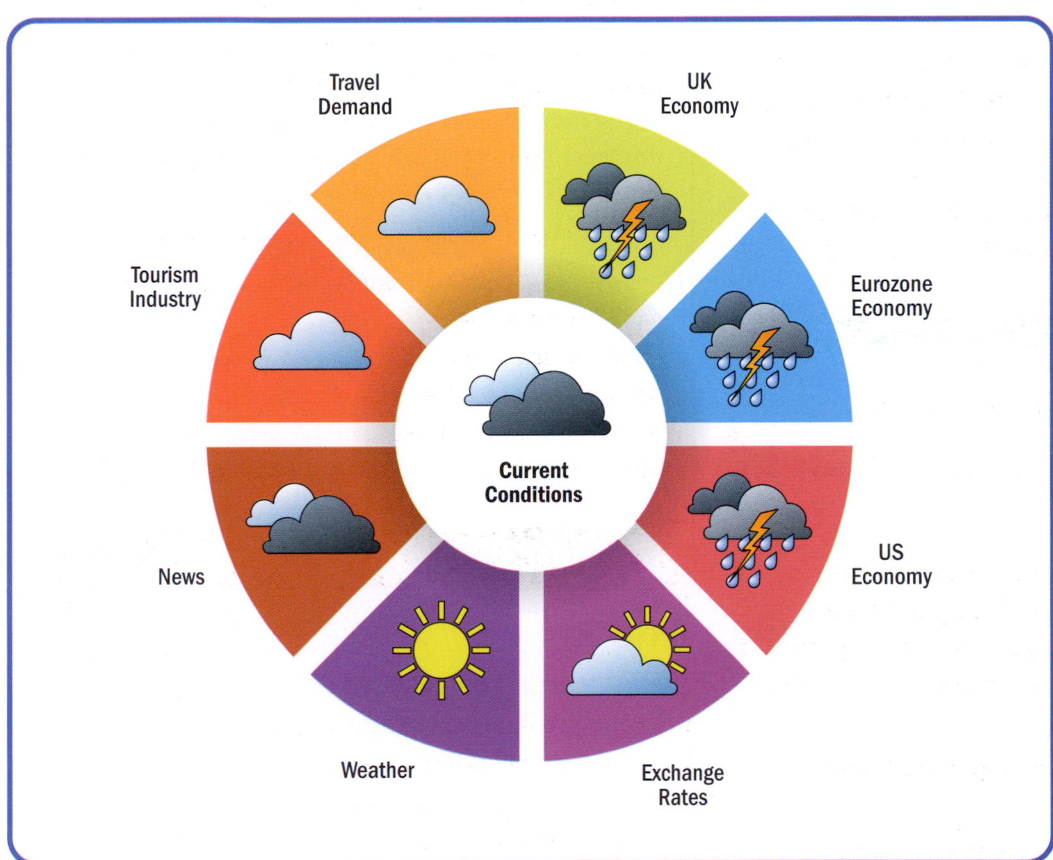

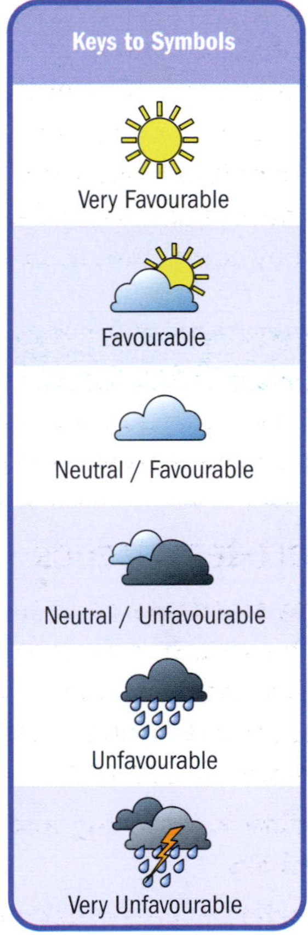

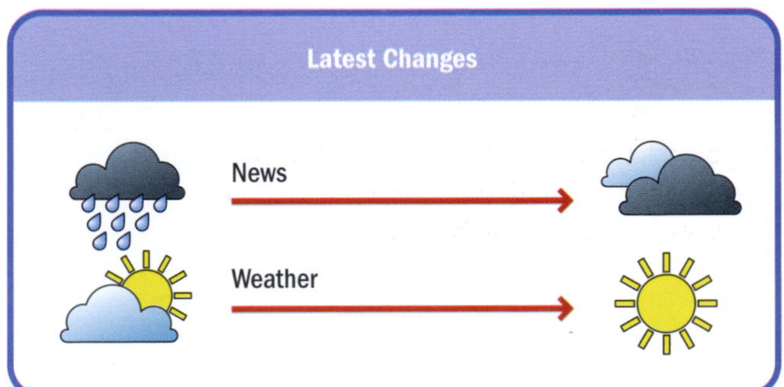

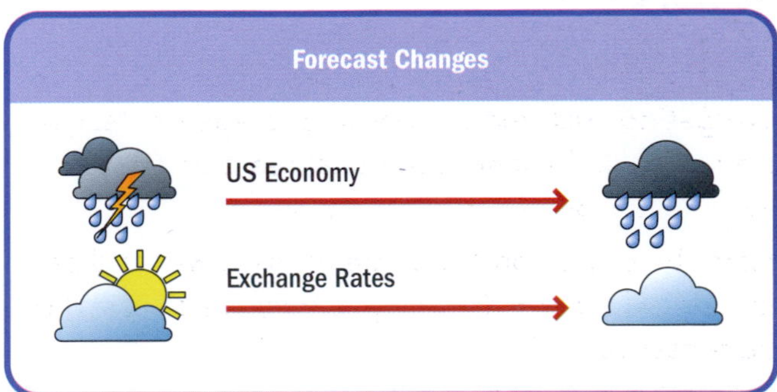

Figure 1.6: Factors contributing to tourism trends in Britain, May 2010

high loads. They need to look at the popularity of destinations and target routes accordingly. The effect of recession is that some of the many routes to Eastern Europe may be axed. However, new routes can also be added. Recent additions have been further afield to Egypt and to the Canary Islands.

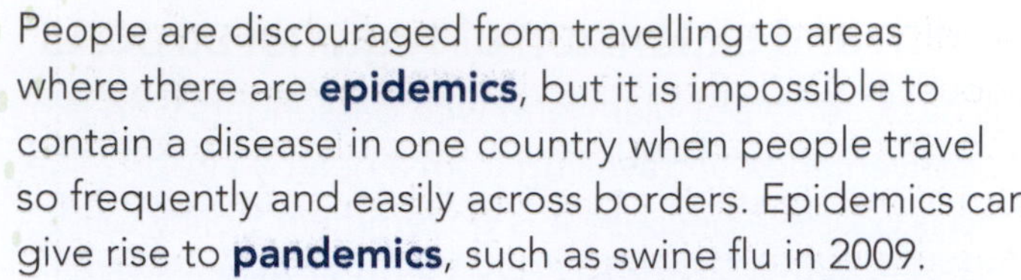

People are discouraged from travelling to areas where there are **epidemics**, but it is impossible to contain a disease in one country when people travel so frequently and easily across borders. Epidemics can give rise to **pandemics**, such as swine flu in 2009.

Activity: Tourism trends

Look at Figure 1.6 on page 25. Draw your own version based on your own research into current trends.

Key terms

Epidemic – an outbreak of a contagious disease that spreads rapidly and widely within an area.

Pandemic – an epidemic of an infectious disease that spreads across a large region; for instance a continent, or even worldwide.

4.2 Factors and their effects

Natural disasters

Natural disasters such as hurricanes and earthquakes bring about a decline in tourism in the affected area. Climatic disasters have a devastating impact on destinations and on their tourist industry.

An example is the earthquake in Haiti in 2010. The earthquake resulted in thousands of deaths. The death toll was appalling but the livelihood of the survivors was also threatened due to the devastation of the infrastructure.

In 2009 floods affected a tourist area of the Lake District, Cockermouth in the UK, bringing devastation to the area and its industries.

Think about it

What do you think are the effects of the flooding on a tourist town?

Health warnings, epidemics and pandemics

In 2009 an outbreak of swine flu began in Mexico. The immediate impact on tourism into Mexico was very serious as the flu quickly spread and people cancelled holidays to avoid it. This echoed the impact of an earlier outbreak of the respiratory disease SARS in 2003.

Activity: Impact of swine flu

Many travel companies suffered losses due to the outbreak of swine flu in Mexico in 2009. The British government advised people to avoid non-essential travel to Mexico. Some people who were on holiday in Mexico at this time chose to end their holidays early and come home. This cost was covered by tour operators.

How are tour operators affected by epidemics like swine flu? What happens to holidaymakers already on holiday when there is an event such as this?

Research some current factors which are impacting on demand for specific destinations. Give examples of what tour operators are doing in response to changes in demand.

Terrorism

The devastating terrorist attacks of 11 September 2001 ('9/11') in the USA also had an impact on the UK and the worldwide tourism industry. People were afraid to fly, particularly American tourists, resulting in a decline in visitors to the UK and a decline in worldwide travel for leisure and business.

The impact of '9/11' has been long-term. Security is high priority at airports. Further plots involving liquid explosives were foiled by Intelligence operations in 2006.

In December 2009, a 23-year-old Nigerian man attempted to set off an explosion on a flight from Amsterdam to Detroit. The attack failed but the United States government put even stricter security screening measures in place following the incident.

The effect of these attempts to attack planes were still serious. In 2006 international travellers were stopped overnight from carrying liquids onto planes. Stringent restrictions are still in place. Liquids must be carried in a see-through plastic bag and each container must not exceed 100 millilitres. These restrictions cause delay and disruption as passengers struggle to understand what is allowed.

Terrorist attacks in destinations also impact on tourism. Recent years have seen explosions in Majorca, Bali and Egypt. We should expect tight security and threats of terrorist attacks into the foreseeable future. Every incident brings more security checks and more difficulty for air passengers to travel freely.

Environmental issues

As society and government policy become more 'green' the awareness of tourists about environmental issues grows. This leads to a demand for responsible travel and an expectation that companies will adopt environmentally friendly policies. There is also pressure from governments to reduce the 'carbon footprint' of travel, particularly air travel. Airlines in the UK have responded by investing in more fuel efficient, quieter planes. These issues are explored in detail in Unit 12.

Cost of travel

Travel is relatively cheap today, particularly air travel, and is no longer available only to the elite. The advent of low-cost airlines has brought down the cost of air travel. Long-haul travel prices are more fluid, but there are often bargains to be had off peak. Air travel is likely to become more expensive if proposed air passenger taxes are introduced.

Rail travel is expensive in the UK but advance booking can result in favourable prices.

World recession

The recession in 2008–10 has had a big impact on tourism, even coining a new term in the UK, the 'staycation' – a holiday staying in the UK rather than going abroad.

You saw some of the trends arising from recession in the last section. As people took fewer holidays in this period, companies started to struggle and some went bankrupt, for example SKY Europe, a low-cost airline operating from Eastern Europe. Those people still employed during the recession could find lots of bargain holidays on offer. However, even the employed are still more reluctant to travel as they might feel insecure about keeping their jobs.

As the economy improves, we can expect tourist numbers to increase.

Currency exchange rates

Currency exchange rates are linked to the recession as they reflect the strength of one currency and therefore the strength of that country's economy in relation to another.

The effects of this is that, when the pound (GBP) is strong against the euro, UK outbound travellers can buy more euros for their money and therefore can have a cheaper holiday in Europe. However, a strong pound would similarly deter Europeans from coming to the UK as it would be more expensive for them.

Travel and tourism organisations keep a close eye on exchange rates as they affect the prices they pay for accommodation and services in resorts.

New developments

You examined transport and technological developments earlier in the unit (see pages 18–21). In general, developments help to increase sales as they represent improvements in the service offer, such as faster travelling times or easier booking.

Activity: Factors affecting travel and tourism

Look in the quality newspapers and find examples of trends or factors that currently affect travel and tourism.

- Review these trends or factors and explain how they affect the industry.
- Analyse how travel and tourism organisations are responding to changing trends and factors.

PLTS

As you explore issues, events or problems from different perspectives when you study current factors you will be an **independent enquirer**.

Assessment activity 1.2

In this activity you will be adding to your preparations for the Road Show promoting the travel and tourism sector to students in schools.

Your audience needs to know about the development of the travel and tourism sector. Add the following to your display or information session:

1 a summary of ten key developments that have shaped the present day travel and tourism sector P4

2 a review of current trends and factors that currently affect the sector (a minimum of three trends and three factors not more than five years old) P5

3 explanatory notes accompanying your review showing the significant effect of developments, trends and factors on the sector M2

4 an analysis of the response of two travel and tourism organisations to the trends and factors you reviewed D2

Grading tips

You can start looking at developments from the 1960s and onwards.

P4 Make sure the developments you choose have affected, or continue to affect, the sector – for example development of new types of aircraft.

P5 Examples of trends to look for are increases or decline in different types of holidays, expansion of one particular industry and changes in spending.

Examples of factors to look for include natural disasters, heat waves, transport strikes, the introduction of new products or technology and outbreaks of war.

M2 Make sure your research is current and that you link recent and current developments, trends and factors to what is happening in the sector today. You should provide clear explanations with supporting statistics.

D2 Select two organisations from the travel and tourism component industries and analyse how changes have impacted on their operations and how effectively they have responded.

PLTS

As you plan and carry out your research you will be practising your skills as an **independent enquirer**.

Exploring ideas about the trends and factors that are currently affecting the travel and tourism sector will help to develop your **creative thinker** skills.

Functional skills

As you select and use different texts to gather your information, you will develop your **English** skills in reading.

WorkSpace

Sarah Turner

Tourist Information Officer

Sarah is a 21-year-old BTEC National Travel and Tourism graduate who currently works in the Tourist Information Centre for the city of Cambridge. 'I've lived in Cambridge most of my life and know all the sights and attractions, so armed with my BTEC Level 3 National Travel and Tourism I find this job really satisfying and enjoyable.'

Her role is to respond to any questions or queries that tourists might have about the city and to recommend to them any activities they might enjoy on their visit to the city. A city such as Cambridge relies on people like Sarah to ensure that tourists have a good time and are satisfied, as tourism spend contributes to the city's economy.

How did you manage to get a job in the Tourist Information Centre and what skills does your job require?

I was able to get a part-time job at weekends here at the Tourist Information Centre while I was doing my BTEC. But to get a full-time position here I did have to do a lot of research and study all of the University colleges, as they are a main tourist attraction.

I have to have excellent customer service as that is essentially what my job is. I found that the BTEC helped me a lot with this. I have to be able to answer any question about the city and its attractions and services. I also have to know the location of pretty much everything in the city – I probably know my way around better than a taxi driver now! The main skills I need are to be as friendly and helpful as I can to the customers.

Where do you see yourself in the future and do you think this is a good job to gain experience?

I've gained some amazing experience here that will help me in the tourism industry. I will continue to work here for another year or so and then I would like to join the tourism department of the city council and get more involved in tourism strategy. I'm sure that my BTEC National qualification and experience working for the Tourist Information Centre should help me move on.

Think about it!

1. Where is your local Tourist Information Centre?
2. Find out what kind of services they offer.
3. What kind of work experience is available there?

Just checking

1. How did the development of low-cost airlines impact on travel and tourism?
2. What is meant by deregulation?
3. What are the elements of a package holiday?
4. Give an example of legislation affecting tourism in the UK.
5. Describe the different methods of distributing travel and tourism products to consumers.
6. Why has Croatia increased in popularity as a holiday destination?
7. What is the difference between scheduled and charter airlines?
8. How do call centres motivate their staff?
9. Who are the major tour operators?
10. What is horizontal integration?
11. What is vertical integration?
12. Which government department is responsible for tourism?
13. What is the role of a tourist information centre?
14. What is the role of the AUC?
15. Describe the two types of motivation to travel and give an example of each.

Assignment tips

- Although lots of statistics are given in this unit, they change all the time. Make sure you know your way around the VisitBritain website to find current figures.
- Every time you come across a useful report, download a copy onto your PC so you can find it again easily.
- You will only know about current trends and factors and their impact if you read newspapers and the trade press.
- Useful websites are:
  www.visitbritain.org.uk
  www.tttglive.com
  www.travelweekly.com

Credit value: 10

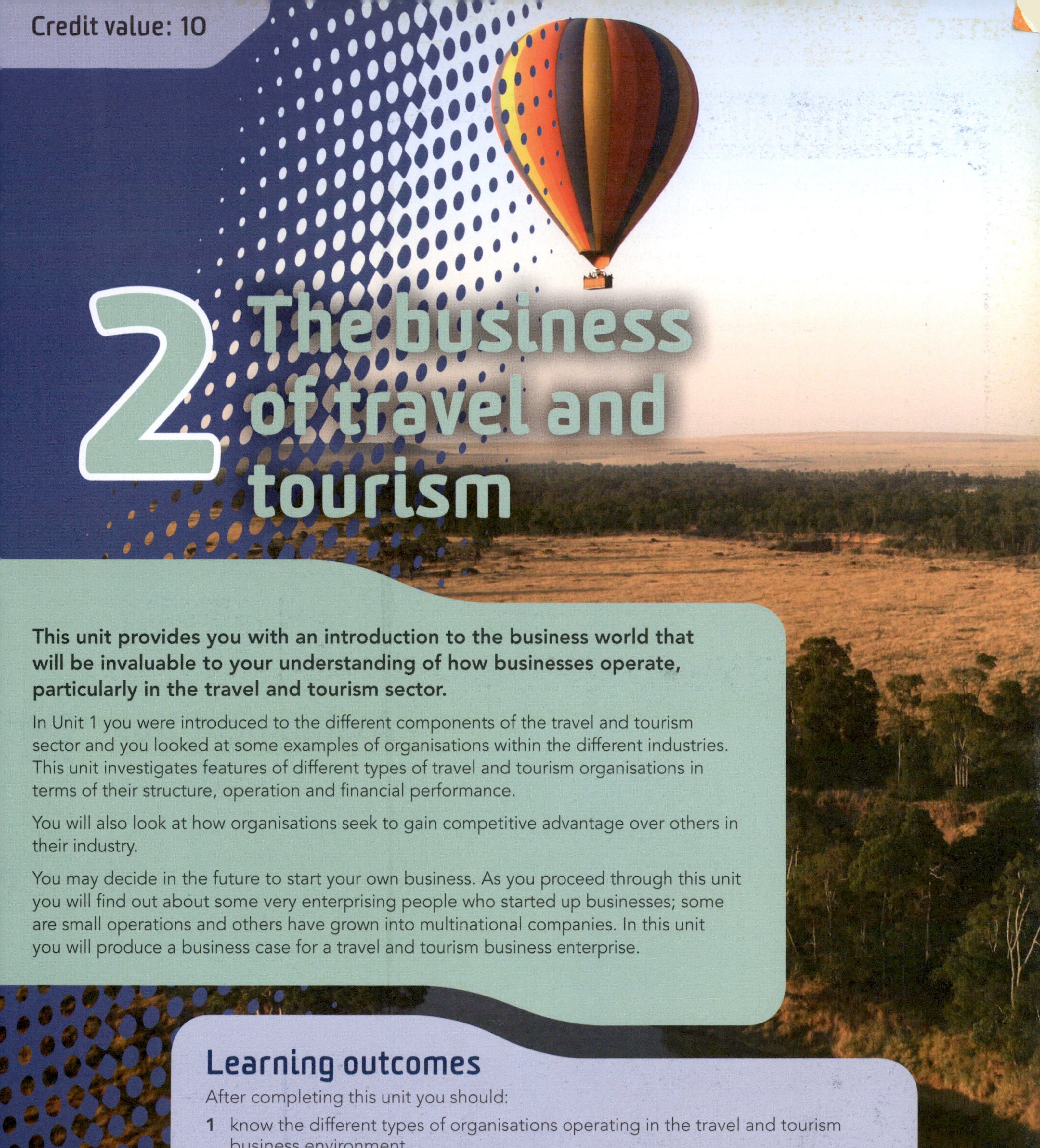

2 The business of travel and tourism

This unit provides you with an introduction to the business world that will be invaluable to your understanding of how businesses operate, particularly in the travel and tourism sector.

In Unit 1 you were introduced to the different components of the travel and tourism sector and you looked at some examples of organisations within the different industries. This unit investigates features of different types of travel and tourism organisations in terms of their structure, operation and financial performance.

You will also look at how organisations seek to gain competitive advantage over others in their industry.

You may decide in the future to start your own business. As you proceed through this unit you will find out about some very enterprising people who started up businesses; some are small operations and others have grown into multinational companies. In this unit you will produce a business case for a travel and tourism business enterprise.

Learning outcomes

After completing this unit you should:

1 know the different types of organisations operating in the travel and tourism business environment

2 know the characteristics of different types of travel and tourism organisations

3 understand how travel and tourism organisations gain competitive advantage to achieve business aims

4 be able to produce a business case for a travel and tourism enterprise within financial constraints.

Assessment and grading criteria

This table shows you what you must do in order to achieve a **pass**, **merit** or **distinction** grade, and where you can find activities in this book to help you.

To achieve a **pass** grade the evidence must show that you are able to:	To achieve a **merit** grade the evidence must show that, in addition to the pass criteria, you are able to:	To achieve a **distinction** grade the evidence must show that, in addition to the pass and merit criteria, you are able to:
P1 describe the travel and tourism business environment, providing examples of organisations **See Assessment activity 2.1, page 37**	**M1** compare the organisational and financial characteristics of two organisations with different business structures and the methods and opportunities they have used to gain competitive advantage **See Assessment activity 2.2, page 47**	**D1** evaluate the links between an organisation's characteristics and their success in gaining competitive advantage and achieving aims **See Assessment activity 2.2, page 47**
P2 describe the organisational and financial characteristics of different types of travel and tourism organisations **See Assessment activity 2.2, page 47**		
P3 review the methods and opportunities used by travel and tourism organisations to gain competitive advantage and achieve business aims, providing examples **See Assessment activity 2.2, page 47**		
P4 produce a business case for a travel and tourism enterprise within financial constraints **See Assessment activity 2.3, page 54**	**M2** present a business case and explain its feasibility in order to meet the objectives **See Assessment activity 2.3, page 54**	**D2** present a professional business case, responding confidently to questions and justifying its feasibility **See Assessment activity 2.3, page 54**

How you will be assessed

This unit will be assessed by one or more internal assignments that will be designed and marked by your tutor. Your assignments will be subject to sampling internally and externally as part of Edexcel's quality assurance procedures. The assignments are designed to allow you to show your knowledge and understanding related to the unit. The unit outcomes indicate what you should know, understand or be able to do after completing the unit.

Gina, 18-year-old BTEC National learner

I was looking forward to this unit because my uncle has his own business. He runs a tourist bus around our town. It runs several times a day and has a commentary on local attractions in different languages. It's very successful and he wants to expand.

I offered to help him, but he didn't take me very seriously. Although he was good at helping me by explaining what type of business he has – it's a private limited company – and who the directors are and what documents they had to complete, he didn't seem to think I had anything to offer him. However, he changed his mind when I told him all I had learnt about raising finance and putting a business case together. I did lots of research with Business Link and found two courses that were useful for him to go on and they were free.

After that he let me help him with his business plan. He is presenting it to his bank for extra funds to expand. If it's accepted I will be helping him set up in another town.

Over to you!

1 Try to think of someone you know who runs their own business. Can you ask them to explain their type of organisation and show you their business documentation?

2 Find out what local support is provided for small and medium businesses in your area.

1 Different types of organisations operating in the travel and tourism business environment

Set off

lastminute.com

Have you heard of lastminute.com? It is the product of a wonderful example of entrepreneurship. Research the story of Brent Hoberman and Martha Lane-Fox at www.lastminute.com. Find out what happened to them. What ventures are they now involved with?

- Which other travel internet sites are you familiar with? What makes you remember them?
- Which other famous entrepreneurs do you know of?

1.1 Travel and tourism business environment

Before looking at the different types of organisation, you need to understand the nature of the UK travel and tourism business environment.

The public sector

This sector includes public sector organisations, regulatory bodies and conservation groups. The role of the public sector is one of supporting and guiding different businesses so that everyone, including tourists, employees and management, can benefit from tourism while minimising problems.

The private sector

Most tourism businesses belong to the private sector. The term refers to the part of our economy that is not under government control. It is owned and resourced by private enterprises.

Geographical regions

All businesses operate in a geographical region. This could be:

- local, for example an independent travel agent operating in your town
- regional, for example a Regional Development Agency (RDA)/Local Economic Partnership (LEP)
- national, for example a tourist board such as Visit Wales
- international, for example an airline operating between different countries
- global, operating worldwide, for example some hotel groups like Accor.

Importance to the international and UK economy

All businesses contribute to the economy, either to the UK economy or to international economies. They do this by providing jobs and contributing to **Gross Domestic Product (GDP)**.

Key term

Gross Domestic Product (GDP) – a measure of the value of goods and services produced in an economy in a year. GDP indicates the wealth and economic development of a country. Countries with developed economies usually have high GDPs and countries with developing economies usually have low GDPs.

According to the World Tourism Organization (WTO), tourism accounts for about 30 per cent of exports of services and over 6 per cent of exports of goods and services globally.

Tourism is said to be the world's largest employer. The International Labour Organization (ILO) predicts that globally over 250 million will be directly or indirectly employed in tourism. In the UK, 10 per cent of total employment is in the tourism sector.

1.2 Types of organisation

Remember that all the organisations described in this section may be operating in domestic, inbound or outbound tourism markets (see page 4).

Organisations in the public sector

Public sector organisations receive their funds from local or central government and usually aim to provide a service. Examples include the national and regional tourist boards and some visitor attractions.

Funds for public sector tourism organisations come from central government through the Department for Culture, Media and Sport (DCMS) or from local councils. These organisations are judged on issues such as numbers of visitors achieved and quality, rather than on financial success.

Activity: Public sector organisations

Find out which travel and tourism organisations in your area are in the public sector. Compare your findings with your group. Are they responsible for domestic, inbound or outbound tourism?

In some countries the state owns and runs companies, re-investing the profits into other state ventures. Many transport facilities are state-owned, although not in the UK where **privatisation** has taken place.

Key term

Privatisation – the government selling assets that were previously in the public sector to the private sector, to raise money.

Case study: Privatisation

The City of Derry airport is owned by Derry City Council. The Council has taken steps to bring in private investment to the airport. The first step was to set up a holding company of which the council has 100 per cent of shares.

The council is seeking expressions of interest from private investors. In 2009 the airport was subsidised by £3.5 million per year. The chairman of the airport committee said that this needs to be reduced, the commercial performance of the airport needs to be improved and the government should set up a new governance regime.

He added that the region needs an affordable and successful airport and that the reform would safeguard investment and growth.

1. Why does Derry City Council want to privatise the airport?
2. What is meant by 'holding company'?
3. What are the advantages and disadvantages of privatisation?
4. Find out what has happened to Derry airport since 2009.

How has the City of Derry sought to bring in private investment?

PLTS

As you carry out research into Derry airport you will be developing your skills as an **independent enquirer**.

Functional skills

When you select, read and understand text to gather information you will be gaining functional skills in **English** (reading).

Organisations in the private sector

Most organisations in the travel and tourism industry are privately owned. These organisations may be huge companies like British Airways or small businesses like those of a sole trader. They usually aim to make a profit and are commercial companies. When they fail to make a profit over a period of time they are likely to cease trading. All theme parks, restaurants, tour operators and travel agents in the UK are privately owned.

There are different types of private ownership ranging from sole proprietor or trader to **public limited company (plc)**. Sole traders are small and run by one person, as the name suggests. A public limited company is listed on the stock market and is owned by its shareholders, who may buy and sell shares as they see fit.

Key terms

Public limited company (plc) – a business that is owned by shareholders. Its shares are bought and sold on the London Stock Exchange. Avoid confusing this type of business with one which is 'in the public sector'. It is not the same thing. A business in the public sector is owned and usually financed and run by national or local government.

Private limited company – a company which is not listed on the London Stock Exchange and usually has limited liability.

Dividends – a share of profits made as a payment to shareholders.

Private limited companies

There are different types of private companies – the differences lie in the amount of liability the owners have if the company goes bankrupt.

Private limited companies issue shares that can be bought and sold only with the permission of the board of directors. If the company goes bankrupt each shareholder's liability to pay the company's debts is limited to the amount of company shares that they own. This means that they cannot be asked to put any further money into paying the company's debts.

It is also possible to set up a private company limited by guarantee. In this case, the owners agree on liability limits when they set up the company. This structure is often used to limit the personal liability of directors.

There are also private unlimited companies, where there is no limit to liability. This is very dangerous as if the company goes bankrupt the directors will be liable for the debt and could lose all their assets, including their homes.

Most small businesses are private rather than public limited companies. A private limited company has to have at least one director and a company secretary – these cannot be the same person.

At the end of the year, the board of directors decides whether to pay **dividends** to shareholders depending on how much money the company has made. Dividends are paid in relation to the number of shares held by an individual. Shareholders have to pay tax on dividends.

Partnerships

This is when two or more people combine to form a company; the maximum number of partners allowed by law is 20. Each partner receives a percentage of the return of the business, depending upon how much they invested. Each partner is responsible for all the debts incurred by the business, no matter which partner incurred them. The partners usually retain the profits in the business and pay themselves a regular salary.

Think about it

If you were to set up in business, would you be prepared to risk everything you have? Many people do as they are so sure they will be successful.

Limited liability partnerships

These are very similar to a normal partnership, but the partners have reduced personal responsibility for business debts. It is the limited liability partnership itself that is responsible for any debts that it runs up, not the individual partners.

Sole proprietor

A small independent firm usually operates as a sole proprietor or sole trader. This means that the owner is personally responsible for all amounts owed to creditors and the government. It also means that should the sole trader not be able to make suitable arrangements to settle any debts, personal possessions will be taken by creditors.

Although this is a simple business set-up, sole traders are very vulnerable because if their ventures fail, they can lose everything including their homes. A sole trader has the advantage of full control over their business.

Franchise

A franchise is a type of ownership which allows an individual to start up their own business, but to minimise the risks by being part of an existing organisation.

An organisation, the franchisor, sets up a contract with the person wanting to enter the business, the franchisee. The contract includes the following:

- permission to trade under the corporate name
- assistance and advice in running the business
- provision of stock and trading materials
- help in finding premises.

In return the franchisee must pay a premium, and a percentage of the revenue earned by the new business.

Activity: Travel and tourism franchise

The Global Travel Group is an example of a travel and tourism franchise. It offers franchisees the chance to start their own travel businesses from home or an office.

Look at the Global website and see what is on offer.

- What are the benefits of taking on a franchise?
- What are the drawbacks of taking on a franchise?

You can find out more about franchising from the British Franchise Association.

Co-operatives

Co-operatives belong to members rather than to shareholders. They operate for the benefit of their members. We will look further at the characteristics of these types of organisations in the next section.

Assessment activity 2.1

P1 BTEC

1 Some of your group were sick with flu and missed the part of the unit that covers the travel and tourism business environment. You must help them out and give them a short description of the following factors in the business environment:
    - public sector
    - private sector
    - geographical area
    - importance to UK and international economy.
2 Research an example and give a brief description of a specific organisation from each of the following categories:
    - public sector
    - government controlled
    - local government controlled
    - membership
    - private sector
    - public limited company
    - private limited company
    - partnership
    - limited liability partnership
    - sole proprietor
    - franchise.
3 Are the organisations responsible for inbound, outbound or domestic tourism?

Grading tip

P1 make sure you cover all the types of organisation listed.

PLTS

As you plan and carry out research to produce your examples you will be developing your skills as an **independent enquirer**.

Functional skills

As you compare, select, read and understand different texts to collect your information you will gain functional skills in **English** (reading).

2 Characteristics of different types of travel and tourism organisations

Now that you understand the business environment, we can look in more detail at the organisational and financial characteristics of travel and tourism organisations. The two sets of characteristics are interdependent, for example a company with shareholders will expect to pay dividends to shareholders.

2.1 Organisational characteristics

Business structure and control

Organisational characteristics include the way the business is structured and controlled and the liability for debt.

Sole traders have the simplest structure with few regulations to worry about. However, it is often difficult for a sole trader to raise capital. The sole trader has complete control and is therefore autonomous and receives all profits after tax. The sole trader is, however, liable for all debt.

Partnerships have a structure of at least two people who share liability for any debt. There is no requirement for a partnership to be registered at **Companies House**. Partners can limit their liability for debt by setting up a limited liability partnership. Partners share control and the profits.

Limited companies can raise capital, issue shares and limit risks. There are more regulations governing the way they are run. Accounts must be filed at Companies House. Limited companies are controlled by the board of directors and shareholders. The management is accountable to the board and to shareholders for any decisions they make.

The board of directors is a group of people who are elected by the shareholders of an organisation and have the responsibility of overseeing the running of the organisation. Public companies usually have **executive directors** and **non-executive directors**. One member of the board will be appointed chairman.

Sometimes the board may be referred to as a board of trustees or a board of governors. If you are studying at a college, for example, you will hear of governors rather than directors, but their function is the same.

Charities usually have trustees, for example Earthwatch Institute (Europe) has a board of trustees who are responsible for the governance of the charity and overseeing its strategy and direction.

Key terms

Executive director – usually a full-time employee of the company who also has management responsibilities.

Non-executive director – someone paid an annual fee to attend a number of board meetings and contribute to decision-making. They are invited onto the board because of their experience and skills.

Companies House – an executive agency of the Department of Trade and Industry (DTI) responsible for company registration in the UK. There are more than 2 million limited companies registered in the UK.

Co-operatives – organisations which are set up and run democratically by members. Any profits made are shared between the members.

Co-operatives are democratically controlled by their members, and they believe in supporting the community and campaigning for a fairer world. A list of co-ops in the UK can be found at www.cooponline.coop. Any liability for debt also falls to the members.

Business organisation

Vertical and horizontal integration

You were introduced to vertical and horizontal integration in Unit 1 (see page 15). Integration can affect the organisation of a business as often all the different functions such as finance, marketing and human resources will be consolidated to cut costs.

Sometimes a business has a policy of acquisition – of buying out other companies. Companies take over other businesses to grow and to reduce the competition. Takeovers happen constantly in travel and tourism.

Takeovers can be friendly or hostile – a hostile bid means that a company management does not want the company to be taken over, but the decision must be made by the shareholders.

In December 2009, Virgin Holidays bought Bales Worldwide. This is an example of horizontal integration as both companies are in the tour operation business.

Another example of horizontal integration occurred in 2009 when Lufthansa completed its takeover of Austrian Airlines. A deal was made with the Austrian government to gradually take over shares in the airline, resulting in a 90 per cent holding by Lufthansa. Shareholders would get a payout of 166 million Euros. In addition, 500 million Euros would be paid to the Austrian state to reduce the airline's debts.

A tour operator could benefit from having its own airline, hotels and/or distribution channels, e.g. Thomson (part of the TUI group) is vertically integrated as it has its own airline, tour operations and travel shops. Shearings is a coach tour operator – they own some hotels and have a number of travel agencies.

Think about it

You can learn how much directors get paid from the organisation's annual report.

Documentation for business set up

If you decide to set up a limited company then you will need to complete several documents and submit them to Companies House.

Certificate of Incorporation

Incorporation is the means of registering a business as a company with Companies House. An application is completed and submitted with all the company details. If the application is successful the Registrar of Companies issues a Certificate of Incorporation – from this point the limited company is formed. In Northern Ireland the process is handled by the Companies Registry.

Memorandum of Association

This document gives the name and location of the company and describes the nature of its business. It also shows the amount of **share capital** in a company and how it is divided.

If you are setting up a business with others you decide on how many shares each will have and sign the memorandum. The money paid for the shares is kept by the company and does not have to be repaid – although dividends from profits will be paid to shareholders. Employees are sometimes given shares in a business or an option to buy shares at a preferential price.

Key term

Share capital – the money raised by selling shares in a business.

Articles of Association

This document explains how the company will be run, what rights the shareholders have and what rights the company directors have.

This extract from the Holidaybreak Annual Report 2008 explains the Articles of Association.

The Company's Articles of Association (the 'Articles') give power to the Board to appoint Directors, but also to require Directors to retire and submit themselves for election at the first Annual General Meeting following their appointment. Specific rules regarding re-election of Directors are referred to in the Corporate Governance Report.

The Board of Directors may exercise all the powers of the Company subject to the provisions of relevant statutes, the Company's Memorandum of Association and the Articles. The Articles, for instance, contain specific provisions and restrictions regarding the Company's power to borrow money. Powers relating to the issuing and buying back of shares are also included in the Articles and such authorities are renewed by shareholders each year at the Annual General Meeting.

The Company is committed to ensuring that it keeps pace with changing legislation and regulation. Accordingly, the Directors propose to recommend to shareholders at the Annual General Meeting that the current Articles be updated to incorporate changes resulting from the implementation of the Companies 2006.

(Source: Holidaybreak plc Annual Report and Financial Statements 2008)

2.2 Financial characteristics

Distribution of profits

If an organisation makes a profit, the directors have to decide what to do with it. The usual course of action is to distribute the profits amongst the shareholders but the board must recommend how much to pay, as in the extract from the Holidaybreak Annual Report above. They may wish to retain some of the profits to expand the company or invest in new projects.

Payments made to shareholders are called dividends (see page 36) and are paid each year or half-year. Sometimes, if a company is doing badly, they are not paid at all.

Retained profits/surplus

Once a business has paid dividends to its shareholders, surplus is reinvested in the business, either to pay off debt or to improve the business. A company may choose not to make a payment to shareholders at all, but to keep all profits for investment. Of course, if a business makes a loss, there is no surplus.

Sources of finance

If you are setting up in business you will need enough set-up capital to run the business until it begins to make a profit. Companies of all sizes also have to raise funds from time-to-time to finance growth, new ventures or takeovers. Various sources of finance are available according to the nature of the business and its ownership.

Banks

Banks are an obvious source of funds. They can offer loans, for a set period and with an agreed repayment schedule. The repayment amount will depend on the loan size and the interest rate. The bank will lend only if the money is guaranteed, which may mean using a house as security or a family member as guarantor. Banks will also probably ask to see a business plan.

Overdraft facilities are also available from banks. These are more flexible than a loan as an individual has an agreed overdraft amount and can borrow what they need up to that limit. It is very quick to arrange an overdraft and you don't need to provide so much security, but if you do exceed the agreed limit you will have to pay penalties and this can be expensive.

Friends and family

Many small businesses are financed by families and can grow to be huge family enterprises. Friends may wish to invest in a business and reap profits without hands-on commitment.

Case study: Grants for tourism

Grant scheme to grow heritage tourism

The Northwest Regional Development Agency (NWDA) today announced a £500,000, three-year extension to the highly successful Heritage Tourism Improvement Scheme (HTIS), a grant scheme which helps unlock the tourism potential of historic sites.

English Heritage has also confirmed a further grant of £75,000 to support the scheme.

Managed by the Lancashire and Blackpool Tourist Board, the region-wide HTIS is supported by a dedicated Heritage Tourism Executive Project Officer, funded by the NWDA and English Heritage.

Funding is available to historic houses, gardens and buildings in the Northwest that are open to the public and are interested in maximising the contribution that they make to the region's visitor economy. The new round of funding will award grants of up to £40,000 for physical improvements that enhance the visitor experience, including car parking, educational activities, disabled facilities and interpretation.

The project aims to grow heritage tourism in the Northwest and ensure it is recognised as a significant player in the region's visitor economy. Historic sites are a big draw for visitors and the Northwest's varied heritage assets have great potential to deliver economic benefits for the region. It is estimated that heritage tourism could be worth as much as £3 billion to England's Northwest every year.

A sum of £350,000 has been invested by the NWDA in the grants scheme to date and this has created six full-time equivalent jobs and levered in over £1.2 million of other investment.

(Source: www.nwda.co.uk – press release 8 April 2009)

1 Find out from where the Northwest Regional Development Agency (NWDA) obtains its funding.

2 Discuss with your group the kind of projects you think would be eligible for this grant scheme.

3 Take a look at the NWDA tourism sector website www.nwtourism.net and find out what projects have benefited from the scheme.

Shareholders

One way of raising funds is to issue shares in a company. Individuals buy shares and become part owners of the business with voting rights. When profits are distributed they are shared amongst the shareholders as dividends. If the company does not make any profit, there are no dividends.

Issuing shares is a type of private equity finance, that is finance raised from shareholders in return for ordinary shares. Public companies must have at least £50,000 of share capital. If a company needs more money to expand, or undertake a new venture, it can issue new shares to raise the finance.

Sometimes many shares are owned by employees. This gives them an incentive to help the company be successful as they will get dividends on top of their salary. For example, 16 per cent of the airline Flybe's shares are owned by staff through an employee share scheme.

Grants

There are many sources of grants. In travel and tourism the Regional Tourist Board (RTB) is able to advise on possible sources. Grants are usually from government or EU funds and are one-off payments which do not have to be repaid, nor does interest have to be paid.

There are strict criteria for eligibility when applying for grants. A grant will not usually be given for the full cost of a project or venture.

Public funding

The European Regional Development Fund was set up in 1975 to stimulate economic development in the least prosperous regions of the European Union (EU).

The EU has three other funds within it. These are the European Social Fund (ESF), the European Agricultural Guidance and Guarantee Fund and the Financial Instrument for Fisheries Guidance. It is the ESF that is relevant to tourism as it provides opportunities for business support and development through training.

The National Lottery is a source of grants. The DCMS has responsibility within government for National Lottery policy, but does not award the grants. There are currently 16 independent distributing bodies responsible for awarding Lottery grants. They include the Olympic Lottery Distributor, the Heritage Lottery Fund and the Arts Council, England.

The following extract describes how the Heritage Lottery Fund aims to distribute the grants for which it is responsible.

The Heritage Lottery Fund has three aims which relate to learning, conservation and participation. Through its grant-making, it aims to:

- conserve the UK's diverse heritage for present and future generations to experience and enjoy;
- help more people, and a wider range of people, to take an active part in and make decisions about their heritage;
- help people to learn about their own and other people's heritage.

(Source: http:/www.lotteryfunding.org.uk /uk/heritage-lottery-fund)

Using money raised through the National Lottery, the Heritage Lottery Fund sustains and transforms a wide range of heritage for present and future generations to take part in, learn from and enjoy. From museums, parks and historic places to archaeology, natural environment and cultural traditions, it invests in every part of our diverse heritage. For more information visit www.hlf.org.uk.

Commercial companies whose aim is to make a profit are rarely eligible for grants, as grants come from public funds.

Activity: National Lottery

Go to the National Lottery website (www.nationallottery.co.uk) and find out which organisations related to travel and tourism have been awarded lottery grants. Remember they are likely to be in the heritage sector. Discuss with your group what the funds were spent on.

Supplying products and services

Products and services may be supplied to make a profit for a business, or they may be supplied at a cost. They are usually supplied to meet a specific demand in the market and may be supplied for individual customers, other business or even government agencies.

Travel and tourism organisations make their profits through the provision of products and services to customers or to other businesses. An example is an airport. An airport is likely to be a public limited company and provides services to airlines, retailers and catering companies. It also provides services to customers who use the airlines and the airport. Through the provision of these services the airport makes a profit.

Financial accountability

Every organisation, from the sole trader to the largest company, has to produce financial records. A sole trader must, at least, record incoming cash and outgoings and produce a tax return. A plc is required to publish a full set of formal accounts.

Sole traders do not have to make their annual accounts public, although they are likely to keep them for their own use. Private and public limited companies, however, must comply with the Companies Act and complete an **annual return**. They must also supply a signed set of accounts to Companies House every year.

Most large organisations incorporate their annual accounts into an annual report. This gives information about the current activities in the business, as well as the figures in the accounts. All shareholders receive a copy of the annual report. All companies in the UK have to have their final accounts **audited** by a professional accountant from outside the company.

Since January 2005, Europe's listed companies have had to conform to International Financial Reporting Standards. The aim of these standards was to create one single set of accounting standards that can be applied anywhere in the world. This made it easier for investors to compare the performance of companies across international boundaries.

Key terms

Annual return – record of key company information which must be provided annually. Annual returns are filed at Companies House in London and are made publicly available.

Audit – check on the accounts and accounting system of an organisation. An audit checks that the accounts show a true and fair view of the affairs of the company.

Inland Revenue

Every sole trader must complete a self-assessment tax return. Tax has to be paid on profits from the business. Expenses can be deducted from income to calculate how much profit is left (if any). If all the internal accounting systems have been properly managed, it is relatively easy to complete the tax return.

Corporation tax has to be paid by companies on their profits. The company must file tax returns with the Inland Revenue.

Activity: Annual report

Study the annual report of a company that interests you. You can ask for a free copy of any annual report from the Financial Times Annual Reports service (ft.ar.wilink.com) or you can find an annual report on a company's website. You may like to study the annual report from Lastminute.com – which is on their website.

Look at cash flow. Can you make any judgements about the financial status of the company? Who are the major shareholders? Make some notes and compare your findings with other companies researched by your group.

Customs

HM Revenue and Customs is a government department. It collects Value Added Tax (VAT) on sales of goods and services. The current rate of VAT in the UK is 17.5 per cent, although it can change. For example, it was temporarily reduced in 2009 to 15 per cent in an attempt to boost the economy by reducing the price of goods and services. Some goods, for example foods, are exempt.

All VAT registered businesses have to complete a VAT return form for each tax period, usually every three months. A business must be registered for VAT once its turnover reaches £68,000, and must charge VAT on its goods and services, and keep records of VAT paid on purchases.

The following information is included in the VAT return:

- VAT charged to customers
- VAT paid by the business to suppliers.

The difference between the amount of VAT received and the amount paid out must be calculated. If a business pays out more than it receives, it can claim this back, but if it receives more than it pays, this amount must be paid to HM Revenue and Customs.

Contribution to global and UK economy

When companies are successful they contribute to the economic well-being of the nation, increasing the gross domestic product (GDP). In times of recession GDP contracts, leading to higher taxes, increased unemployment and spending cuts.

Case study: Holidaybreak

Read the following extract from the Annual Report and Financial Statements 2008 of the company Holidaybreak plc.

The Board of Directors

The Board of Directors is currently made up of six Executive Directors, four non-executive Directors and the Chairman. The positions of Chairman and Group Chief Executive are not combined, ensuring a clear division of responsibility at the head of the Company. The Board considers its non-executive Directors and its Chairman as independent from management and each other being free from any business or other relationship which could materially interfere with the exercise of their judgement. Collectively, the non-executive Directors provide broadly-based knowledge and experience to the Board's deliberations. The complementary range of financial, operational and entrepreneurial experience ensures that no one Director or viewpoint is dominant in the decision-making process.

Appointments to the Board are made after receiving recommendations from the Nomination Committee.

The practice is to appoint non-executive Directors whose appointment, provided they have indicated a willingness to serve a term of three years, is subject to a twelve month rolling notice from the Company and also subject to re-election and to Companies Act provisions relating to the removal of a Director. Re-appointment is not automatic. New Directors appointed by the Board must submit themselves for re-election by shareholders at the Annual General Meeting following their appointment.

Thereafter, the Company's Articles of Association require that all Directors stand for re-election at intervals of not more than three years. The Chairman will confirm to shareholders when proposing re-election that, following formal evaluation, the individual's performance continues to be effective and they continue to demonstrate commitment to the role.

Directors have unfettered access to the advice and services of the Company Secretary. The Company Secretary is responsible for ensuring good information flow, that Board procedures are complied with and provides advice on corporate governance and regulatory compliance. Directors can, where necessary for the discharge of their duties, obtain independent professional advice at the Company's expense.

(Source: Holidaybreak plc Annual Report and Financial Statements 2008)

1 Describe the organisational and financial characteristics of Holidaybreak.

2 Discuss the key features with your group.

The tourism industry's contribution to GDP is measured in terms of the revenue generated by tourists. International measures of tourist arrivals and spending (receipts) show how much tourism contributes to the global economy.

In 2009, the travel and tourism economy is expected to account for 9.3 per cent of global GDP (key term on page 34) and to generate over 210 million jobs, or 7.4 per cent of global employment.

3 How travel and tourism organisations gain competitive advantage to achieve aims

3.1 Aims of organisations

Company aims vary, particularly according to whether they are profit-making or non-profit-making.

A profit-making company must make money to stay in business and to satisfy the shareholders, who, after all, have invested in order to make money. However, a profit-making company may have other aims too, although these will be determined with the main aim of making money.

Here are some examples of possible aims other than profit-making:

- to increase revenue
- to be environmentally friendly and support responsible tourism
- to improve product quality
- to meet a demand
- to increase market share.

A non-profit-making company is likely to share some of these aims but will put any money earned back into the company to achieve further aims or will donate it to the cause it supports.

The best way to understand company aims is to look at some specific examples. First, look again at Holidaybreak plc.

> Holidaybreak is focused on cash generation. In the medium- and longer-term, our strategy is to grow the portfolio of brands under the Holidaybreak umbrella organically and by acquisition with an emphasis on organic growth initiatives. We continue to focus on leveraging our core strengths – a relentless focus on value and on the consumer.
>
> © Holidaybreak plc
>
> *(Source: Holidaybreak plc Corporate Factsheet 2009)*

Think about it

What do you think the difference is between 'organic growth' and 'acquisition'?

Activity: Comparing aims

- Compare the aims of BALPPA with those of Holidaybreak. How are they similar and how do they differ? Draw up a comparative table.
- BALPPA is a non-profit-making organisation. Give your ideas on whether it seeks competitive advantage and with whom.

These are the stated aims of a non-profit-making trade association in the visitor attractions sector, The British Association of Leisure Parks, Piers and Attractions (BALPPA).

BAPPLA aims:

- to represent the needs and concerns of the industry to HM Government departments, policy-makers and influencers
- to promote safe practice throughout the industry
- to promote and defend the interests of the industry
- to provide advice, information and services to members, to provide forums for discussion of their interests and concerns, and to promote professionalism, profitability, and best practice in the industry
- to act as an authoritative source of information concerning the industry to the media and other opinion formers.

3.2 Gaining competitive advantage

Companies use various methods and opportunities of gaining **competitive advantage**.

Key term

Competitive advantage – an advantage gained over competitors by giving better value to customers so that they choose your product and not the competitor's product.

Providing added value

Customers do not always choose a product or service on price alone. If that were the case there would be no business class on airlines – everyone would travel in economy.

Sometimes a company can be more competitive by having a better product. Grand Central Railway is an example (see page 45).

Providing new and innovative products and services

Airlines add new routes to gain competitive advantage. For example, in 2009 Jet2 added four new routes for summer 2010 to Dubrovnik, Split, Reus and Prague. This means it serves 28 destinations from Manchester, more than any other carrier.

Case study: Grand Central

Grand Central Railway Company Ltd is a privately owned train operating company, running services between London, Yorkshire and the north of England since 2007. It offers passengers the following services.

- Passengers in standard accommodation enjoy higher levels of comfort than with most other train companies with improved seating and leg room. Seats are lined up to ensure everyone gets a window seat.
- Carriages have added space for luggage and power points for laptops and phones. Power points are provided in both first and standard class. Free WiFi is available throughout all Grand Central services.
- Seat reservations are provided free of charge on all Grand Central services.
- Monopoly, Cluedo and chess boards are available on every table. Playing pieces can be purchased from the buffet or feel free to bring your own. Great to help you while away your journey.
- Independent industry research has put Grand Central in second place for customer satisfaction compared to all other GB rail companies (Autumn 2009 Passenger Focus).

(Source: www.enjoyengland.com)

Visit www.grandcentralrail.com to find out more about the service.

1 Do you think the service represents added value in comparison with competitors?

2 Suggest what else could be offered to improve the service.

Total quality management (TQM)

This is a business philosophy which arose from the Japanese management approach known as Kaizen. It involves all members of an organisation constantly trying to improve quality in the processes they use, the products and services they produce and the culture in which they work. It can be summed up as a management approach to long-term success through customer satisfaction.

TQM has three stages:

- Setting quality targets – to ensure high standards of customer service.
- Quality development – setting up procedures and systems to achieve the standards.
- Quality assurance – monitoring the quality to make sure standards are upheld.

Providing excellent customer service

Customer service is a key aim for most companies and striving to achieve excellence is vital to success. You saw in the case study that Grand Central added extras to its product to meet customer needs, but excellent customer service is more than that. The attitude of the staff who meet the customers is the most important factor. This is explored in Unit 4.

Training and development of staff

Many would argue that this is the most effective means of achieving competitive advantage and that without excellent staff a company will not survive. Staff need to project a favourable company image, know their product and deliver good service. This cannot be achieved without good training.

Staff need different types of training according to their job role, but all should undertake induction training and understand their responsibilities in terms of health and safety. Regular training helps staff to perform effectively and to keep updated with developments affecting the business.

Targeted advertising and promotion

Advertising is an essential tool for being competitive. Travel companies spend a lot of their budgets on advertising. It is impossible to say which adverts contribute to company success, as there are so many other factors involved.

Some of the traditional advertising budget might be better diverted to paying for prime positioning on search engines. This will ensure the company's name appears on internet searches, targeting the increasing numbers of customers who research and book travel online.

The key to advertising is reaching the right target audience. For example, if a holiday advertisement appears in the travel section of a newspaper, it is likely that anyone reading this section of the newspaper will also be interested in reading about this product.

Eurotunnel and Eurostar are different companies involved in promoting travel through the Channel tunnel. Eurostar is for foot passengers travelling by train from London and Ashford International to the Continent, whereas Eurotunnel is for passengers and their vehicles from Folkestone to Calais.

Figure 2.1: How do different companies try to reach the right target audience?

Innovative pricing policies

Competitive pricing is a strategy that is used to great effect in tour operating and in the low-cost airline business. Where products are almost homogenous (that is, there is very little difference perceived between them) price is very important. This is not always the case with a flight. The further people are travelling the more important service and comfort become. With short-haul air travel, however, many people are prepared to forego service and comfort for a cheap price.

The problem that often occurs with such a pricing strategy is that competitors continue to undercut each other until prices get so low that they are unrealistic, margins are cut to the bone and businesses start to drop out of the market. There have been many airlines which have failed in recent years.

Mass-market tour operators operate on such low margins that unforseen events such as a terrorism attack or extreme climatic conditions can wipe out their profits for the year.

Locational advantage

Location is most important for travel and tourism companies who depend on customer **footfall**. Travel agents depend on customers being able to access their services personally, as do Tourist Information Centres (TICs). You will therefore notice these types of business in town centres. Call centres and tour operators have no need to be in central locations and can reduce costs by seeking cheap out-of-town locations.

Key term

Footfall – refers to the number of customers walking into retail premises.

Sales techniques

Using high-pressure sales techniques can put customers off, so staff need to be trained in using sales techniques effectively. This is particularly important for call centre staff who are selling over the telephone. In travel agencies, staff concentrate on add-on sales such as insurance, car hire and excursions.

Integration and consortia

Horizontal and vertical integration were discussed on page 15. Integration helps a company be competitive as it gives the company control over different stages of producing and distributing products.

Independent travel companies may choose to join a consortium. Examples are Freedom Travel Group and the Hays Travel Independence Group. These consortia offer benefits such as access to reservation technology systems, centralised payment and ABTA – The Travel Association protection.

You can learn more about marketing strategies in Unit 5 (see pages 129–138) and find out how travel agencies attain competitive advantage in Unit 9 (see pages 254–256).

Assessment activity 2.2

P1 P2 P3 M1 D1 BTEC

LEGO

2008 was a successful year for LEGO products all over the world. This was reflected by considerably higher sales and much better earnings compared with the previous year and with expectations. The LEGO Group's profit for the year before tax amounted to DKK 1,852 million in 2008 against DKK 1,414 million in 2007. The results are considered highly satisfactory.

Increasing sales

The LEGO Group saw an 18.7% increase in revenue from DKK 8027 million in 2007 to DKK 9526 million in 2008. All the LEGO Group's markets saw significant sales increases in 2008. This despite the fact that, overall, the global market for traditional toys saw a moderate decrease in 2008. The highest growth was achieved on the English-speaking and the Eastern European markets.

Also in 2008, the classic product lines like LEGO City, LEGO Creator, LEGO Technic and LEGO Star Wars accounted for most of the increased sales. Moreover, the licensed product line LEGO Indiana Jones achieved considerably higher sales than expected at the beginning of the year.

Shared vision

LEGO Group strategy for the period to 2010 goes under the name of Shared Vision. The strategy is made up of many components – but its core remains unchanged. Its objectives are to:

- be the best at creating value for our customers and sales channels
- refocus on the value we offer our consumers
- increase operational excellence.

The strategy underlines the continued importance of focusing on profitability within the organisation. The situation facing all toy manufacturers at present is that they are pressured from many quarters – by consumers, customers and competitors. The LEGO Group meets this challenge with a determination to bind consumers, fans and retailers even closer to the organisation.

At the same time, the Group will increasingly refine and improve its product range to enable its new products to compete, for example, with the many electronic products on the market.

It continues to be the LEGO Group's primary purpose to supply good, healthy play – developing children and helping them to face the challenges of tomorrow.

(Source: www.lego.com. LEGO is a trademark of the LEGO Group, here used with special permission.)

Youth Hostel Association (YHA)

YHA (England & Wales) Ltd operates a network of more than 200 Youth Hostels across England and Wales. Over 300,000 members receive a warm welcome, comfortable accommodation, good food and affordable prices.

YHA's charitable objective forms the basis of all our work: to help all, especially young people of limited means, to a greater knowledge, love and care of the countryside, and appreciation of the cultural values of towns and cities, particularly by providing Youth Hostels or other accommodation for them in their travels, and thus to promote their health, recreation and education.

The business plan is being reviewed and rewritten to consolidate change programmes and to give a clear focus based on our vision and aspiration to double the number of young people who experience YHA over the next five years.

The world around YHA and the market in which we operate is rapidly changing and we have to address the prospect of severe economic conditions in the general economy. Our charitable object is at the core of our activity. We need to retain a focus on disadvantaged people as well as those of limited means.

Some core programmes are already aligned with our object and there is more we can do. Government agendas on health and wellbeing, physical activities for school-aged children and the need for better community cohesion offer us an enormous opportunity to really make a difference to the lives of many young people and families.

The Department for Children, Schools and Families (DCSF) has confirmed its support for the Do it 4 Real programme during 2008 and is providing £4.75 million. The planned programme for 2008 has camps at 27 locations in the summer. In all, we aim to help a further 10,000 young people enjoy the benefits.

(Source: www.yha.org.uk)

1. Describe the organisational and financial characteristics of the LEGO Group and the YHA. P1
2. Carry out research to find out and explain how the LEGO Group seeks to gain competitive advantage in order to meet the company aims. P3
3. Carry out research to find out and explain how the YHA seeks to gain competitive advantage in order to meet its aims. P3

Assessment activity 2.2 continued

P1 P2 P3 M1 D1 BTEC

4 Use the information you have gathered for P2 and P3 to compare the organisational and financial characteristics of the two organisations, as well as the methods and opportunities they have used to gain competitive advantage. M1

5 Evaluate the links between either the LEGO group's or the YHA's characteristics and their success in gaining competitive advantage and achieving aims. D1

Grading tips

P3 When you are discussing competitive advantage, give examples of the different methods relating to these companies. Ensure you cover financial, image and products.

P2 M1 Make sure you include all of the following in your description and comparison:

- business structure
- business organisation
- control
- documentation needed for start-up
- liability
- distribution of profits
- sources of finance
- supply of products and services
- financial accountability
- contribution to economy.

D1 Remember to include financial aims, image aims and product aims. Ensure that your analysis is in depth and demonstrates a thorough understanding of the characteristics, methods and opportunities utilised for success in the sector.

PLTS

When you analyse and evaluate information, judging its relevance and value, you will be an **independent enquirer.**

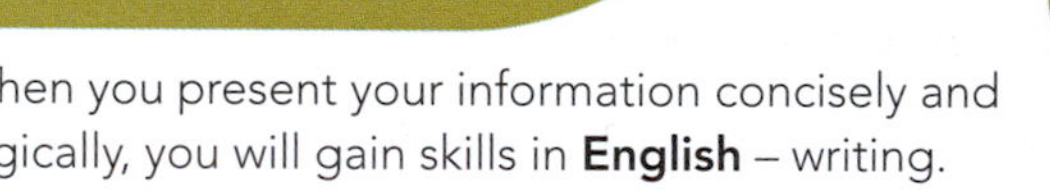

Functional skills

When you present your information concisely and logically, you will gain skills in **English** – writing.

4 Produce a business case for a travel and tourism enterprise within financial constraints

In this section you are going to find out how to put together a business case for your own travel and tourism enterprise. The business case is a proposal which will demonstrate the feasibility of your idea for your business venture.

4.1 Enterprise

You need to think about what kind of enterprise is viable for you to undertake. You may want to produce a business case to plan a one-off event such as a charity fundraiser. Or you may want to work on a profit-making travel and tourism venture that you can start up when you finish your course. Ideas include tour-guiding services, setting up a cycling tour in your locality, or setting up a guest house and hospitality services.

When people set up in business it is usually because they have spotted a need for a product or service that is not currently being met. This is known as a 'gap in the market'.

A business case is not just for start-up businesses, it is also necessary to make a business case for a new product or service in an existing company. Organisations only want to invest money in new ideas when they are shown to have a good chance of succeeding.

A useful source of funding for young people starting up in business is the Princes Trust. The Trust's 'Startups' programme was set up in 1983 to help 18–30 year olds start their own businesses. It provides financial help and business support for entrepreneurs in England, Wales and Northern Ireland. The Prince's

Scottish Youth Business Trust is a very similar scheme run for 18–25 year olds in Scotland. Find out more at www.princes-trust.org.uk and www.startups.co.uk.

Think about it

An example of a SMART objective for an airline might be to increase the sales of their fast-track boarding product by 10 per cent in six months. This is very **S**pecific, it can easily be **M**easured, it is **A**chievable and **R**ealistic as the target is not too great, and it is **T**imed to be achieved in six months.

4.2 Business case

A business case has the following elements.

- **Executive summary** of the essential elements of the business as an introduction – this serves as a quick overview of the business.
- Short description of your business opportunity, that is, who you are, what you want to sell or offer and to whom. Include your **mission statement**.
- **Objectives** – these should be tested against the SMART theory to make sure they are feasible. SMART objectives are:

  Specific – clear and concise

  Measurable – how will we know if we achieved them?

  Achievable – must have the skills and resources to achieve them

  Realistic – not overly ambitious

  Timed – deadlines.
- **Organisational structure** (brief) – is your business to be run by you as a sole proprietor or have a different business structure?
- **Human resources** – what staff will the enterprise need? In what roles? How much will staff cost?
- **Marketing and sales strategy** – what research is needed? What about the pricing strategy? What about distribution channels? How will you advertise or promote the business? Who is your target market? Who is the competition?
- **Timescales** – in your plan you should show what is going to happen and when. Show also who is responsible for each task.
- **Financial resources** – consider what the costs of the business will be and the potential revenue. Indicate where your funding is coming from. Is a loan needed? Are you eligible for a grant? Think about financial constraints and stay within them. Carry out a cash-flow forecast – see page 50 for ways of doing this.
- **Feasibility** – throughout your plan, you need to demonstrate that you have carried out research and that you can achieve your objectives in the timescale given. You will have shown where your income is coming from and how it will meet costs. You will have a given a rationale for your business idea showing that there is a demand. You will have thought about the competition and how you can gain advantage over them.
- **Risk analysis** – one part of assessing feasibility is to undertake risk analysis. You think about all the possible risks and try to mitigate them – that is, you think about the steps you can take to minimise the risks. Table 2.1 shows an example of a risk assessment.
- **Presentation** – make sure the business case is professionally presented. It is usual to present a business case orally, possibly to someone who may be investing time or money in it. If so, be well prepared and know the facts. Prepare slides and cards to prompt you. Even if you are doing an oral presentation, your business case should be written up neatly and clearly with title and contents pages and sections clearly labelled. It should be bound and copied to submit to interested parties.

4.3 Cash flow

If you are setting up a business you will be expected to present a **cash flow** forecast as part of your business case.

Key terms

Mission statement – a brief summary of the overarching aim of a business or other organisation.

Cash flow – the assessment of money coming into a business and money going out at any given time.

Table 2.1: Part of Holidaybreak's risk assessment from their annual report

Key risks	Impacts	Mitigation strategy
Cash generation in current financial climate	Due to external factors, we may not generate sufficient cash for re-investment in our businesses (e.g. activity centres, mobile-homes) or for acquisitions.	The Group will focus on increasing cash generation across its businesses and selling off non-core assets.
Health, safety and security	The risk that the Company fails to manage health, safety and security issues may lead to significant financial and operational costs.	Our businesses are committed to ensuring the highest standards of health, safety and security in their operations and monitor and conduct regular audits when appropriate. All divisions produce monthly health and safety reports. Issues noted as significant are considered at the Board meeting.
Failure to retain key employees	We may be put at competitive risk if we fail to retain key employees.	Our people, including call centre and administration staff, tour leaders, couriers and activity staff, are our most important assets. We believe our training programmes and remuneration arrangements provide the necessary incentives to retain key staff. Next year we will be introducing a senior executive development programme.

(Source: Holidaybreak plc Annual Report and Financial Statements 2008. © Holidaybreak plc)

You will have heard of the expression 'strapped for cash'. It may refer to you when you are waiting to get paid for a Saturday job and yet you need money to buy a birthday present or have a night out. In business terms it may mean that you are waiting for payments due in from customers and yet you don't have the cash right now to buy stock or pay an essential bill.

What happens to you in this situation? Do you decide to manage better next month and either borrow money or forego the night out? A business might not have the opportunity to do better next month as by then it may have gone bust. It is essential that it manages cash flow so that these difficult cash situations don't occur.

If you are setting up a business you will need some cash reserves to keep you going until payments from customers start to come in.

Companies may make a profit when everything owed is paid in, but may have problems throughout the trading period. These problems can be significant in the travel business when, for example, flights and hotels have to be booked a long time before the customers pay for them.

Cash inflow includes:

- payments for sales from customers – that is, receipts from sales and VAT on sales
- the cash put aside to start up the business – start-up capital
- interest on savings
- shareholder investments
- overdrafts or loans
- cash outflow includes:
  - payments to suppliers, e.g. hoteliers, transport
  - payments on fixed assets, e.g. company office
  - loan repayments
  - overheads, e.g. rent, wages, electricity and telephone bills
  - purchase of fixed assets, e.g. computers
  - stock, e.g. stationery or raw materials.

Net cash flow shows the difference between total payments and income.

Preparing a cash flow forecast

The forecast can be divided into three parts:

- forecast revenue – that is, cash inflow
- forecast expenses – that is, cash outflow
- net cash flow (the balance).

Think about it

Cash flow and profit are not the same thing. Think of your bank balance at the end of the year – you may be in the black (that is, in credit), but have had occasions during the year where you struggled to pay for things.

	April	May	June	July	Aug	Sept
Revenue (inflow)						
Sales	–	5500	5500	5500	5500	5500
Expenses (outflow)						
Rent	1000	1000	1000	1000	1000	1000
Computers etc.	250	250	250	250	250	250
Salary	2000	2000	2000	2000	2000	2000
Electricity	0	0	0	0	0	75
Travelling	200	200	200	200	200	200
Total expenses	3450	3450	3525	3450	3450	3525
Net cash flow	–3450	2050	1975	2050	2050	1975
Opening balance	3000	–450	1600	3575	5625	7675
Net cash flow	–3450	2050	1975	2050	2050	1975
Closing balance	–450	1600	3575	5625	7675	9650

Note there is no revenue in the first month

All the monthly expenses added up

Opening balance is always the same as the closing balance from the month before

The difference between inflow and outflow

Closing balance is the difference between opening balance and net cash flow

Figure 2.2: Cash flow forecast for a website designer. (All figures are in £.)

Figure 2.2 is an example of a travel website designer whose trading follows the tax year from 1 April to 31 March the following year. This is the cash flow for six months:

- Sales are forecast to be £5500 per month. Customers are given credit terms of one month, so the cash inflow occurs one month after the sale.
- Expenses will be:

  rent £1000 per month – no arrears

  computers, printing, stationery, etc. £250 per month

  salary £2000 per month – payable each month

  electricity £75 per quarter – first payment in June

  travelling £200 per month.
- The carried forward bank balance is £3000.

This information can be entered into a table or spreadsheet.

Table 2.2 on page 52 is an example of a cash flow **consolidated account** for a restaurant chain.

Key term

Consolidated account – no longer a forecast, but an actual account of cash inflow and outflow for the year.

Activity: Adjusting a cash flow forecast

Study the example shown in Figure 2.2 and make sure you understand it. Then think about what would happen if:

- sales are expected to dip to £500 in June
- the company decides that from May it will advertise at a cost of £700 every two months
- the car is scheduled for service at a cost of £1000 in August.

Update the cash flow forecast using a table or a spreadsheet.

Functional skills

As you identify what mathematical methods are needed to update the cash flow forecast and apply them, you will gain functional skills in **Maths**.

Think about it

Accounting software is available to help with completing cash flow forecasts. See if your teacher or tutor has a package you can use for practice.

Activity: Preparing a cash flow forecast

Stephen and Al Brown run a bed and breakfast business, the St Raphael Guesthouse, with 12 rooms on offer. Al is concerned about the way the business is operating. He has looked at the figures for the last few months and is worried that they will have to borrow more money. Al knows that there is £1000 in the business bank account. He is preparing a cash flow forecast for the coming financial year.

- Use a spreadsheet to prepare the cash flow forecast.
- Should Stephen and Al be worried? Why do you think problems occurred? Give a possible explanation.
- Make realistic recommendations to resolve the problems.

Al suggests to Stephen that they should get an overdraft of £12,000 to refurbish three annex rooms that are not currently used. This would increase monthly room sales by £800 and give another £120 in food sales.

- Update the cash flow forecast for the month following the refurbishment.

	Apr	May	June	July	Aug	Sept	Oct	Nov	Dec	Jan	Feb	Mar
Revenue (cash inflow)												
Sales												
Expenses (cash outflow)												
Net cash flow												
Opening balance												
Net cash flow												
Closing balance												

Cash inflow	
Room sales	May to October £5000 per month
	November and December £3000
	January and February £3500
	March and April £4000
	Guests pay immediately
Food and bar	£1000 per month in May to October
	£500 per month in other months
Cash outflow	
Wages	£4000 per month
Repainting	£900 in May
Maintenance	£100 per month
Heating and lighting	£50 per month
Advertising	£20 per month
Other expenses	£200 per month from May to October and thereafter £150 per month

Case study: Safari Specials

Joe Jensen, the managing director of Safari Specials, was devastated to report to his staff that the company had gone bust after 12 years in business. Jensen was unable to pay his bills and tried in vain to secure a rescue package from the banks.

Trade had been going very well about four years ago and Jensen decided to move into a new office and employ new staff. Overheads increased from £900,000 in 2009 to £1.6 million in 2010. Just after, a key manager left and set up in competition with Safari Specials taking staff with her.

Jensen decided to take action. He cut staff and cut capacity, reducing the number of safari destinations on offer. However, it was too late. Jensen had accommodation bills that were due, as he had committed to long-term contracts for accommodation that had to be paid for in advance, as well as flights to pay for. The company folded with debts of about £4 million.

A competitor suggested that the company had overcommitted on flight seats for May and June, many of which remained unsold.

1 Identify the cash flow problems experienced by Safari Specials.

2 Suggest how Jensen might have managed the cash flow situation.

PLTS

When you consider the influence of circumstances on decisions and events, you will be an **independent enquirer** and **reflective learner**.

Cash flow management

Cash flow has to be controlled – businesses can't afford to wait and see what happens and hope for the best. By keeping an eye on cash flow, you can identify potential problems and deal with them straightaway. Before making any major buying decisions you can make sure you have enough cash and, if necessary, arrange to borrow. It is a good idea for a business to have a contingency fund so that there is some cash for emergencies.

Ways to improve cash flow

Improving cash flow means getting money in as quickly as possible and delaying payments out as long as possible.

Getting the money in

- Ask for information. A business needs to know if its customers are credit worthy. For example, if a customer pays for a holiday by credit card the travel agent is assured of payment – the credit card company has already vetted the customer's credit worthiness. For business customers, a company can get a credit reference from a bank. This doesn't guarantee payment, but does give some confidence in ability to pay.
- Ask customers to pay upfront.
- Chase non-payers immediately.
- Borrow money (if you can afford to pay it back!).

Stopping the money going out

- Keep a tight control on stock and orders from suppliers.
- Check payment terms with suppliers – negotiate good credit terms.
- Don't buy equipment and assets, lease them.

4.4 Financial constraints

You considered financial constraints in your business case. Everyone's situation is different and people start ventures with different funds. If you are looking for a bank loan you must be able to explain what the money is for and how you will be able to pay it back. Look back in this unit to remind yourself of sources of finance.

4.5 Feasibility

When you produce your business case you demonstrate the feasibility of your ideas. Remember that the person assessing your proposal will be checking that you have done your research adequately and that your idea is realistic and has the potential to reach its objectives.

Assessment activity 2.3

You have inherited some money and so you have decided to set up a travel and tourism business. The money will go a long way to funding the business, but you will also need a bank loan.

You are required to put together a feasible business case for your travel and tourism business enterprise. You must determine the overall finances needed for the enterprise and then keep within those constraints in your planning.

Your business case must be thoroughly researched and include:

- clear objectives (e.g. make a profit within given timescale)
- how you are filling a gap in the market
- how you will gain competitive advantage
- cash flow forecast
- details of intended marketing materials
- clear timescale for set up
- operation of the enterprise.

You will present your business case to the bank. Be prepared to make an oral presentation supported by a written submission. Expect to answer questions on your proposal.

Grading tips

P4 Your business case must have full details including a cash flow forecast, details of your intended marketing materials and clear timescales for the setting up and operation of the enterprise.

M2 You must be able to explain the feasibility of the business case and justify how it will meet its objectives. Your case must be sound and you must be confident.

D2 Your business case should be of a professional standard in terms of format, presentation and any supporting materials. You will be able to confidently justify its feasibility.

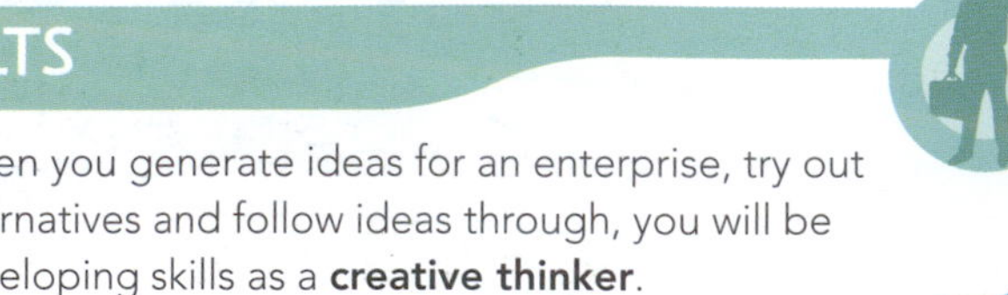

PLTS

When you generate ideas for an enterprise, try out alternatives and follow ideas through, you will be developing skills as a **creative thinker**.

Functional skills

When you select and apply a range of mathematics as you produce your cash flow forecast, you will gain functional skills in **Maths**.

WorkSpace

Tom Li

Travel and Tourism Analyst

Tom is an analyst for a bank in London. Analysts work in the stockbroking business, tracking the market performance of a set group of companies. Joe is responsible for tracking airlines and bus companies across Europe.

Tom has a degree in French, but any degree is acceptable. The important skills are understanding how the stock market works, being able to interpret financial reports and understanding the industry you are tracking.

Tom's role is to make judgements about the performance of his allocated companies and produce reports and advice for money managers, to help them decide whether to buy or sell shares the companies he is tracking.

Can you tell us what happens on a typical day?

I am at my desk by 7 a.m. At 7.20 a.m. we have a meeting where I report to our sales team about latest market conditions. The sales team use the information to deal directly with money managers, selling or buying shares.

At 8 a.m. I am ready to call clients. I might be speaking to industry analysts – they are people who are doing a similar job to me, but employed by companies.

I also call the airline and bus companies, speaking to finance directors or whoever is in charge of investor relations. It is important for companies to have a strong share price to show that they are in a strong market position. A weak share price makes a company vulnerable to takeover.

For the rest of the day, I might be compiling research reports, creating spreadsheets on results or updating models for sets of results.

Often, I attend result meetings given by a company's chief executive like Willie Walsh from British Airways or Michael O'Leary from Ryanair. The results are important in helping me form judgements about trading and a chance to catch up with other analysts from different banks.

It's a long day – I might be leaving at 6 p.m.

Think about it!

1 How could you keep track of what is happening to airline and bus companies?

2 How might Tom's work be affected by other trading sectors?

Just checking

1 What are the differences between public, private and voluntary organisations?
2 What is the difference between an executive director and a non-executive director?
3 What is a dividend?
4 Why might a dividend not be paid?
5 Give three examples of sources of finance for setting up a business.
6 What is a Memorandum of Association?
7 Give three examples of cash inflow.
8 Give three examples of cash outflow.
9 Give two examples of overheads.
10 Why is it necessary to manage cash flow?
11 Why are timescales important in planning a business case?
12 What is meant by total quality management (TQM)?
13 What types of travel and tourism organisations need town centre locations?

Assignment tips

- Think very carefully about your enterprise idea before starting your business case proposal. Choose something that is manageable.
- You don't have to carry out the enterprise – just produce the business case.
- Use Business Link to help you with the elements of the business case: www.businesslink.gov.uk.
- Look at your regional tourist board website to find out what grants are available.
- Find examples of entrepreneurship at www.realbusiness.co.uk.

Credit value: 10

3 The UK as a destination

This unit will provide you with the opportunity to explore tourism in the UK. It will build on the knowledge you already have and introduce you to key products and customers.

The UK boasts a wide array of attractions, from beautiful coastlines and National Parks to cultural and historical gems and purpose-built attractions that cater for all types of visitor. In this unit you will learn the location of key destinations in the UK, as well as gateways and geographical features. You will study the factors that contribute to the appeal of destinations, including the natural appeal, the location and access and the attractions which are to be found at a destination.

You will also explore the differing needs of domestic and inbound visitors and how the travel and tourism sector in the UK meets those needs. Travel and tourism changes constantly, affected by factors within the sector and those outside it. You will explore the impact of these different factors on the sector.

Before you study any of these areas, you will first learn how to use different reference materials to investigate travel and tourism in the UK.

Learning outcomes

After completing this unit you should:

1 be able to use reference sources to provide information on the UK as a destination (LO5)
2 be able to locate UK gateways, tourist destinations and geographical features (LO1)
3 know the needs of inbound and domestic visitors to UK tourist destinations (LO2)
4 know the features and facilities that attract visitors to UK destinations (LO3)
5 understand how UK inbound and domestic tourism is affected by internal and external factors (LO4).

Note that LO5 is covered first here to provide information on reference sources before working through the rest of the unit.

Assessment and grading criteria

This table shows you what you must do in order to achieve a **pass**, **merit** or **distinction** grade, and where you can find activities in this book to help you.

To achieve a **pass** grade the evidence must show that you are able to:	To achieve a **merit** grade the evidence must show that, in addition to the pass criteria, you are able to:	To achieve a **distinction** grade the evidence must show that, in addition to the pass and merit criteria, you are able to:
P1 locate gateways, tourist destinations and geographical features of the UK without the use of reference material **See Assessment activity 3.1, page 64**		
P2 describe the needs of inbound and domestic visitors to UK destinations **P3** describe the features and facilities that attract visitors to three UK destinations **See Assessment activity 3.2, page 82**	**M1** analyse how one UK destination attracts inbound and domestic visitors and meets their needs **See Assessment activity 3.2, page 82**	**D1** evaluate the effectiveness of one UK destination in attracting and meeting the needs of inbound and domestic visitors, making recommendations for addressing gaps or weaknesses in provision **See Assessment activity 3.2, page 82**
P4 explain how internal and external factors affect UK inbound and domestic tourism **See Assessment activity 3.3, page 88**	**M2** analyse how three factors are currently affecting UK inbound and domestic tourism **See Assessment activity 3.3, page 88**	**D2** evaluate the potential impacts of two factors on the future of UK inbound and domestic tourism **See Assessment activity 3.3, page 88**
P5 use appropriate reference sources to provide information on the UK as a destination **See Assessment activities 3.2 and 3.3, pages 82 and 88**		

How you will be assessed

This unit will be assessed by one or more internal assignments that will be designed and marked by your tutor. Your assignments will be subject to sampling internally and externally as part of Edexcel's quality assurance procedures. The assignments are designed to allow you to show your knowledge and understanding related to the unit. The unit outcomes indicate what you should know, understand or be able to do after completing the unit.

Kate, 18-year-old BTEC National learner

This unit was kind of the reverse of other units as we usually think about where British people go as tourists rather than who comes to us. So, it was interesting to find out what kind of people come here and what they are looking for on their trips. There was a difference between nationalities – we found out that the French love to shop and that the Brazilians are most likely to go to restaurants.

I loved doing the maps, although you have to be able to locate places without any help from atlases, so I had to practise a lot to be able to do that. We were all a bit embarrassed about how little we know about the UK. Most of us had been on holiday to Europe and not very much in the UK. We decided to take a couple of day trips to visit some UK places. We went to York which helped us with our case study and then we went to London. We are going to visit the seaside next.

There is quite a lot to do for the assessments and at first I forgot to write down all the resources like websites that I used. I realised how important this is when I wanted to go back to a website with information about what British people do on holiday in the UK. I never did find the website again. My tutor gave me a tip – I have a document headed 'Resources' and each time I use a website I copy and paste the address into that document.

Over to you!

1 How much do you know about UK destinations?

2 How is your UK geography?

3 Look at the assessments for this unit and think about resources you will need.

1 Be able to use reference sources to provide information on the UK as a destination (LO5)

Set off

UK holidays on the increase

A Mintel report on domestic tourism, published in 2009, found that, for the first time in five years, more British people took domestic (UK) holidays than went abroad. In the midst of recession, cheaper budget breaks were available as hoteliers and operators offered discounts. The strength of the Euro against the pound made Europe expensive for UK outbound travellers. Also a hot 'barbeque' summer was predicted for the UK, although this didn't happen.

- Where do you take your holidays? Do you prefer to stay in the UK or go abroad?
- What do you think the UK offers holidaymakers? Think about attractions, accommodation, weather and eating out.

1.1 Reference sources

You need to become proficient in using a range of reference materials to investigate UK destinations.

Atlases

A good atlas is essential to anyone working in travel and tourism. You will find these at any public library or to buy online.

The *World Travel Atlas* (Columbus Press) has been designed for the travel trade and for students. It is a good source of facts and figures which are updated every year.

The internet

The internet is a wonderful source of information. However, there are so many websites that you will have to learn how to search properly to find what you want and to make sure the information is reliable.

First, make sure you are familiar with search engines such as Yahoo and Google. You have the option of searching UK or worldwide and it is often easier to limit yourself to UK searches to begin with. If you enter 'Travel and tourism' you will find thousands of websites listed and many will have little relevance to you. However, it is worth spending some time surfing these websites and bookmarking those which are useful in your favourites list. (If you do not have your own computer, make a note of the addresses.)

Some websites are themselves directories and link to other useful tourism information sites. Examples are:

- www.intute.ac.uk/geography
- www.tourismeducation.org

If you are searching for information on UK destinations the following websites will help you:

- www.visitbritain.com
- www.enjoyengland.com
- www.visitwales.com
- www.visitscotland.com
- www.discovernorthernireland.com

Set some time aside to familiarise yourself with these websites so that you know what can be found on them.

Brochures

These give a lot of destination information. They are visually appealing and easy to understand. But remember that their purpose is to sell and therefore they are likely to give a biased view, which is always positive.

Brochures are produced by tour operators, often with several editions in one year. The brochures are distributed to travel agents who use them to sell holidays. You will need them for your studies and you can collect them free at any travel agency. It is best not to take too many at one time! You can also order brochures from tour operators online or by telephone.

Statistical data

The internet means that you can access data about UK tourism.

- VisitBritain's trade site (www.visitbritain.org) publishes useful statistics and this should be your starting point.
- You should also familiarise yourself with the website for official UK statistics (www.statistics.gov.uk).

You will look at statistics later in this unit when examining key trends affecting UK tourism.

Timetables

Timetables are published by all transport carriers and providers, and are readily available in published form and on the internet. Airports amalgamate the timetables of their carriers and post them on their websites.

You can look up routes and times for coaches, ferries and trains, as well as airlines.

Useful websites are:

- www.thetrainline.com
- www.nationalrail.co.uk
- www.nationalexpress.com
- www.ferrybooker.com

Travel guides

These are extensively available in bookshops and libraries. They are constantly updated, so do check the dates of library editions as many libraries cannot afford to update their whole collection of travel guides regularly. Some of these guides are very well produced and include maps, hotel and restaurant recommendations and plenty of information on what to see and do. They are ideal for finding out what there is to do in a destination and how to get there.

Hotel guides

All major chains produce their own guides listing their hotel locations, facilities and services. Remember that these are sales tools like brochures and will present only positive information.

Travel agents refer to travel trade hotel guides. These give independent reviews of hotels and are useful for checking hotels before you visit them.

Travel trade press

Your library should have copies of travel trade journals, which give up-to-date features on the industry and on specific destinations. If you wish you can subscribe to these publications with a student discount. Alternatively, *Travel Trade Gazette* and *Travel Weekly* are both available on-line.

Newspaper reports

The national and regional press also carry regular travel pages, which are full of informative features and advertising.

Television and radio programmes

Holiday and travel programmes feature reports on UK destinations, as well as those abroad.

2 Be able to locate UK gateways, visitor destinations and geographical features (LO1)

2.1 Gateways

UK airports

Airports are gateways to travel destinations and air travel is the most favoured form of travel for inbound visitors to the UK.

Gateway airports are always the busiest types of airports, handling a lot of international traffic and passengers. Sometimes the gateway is to another flight. Transfer passengers are those who fly to a **hub airport** and transfer to another flight.

London is served by four major airports: Heathrow, Gatwick, Stansted and Luton. There is also a small airport in the Docklands area of London, London City Airport. This airport is used mainly by business travellers.

Key terms

Gateway airport – a major point of arrival or departure in a country, served by international scheduled services.

Hub airport – an airport, usually major, that serves many outlying destinations and allows passengers to fly in and transfer to other flights. The outlying airports are known as 'spokes'.

To cope with increased demand for air travel, many gateway airports have had to expand capacity. For London, Heathrow now has a fifth terminal and Stansted has plans for a second runway.

There are over 50 regional airports in the UK, but distances are not so great as to make air travel a preferred option within the UK. However, services from cities in Scotland and Ireland to London do very well.

Airports are identified by three-letter **airport codes** (see International Air Transport Association (IATA) codes, Unit 7 page 186).

Key term

Airport code – every airport in the world has a unique three-letter code to identify it. You can find these codes at the Airline Codes website www.airlinecodes.co.uk.

Table 3.1: Top ten UK airports (by passenger numbers) in 2009

1	Heathrow	65.7 million
2	Gatwick	32.4 million
3	Stansted	20.7 million
4	Manchester	19.5 million
5	Luton	9.5 million
6	Birmingham	9.3 million
7	Edinburgh	9.0 million
8	Glasgow	7.5 million
9	Bristol	5.7 million
10	East Midlands	5.0 million

(Source: Civil Aviation Authority – UK Airport Statistics)

Activity: Locating airports

1 Locate each of the airports from Table 3.1 on an outline map of the UK (you could copy the outline in Figure 3.1).

2 Find out the airport codes for each of the airports.

3 You will notice that Heathrow is by far the busiest airport. Visit Heathrow's website (www.heathrowairport.com) and find out the following:
   - Who owns Heathrow airport?
   - What other airports does this company own?

4 Find five examples of domestic (inside the UK) cities linked by air to Heathrow. For each example, state the airline operating the flight.

Passenger seaports

Like airports, seaports are gateways. They are embarkation points for ferry services and also for cruise passengers. Cruise passengers from the UK may fly to a port to start their cruise or may leave by sea from the UK, usually from Southampton.

Major passenger ports are situated along the south coast, providing Channel crossings to France, Spain and the Channel Islands and along the east coast, providing crossings to Belgium, Germany, the Netherlands, Denmark, Norway and Sweden.

There are also numerous crossings between Wales and Ireland and Scotland and Ireland.

Channel tunnel termini

There is a Eurotunnel access port at Folkstone and also Eurostar access ports at Ashford and London St. Pancras, providing rail access to Europe (see page 194 for further information).

Figure 3.1: Map of the UK

Figure 3.2: Main sea routes

Activity: Locating seaports

On the map in Figure 3.2 locate the following seaports:

- Dover
- Belfast
- Larne
- Stranraer
- Holyhead
- Portsmouth
- Harwich
- Southampton
- Hull
- Fishguard
- Eurotunnel access port of Folkestone
- Eurostar access ports of Ashford and London.

2.2 Tourist destinations

Capital cities

The UK's capital cities, Belfast, Cardiff, Edinburgh and London, are important destinations for domestic and inbound visitors alike, with London receiving the most visitors.

Activity: Capital cities

1. Choose one of the capital cities and find a guide for that city.
2. Describe three main features of the destination that would appeal to inbound visitors.
3. Consider whether these features would also appeal to domestic visitors and say why.

Coastal resorts

Coastal resorts provide something for all the family – sea, beach and some form of entertainment. In Assessment activity 3.1 you will need to be able to locate coastal towns on a map of the UK. Some are important for business tourism as they provide extensive conference facilities. Examples include Brighton, Bournemouth and Blackpool.

Countryside areas

The UK has many beautiful countryside areas such as the Lake District and the Scottish Highlands which attract visitors.

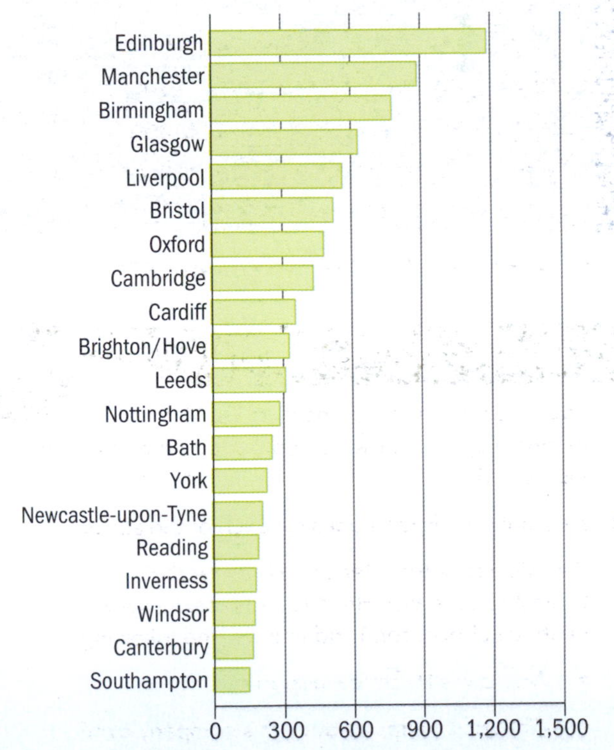

Figure 3.3: Top 20 UK towns visited (excluding London) by number of overnight visits

(Source: Travel Trends, 2008)

Activity: Top towns

Figure 3.3 shows the top 20 towns visited by overseas residents in 2008, excluding London. London received over 14.8 million visitors.

1 Locate and name these destinations on a blank map of the UK.

2 For each town and city name the nearest airport and motorway or major road. Locate these on the map.

3 Choose one of the towns and try to find out the visitor numbers for that town. You should be able to find these on the local government website or via the Tourist Information Centre (TIC).

- Produce a short report with tables on the numbers of visitors, length of stay, purpose of visit, etc.
- What conclusions have you drawn from your findings?

Cultural or historical towns and cities

Cities and towns have traditionally been on the 'tourist trail' for incoming visitors because of their cultural and historic appeal. London is the most popular, but overseas visitors are usually keen to see places such as Bath, Stratford, Oxford and Edinburgh. City breaks are one of the fastest-growing sectors in UK domestic and inbound tourism.

Geographical features

You need to be able to locate various geographical features. These include rivers, lakes (e.g. Loch Ness), mountain ranges (e.g. Snowdonia) and upland areas (e.g. the Pennines), islands (e.g. Arran) and forests (e.g. the New Forest). These features are discussed in section 4.2.

Think about it

In 2009 *The Telegraph* newspaper carried out a poll. Only 6% of those polled knew the name of Britain's tourism minister. Do you know it? At the time of the poll it was Barbara Follett.

Assessment activity 3.1

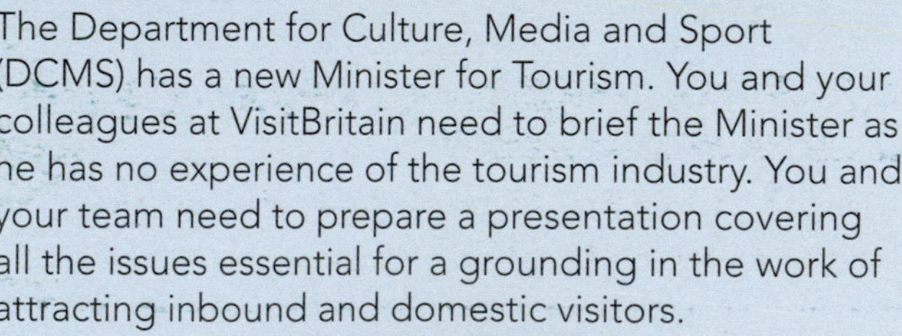

The Department for Culture, Media and Sport (DCMS) has a new Minister for Tourism. You and your colleagues at VisitBritain need to brief the Minister as he has no experience of the tourism industry. You and your team need to prepare a presentation covering all the issues essential for a grounding in the work of attracting inbound and domestic visitors.

(Note: All the assessments for this unit relate to this scenario.)

Without using reference sources produce a map, or series of maps, which show the Minister where our important gateways, tourist destinations and geographical features are located.

You must include:

- all capital cities
- six coastal resorts
- six historical or cultural cities or towns
- four countryside areas
- a body of water, for example a lake
- a woodland area or forest
- a river
- a mountain range or upland area
- an island
- four international UK airports (include their three-letter codes)
- four UK passenger seaports
- two UK Channel tunnel terminals.

Grading tip

P1 You must be able to locate accurately all the features without access to reference sources, so do not attempt the assessment until you are confident.

Make sure that all the geographical features you choose are ones that attract tourists and do not repeat any of the locations.

3 Needs of inbound and domestic visitors to UK tourist destinations (LO2)

There are a number of different types of domestic and **inbound visitors** with different motivations for their visits.

Key term

Inbound visitors – people who visit a country which is not their country of residence for the purposes of tourism. If the visitor comes from France to the UK then they are outbound from France and inbound to the UK.

3.1 Inbound visitors

How do we know who comes to visit the UK? All the information you need can be found from statistics produced from the International Passenger Survey. Go to www.statistics.gov.uk and search for the report entitled *Travel Trends*.

From this source we know that the latest figures show a decline in the number of overseas visitors to the UK by nearly a million between 2007 and 2008. This sounds a lot, but happily the visitors who did come spent more than ever, spending a record £16.3 billion – that is 2.3% more than the previous year.

Visitors who come to the UK are fairly evenly divided between those who come on business, those who visit friends and relatives and those who take a holiday.

Activity: How many visitors?

- Find the latest *Travel Trends* report. Find the latest figures for inbound visitors to the UK. Look at arrivals and receipts (spending).
- Work out the percentage difference between the 2008 figures and your latest figures. Produce a chart to show your figures.

It is also interesting to know where our visitors come from. We can then start to think about their particular needs in terms of culture or food.

Our top ranking visitors are the French and the Irish from the Irish Republic. Those visitors from the north of Ireland are domestic visitors, because Northern Ireland is part of the UK.

Figure 3.4 shows the nationalities of the top visiting countries from 2008.

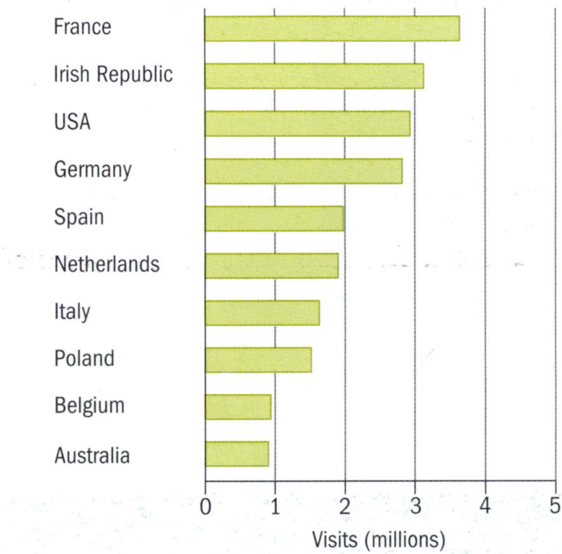

Figure 3.4: Who visits Britain? *(Source: Travel Trends, 2008)*

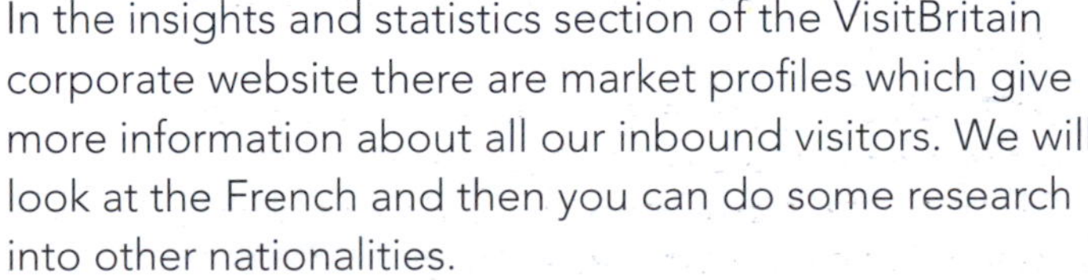

In the insights and statistics section of the VisitBritain corporate website there are market profiles which give more information about all our inbound visitors. We will look at the French and then you can do some research into other nationalities.

The market snapshot tells us quite a few facts.

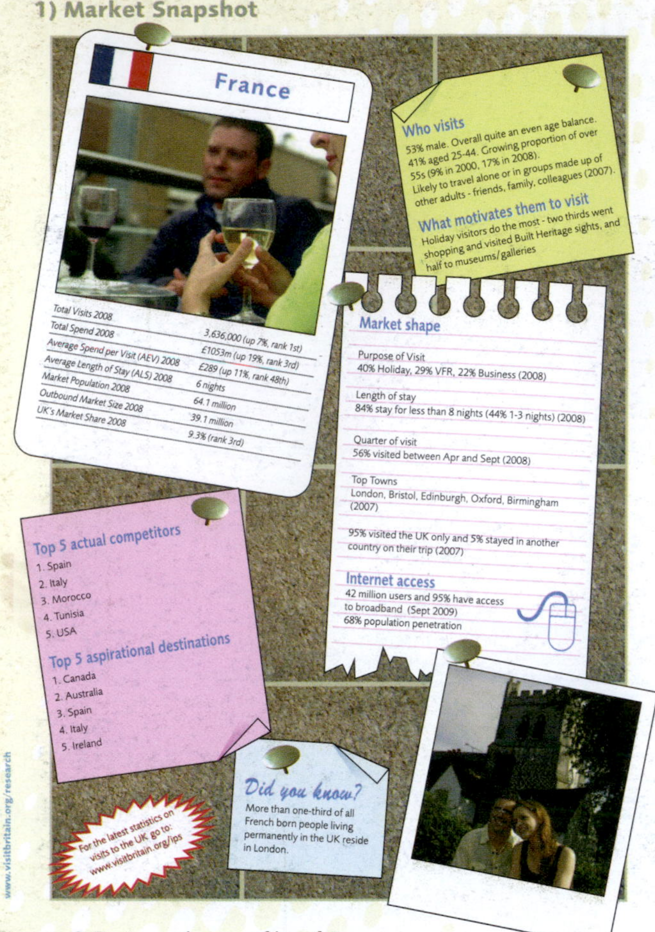

Figure 3.5: A market profile of France.
(Source: www.VisitBritain.org)

Activity: Visitors to the UK

Go to the insights and statistics section of www.visitbritain.org and find the report on France in the publications section.

- Study the market snapshot.
- How does it help a tourist organisation to know this information about visitors?
- Advise a French person visiting your town what would be interesting for them to do.
- What difficulties might they face?

As a group, divide up the other nine nationalities in Figure 3.4 between you.

- Produce a poster with a market snapshot showing key information about the visitors.
- Liaise with the other groups so all your posters make a co-ordinated display.
- Use VisitBritain's market snapshots to help you, but find your own information as well. Do not copy VisitBritain's displays, but invent your own.

3.2 Domestic visitors

Key term

Domestic visitors – people who are travelling in their own country for tourism purposes.

Who are domestic visitors?

People in the 35–54 age group are most likely to take holidays in the UK. These are also the people most likely to be parents and that might restrict their choice of destination. Older age groups are likely to be an important future market as there are increasing numbers of affluent people aged over 55. These people belong to the group known as **domestic visitors**.

Although knowing the type of customer in terms of age and family grouping is useful, it is even more useful to know what motivates them as visitors in order to best suit their needs. Enjoy England uses a research tool known as the ArkLeisure model to help them understand consumers' needs, motivations and attitudes to England as a destination. This is a segmentation model. You can learn more about segmentation in Unit 5 (page 123).

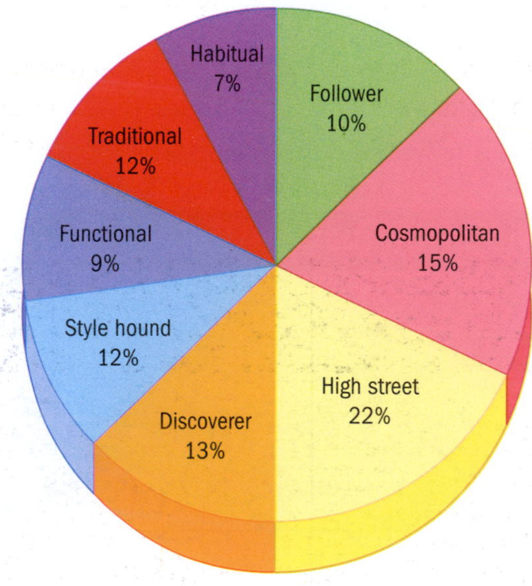

Figure 3.6: There are eight segments in the ArkLeisure model

Case study: Marketing England

The Enjoy England study *England Marketing* focuses on just three of these segments. These were selected as they are most active in the short-break market and most likely to be influenced by the *England Marketing* message. A summary of the three segments is shown in Table 3.1.

Table 3.1

Segment	Core values	Market size and lifestage	Holiday habits
Cosmopolitan	Strong, active, confident individuals, risk-takers who seek new experiences and challenges, both physical and intellectual. High spend market – like individual attention and will pay for it. Appreciate art and culture.	19% of the population, even breakdown of ages, 32% have children at home, 57% are socio-economic group ABC1	
Discoverers	Independent of mind and keen on value for money. Quite high spenders if the product is right. Little influenced by style or brand, but value good service. Arts and culture not really important to them.	13% of the population, even split of ages, 30% have children at home, 55% ABC1	
High Street	Interested in fashion brands that care what others think. Prepared to try new things as long as tried and tested by others, therefore experiences are more likely to be new to them rather than to the market.	18% of the population, even split of ages, 32% have children at home, 51% ABC1	

(Adapted from Enjoy England: International and Domestic market profiles)

On a copy of this table, complete the last column suggesting what holiday habits the group might have .

Domestic tourism (excluding day visits) was worth over £21,000 million in 2008. Holidays make up the largest proportion of domestic trips, especially short breaks (1–3 nights).

Table 3.2: Purpose of domestic trips in the UK

Purpose	2007 (Jan–Dec) millions	2008 (Jan–Dec) millions	% change
Total	123.458	117.715	–4.65%
Holiday	76.828	75.428	–1.82%
1–3 nights	49.543	49.767	+0.45%
4+ nights	27.285	25.661	–5.95%
Visiting friends and relatives (VFR)	24.708	20.626	–16.52%
Business/work	18.745	18.199	–2.91%

(Source: VisitBritain)

Day visits are also important to the economy, although their number and value is calculated separately. Remember that, officially, day visitors are not tourists as tourism includes an overnight stay.

The last *Leisure Day Visits* survey was in 2005 and there is a need for a new survey to be introduced. We do know that day visits account for half of all tourism expenditure.

The motivation for a day trip may be very different from a holiday, and it is more likely to be planned at the last minute. Figure 3.7 (page 68) shows the motivations of domestic tourists in England.

Activity: Motivations

Discuss with your group how the motivations for taking a holiday might differ from those for a day trip.

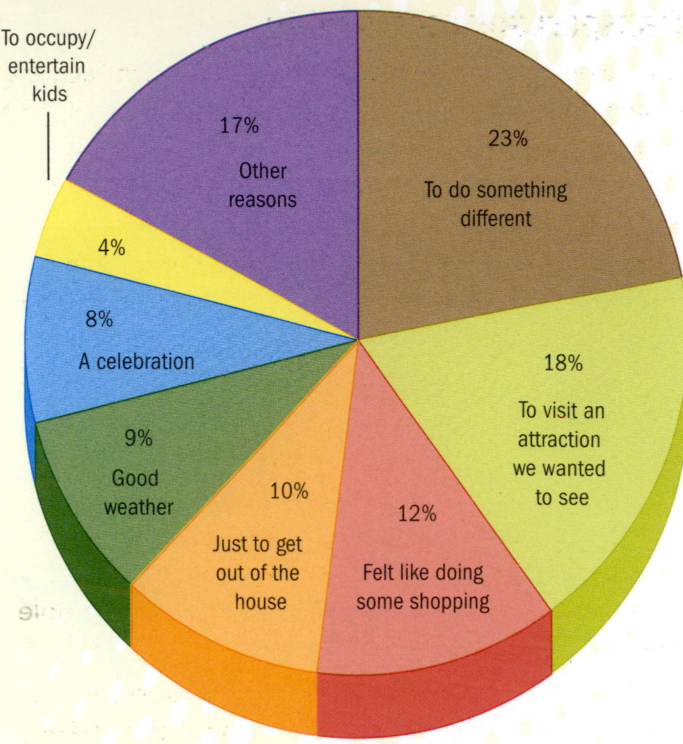

Figure 3.7: Main reason for taking day trips *(Source: VisitBritain)*

Activity: Debate

Working in your group, debate the motion 'Holidays in the UK are preferable to going abroad for young Britons'. Your tutor will assign you to speak either for or against the motion. Prepare your arguments from the point of view of domestic tourists. The usual debating rules apply.

Points to consider include:

- ease of access
- activities you like to do
- transport
- sightseeing
- safety and security
- language.

PLTS

As you work together, debating in groups, showing fairness and consideration to others and taking responsibility for their contribution to the debate, you will be developing skills as a **team worker**.

3.3 Domestic and inbound visitor needs

Access to information

The internet can help all travellers plan their journeys and holidays. Incoming visitors need information on transport, accommodation, attractions and events. The VisitBritain website and the national and regional tourism board websites, and their links, allow inbound visitors to do a lot of research before they arrive in the country.

Inbound visitors cannot always access information in English. It needs to be available in their own language. VisitBritain has added a local language website facility, with websites added for the Czech Republic, Greece, Hungary, Malaysia and Thailand.

Inbound visitors may also require information from other sources in their own countries. The provision of overseas offices by VisitBritain is one means of giving access to this information. Tour operators in overseas countries also supply information about the UK. They will print brochures in local languages so that information is easily accessible.

Deciding, planning and booking patterns

According to enjoy England, almost two thirds of visitors to the UK obtain information about the destination they are travelling to from previous experience (63 per cent). Advice from friends and relatives (61 per cent) and the internet (48 per cent) are also strong influences.

Table 3.3: Sources of information when choosing a holiday destination in England

Source	%
Previous experience	63%
Advice from friends and relatives	61%
Internet	48%
Tourism brochures	24%
Travel agents	23%
Articles in newspaper/magazines	14%
Travel books	13%
Accommodation guides	10%
Advertisements in newspapers/magazines	8%
Television/radio programmes	7%
Items in the post	7%
Television/radio advertisements	3%
Tourist board stand at shows	3%

(Source: www.enjoyengland.com)

Domestic visitors need the same information and can get it from travel agents, tourist boards, direct from attractions and from TICs.

Language

The British are not best known for their linguistic abilities and yet inbound visitors cannot always be expected to speak English. They need to have information readily available in their own language. This does not often happen, even with common languages such as French and Spanish. Few restaurants provide translated menus and transport information is not often available in other languages. Hotel staff who can speak a number of languages are rarely found outside large cities. In addition, cultural differences between visitors and UK residents need to be accommodated.

The sector that performs best in terms of language interpretation is the attractions sector where, in order to appeal to UK-inbound visitors, information in the form of leaflets and tapes is often in several languages.

The importance of welcoming visitors in their own language is recognised by the *Welcome to Excellence* training programme, Welcome International, provided for tourist staff by Regional Tourist Board Partnership. The course also raises awareness of cultural differences. The course covers:

- the international tourism industry
- how to communicate effectively
- how to greet visitors in their own language
- identification cultural expectations.

Accommodation

Providers of accommodation should be aware of the expectations of different groups. For example, international women travellers will expect good security in the hotel and places to eat and drink where they feel comfortable. Some visitors, for example from the USA, may be used to very spacious rooms with high standards of cleanliness and service. London hotels tend to have smaller rooms and, because of pressure on space, may not provide facilities like gyms and swimming pools.

Cost may also be a consideration of many visitors. Young people on educational visits are likely to book low-cost hotels or hostels. You can find out what types of accommodation tourists stay in by looking at *The UK Tourist*, an annual report published by VisitBritain.

Transport and accessibility

Accessibility means that tourist facilities and attractions should be available to as many different groups as possible without restriction. It also means meeting individual requirements including access for people with disabilities (physical or learning) or families.

When choosing to visit a destination, it is important that people know about access, so that if, for example, the streets are narrow and cobbled, a family with a child in a pram can choose to go elsewhere.

Airlines and ferry companies cater for outbound and inbound visitors, but UK-based companies have to make greater marketing efforts in foreign countries to establish their reputation. Some low-cost airlines have had success in this way to the extent that they have established bases in other countries: for example Ryanair has a base in Frankfurt-Hahn.

Inbound tour operators will be less familiar to you than outbound ones, as their marketing activity takes place overseas, attracting visitors to the UK. These tour operators are represented by Ukinbound, a trade organisation which has over 250 members in all sectors of tourism.

When inbound visitors arrive at an airport they will find tourist information services, transport information and accommodation desks to help them move on to their destination. Some may hire cars which are easily collected and returned at the airport. Others will use public transport. Whatever they choose, tourists need a safe, efficient and clean transport system.

By car

Most domestic visitors travel by car (73 per cent of trips are taken by car according to the UK Tourist Survey). The car traveller needs an adequate, uncongested road network and service stations at regular intervals en route.

When travelling by road, different types of tourists will have different requirements. Those with plenty of time and no small children may make the journey an integral part of the trip, enjoying driving and stopovers en route. Others may want to arrive at their end destination as quickly as possible. Tourists also have to consider what transport is available within the destination, as well as getting to the destination.

Driving is not such a popular option for inbound visitors as drivers from many countries have to contend with driving on the left-hand side of the road with a steering wheel on the right if they hire a car in the UK.

Public transport

Domestic visitors are familiar with our systems and are more likely to get to grips with booking tickets on different forms of transport than overseas visitors.

Overseas visitors are much more dependent on public transport than domestic visitors. Transport systems which meet the needs and expectations of inbound visitors, especially those coming from countries with excellent train services, would certainly meet the needs of domestic visitors.

Inbound visitors need:

- good public transport directly from airports to cities and towns – Heathrow and Gatwick are quite well served, but some regional airports are not
- access by lift and escalator, with space for luggage
- clear information about services across transport systems
- the ability to buy tickets which can be used for through-journeys across transport systems
- catering en route, for example buffet cars on trains.

At the end of 2004, the Department of Transport launched a new website, www.transportdirect.info. The aim of Transport Direct is to provide, in one place, everything anyone needs to know about getting round Great Britain. It claims to be the first ever website to provide national coverage for information about all types of transport.

Travellers can enter their departure point and their destination and get a breakdown of the journey by public transport with details of trains and buses, times and even walking times between connections. Information for domestic air routes is also given. Details of the equivalent car journey can also be found for comparison.

Activity: Transport Direct

Go to the website at www.transportdirect.info

- Imagine you are a visitor arriving at Heathrow and need to find out how you would get to Lancaster by public transport.
- Are there any limitations to the website from the incoming visitor's point of view?
- Discuss your use of the website with your group.

Transport Direct is operated by a consortium, led by Atos Origin. The non-profit service is funded by the UK Department for Transport, the Welsh Assembly Government and the Scottish Government.

Figure 3.8 shows the route by public transport for a visitor arriving at Gatwick and travelling to Manchester.

Customer service

All tourists have a right to expect a high standard of customer service from the transport and travel services that they use. To try and maintain consistent high standards, tourist boards offer customer service training to people who work in travel and tourism. You may have come across courses such as *Welcome Host* and *Welcome All*.

Tourists will also use guides for quality recommendations on places to visit and for restaurants. These may be international guides such as Michelin or Fodor.

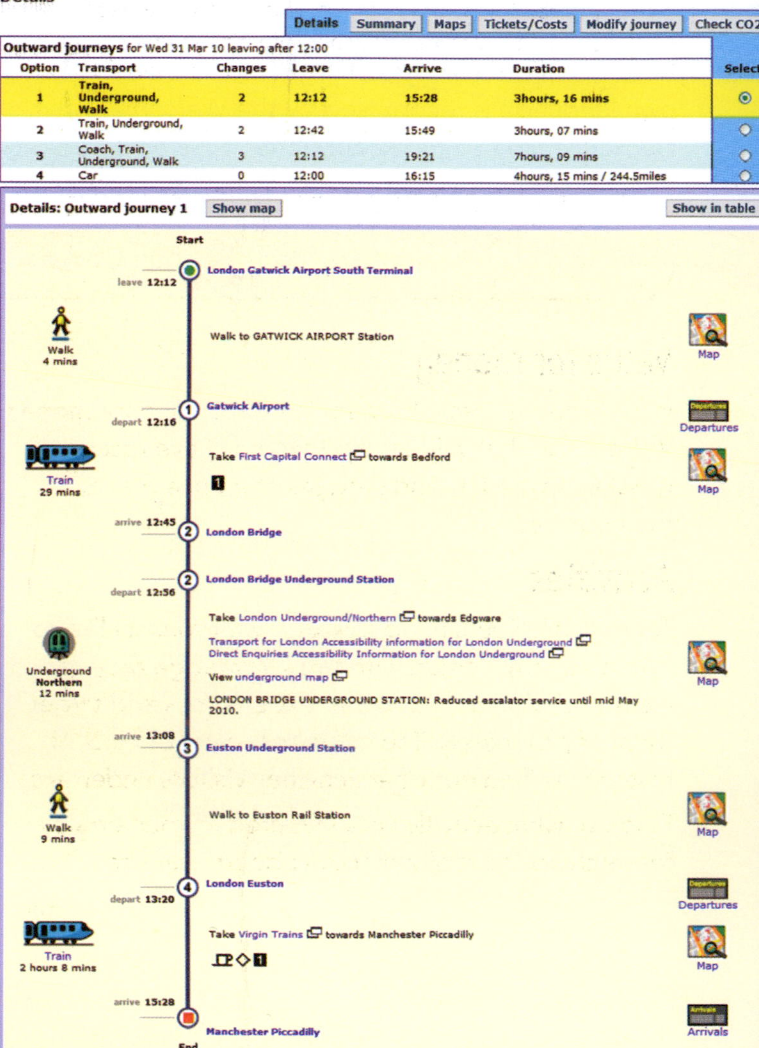

Journey(s) found for London Gatwick Airport to Manchester Piccadilly Rail Station
Details

Details | Summary | Maps | Tickets/Costs | Modify journey | Check CO2

Outward journeys for Wed 31 Mar 10 leaving after 12:00

Option	Transport	Changes	Leave	Arrive	Duration	Select
1	Train, Underground, Walk	2	12:12	15:28	3hours, 16 mins	
2	Train, Underground, Walk	2	12:42	15:49	3hours, 07 mins	
3	Coach, Train, Underground, Walk	3	12:12	19:21	7hours, 09 mins	
4	Car	0	12:00	16:15	4hours, 15 mins / 244.5miles	

Details: Outward journey 1 Show map Show in table

Figure 3.8: A sample journey plan from Gatwick to Manchester

Case study: Enjoy England Quality Rose

The Enjoy England Quality Rose reassures you before you check into your holiday accommodation that it will be just what you want, because it's been checked out by independent assessors. Enjoy England assessors work all year round, ensuring that the standards you find are what you would expect. Since we've done all the work, you can relax, book with confidence and get on with the real business of having a fantastic break.

The Quality Rose is the mark of England's official, nationwide quality assessment scheme and is an independent, reliable, impartial assessment of quality, covering just about every type of place you might want to stay. The variety of accommodation on offer is truly astonishing: from caravan parks to stylish boutique hotels, farmhouse B&Bs to country house retreats, self-catering cottages by the sea to comfy narrowboats perfect for getting away from it all. There are nine main types of accommodation, with a host of different options in each.

But whatever your budget or preference, you can be sure of finding something to suit. Think of the Quality Rose as your personal guarantee that your expectations will be met.

Our objective quality ratings give you a clear indication of accommodation standard, cleanliness, ambience, hospitality, service and food. Using a clear star rating system (1–5 stars), they provide the reassurance you need about what to expect before you arrive. Generally, the more stars, the higher the level of quality.

For individual types of accommodation, the quality rating allows you to distinguish between both the quality of the accommodation and the facilities on offer. For hotels, one and two star hotels tend to be smaller operations that do not offer room service or have telephones in the rooms, but the quality of the service and hospitality, bedrooms, bathrooms and food may be of a high quality.

Look out for the Silver and Gold awards for hotels and guest accommodation whose quality outperform their star rating.

(Source: www.enjoyengland.com)

1 Explain how a system such as the Quality Rose is reassuring for tourists.

2 What other indications of quality and good customer service could a tourist look for?

Value for money

Price is not necessarily an indicator of value for money. Visitors feel that value is good if they have received excellent products and services at a price that fits their budget.

Activities

Tourism providers need to know what tourists like to do on holiday. Armed with this knowledge they can create suitable products and experiences and target them appropriately. Tourist Boards carry out lots of research to find out what activities visitors undertake.

Find out what activities are favoured in your area by researching the regional tourist board website.

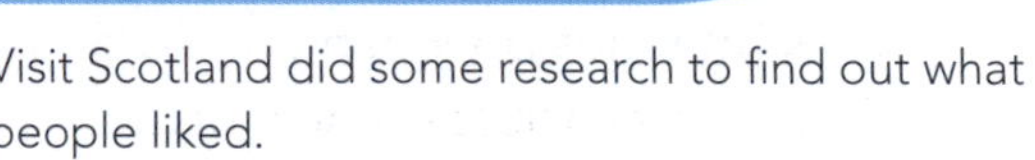

Did you know?

Visit Scotland did some research to find out what people liked.

- Sightseeing is important – searching for the Loch Ness monster and following the route of *The Da Vinci Code* novel.
- A sport called Sphering is fun – it involves going downhill in a huge balloon.
- Drinking is popular, as is visiting old pubs.
- Scotland is the European Capital of Adventure and tourists enjoy adventure sports.

4 Know the features and facilities that attract visitors to UK destinations (LO3)

Tourists are interested in visiting all kinds of destinations, depending on their interests and motivation. They may wish to visit our capital cities, coastal resorts such as Brighton or Blackpool, cultural and historical towns and cities such as Windsor or Bath. Countryside areas such as the Lake District and Snowdonia are attractive for their beauty and for those tourists who like outdoor activities.

Activity: UK destinations

Collect information about two different destinations in the UK. You could choose your own locality and a historic city or seaside resort. Produce a poster which shows all the facilities and features that attract visitors to each destination.

- Present your poster to your group explaining how each destination attracts visitors. Point out the differences and similarities in appeal.

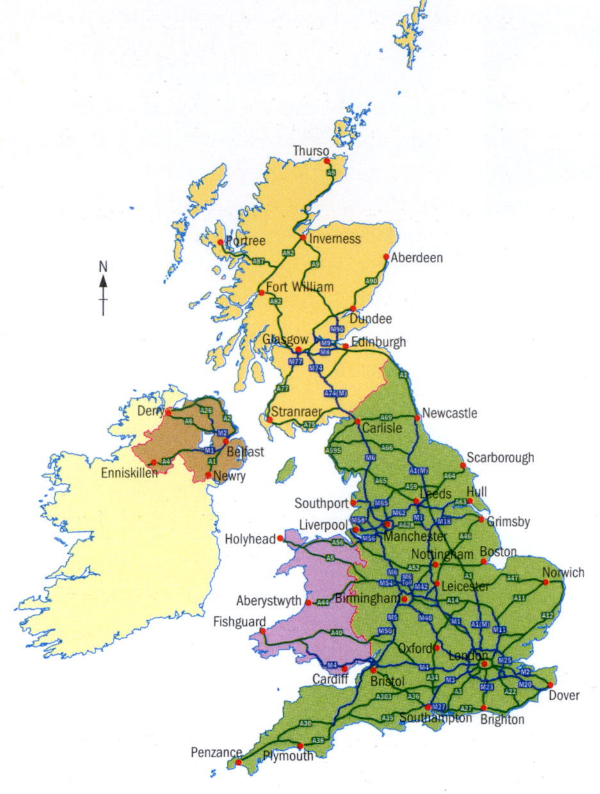

Figure 3.9: UK road map

4.1 Location

The map of the UK road network shows how easy it is to reach destinations by road in the UK. However, in northern Scotland the roads become sparser and access becomes more difficult. There is also an extensive rail network in the UK with fast and frequent journeys available, particularly from the north to the south.

Once inbound visitors arrive at a gateway (a seaport or an airport), they can easily reach their destination by private or public transport.

Roads

Domestic travellers within the UK are more likely to travel by road than by any other means. Car ownership is at its highest ever – it was mentioned earlier that 73 per cent of domestic trips are made by car.

The appeal of travelling by road in the UK is:

- there is an extensive road network with few tolls
- it is easy to find petrol stops and service stations
- roads are well signed
- you can carry whatever baggage you want
- it is easy and comfortable for families with children.

However:

- roads can be congested in holiday periods
- inbound visitors may have trouble driving on the left
- fuel is expensive.

Tourists with limited budgets may choose to travel by coach. There are some excellent services in the UK, especially for longer distance express services across the country where coach travel offers a good alternative to rail travel at competitive fares.

The appeal of travelling by coach in the UK is that:

- there are services from all major towns
- it is cheaper than other forms of road transport.

However, journeys take longer compared with other modes of transport.

Rail

The UK has a complex rail network, with services run by different rail operators. Maps of the network can be found on the National Rail Enquiries website.

London has a comprehensive underground rail system, and Glasgow and Newcastle have metro systems. The London Docklands Light Railway has been very successful in improving transport links and reducing road congestion.

The Channel Tunnel opened in 1994 and provides a vital rail link with France and Belgium.

The appeal of travelling by rail is:

- it is comfortable and can be very fast on express services
- most towns have a railway station.

However:

- it is expensive, although it is possible to get some very cheap rates by booking ahead
- overseas visitors might find the pricing of tickets complex.

Domestic air travel

In terms of fatalities per passenger kilometre, air is the safest mode of transport. It is possible to travel from most regional airports to London and there are excellent daily connections between Scotland and London.

Activity: Airport passengers

Find out the numbers of passengers at your nearest airport. You should be able to find them on the airport's website. Find out where visitors are coming from. Are they domestic travellers, inbound or outbound? Compare your findings with another member of the group. Produce a chart showing the results of your research.

The appeal of air travel is:

- it is often cheap
- the journey is fast.

However:

- onward connections are also needed
- airport check-in and travel to and from the airport adds time to the journey.

Sea

The UK is linked by ferry to its neighbours in Ireland and also to France, Holland and Scandinavia. Because of competition from air travel and the Channel Tunnel, operators have added many extras to their services to entice people to travel by ferry.

Domestic tourists who travel by sea are most likely to be leisure or VFR (visiting friends and relatives) travellers. They may be going to the Channel Islands, the Isle of Wight or the Isle of Man on holiday. Many tourists cross to Ireland to visit family, although these routes face competition from the low-cost airlines.

Case study: Ferries

Ferry firms promote value with new ads

The appeal of ferry travel over airlines is being reinforced by a new Irish Ferries advertising campaign. The push in national press, on TV and on-line is designed to drive out any remaining misconceptions that ferry travel is the 'poor relation'.

Stena Line also launched a new £3 million advertising campaign focusing on the core family and singles travel market. The TV campaign will be reinforced by national radio, press and on-line ads that and will run over six months.

Irish Ferries' head of passenger sales Declan Mescall said: "While Irish Ferries remain the low fares ferry company, we are also driven by our high standards and proud level of customer service, in stark contrast to the low service airlines. Having invested €500 million in our services in recent years we are now primed to drive home the message to any remaining 'doubters' that a ferry is not just a cost-effective way to travel to Ireland, but also a very pleasurable one, with a check-in time of just 30 minutes, five-star on-board facilities, no restrictions on luggage and no 'hidden extras'."

Phil Davies 16 March, 2009

(Source: www.travelmole.com)

1. Summarise the appeal of travelling by ferry.
2. Find out which services appeal to families and the singles market.
3. Imagine you are a single person travelling from Ireland to England. Draw up a table comparing the appeal of a ferry journey against air travel.

4.2 Natural features

Natural attractions appeal to tourists who want to appreciate and enjoy the world's wonders, such as the lakes and mountains in the UK's Lake District, or beautiful beaches.

Every tourist area will have some kind of natural attraction in, or near, to the destination that can be promoted to tourists. Particular features of the **topography** will appeal to different types of visitors. Here are some examples.

Key term

Topography – the shape and composition of the landscape, including mountains and valleys, and the pattern of rivers, roads and railways.

Beaches

Much of the coastline of the UK is protected. About 33 per cent of the coast in England and 42 per cent in Wales is protected under the Heritage Coast scheme. In England, the heritage coasts are managed by Natural England, while the Countryside Council for Wales (CCW) administers the coasts in Wales.

The United Nations Educational, Scientific and Cultural Organisation (UNESCO) awarded Natural World Heritage Status to the coast of Dorset and East Devon in December 2001, in recognition of its unique pedigree which spans 185 million years.

Scotland has a different system of 'Preferred Conservation Zones'.

Beaches appeal to many types of tourists, as there is so much to do. If it is sunny, adults and children can relax on the beach enjoying the sea and sand. The more active can go rock climbing, fishing, walking and cycling. In the south west (Cornwall) the beaches are famous for surfing.

Coasteering is an example of an extreme sport. It combines swimming and climbing with cliff jumping. The aim is to climb along rocks by the sea and when it is impossible to go any further on the rocks to jump into the sea and swim to the next set of rocks. This is a potentially dangerous sport which should only be undertaken under the guidance of a qualified instructor.

Rivers and lakes

Lakes, rivers and mountains can provide the setting for a wide variety of leisure and sporting activities, for example walking, mountaineering and fishing.

In the UK there are nearly 6500 kilometres of rivers and canals. Many of these waterways are managed by British Waterways, a public corporation which looks after more than 3220 kilometres of canals and rivers in the UK. Its role is to conserve and enhance the waterways.

Rivers also provide lots of scope for activities such as boating, including using motor boats, canoeing and rowing. In Oxford and Cambridge, tourists love to go punting on the rivers. British Waterways is trying to enhance our canals and rivers and encourage people to visit them as part of their day-to-day business, as well as for leisure activities.

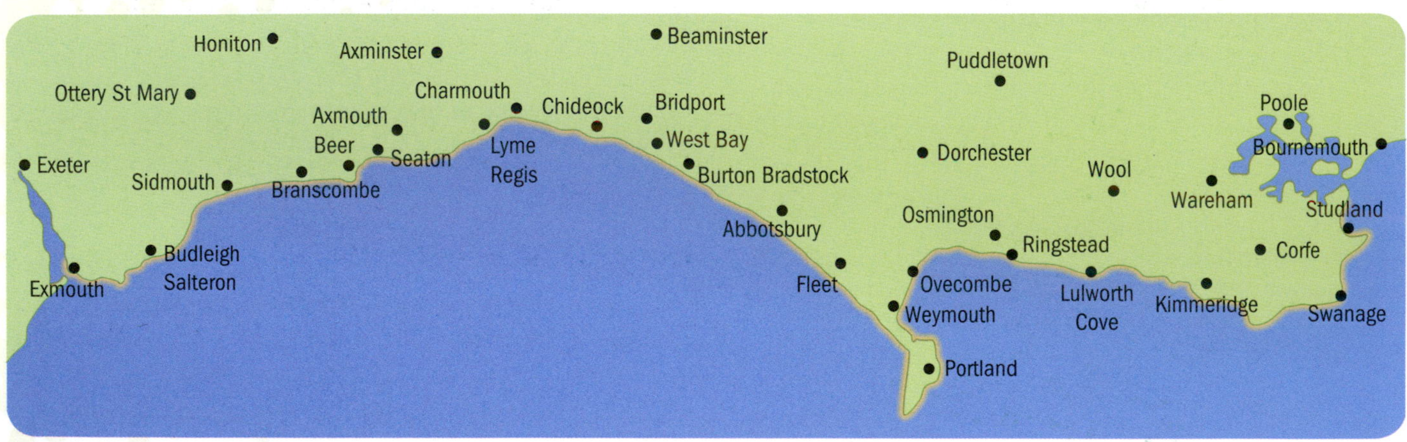

Figure 3.10: Heritage coast

The Lake District in Cumbria attracts tourists for walking and admiring the spectacular scenery or boating on the lakes. Windermere is the largest lake in the Lake District, at 17 kilometres long. The largest lake in the UK is in Northern Ireland. It is called Lough Neagh and covers 383 square kilometres.

National Parks

About 9 per cent of the land area of England and Wales is designated as National Park land. These parks were created in the 1950s and 1960s to protect areas of particular beauty and areas with special ecological features. They provide valuable recreational areas for visitors. In the UK there are 15 National Parks.

In recent years some new National Parks have been designated: Cairngorms National Park and Loch Lomond and the Trossachs National Park, both in Scotland.

Activity: Tourism in the National Parks

Choose one of the National Parks and describe the features that attract tourists. See if you can find statistics about numbers of visitors to the park. Does the park attract more inbound or more domestic tourists and why? What might be the negative impacts of attracting visitors?

Figure 3.11: National Parks in the UK

The parks are not publicly owned. In fact, large areas are owned by private landowners. The National Trust owns about 12 per cent of the Peak District National Park, more than 25 per cent of the Lake District National Park and areas of other parks.

National Park Authorities run National Parks and are given funding to do so by the government. These authorities have powers to control development and manage tourism.

Areas of Outstanding Natural Beauty (AONB)

An AONB is a landscape which has such great beauty, that it is important to protect it. It may be a coastline, a water meadow, a moor or downland.

There are 40 AONBs in England and Wales. About 18 per cent of the countryside of England and Wales is protected in this way. The AONBs are important national resources and were given further protection under the Countryside and Rights of Way Act (2000).

In addition, there are many botanical parks in the UK. Possibly the most famous is Kew Gardens in London. Also, in London there are several royal parks, for example St James's Park and vast areas of heath such as Hampstead Heath. The heaths are most popular with local people for recreational activities and walking, but some are also attractive to tourists. Greenwich Park, with its observatory, is one of the most popular London attractions.

Mountains

The UK has several mountainous areas in Scotland and Wales. Ben Nevis is the highest mountain in Scotland at 1344 metres. Snowdon is the highest in Wales at 1085 metres. In England the highest peak is Scafell Pike at 978 metres.

Mountainous areas are popular with walkers, although the terrain can be tricky so it suits experienced walkers best.

Gorges and waterfalls

A gorge is a deep ravine created by water running through it. It has steep sides and often has waterfalls. These features provide spectacular scenery.

Examples in the UK include the Falls of Glomach in the Highlands of Scotland, one of the highest waterfalls in the UK. In Wales, the gorge at Ceunant Llennyrch, in the Brecon Beacons, has sides 30 metres high and a waterfall called Rhaeadr Ddu. Some of the water from this waterfall was once used for hydroelectricity. In England, the Aysgarth Falls in Wensleydale have attracted visitors for over 200 years.

Lydford Gorge in Devon offers:

- woodland trails through a deep-cut ravine alongside the river Lyd
- a 30-metre Whitelady waterfall
- 'walk the plank' over the Devil's Cauldron whirlpools
- wildlife-watching hides located along the Railway Trail
- organised children's activities.

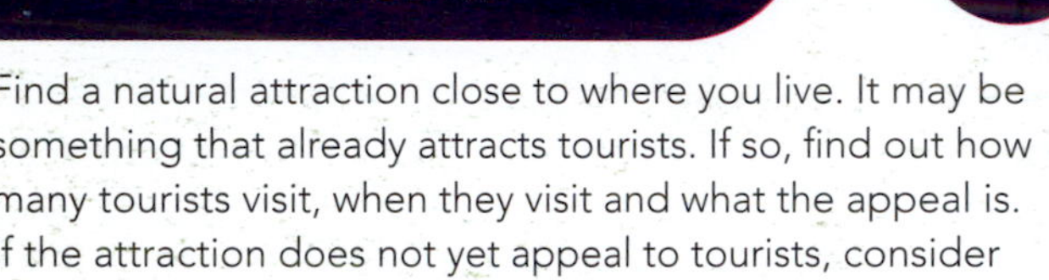

Activity: A local natural attraction

Find a natural attraction close to where you live. It may be something that already attracts tourists. If so, find out how many tourists visit, when they visit and what the appeal is. If the attraction does not yet appeal to tourists, consider the potential and suggest what developments could be made to encourage tourists to visit.

Prepare some notes for a presentation on your findings to the rest of your group. Think about your audience when making your presentation – adapt your language appropriately.

Why do visitors like gorges and waterfalls, such as this one in Scotland?

Case study: Bow Back Rivers

The Bow Back Rivers are a 5½ km network of industrial tributaries of the River Lea which criss-cross the Olympic Park in East London. They have been used for many hundreds of years for industry, transport and flood relief. They are not in too poor a condition considering that they have suffered from contamination from local industries, from pollution and fly-tipping from neighbouring businesses, as well as the decline in commercial boat movement.

The rivers are largely unknown and rarely visited. Despite the continuing problems of pollution, however, the waterways today host a range of wildlife habitats, have a relatively good network of towpaths and even a small community of narrowboats.

Restoration of the Bow Back Rivers has been a national priority since 2002 and is one of the Mayor of London's policies in the London Plan.

After London was chosen to host the 2012 games, the Defra agencies (Environment Agency, Natural England and British Waterways) and a range of other stakeholders worked with the Olympic Delivery Authority (ODA) on a plan to maximise the use of the waterways for wildlife, navigation, people and flood conveyance. The proposals extend beyond the Olympic Park – from Hackney to the Thames – and seek to create the most sustainable waterway restoration possible.

(Source: www.britishwaterways.co.uk/olympics)

1. What is the main purpose of the restoration?
2. Find out more about the role of British Waterways.
3. Find out about other restoration projects which are underway in East London in preparation for the 2012 Olympics.

World Heritage Sites

World Heritage Sites attract tourists in large numbers. These are sites designated by **UNESCO** under the World Heritage Convention of 1972. There are over 890 World Heritage Sites designated worldwide including 28 in the UK.

Key term

UNESCO – The United Nations Educational, Scientific and Cultural Organisation seeks to encourage the identification, protection and preservation of cultural and natural heritage around the world considered to be of outstanding value to humanity.

UNESCO is a global organisation and not specific to the UK. In the UK the DCMS makes sure that the UK complies with the convention. It can also nominate sites in England as potential World Heritage Sites. Nominations in Wales, Scotland and Northern Ireland are made by the respective administrations.

The UK currently has 28 World Heritage Sites. Here are some examples:

- City of Bath
- Hadrian's Wall
- Heart of Neolithic Orkney
- Giant's Causeway and Causeway Coast
- St Kilda.

Activity: Locating the UK's World Heritage Sites

Find the list of UK World Heritage Sites from the UNESCO website (portal.unesco.org). Make sure you know what and where each of them is.

- Choose one in the UK and try to decide what makes it outstanding. Discuss your findings with your group.

What makes World Heritage Sites, such as Giant's Causeway, attractive to visitors?

4.3 Built attractions

These attractions include castles, museums, historic houses, theme parks and cathedrals. Some modern attractions are also built to enhance the existing tourism potential of a destination, such as water parks and fairgrounds at a seaside resort.

Case study: Top tourist attractions

What's the most popular UK attractive for overseas tourists?

Trafalgar Square is the top tourist attraction for international travellers visiting the UK, according to a survey by First Rate Exchange Services.

Its poll of visitors from the US, Ireland, Spain, France and Germany found Tower Bridge and Buckingham Palace were the next popular.

These sites, combined with London's magnitude of museums, made London the main port of call for 72% of these international visitors.

A visit to Buckingham Palace is a must for Americans, with 51% saying visiting the Queen's London home was top of their tourist trip table.

For the Irish, Oxford Street is the most popular destination, and a visit to the Bullring Shopping Centre in Birmingham also features their top 10.

The French are the most likely to venture out of the capital with Edinburgh Castle, Oxford University and the White Cliffs of Dover featuring highly on their holiday hot spots.

The top 10 attractions for inbound tourists were:

1. Trafalgar Square
2. Tower Bridge
3. London Museums
4. Buckingham Palace
5. Oxford Street
6. London Eye
7. Windsor Castle
8. Edinburgh Castle
9. Stonehenge
10. Globe Theatre, London

The list is based on research undertaken by Toluna, with a base size of 2,500 inbound tourists during April 2009.

By Bev Fearis

Source: Travelmole

1 Seven out of ten of the top tourist attractions are in London. How successful is London in meeting the needs of inbound and domestic visitors?

2 Hold a discussion in groups of four. Two people think of all the positive factors that meet the needs of tourists. The other two think of all the ways London doesn't meet tourists'needs.

3 Share your thoughts with the larger group and come to a consensus.

4 Make recommendations as to how London could further its appeal.

5 Find out if the top attractions are still the same.

Case study: Burghley House

Burghley House is the largest and grandest house of the first Elizabethan age built between 1555 and 1587. As well as 35 major rooms on the ground and first floors, there are more than 80 lesser rooms and numerous halls, corridors, bathrooms and service areas. It also has beautiful walks around the historic parkland laid out by Capability Brown.

Investigate Burghley House on the internet (www.burghley.co.uk) and answer the following questions.

1 What is the appeal to visitors of Burghley House?

2 What kind of visitors are most likely to visit and why? Are they domestic tourists, incoming visitors or day visitors?

3 Which organisation(s) are involved in running the house?

4 Choose a historic property in your area and answer the same questions.

Castles and palaces

Our heritage includes many famous castles. Some are ruins and definitely unoccupied, but others are very much in use, for example Windsor Castle. Scotland and Wales have many spectacular castles, such as Edinburgh and Stirling Castles in Scotland, and Caernarvon and Conway Castles in Wales.

Palaces are also very appealing to tourists and Buckingham Palace is one of London's major attractions.

Unoccupied royal palaces are looked after by the Historic Royal Palaces Agency, a charitable organisation set up by DCMS. The organisation is responsible for the upkeep and conservation and also manage public opening. The palaces it takes care of are:

- The Tower of London
- Hampton Court Palace
- Kensington Palace State Apartments (including the Royal Ceremonial Dress Collection)
- The Banqueting House
- Whitehall
- Kew Palace with Queen Charlotte's Cottage.

Museums

There are over 2000 museums in the UK, catering for every interest. In London, our vast museums are very attractive to visitors both from home and abroad. They include the British Museum, the Natural History Museum, the Science Museum and the Victoria and Albert Museum. In addition, art galleries are appealing to visitors and these can be found in most cities.

Theme parks

Theme parks are sometimes better known as amusement parks. They are purpose-built and usually have a collection of rides and other forms of entertainment such as game stalls and shows. They provide a fun day out for families.

Probably the most famous theme park is Alton Towers. In the same organisation are Chessington World of Adventures and Thorpe Park. This has lots of water rides so people who visit tend to get wet! However, there are theme parks in every region. Some are built to enhance seaside areas like Blackpool Pleasure Beach.

How do theme parks appeal to a range of people?

4.4 Facilities

Hotels and other accommodation providers, such as bed and breakfasts, campsites, holiday parks and rented cottages, attract inbound and domestic visitors. Those hotels in international groups often have an advantage as they can market globally and visitors to the UK who are familiar with a brand in their home country may look for it here. Smaller establishments can use the services of tourist organisations to help them promote themselves to tourists.

Eating out is a necessity for most tourists, although the UK is not famous for its cuisine. However, it has improved and restaurants and cafes are available for every taste and price bracket. Tourists may be interested in eating in Michelin Star restaurants in London, or Heston Blumenthal's The Fat Duck in Bray (voted third best restaurant in the World in 2010).

Shopping is often an important activity for tourists. The shops in London are unrivalled anywhere in the world and shopping areas, such as Oxford Street and Covent Garden, are major attractions.

Entertainment may attract visitors. The West End theatres in London are a good example of this, as are Shakespeare's plays in Stratford-upon-Avon.

Sport is a big attraction, particularly major events such as the Olympics which is expected to attract many visitors to London and the UK in 2012. Visitors will need guidance on how to get around the area by bus, train and the Underground.

4.5 Features

VisitBritain has campaigns promoting various activities aimed at overseas visitors to try to encourage them to come to the UK. You can find current examples on the VisitBritain website. Here are some examples of features that attract visitors.

Media influences

If a town, or attraction, has been featured in the media then visitors often want to go there. Historic houses used in television dramas or places featured in Harry Potter movies are very popular.

Famous people

Visitors like to visit the home place of famous people. Whole industries have built up around Stratford-upon-Avon, home of Shakespeare, and Haworth in West Yorkshire, where the famous Brontë family of writers lived. Visitors are alerted to houses where famous people were born or lived by blue heritage signs on buildings, known as blue plaques. There are over 800 in London.

Have you seen any blue plaques?

Events might be linked to famous people. In 2009, in Scotland, over 100 events were organised to celebrate the 250th birthday of the poet Robbie Burns.

Royalty

Royal palaces, and events such as the Changing of the Guard, are very attractive to visitors. Many overseas visitors are fascinated by the British royal family and the pomp and ceremony that go with it. Remember that many of the UK's visitors are from republics and therefore have no royalty.

Events

Many events provide an opportunity to see local or national customs, such as bonfires on 5th November or Christmas celebrations. Other examples of special events are the many music festivals in the UK, although these are more likely to attract domestic rather than incoming visitors.

In the summer, festivals in Reading and Leeds attract rock music lovers to those areas. Glastonbury is also a famous music festival venue.

Sporting events are very appealing to tourists. Football and cricket matches in particular attract both day visitors and inbound visitors.

Local customs and traditions

Events such as the Notting Hill Carnival attract domestic tourists to London.

The Notting Hill Carnival takes place every August Bank Holiday weekend. The festivities last for three days. The first carnival was in 1964 and was started by West Indian immigrants in the area. These were mainly Trinidadians who wanted to replicate the flavour of their wonderful carnivals at home. The first carnival was fairly small, but now it is a massive spectacular attracting up to 1 million people.

Activity: Carnival

If you can, visit the Notting Hill Carnival. Otherwise, find out about a similar (possibly much smaller-scale) event in your area that represents the local culture. Describe the event in detail. Find out if the event attracts tourists and if that is its purpose. Compile some facts and figures on the event and share your findings with your group.

The carnival reflects the multicultural nature of British society, with people celebrating their own musical and artistic traditions from around the world, for example the Philippines, Central and South America and Bangladesh as well as the Caribbean.

For two days of the carnival there are three live stages featuring local bands, as well as song artists from other countries. Visitors can buy Caribbean foods at street stalls or buy traditional arts and crafts.

Perhaps the most exciting part of the carnival is the long procession which takes place. People parade in magnificent costumes, alongside steel bands.

Case study: The appeal of York

York is a popular city destination for both domestic and overseas visitors.

Most visitors arrive in York by car as it is easily accessible by road, though York also has good rail links. There are regional airports within reach, but international visitors are likely to travel via London or Manchester.

The city has many historic and cultural attractions, the most famous being York Minster, the Castle Museum, the National Railway Museum and the Jorvik Centre. The last two are purpose-built attractions.

Motivation for visiting the city varies according to the type of tourist. Many visit to see a historic city, but there are those who come for the good shopping or to be entertained at the horse races.

Geographically, York benefits from its proximity to beautiful countryside – the North York Moors and the Yorkshire Dales. Many tourists combine a visit to the countryside with their city visit.

Local attractions include:

- Jorvik Centre – a ride back to Viking life to AD 975, with many items on display from an archaeological dig on the site
- York Minster – the largest gothic church in England
- medieval city walls
- nearby stately homes – Bishopthorpe Palace and Sutton Park
- shopping in the streets of Stonegate and Petergate.

Repeat business is important to York, otherwise overall visitor numbers would fall. A series of one-off, or annual, events is arranged in order to attract visitors. Look at the York Tourism website (www.visityork.org) for the latest examples.

Information about tourism in York is provided by City of York Council for 2008/9:

- over 4 million visitors to York
- £364 million spent by visitors to York
- 10,000 jobs in York created by tourism
- 59 per cent travel to York by car, 27 per cent by train and 3 per cent by regular bus.
- nearly 11,000 year-round and seasonal bedspaces
- 50.6 per cent bed occupancy, 64.2 per cent room occupancy
- the largest number of visitors is in the 45–64 age group
- there is a trend towards older visitors (over 55)
- 55 per cent of visitors were staying overnight, significantly higher than the regional average of 35 per cent
- 45 per cent were day visitors – much lower than the regional average of 65 per cent
- 80 per cent of visitors have been to York before – a strong showing for repeat business
- the most important overseas markets are the USA, Germany, Netherlands and Belgium – 13 per cent of visitors are from overseas.

(Source: City of York Council)

1. What is another term for the amount of money spent by tourists?
2. Why is there a difference between bed occupancy and room occupancy?
3. How could York attract more young people?
4. Fewer overseas visitors went to York between 1996 and 2009. Can you suggest why this was so?
5. Do some research and identify five attractions in York, or the surrounding area, that might appeal to a visiting couple in their fifties from the USA.
6. Analyse why York's attractions appeal to both domestic and inbound visitors.

Assessment activity 3.2

Remember the new Minister for Tourism you met in your first assessment? (See page 8.) The Minister needs information on the needs of domestic and inbound visitors. Identify the needs of the tourists described below.

- A couple from Sheffield are visiting London by train for a short break. They have been twice before and are keen fans of theatre and musicals.
- Myra and fellow students, on a BTEC course in Retail Business, want to visit the Metro Centre (shopping centre) near Newcastle. They want to stay over and have a night out in Newcastle.
- A German couple are visiting London for the first time. They do not speak English. They want to watch tennis at Wimbledon and see something of the capital.
- A family from the USA, two parents and five children, want to trace their heritage. They will visit London for two days then spend a week in their ancestral home city of Belfast in Northern Ireland. P2

Make sure you address all of the following for each group of visitors:

- access to information
- accommodation
- costs and standards
- transport
- accessibility
- customer service
- quality assurance
- value for money
- activities.

The Minister should be informed about the features and facilities of at least three UK destinations that attract tourists. Your three destinations must include one coastal resort, one countryside area and one historical or cultural town or city. The Minister might be tiring of presentations now, so prepare a visual display which you can supplement with explanatory notes or dialogue. P3

Analyse how one of the destinations chosen for your display attracts inbound and domestic visitors and meets their needs. Add this information to your display. M1

Think about the same destination you studied for the last task and evaluate the effectiveness of the destination in attracting and meeting the needs of inbound and domestic visitors. Make recommendations for addressing gaps or improving provision. D1

Grading tips

P3 Make sure you address all of the following for each destination:

- location and accessibility
- natural features
- built attractions
- facilities (range of accommodation, eating out, sport and leisure, entertainment, shopping and local transport)
- other features relevant to that destination.

Make sure you refer to all types of visitors in your presentation.

M1 You must focus your analysis on at least four different types of visitors, so why not use those you considered earlier in the assessment?

D1 and P5 Ensure you use a range of information sources and you reference these accurately.

Functional skills

When you present information clearly to others you will develop **English**–speaking skills.

PLTS

As you explore your destination from the perspective of the visitor you will develop skills as an **independent enquirer**.

5 Understand how UK inbound and domestic tourism is affected by internal and external factors (LO4)

Activity: Important terms

Match up these terms and their definitions.

Term	Definition
Incoming visitors	People travelling in their own country for tourism purposes
Domestic visitors	A country from where visitors originate
Inbound visitors	The amount of money visitors spend on tourism in a country
Day visitors	People who visit a country which is not their country of residence for the purposes of tourism
Tourism generator	The number of visitors coming to a country
Receipts	People who visit a country which is not their country of residence for the purposes of tourism
Visitor flow	People going on an excursion and not staying overnight
Arrivals	Tourists leaving their country of residence to visit another country
Tourism receiver	Visitors travelling for the purpose of business
Outbound tourists	A country that is a destination for tourists
Business visitors	Tourists going on a holiday
Leisure tourists	Visitors travelling to visit a friend or relative
VFR	The number of visitors coming in and going out of a country

Factors affecting tourism may be internal (that is, within the UK) or external (occurring outside the UK) and therefore are more difficult to control. All factors have an effect on tourism in terms of visitor numbers, how long people stay on a trip, the volume and value of inbound and domestic tourism, how often people visit and on generating countries and regions.

As we discuss the factors that affect tourism, we will consider their effect in these terms.

5.1 Internal factors affecting the tourist market

Health, safety and security within the UK

The UK has stringent health and safety legislation so tourists can expect to be as safe, or safer, than they would be in their own countries. This also applies to security. However, people tend to behave differently when they are on holiday and may not be as aware as they normally are of difficult situations. People who are unfamiliar with their surroundings and the local culture are more vulnerable to crime than others.

Domestic tourists may also be more vulnerable when visiting a part of the country they are not used to. The Metropolitan Police, for example, have issued advice for tourists visiting London and an extract is shown on page 84. You will note that much of the advice relates to common-sense precautions for any large city.

Terrorist activity, such as the London Underground bombings in 2005, has the effect of temporarily deterring visitors because they are worried about their safety. The Association for Leading Visitor Attractions (ALVA) reported 'a considerable' impact, although attractions outside the centre benefited, for example Kew Gardens.

ADVICE FOR TOURISTS

- Keep your bag or camera where you can see them by wearing them in front of you, not over your shoulder. This is especially important if you are in a crowded area, such as on a bus or an underground train.
- When in restaurants, bars, theatres or cinemas never leave your bag on the floor or over the back of your chair. Keep it where you can see it.
- Only buy theatre or concert tickets from reliable sources and not from 'touts' in the street.
- If you're out and about at night on foot try to keep to busy, well-lit areas.
- When travelling by bus or train try to avoid using stations in isolated places. When possible sit near the driver on buses, and on trains try to make sure you sit in a compartment where there are other people.
- Only use taxis that have been licensed. These are easily recognised by a licence on display.
- Take extra care when crossing the road. Always remember to look both ways as traffic may be coming from a different direction than you are expecting.

(Source: www.met.police.uk; © Metropolitan Police Authority)

Recession and strength of the pound

When the UK economy is doing well, the pound sterling is strong. However, a strong pound actually deters visitors from overseas because when they exchange their own currency for sterling they get fewer pounds for their money, so visiting the UK becomes more expensive. When sterling is weak, as in a UK recession, then overseas visitors get more pounds for their money and find the UK very cheap. A recession can occur in any country and affects travel and tourism in the same way.

In 2009 there was a global recession and it affected travel and tourism everywhere. According to VisitBritain statistics, visits from North America were down 21 per cent from 2008. Visits from accession (to the European Union (EU)) countries were down by 24 per cent. Visits from other parts of the world were down by 17 per cent. London was the city that tourists stayed in the most, but it still had fewer visitor numbers than usual.

As countries emerge from recession, people start to travel again. In 2009, there was an increase in visitors to the UK from Germany as that country came out of recession.

Exchange rates change every day and you can find them reported in banks, on the internet and in the newspapers.

The recession affects domestic tourism as well as international tourism. People take fewer trips and even when they do go away they tend to spend less money.

Table 3.4 shows the volume and value of domestic tourism in the UK in 2008.

Table 3.4: Tourism trips taken in the UK 2007/8

	2007	2008
Trips (millions)	123.458	117.715
Nights (millions)	394.413	378.388
Spending (£ millions)	21,238	21,107
Average nights per trip	3.19	3.21
Average spend per trip	£172	£179
Average spend per night	£54	£56

(Source: The UK Tourist from The United Kingdom Tourism Survey 2008, VisitBritain)

Activity: Percentage change

Copy the table and add another column and calculate the percentage change. Check the current survey and find new figures. What are the changes? Discuss the reasons for changes with your group.

Accessibility

The UK remains one of the best connected countries for international tourism, with hundreds of air routes, sea routes and the Channel Tunnel bringing tourists into the UK. Many low-cost airlines serve the UK, bringing increased traffic between Europe and the UK. Such services also increase outbound travel.

Accession to the EU has added to the appeal of the UK for new member states. Low-cost air travel, including

Case study: Marketing campaigns

Visit Wales is responsible for marketing Wales, both to domestic tourists and to inbound visitors. Here is an example of one of their marketing campaigns from 2009.

Current UK campaign

The campaign promotes 'holidays are changing' and that more people are waking up to the fact that holidays in Wales can offer a real alternative to the formulaic packaged holiday.

Looking at what products are strong for Wales and of interest to our audience, the campaign focuses on: Food, The Environment, Activities, Welsh Style, Accommodation and The Family, placing the country at the heart of a new holiday movement.

The campaign will target the independent explorers and its sub-audiences (personal, family and active explorers). Have a look at the target markets page for more information.

In addition, due to the economic downturn and strength of the euro, we have allocated a proportion of the budget to target people that would normally be looking at France for their main holiday (known as domestic switchers) and trying to target them with a Wales message.

We will be doing this through:

- a spend on mailing customers identified as France holiday takers
- buying search words that relate to French holidays
- running on-line advertising in environments where people would be searching for their holidays as part of our on-line activity.

(Source: new.wales.gov.uk)

1 Summarise the features of Wales that will also appeal to people who usually holiday in France.

2 How does 'buying search words' help boost tourism in Wales?

3 How will the tourist board get hold of customers' names and addresses in order to mail them about Wales?

low transatlantic fares, makes the UK more accessible to all. Markets such as China and India will generate more visitors as air travel agreements between those countries and the UK come into play.

Accessibility impacts on visitor numbers as it makes it easier for people to travel to the UK. It also affects frequency – it is easy to travel to, so why not go more often?

Availability of products and services

Tourism in the UK is subject to seasonal trends and prices fluctuate with seasons. Hotel and transport prices are at their most expensive in peak times, such as the summer school holiday and the Christmas period. Rooms are less likely to be available at such times. Restaurants are quickly booked too.

The key for tourists is to plan well ahead if they want to holiday at peak times. Inbound visitors need information about opening hours of bars, restaurants and shops, as they may differ from their home country.

Quality of goods and services

Consumers are becoming more discerning and the UK tourist market is responding with help from marketing agencies such as VisitBritain. Since January 2006, VisitBritain has promoted only quality assessed accommodation. Those who do not meet the criteria will not be promoted. In general, the UK has a reputation for good quality and high standards of customer service.

VisitBritain also carries out research into visitor perceptions of the UK. The results of this type of research help to improve quality standards.

5.2 External factors affecting the tourist market

Exchange rate

The exchange rate continues to exert an influence on visitor numbers. Rates to watch are sterling/euro and sterling/dollar. An improvement in the strength of the dollar could bring a greater rise in visitors from the USA.

Travel restrictions

Travel restrictions may impact heavily on the numbers of inbound visitors. Restrictions fall into the following categories.

Security-related restrictions

In August 2006, the British intelligence service claimed to discover a terrorist plot to blow up some aircraft in mid-air. Very stringent hand baggage rules were put in place.The extra inconvenience and fear of terrorism deterred some people from travelling.

Customs restrictions

These relate to alcohol, tobacco and gifts. Leaflets are available explaining the restrictions to visitors. These are unlikely to affect large numbers of tourists.

Immigration restrictions

Residents of EU member states are free to travel without restriction throughout Europe. Consequently the UK has seen a huge increase of inbound tourism from Europe since the accession of member states from eastern Europe in 2004.

Some visitors require visas to enter the UK. These have to be applied for and can be expensive.

Activity: Allowances

Visit the HM Revenue & Customs website (customs.hmrc.gov.uk) and find out what the current allowances for alcohol, tobacco and gifts are for visitors to the UK from within and outside Europe. Send an email to a friend visiting from the USA and tell them what they can bring into the UK.

Emergence of new markets

Asia Pacific, the Middle East and Africa are the fastest growing areas for visitors to the UK, according to VisitBritain's Global Insights. They are likely to grow by 9 per cent a year up to 2012. China is another important market as outbound visits from China are forecast to grow by 84 per cent by 2012.

As new markets emerge we see a difference in ranking of generating countries and regions. Table 3.5 shows the top ten markets by volume and value.

Table 3.5: International travel - leading destination countries 2007 and 2008

Rank	Arrivals			Rank	Receipts		
	2007 Millions	2008 Millions	% change 2008/7		2007 US$bn	2008 US$bn	% change 2008/7
1 France	81.9	79.3	–3.2	1 USA	96.7	110.1	13.8
2 USA	56.0	58.0	3.6	2 Spain	57.6	61.6	6.9
3 Spain	58.7	57.3	–2.3	3 France	54.3	55.6	2.4
4 China	54.7	53.0	–3.1	4 Italy	42.7	45.7	7.2
5 Italy	43.7	42.7	–2.1	5 China	37.2	40.8	9.7
6 UK	30.9	30.2	–2.2	6 Germany	36.0	40.0	11.0
7 Ukraine	23.1	25.4	9.8	7 UK	38.6	36.0	–6.7
8 Turkey	22.2	25.0	12.3	8 Australia	22.3	24.7	10.6
9 Germany	24.4	24.9	1.9	9 Turkey	18.5	22.0	18.7
10 Mexico	21.4	22.6	5.9	10 Austria	18.9	21.8	15.4

Source: World Tourism Organization (UNWTO) © (Data as collected by UNWTO, 2009)

Activity: Campaigns

- Find an example of a marketing initiative from VisitBritain, or one of the National Tourist Boards, to promote incoming tourism from a specific country. Report back on the campaign to your group.
- Draw up ideas for a campaign to promote your own area to domestic tourists from other parts of the country.

Think about it

How do you think we know how many visitors come to the UK? The data are collected in the International Passenger Survey for the Office of National Statistics. A sample of people is questioned at airports and seaports. People travelling outbound are also questioned. Around 250,000 interviews are carried out per year representing 0.2 per cent of all travellers.

Competition from other destinations

The UK has to be more appealing than other destinations in order to win tourists. There are many factors, as we have seen, which affect a visitor's decision on where to travel. Table 3.5 (page 86) shows how the UK compares with other destinations worldwide in attracting visitors.

Activity: Analysing data

Study Table 3.5.

1. Why is there a difference in ranking between arrivals and receipts?
2. Why do you think the USA ranks first as a destination in terms of receipts?
3. Why has China risen in popularity as a destination?
4. What do you think happened to Mexico's position following the collection of this set of data?
5. Prepare some presentation notes explaining why tourists should visit the UK rather than the top five destinations.

Weather

The weather plays an important role in determining where tourists choose to go. A poor summer in the UK always leads to increased bookings for holidays abroad the year afterwards. The weather is not an attraction for inbound visitors to the UK – we rely on the appeal of our heritage and other attractions.

How does the weather affect inbound and domestic tourism?

Assessment activity 3.3

Although the Minister understands the workings of the DCMS, as it is the government department he is assigned to, he has not researched factors which affect tourism. You need to help him with this too.

1 Prepare (using a programme such as PowerPoint®) presentations which clearly **explain** at least five external and internal factors on UK inbound and domestic tourism. P4
2 **Analyse** how three factors are currently affecting UK inbound and domestic tourism. M2
3 **Evaluate** the potential impact of two factors on the future of UK inbound and domestic tourism. D2

Grading tips

P4 Use recent statistical data (within the last five years) for domestic and inbound tourism to support your explanations of the effect of at least five factors affecting the sector. Make sure you cover both domestic and inbound tourism.

P5 Ensure you use a range of reference sources including atlases, the internet, brochures, statistical data, timetables, destination guides and other sources. Ensure you complete a bibliography.

M2 Analyse rather than explain – this means stating exactly how three current (within the last year) factors have affected tourism. You must analyse three factors.

For example, factors affecting visitor numbers from Eastern Europe could be:

- the increase in provision of low-cost flights between Eastern Europe and the UK
- the introduction of flights to Eastern Europe from regional airports.

You need to explain why these factors affect numbers and produce statistical evidence of the increases/decreases.

D2 Assess what the future impact of two factors will be. Use two of the three factors that you have already analysed. For example, if a factor is that even more flights will be provided from regional airports, what will happen to visitor numbers and patterns of tourism?

Functional skills

Selecting and using appropriate sources of ICT-based information to meet the task requirements will help you develop your **ICT** skills.

PLTS

Supporting your conclusions with relevant evidence, using reasoned arguments will help develop your skills as an **independent enquirer**.

WorkSpace

James Turner

PR Manager

I work for a Scottish tourist company that promotes Scotland to visitors and it is my job to ensure that the right message about Scotland, and everything we offer, gets out to the media. My job carries a lot of responsibility, but it is fascinating and I am always happy to go to work in the morning.

I manage a team of people who will be working on individual campaigns. I have to monitor them and know exactly what is going on at any time with any campaign. If something is late or overspent, ultimately it is my fault. I am given a budget for public relations each year and then I plan campaigns within that budget. The budget might be as much as £100,000. Of course, the campaigns must be related to our strategic objectives.

This year a major campaign has been our Homecoming Scotland celebration. We have had about 100 events celebrating the 250th birthday of Robbie Burns. My team handles press enquiries about the events, organises press releases and press launches for events. I spend a lot of time networking with media contacts. It is important to have good relationships with the media so that we can get events covered in the way we would like.

Members of the team attend exhibitions to promote Scotland, so recently we were in London at the World Travel Market.

I had to be a graduate to get this job and I also have a postgraduate Diploma in Public Relations. I had been working in PR in London before I took this job, but I am Scottish and I needed to show that I had a very extensive knowledge of Scotland and its tourism products to get this job. My bosses were looking for initiative and at my interview I was asked lots of questions about how I had developed previous campaigns. Creative thinking is very important too, as in PR we have to try to find new approaches to campaigns and events to catch the attention of the media.

Think about it!

1 How would you begin to organise a press launch?

2 How would you know whom to contact?

3 What other skills do you think are needed for this job?

Just checking

1 Why are day visitors important to the economy?
2 Give two examples of historic attractions.
3 Explain why most domestic tourists travel by car.
4 How is the International Passenger Survey carried out?
5 Why do France, Germany and the Irish Republic generate large numbers of incoming visitors to the UK?
6 Explain why China is an emerging market.
7 What is the difference between arrivals and receipts?
8 Which two countries generate most visitors to the UK?
9 What travel restrictions might deter tourists from visiting the UK?
10 Give four examples of islands lying close to the UK.
11 Give three examples of types of domestic tourist.
12 What is a National Park?
13 Name three National Parks.
14 What is the role of UNESCO?

Assignment tips

Your assessments for this unit relate to supporting the Minister for Tourism. Get familiar with the DCMS website at www.culture.gov.uk and find out what their latest activities are.

- Record all the sources you use for research as you go along.
- Look at maps, and a British atlas, and know the locations of gateways and key destinations before you do Assessment 3.1.
- To achieve P5 in this unit you must keep records of all the sources of information you use for your research on UK destinations. You should give details of every source and say how and where you used each source. Start this now. Get a notebook for this purpose or create a Word document. If you are working electronically, make sure you keep a back-up file.
- When you submit each section of your assignment, you should add a bibliography: that is, a comprehensive list of all the sources you have used. If you keep a detailed log throughout the unit and complete your bibliographies, you may achieve P5.
- Sign up for the VisitBritain newsletter (industryupdate@visitbritain.org). All the latest news and research findings will drop into your inbox.
- You will find TravelMole a really useful on-line resource, but you need to register first (www.travelmole.com).

Credit value: 10

4 Customer service in travel and tourism

Providing excellent customer service is essential to remain competitive in any business. In travel and tourism, it is paramount. Products and services are often intangible and it is the quality of the customer service that helps the customer choose the right product for their needs.

Many organisations provide similar products and services and the customer often has a preference for the organisation with high levels of service. This unit will develop your understanding of what excellent customer service means in practice for tourism organisations and will give you the opportunity to develop skills so that you can deliver excellent customer service.

Your own customer service and selling skills need to be of the highest standard to work in the travel and tourism sector. You will find out about the skills needed and practise using them in different situations.

Learning outcomes

After completing this unit you should:

1 understand the importance of providing excellent customer service in travel and tourism organisations

2 know how travel and tourism organisations adapt customer service to meet the individual needs of customers

3 know the customer service skills required to meet customer needs in travel and tourism contexts

4 be able to apply customer service and selling skills in travel and tourism situations

Assessment and grading criteria

This table shows you what you must do in order to achieve a **pass**, **merit** or **distinction** grade, and where you can find activities in this book to help you.

To achieve a **pass** grade the evidence must show that you are able to:	To achieve a **merit** grade the evidence must show that, in addition to the pass criteria, you are able to:	To achieve a **distinction** grade the evidence must show that, in addition to the pass and merit criteria, you are able to:
P1 explain the importance of providing excellent customer service in travel and tourism organisations **See Assessment activity 4.1, page 103** **P2** describe customer service provision in travel and tourism organisations to meet the individual needs of different types of customers **See Assessment activity 4.1, page 103**	**M1** assess how customer service provision meets specific customer needs in travel and tourism organisations **See Assessment activity 4.1, page 103**	**D1** make recommendations for how a travel and tourism organisation can improve its customer service provision to meet specific customer needs **See Assessment activity 4.1, page 103**
P3 describe the customer service skills required to meet customer needs in travel and tourism contexts **See Assessment activity 4.2, page 114**		
P4 demonstrate customer service skills in travel and tourism situations **See Assessment activity 4.3, page 116**	**M2** deal independently with customers in travel and tourism situations **See Assessment activity 4.3, page 116**	**D2** demonstrate good product knowledge, customer service and selling skills to provide a consistently high standard of customer service in different situations **See Assessment activity 4.3, page 116**
P5 demonstrate selling skills in a travel and tourism situation **See Assessment activity 4.3, page 116**	**M3** demonstrate effective selling skills in a travel and tourism situation **See Assessment activity 4.3, page 116**	

How you will be assessed

This unit will be assessed by one or more internal assignments that will be designed and marked by your tutor. Your assignments will be subject to sampling internally and externally as part of Edexcel's quality assurance procedures. The assignments are designed to allow you to show your knowledge and understanding related to the unit. The unit outcomes indicate what you should know, understand or be able to do after completing the unit.

Matthew, 18-year-old BTEC National learner

I did a BTEC First Diploma before this course and Customer Service was one of the units. I also have a part-time job in a shop, so I have experience of dealing with customers. We get training in the shop too, so I think I am a bit of an expert!

However, I still found lots of new things in this unit. For example, I had never been taught how to sell before – even at the shop. Now I see that understanding the stages and how to close are really useful. I see now that some of my colleagues are too pushy and put people off buying.

When it came to the first assessment I asked my tutor if I could use my shop as one of the organisations to study. She said that it wasn't suitable as it wasn't in travel and tourism, but that the experience I had there would help me in the role-plays for the last assessment.

My aunt works as cabin crew for an airline so she got me some information about their customer service and our tutor arranged for the Tourist Information Centre (TIC) to send one of their staff to talk to us. Those were the two organisations I used for my first assignment. They had very different policies, even though both were very clear about good customer service being important for success.

Over to you!

1 What experience do you have already of customer service?
2 What contacts can you think of to help you get information on customer service policies in travel and tourism?

1 The importance of providing excellent customer service in travel and tourism organisations

Set off

What makes good customer service?

A common interview question on application forms is to ask you to think of an example of when you provided excellent customer service. Try this now. It might be an example from your part-time job, from an event at your college or school or from a voluntary activity.

Share your examples with the group and try to decide what the common elements are that make the service really good.

1.1 Customer service

What exactly do we mean by customer service? Do we mean how friendly the travel consultant was, how quickly a phone call was returned, the personality of the receptionist or the cleanliness of the aircraft?

All of these things contribute to our experience of service in travel and tourism. As a travel and tourism employee you are going to have to recognise and deliver a high standard of customer service to ensure that customers trade with you rather than your competitors.

First impressions

It takes customers just ten seconds to form their first impressions. First impressions count!

These first impressions could be formed by seeing:

- a queue of customers – or being served immediately
- staff talking to each other and ignoring their customers – or being greeted with a smile
- scruffy staff who are chewing gum – or well-dressed staff with a professional appearance
- staff slouching over desks – or positive behaviour and body language
- eating in the office – or clear and tidy desks.

Once a negative first impression is formed, it is very difficult to change it.

Organisations need to ensure that they retain their customers. It is essential that everyone working in travel and tourism is aware of the importance of first impressions and ensures that they help to make it positive. Presentation and non-verbal communication are important elements of a first impression.

Company image

The images customers have of companies will influence where they choose to buy their products and services.

An image is personal and depends on your own experiences, expectations, things you may have read and word of mouth. Your image of a holiday destination may be formed by holiday brochures; someone who has seen the same resort featured on a 'holiday horrors' programme will have quite a different image.

All organisations try to develop positive images. They do this through **mission statements**, websites, **logos**, **corporate images** and ensure they present an air of efficiency. The appearance and location of premises are also important for many organisations. If you see a scruffy shop front and untidy window display you will probably form a negative image.

Key terms

Mission statement – a concise statement about an organisation's purpose. Mission statements vary, but usually contain information about products, services, beliefs and values.

Logo – a symbol used by an organisation (for example, the tick is the logo of Nike and the happy face the logo of TUI).

Corporate image – the impression created and presented by a company; how a company is perceived.

Activity: Creating an image

1 Work with a partner. Think about your images of the following organisations and destinations. What has formed your images?

- Virgin Atlantic Airlines
- Manchester United
- Ibiza
- Venice
- Ayia Napa (Cyprus)
- Australia
- a local hotel
- Hilton Hotels

2 Choose two travel and tourism organisations. Using the internet, find out what their mission statements are. What images are they trying to create through their mission statements and logos?

Organisational efficiency

This includes effective systems and procedures for dealing with customers, which are communicated to all employees. For example, ensuring calls are returned when promised, sending travel documents in good time and dealing with special requests.

Speed and accuracy of service

An important factor in the provision of customer service is that it is fast. No one wants to be kept waiting. Customers expect to be greeted straight away; the expectation is that telephones should be answered within three rings and e-mails to be responded to within 24 hours.

In order to provide information quickly and efficiently, you need several skills.

- You must be organised. You don't have to know everything – but you must know where to find out about everything. If a customer wants to book a cross-country skiing holiday, you should know where to find the specialist information.
- You need product knowledge – for example, ideally you will know where cross-country skiing occurs. However, if you don't it is important that you can quickly look it up on the internet, bespoke software or in the World Travel Guide (www.worldtravelguide.net) and establish the location of relevant destinations.
- Product knowledge also includes information about your organisation – what it sells, who to refer complaints to, opening times, and how to use the computer and telephone systems effectively. All of these will help you to provide a speedy and accurate service.
- Your expertise in using the available technology will determine whether you provide an efficient service. If you lose people when transferring them on the phone, use the incorrect airport code on the computer reservation system or lose an unsaved document you have just produced, you will not be able to give a good service to your internal or external customers.

Consistency

Consistency of service is also important. This means a high level of service is given all the time to every customer.

Products and services offered

All travel and tourism organisations have to ensure that they are providing products and services that meet customers' needs and need to assess this continuously. Does the hotel restaurant offer sufficient variety? Are there adequate reception staff on duty at all times of the day? Should the lifeguard hours be extended? Are the evening entertainments suitable?

Meeting customers' needs and exceeding expectations

The aim is not to meet customers' needs, but to exceed them. This can be achieved by providing the right products and services and presenting these to the customer using excellent customer service skills.

Customers buy products or services because they believe they need them – for example a drink, a car or a holiday. Expectations refer to what the customer expects from the product or service. A drink may satisfy a need (thirst), but not meet expectations if it does not taste as good as the customer thought it would. If a customer enters a travel agency looking for a summer holiday for a family of four, they may also have certain expectations about the costs, ideal locations and activities available. You could meet the need (by selling a holiday for the family), but to exceed expectations you will also have to provide details of, for example, excursion possibilities, airport transfers, free child places and car hire.

Customers require some information in almost all encounters with travel and tourism organisations. Some staff are employed simply to provide information, for example at the customer information desk at an airport or a visitor attraction. Similarly, it is the primary role of all staff within a Tourist Information Centre (TIC) to provide accurate information on such issues as car parking, visitor attractions, transportation and accommodation.

Sometimes customers have already bought their product, for example a holiday, but need further advice on how to reach the airport or what help they can expect for someone with special needs. Many organisations provide customer service helplines for these situations or add a 'frequently asked questions' (FAQ) section to a website to try and pre-empt customers' questions.

Dealing with complaints and problems

Customers are usually realistic and appreciate that problems may arise. Sometimes problems may be out of the company's control. For example, a taxi strike in a destination will disrupt travel and is out the control of the tour operator. The company can still deliver great service by dealing with the problem efficiently and satisfying the customer. Some companies reassure customers in advance that their problems will be dealt with.

1.2 The importance of good customer service to the organisation

Keeping existing customers satisfied

Remember that with many travel products and services such as flights and holidays, customers may book a long time in advance. They have parted with their money, but not yet had the benefit of their purchase. The organisation must keep these customers happy up to the point of taking their flight or holiday and beyond.

They do this by keeping in touch with the customer. For example, an airline might send a reminder text about the flight or inform the customer of any extra services on offer. Tour operators or travel agents send out information to help the customer plan their holiday. This might include destination information and advice or details of excursions on offer.

Increasing customers' loyalty and ensuring repeat business

Loyal customers are those who come back again and again, giving what is known as 'repeat business'. Increased sales and profits may result from repeat business. Satisfied customers tell other people, who then wish to use the same organisation to buy their products.

Case study: Thomson Holidays

Thomson's Moneyback Guarantee

With Thomson Holiday, what you see on-line is what you get on your holiday. If you arrive and you find that we've failed to live up to the promise, here's what we'll do:

- Within one day of arrival let us know the problem. We'll then spend 24 hours doing everything possible to put it right.
- In the unlikely event we can't solve the problem to your satisfaction within 24 hours, at your request, we'll fly you home and give you all your money back.

Thomson's No Worries Guarantee

If there's anything you are unhappy with during your holiday, let us know immediately and if it can't be resolved straight away, we guarantee to be on the case within 60 minutes. Our resort teams have the necessary authority, training and skills to take the problem off your hands, deal with it quickly and restore your peace of mind.

(Source: www.agent-travel.co.uk)

1. What kind of problems do you think Thomson might have to deal with?
2. What benefit to Thomson is there in offering these guarantees?

Think about it

A loyal customer of the coach holiday specialist Shearings booked 16 coach trips in 2010 worth more than £5000. The customer is 91-years-old and knows that he is well looked after by the company. He knows all the drivers too. How can good customer service continue to benefit the company?

Enhancing an organisation's image

Image is influenced by the reputation of the company, the service people receive from sales consultants, experience of the product or service and after-sales service. One way companies try to manage their image is through their **public relations** campaigns. You will learn more about PR in the marketing unit.

Providing an edge over the competition

This is known as **competitive advantage**. There are lots of ways this can be achieved: by having superior products, by superb advertising campaigns or, of course, by giving excellent service.

Attracting new customers

There are many ways of attracting new customers, through special promotions and marketing activities. A reputation for excellent customer service also attracts customers as people want to feel reassured, especially when spending large amounts of money.

New customers are needed even when there is a good base of **customer loyalty**. Consider the cruise market as an example. Much effort has been made by the cruise sector to attract new markets, including younger people and families. If they did not do this their customers would literally die off!

Key terms

Public relations – the attempts made by an organisation to have a good image and maintain goodwill with the general public.

Competitive advantage – an organisation strives to be better than (have an advantage over) its competitors. This could be through better pricing or a more attractive product. It could also be through a higher level of customer service.

Customer loyalty – if customers receive consistently good service from an organisation they will want to use it again. They become loyal to that particular organisation because they can rely on its products and services.

Did you know?

Front-line staff, that is those dealing directly with customers, may be the only people from the organisation that customers meet. Examples include cabin crew, check-in staff and resort representatives. These staff have a key role in determining customer satisfaction levels.

Consequences of poor service

You have seen why the provision of excellent service is important to organisations. To ensure excellent service is maintained staff training is required, products have to be up-to-date, the company's premises must be well maintained and levels of service regularly monitored and evaluated.

It is clear that the provision of excellent customer service is costly. However, the consequences of poor service are even more costly.

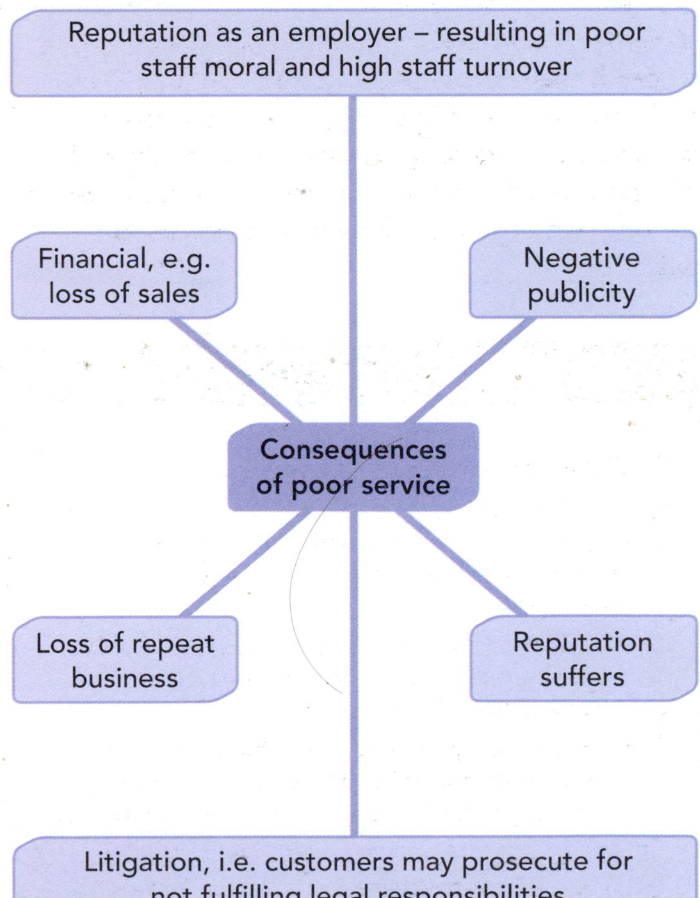

Figure 4.1: The consequences of poor service

Activity: What happens when resources are inadequate?

Select two organisations with which you are familiar and list the resources needed to provide excellent service. Then list all the possible consequences of poor service.

Present your information in a table like the one below. In this example the organisation selected is a travel agent.

Resources needed to provide excellent customer service	Consequences of providing ineffective customer service
Sufficient numbers of well-trained staff to deal with customer queries	• With insufficient staff, customers may go elsewhere and sales lost • Untrained staff will not be able to sell suitable holidays – customer needs will not be met
Office cleaners to keep the premises clean and tidy	• Staff will not feel valued if the office is not clean • Customers will receive a poor first impression
Up-to-date software...	

Consequences of poor customer service include the following.

- Financial – customers will stop coming, resulting in a decrease in sales and profits. Repeat business will begin to fall as an organisation's reputation suffers.
- Staffing problems – if an organisation develops a reputation as a poor employer the best staff will start to leave, taking their experience with them. A high staff turnover will impact on customer service levels as new staff will take time to train. Staff morale will be poor – it is difficult to be cheerful to customers when the office environment is a bit flat!
- Bad publicity – extreme situations may lead to adverse publicity, which can have disastrous results for the reputation of the company.
- Legal problems – if customer service levels slip so badly that organisations don't fulfil their legal obligations, litigation can follow. Travel companies have commitments to their customers, not just to satisfy their needs, but also in law.

Activity: Making an impact

Imagine you work for a hotel. List the ways in which excellent customer service impacts on customers, staff and the organisation.

1.3 Importance to the customer of excellent customer service

If the principles of good customer service are followed, satisfied customers will feel they have been greeted warmly, dealt with by friendly and efficient staff and received the goods or services they want. They will go away having had their needs met and expectations exceeded – they will have purchased the ideal holiday, found the perfect hotel or eaten the best food. You will look at customer needs in more detail in the next section.

Over the long-term, customer loyalty will develop so that a customer would not wish to go elsewhere. They will also recommend the products and services to their friends. Such recommendations are a great way to get repeat business.

Customers can sometimes be **internal customers** – that is, people who work for the same organisation, but need service and support from each other. Cleaners and maintenance staff in a hotel, for example, make sure that the environment is clean, safe and secure for other staff members as well as **external customers**.

Key terms

Internal customers – colleagues and other members of staff who work within the same organisation to provide products and services.

External customers – people from outside the organisation who buy the products and services.

Benefits of excellent service

To Employee
- job satisfaction
- job security
- possible pay rise
- incentives/bonuses

To Employer
- increase sales and profits
- good public relations (PR)
- reduced complaints
- competitive advantage
- loyal customers (repeat business)

To Customer
- needs met
- expectation exceeded
- loyal to the organisation (don't need to shop around)
- recommend it to others

Figure 4.2: The importance of good service

Activity: What makes excellent service?

Recall a situation when you received excellent customer service. Work in pairs and describe the incident to your partner.

- What aspects of the service made it excellent?
- How did it make you feel?
- Have you ever used a particular organisation or bought a product simply because it was recommended to you?

1.4 The importance to the employee of excellent customer service

Happier working environment and higher self-esteem

A happy working environment is one where everyone works as a team and supports each other. If systems and procedures are correctly followed and people strive to do their job, there is less stress for everyone. Knowing that you are doing a good job and working well in your team is also a boost to self-esteem.

Job satisfaction

Providing excellent service, and as a result dealing with satisfied customers, is very rewarding for employees. It is satisfying to be thanked for kindness, efficiency, solving a problem or providing advice. Positive feedback from customers provides job satisfaction and a feeling of well-being.

Job security

If an employee has a good sales record, with positive customer feedback and customers who return, it is more likely their position in the organisation will be secure. This may enhance their prospects for training and promotion and may give them a sense of personal satisfaction as well as financial security

Promotion

For some individuals, providing good service will lead to promotion – perhaps with a pay increase or bonus (incentive). Those promoted are then in a position to set high service standards.

The overall result of excellent service and satisfied customers is a staff team that is productive and positive.

2 How travel and tourism organisations adapt customer service to meet individual needs

2.1 Different types of customers

In order to meet customer needs and exceed expectations, it is first necessary to understand customers' needs. But this is easier said than done. After all, there are many different types of customers, all of whom have different needs.

To be able to provide excellent customer service, organisations must understand their customers, recognise their differing needs and provide products and services that meet their requirements. For example, a tour operator will provide a different holiday and range of excursions for a single person than for a group of young people wanting to go clubbing or a couple wanting to escape the British winter. Similarly, on a day trip to a theme park, a young couple will have different needs from a family with two children.

Individuals

Individuals may be travelling alone or may be with a partner, for example. By individual we really mean anyone who is not in a group.

Leisure travellers include those who are on holiday or visiting friends and relatives. Their needs are very different depending on the purpose of travel and the type of holiday desired.

Business customers can be quite lucrative as they are often travelling at peak times and require convenience and comfort to be ready for work when reaching their destination. Usually the expenses of business travel are paid by the customer's company not by the individual.

Groups

Groups include school groups, special interest groups and friendship groups.

Some groups may all know each other and have similar needs (such as a group of young men wishing to go on a day trip white-water rafting). They may be happy to be treated as a single entity for the purpose of their day trip.

However, a coach party of Americans who have booked a Blue Badge Guide for their tour of Cambridge may all have differing needs. Some will want to visit the colleges, others may wish to go shopping and others may want to enjoy an afternoon's punting on the river.

For those dealing with groups, it is important to remember that the group is actually made up of many individuals – and to consider their individual needs. This can be very demanding.

2.2 Individual needs

Products and services

Travel and tourism organisations provide products and services to meet customers' needs. Products and services provided by a travel agency might include:

- a week's summer sun holiday for a family of three
- a cruise for a recently bereaved single woman
- a first-class flight for a business person who needs to attend a meeting in Prague
- a cultural holiday in Cuba for a group of women in their thirties
- day excursions
- insurance
- overnight hotel accommodation at the airport
- car parking
- advice about currency and temperatures.

Stated and unstated needs

Ideally a customer will tell you what product or services they want – that is, they will have **stated needs**. However, sometimes key information remains unstated. Often customers simply imply what they want. The customer who says 'Spain was a bit too hot last year' is really meaning that they would like somewhere cooler this year. Occasionally you will need to anticipate customer requirements. To establish **unstated needs** or **anticipated needs** requires careful questioning.

Key terms

Stated needs – needs the customer tells you about; for example 'I would like to book a single room for tomorrow night'.

Unstated needs – needs that will affect the customer's choice of product, but which they do not tell you about; for example, they do not say 'We went to Majorca last year and don't want to go there again'.

Anticipated needs – those products or services that you think the customer might need; for example airport parking.

You know that in order to provide excellent customer service you must meet customers' needs. Clearly you have to establish what these needs are before you can respond to them. In the ideal situation the customer responds to the simple question 'How may I help you?' with a statement about their needs, for example 'Please could you book me on a train to Edinburgh?' Stated needs are the easiest to deal with.

Anticipated needs

Good customer service involves trying to anticipate some of your customers' needs. The single mum who has implied that she is on a tight budget may want lots of free activities for her children. The business person booking into a hotel for one night may want to make use of the express checkout facility. Similarly, good customer service means offering kids' clubs for family holidays or regional departures for local people – even though these have not been asked for.

Special needs

Some customers may have special needs which require additional and sensitive customer service. This may be because they have:

- special dietary needs
- mobility problems (e.g. wheelchair users)
- a hearing impairment
- a visual impairment
- speech difficulties
- a medical condition, for example a heart complaint which means a ground floor room is required.

It is clear that all customers with special needs must be treated individually. Many people are unsure how to deal with people with special needs and this can result in customers feeling insulted or patronised.

Read the following extract from *Welcome All*, customer service training for the tourism sector. It explains how to provide a high level of service to people with a visual impairment.

Assisting customers with a visual impairment

- Look out for visual signs, such as a white stick or guide dog.
- When meeting a visually impaired customer, introduce yourself.
- Remember that you cannot rely on your body language to communicate a message.
- Make sure that you say when you are leaving.
- Be prepared to read information out.
- Offer to guide the customer to their destination.
- Provide information in large print, in Braille or on audio cassette.
- Use spoken announcements.
- Be prepared to welcome guide dogs.

(Source: Welcome to Excellence: Assisting Customers, Welcome All, Regional Tourist Board Partnerships Limited)

There are important reasons why it matters to you and your organisation to provide an accessible environment and a high standard of service to disabled customers:

- According to a Family Resources survey there are an estimated 10 million people with disabilities in the UK. They should not be excluded from accessing the same facilities and services as everyone else.
- You have a legal responsibility under the Disability Discrimination Act 1995.
- There is a strong business case for attracting customers with disabilities.
- The reputation of your organisation is based on the service standards that you offer all your customers.

Activity: Asking the right questions

Imagine you are working in a travel agency and a customer has stated some of their needs. Write down some of the questions you could ask to find out more about their needs. The first one has been completed to get you started.

1 We are on a tight budget.

Qs: *How much are you planning to spend?*
Does that include extras such as insurance and transport to the airport?

2 We will be on our honeymoon and want to make sure we get a double bed.

3 My husband is 80 next year.

4 I sometimes use a wheelchair.

5 It is our first wedding anniversary while we are away.

6 While we were on holiday last year my partner was very ill.

7 My son is epileptic.

8 I really need a break from the kids.

9 I am pregnant.

Practise asking different kinds of questions with a partner who wants to book a holiday.

Customers with cultural and language needs

There will be many situations in the travel sector where you will have to deal with people who do not speak English and people from other **cultures**. Your excellent customer service skills must be maintained.

Key term

Culture – the shared traditions, beliefs and values of groups of people.

Such customers may include:

- UK residents from a variety of cultural and ethnic backgrounds. They may not speak English as their first language.
- The many international visitors to the UK from different cultural backgrounds. While many of these visitors will speak English it will not be their first language and misunderstandings can easily occur.

Think about it

Different customers can be motivated by different factors, but may purchase the same product (for example, a weekend in New York may be a well-deserved break for one customer, a chance to see some art galleries for another, or simply the opportunity to see a friend for another).

Other needs

Needs may be related to many factors besides those already mentioned. These needs may relate to age, gender, socio-economic group or special circumstances. The activity opposite explores some of these needs.

Table 4.1 summarises some hints for coping with different customer types.

Activity: Meeting needs

Investigate a large hotel, an airport, an airline or a mass-market tour operator. What particular products or services does this organisation provide to meet the needs of different customers?

You may wish to consider the needs of single women travellers, business customers, children travelling alone (airlines only), people of different ethnic origins, group bookings, people of different religions and disabled travellers.

Table 4.1: Key points about different customer types and how their needs vary

Groups	• A group is a collection of individuals, each with differing needs. Make sure you treat people as individuals. • Try to ascertain who is the group leader/organiser before you commence. • If speaking to a group, gather them into an enclosed space. Make sure everyone can hear you.
People of different ages	• People's needs vary with age – a couple in their twenties will have different needs from those in their fifties and again in their seventies. • Don't be ageist. • Do not presume. Not all older people want culture and younger people beaches – ask open questions to establish their needs.
Business customers	• Business customers are usually under pressure, want an excellent service and are prepared to pay for it. • Time is important and they may need to work on journeys so consider offering additional products and services, for example express check-in, quiet coach on a train journey, etc. • Business travel may not be considered to be a perk of the job – many people would prefer to be at home rather than spending three days sorting out problems in an industrial city where no one speaks English. Think how you can make life easier for them, for example an early morning flight rather than travelling the night before.
Special needs	• Special needs can apply to a range of people. Examples include dietary needs (e.g. vegan passenger on a plane), physical (e.g. child in a wheelchair visiting a theme park), sensory (a hearing or visual impairment), anyone needing assistance (e.g. minors travelling alone, adults travelling with children, elderly passengers). • Ask open questions to establish needs. • Be sensitive, but do not be afraid of giving offence – many complaints arise simply because the right questions are not asked.
Language differences	• Don't shout! • Be patient – how many languages do you speak?
Cultural differences	• Be sensitive. • Educate yourself – make sure you have a basic awareness of the beliefs of key religions and also what causes offence.

Assessment activity 4.1

You have just gained a work experience placement with an independent travel agency in your home town. The manager, Shena Bajart, calls you into her office on the first day of your work experience to discuss what you will be doing.

The agency is doing quite well, but Shena is concerned that a competitor is setting up at the other end of the high street. She wants to improve the customer service her staff provide to ensure competitive advantage.

Shena asks you to carry out the following tasks.

1. Prepare a short presentation which will explain to staff why excellent customer service is important in travel and tourism organisations. **P1**
2. Research how customer service is provided in two travel and tourism organisations. Shena would like you to use this information to write a report in which you do the following:
   a. Describe how customer service in the two organisations meets the individual needs of different types of customers. Make sure that you cover the full range, referring to the content and assessment guidance in the unit specification for detail required. **P2**
   b. Evaluate the service provided by the two organisations, assessing how they meet specific customer needs. **M1**
   c. Make recommendations as to how improvements could be made to meet specific customer needs in one of the organisations. **D1**

Grading tips

P1 Make sure that you include the importance of the organisation to the customer and the employees.

M1 You must make clear links between the service offered and how it meets specific needs.

D1 Think about changes you could recommend, for example to products, ideas to speed up service and reduce queues and ideas to improve the company image.

PLTS

When you carry out your research you will be practising your skills as an **independent enquirer**.

Functional skills

When you compare, select, read and understand texts to find your information you will be practising your **English** skills in reading.

3 Customer service skills required to meet customer needs in travel and tourism contexts

Some people are naturally good at providing excellent service. They have an outgoing personality, appear to be always positive and are not intimidated by difficult situations. Other people have to learn these skills.

3.1 Communication skills

Your communication skills need to be of the highest standard – this includes both written and oral communication.

Face-to-face communication

We are all used to face-to-face communication. When shopping, getting on a bus, greeting friends and working in a team we all communicate directly with each other face-to-face. However, it is important to know how to use this form of communication to its full advantage when dealing with a customer. For example, personal presentation is very important – it will give a good or bad first impression. You must also consider your tone of voice and be very aware of your body language – it will communicate more to your customer than the words you say.

The advantage of face-to-face communication is that you can read your customer's body language, use brochures, leaflets and other materials to help you get information across to your customer, and answer any questions as they arise. Face-to-face communication is often on a one-to-one basis. However, it can also involve groups of people, for example at a staff meeting or a welcome party in a resort.

Activity: Assess yourself

Carry out a self-assessment for the following skills. Give yourself a score between 1 and 5, where 1 is excellent and 5 is poor.

Discuss your self-assessment with a partner. Do they agree with your scores? Think about what you might do to improve your skills.

Skill	Score 1–5
Spelling	
Handwriting	
Greeting people	
Developing conversations	
Positive body language	
Good tone of voice	
Telephone skills	

PLTS

When you carry out your self-assessment you will be practising your skills as a **reflective learner**.

Telephone communication

To be able to communicate well on the telephone you need good listening skills. Remember that you must listen to the tone of voice as well as the words being said. It is particularly important to speak clearly and check understanding when on the phone – as you cannot read the body language or any other non-verbal information such as gestures and facial expressions.

Other techniques for good telephone communication include:

- be clear – use short sentences and phrases
- avoid jargon
- be concise
- pronounce your words clearly
- speak slowly
- make sure there is minimal background noise
- smile!

You should smile when speaking to customers on the phone because it will show in your tone of voice and be reflected in the customer service you provide.

Many travel and tourism organisations require all their staff to answer the phone in the same way. For example, 'Good afternoon, Travel First. Harry speaking. How may I help you?' This is to ensure consistently good service and to present a corporate image. Many jobs in travel and tourism are in call centres so telephone skills are essential for those jobs.

Building rapport

A warm welcome is the first stage of building a good **rapport**. There are many aspects to creating a welcome. It is more than just smiling and saying 'How can I help you?' The environment should be clean, tidy and inviting. Staff need to be displaying positive body language and there should be an atmosphere of quiet efficiency. Rapport is about having a good relationship with the customer so it encompasses listening, thinking about body language and using the right questions.

Key term

Rapport – positive relationship. You need to build a positive rapport with your customer that is based on trust and confidence.

Create a pleasant working environment with no interruptions or background noise, and a clear desk.

Use positive body language – smile, use open gestures.

Create a welcome

Greet your customers warmly – offer a seat or drink if appropriate. If they are regular customers, ask how they are.

Use a positive and enthusiastic tone of voice.

Figure 4.3: Building rapport

Effective listening

How good are you at listening? Do you interrupt when your friends are talking, look away or think about something else?

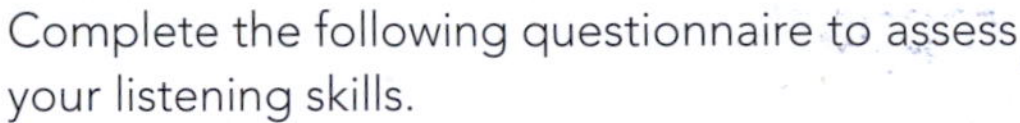

Activity: Listening skills

Complete the following questionnaire to assess your listening skills.

Do you:

1. Face the speaker?
2. Keep focused on the speaker, maintaining eye contact?
3. Nod and smile when appropriate?
4. Think about other things?
5. Look for body language and listen to the tone of voice (to give you more understanding)?
6. Think about your answer while the speaker is still talking?
7. Interrupt before the speaker has finished?
8. 'Tune out' or get bored?

Consider questions 1–8. Which indicate that you are listening?

Use these (and any others you can think of) to produce some guidelines called 'Improve your listening skills'.

Activity: Active listening

Non-verbal behaviour is an important aspect of listening. Carry out this activity to assess its impact.

- Work in pairs. Each of you should choose a topic to talk about (make sure it is something you know a lot about and can talk on for a few minutes).
- Each speaker should talk about their topic twice.
- The first time, the listener will practise **active listening** (nodding, smiling, maintaining eye contact).
- The second time the listener will demonstrate (through behaviour) that they are not listening. This could include looking away, tapping a pencil or yawning. Remember, the listener is practising non-verbal behaviour, so must not speak.

What impact does active listening have on the speaker? What impact does it have on the speaker when it is clear that they are not being listened to?

Key term

Active listening – demonstrating through words and actions (body language) that you understand what is being said to you. For example, you can make appropriate responses ('Wow', 'Oh dear') or ask questions ('So are you saying that he shouted at you?').

Questioning

Asking the right questions is an important aspect of customer service skills. Whatever your future role in travel you will be asking questions of colleagues and customers. In some situations the type of question you ask is as important as the words used. This is especially so when selling products and services or dealing with a difficult situation.

There are different types of questions: for example, closed, open, reflective and leading. These are identified in Table 4.2, together with examples and the limitation of each type of question.

In most situations you will need to ask open questions, for example when establishing a customer's needs. In some cases reflective questions may be useful, for example when dealing with a complaint or making a sale. Table 4.3 gives you some important 'dos and don'ts' to remember when asking questions.

Table 4.2: Question types

Type of question	Definition	Examples	Use	Limitation
Closed	One that can be answered only by 'yes' or 'no'.	Have you sent in your booking form? Will you be staying for dinner? Have you received your tickets?	To clarify facts. Should not be used if trying to gather details.	Closed questions will not provide further information for discussion.
Open	One that cannot be answered by a 'yes' or 'no'. They start with words like *what, when, how, who, why, where* or *which*.	What did you enjoy most about your holiday? Why are you upset? How can I help you solve this problem? Where have you been on holiday before?	To start a discussion or conversation, to gather information.	A talkative person may answer at length and take up a lot of your time!
Reflective	One that checks understanding and gives a person the chance to think about what has been said.	So you feel the hotel staff were unfriendly? So you want somewhere sunny, but you are not looking for a beach holiday?	Allows you to check understanding and for the customer to add to what has been said.	Takes time. You may lose the thread of the previous discussion.
Leading	One that suggests what the answer should be, or leads the person into answering in a certain way.	So you feel that if the flight had not been delayed you would have had a nice holiday?	Try to avoid using leading questions.	Indicates what you are thinking and is unlikely to obtain a full or true answer.

Developing dialogue

Using effective questioning and listening skills together will enable you to develop a **dialogue** with the customer. Both skills will help you to establish customer needs. Throughout all of this you continue to build a relationship with your client – getting to know them and their requirements.

Table 4.3: Do's and dont's

Don't use	Do use
Did you enjoy your holiday?	How was your holiday? Tell me what you enjoyed about your holiday.
Did you learn a lot at the welcome meeting?	What sort of things did the resort representative tell you at the welcome meeting?
Do you want to go to Ibiza because of the nightlife?	What is it that makes you want to go to Ibiza?
You've been to Spain a lot, haven't you?	What destinations have you been to before?

Activity: Changing questions

1 Change the following closed questions into open questions:
- Can I help you?
- Are you OK today?
- Do you like the view from your balcony?
- Would you like to go to Greece again this year?

2 Change the following closed questions into reflective questions:
- Is your budget £400 per person?
- Don't you want to go to Spain?
- Was it the airline's fault?

Key term

Dialogue – an easy, flowing conversation in which you are asking open and relevant questions will help you establish customers' needs while also building rapport.

Non-verbal communication

Non-verbal communication (NVC) is the main way in which we communicate to others how we feel, although we may not be aware that we are doing so! It is estimated that we convey more messages by the way we stand, use eye contact, hold our heads, gesticulate and use facial expressions (that is, use our body language) than we do with words. It is essential that you are aware of your body language in order to convey a positive message (build rapport) with your customers.

Key term

Non-verbal communication (NVC) – communicating without saying anything. The most common type of NVC is body language – how we use our hands, facial expressions and gestures to convey our feelings.

Activity: Body language

Work in pairs. Take it in turns to choose one of the feelings listed below and act it out. Use facial expressions, gesticulate, etc. but don't speak!

- angry
- exhausted
- confused
- excited
- upset
- cheerful/happy
- bored

How successful is your partner at interpreting your body language?

Similarly, our tone of voice can indicate how we are really feeling. We can use the same words in two different situations but our tone of voice may make the words carry an opposite meaning. It's not what we say but how we say it that makes the difference.

Your body language and tone of voice will determine whether the word 'hello' is meant as a cheery sign that you recognise someone, a threat, a put down or an ecstatic greeting. A good actor will be able to convey at least a dozen different meanings with the word 'No'.

An important aspect of providing good customer service is recognising customers' feelings. Watching body language and listening to the tone of voice are the best ways of working out what your customer is really feeling.

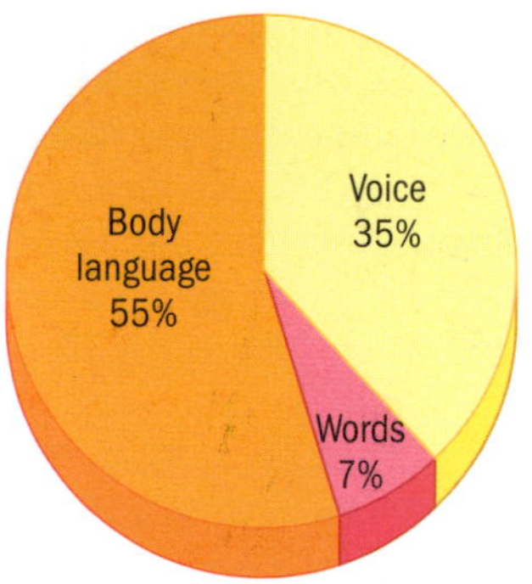

Figure 4.4: How we understand messages

Figure 4.5: How are these people feeling?

Case study: Training cabin crew in customer service at Virgin Atlantic

Your course will incorporate the core elements of exceptional customer care, vital to the success of our airline as well as the cabin services that you will be offering and what our customers have come to expect. After all, it only takes ten seconds to make a first impression on our customers and we won't get a second chance, so we must get it right from the start. Our objective onboard is to exceed the expectations of the customer to ensure they become loyal and choose to fly with Virgin Atlantic again.

Our aim in training is to ensure that you leave our course feeling confident to deliver the services that we offer on board, and able to display the customer service skills that we are renowned for.

You will not get a second chance to make a first impression.

(Source: Virgin Service Training Manual)

1. Why is customer service important for the airline?
2. A lot of emphasis is put on 'first impression'. How does a member of cabin crew make a good first impression?
3. How could the expectations of the customer be exceeded onboard?
4. Give three examples of how cabin crew can give consistent service.

Written communication

Although most written communication will be word-processed, there are occasions when you will need to write information by hand. Examples include completion of an enquiry form, taking a telephone message or leaving a message for a colleague. In some roles, for example when working as a resort representative, weekly reports may also need to be handwritten. Your handwriting needs to legible and your spelling correct. Use of text message spellings is not acceptable.

Activity: Choosing the best way to communicate

Work in small groups. Copy and complete the table below, then compare your answers with other members of your group.

Remember that written communication is more formal than face-to-face communication. It is therefore sometimes used to confirm decisions that have previously been discussed. In some of the choices in the table, you may decide that face-to-face communication, or a telephone conversation, is needed as well as some form of written confirmation.

Message	Method of written communication to be used
The manager of a travel agency wants to advise a customer of a change of hotel.	
A resort rep wants to let head office know that a customer has made a serious complaint about the hotel. She thinks other customers will also complain.	
Two hotel receptionists have agreed to swap shifts. They want to tell their manager.	
Head office has decided to make 20 airline staff redundant.	
A customer has had a great holiday and decides to tell the travel agent and tour operator.	
A visitor to a museum has been overcharged. He realises this only when he gets home.	
After two weeks of reading about two destinations, Jamal wants to confirm a holiday with the travel agent.	

Role-play or produce the documentation for each situation.

When filling in any document, bear in mind that it could potentially be used in a court of law. Therefore take your time over it, be professional and make sure the information is full, accurate and legible. Times and dates must be included. Give facts, not opinions.

It is important that the correct form of written communication is used. For example, e-mails and faxes are an excellent method of communication if speed is important. However, they are informal and should not be used, for example, to deal with a complaint. Similarly, a memo would be used only for internal customers.

3.2 Presentation

Personal presentation is an important element of a first impression. Your personal presentation reveals how you feel about yourself, your customers and your level of professionalism. Travel and tourism is such a 'people' business that you should be aware of the importance of personal presentation and the impact it will have on customers and their confidence in your ability to provide a good service.

Customers will judge you (and the organisation you work for) on:

- your appearance – what you are wearing, whether it is neat and tidy or in need of ironing
- how you care for yourself – is your hair neat, jewellery discreet and nails clean?
- your body language – how you express yourself through your behaviour
- how you greet your customer – are you enthusiastic and smiling?

In order to encourage good personal presentation, some organisations provide staff with a uniform. This is usual for staff in roles dealing directly with customers such as in a travel agency, as an overseas rep, as a local guide or in a tourist information centre.

There are many benefits of staff being in uniform:

- customers immediately know who the staff are – this is particularly important in some roles, for example as an overseas resort representative or a ride attendant at a theme park
- a corporate image is developed
- staff feel they are part of the company – and the team
- the organisation has direct control over what staff wear.

Guidelines regarding the wearing of the uniform, caring for it and other aspects of personal presentation are usually provided. For example, Virgin Atlantic requires its female cabin crew to manicure and varnish their nails.

Think about it

Uniforms are not usually provided for staff who do not deal with customers. Examples include tour operators' head office staff, airline administration staff and back-office staff at tourist attractions. However, many do provide a dress code. Why do you think they consider this necessary?

Presentation of the working environment is also important. It too must be clean and tidy. The office or sales environment should be organised and files easily located.

For example, if purchasing a holiday in a travel agency, customers would expect:

- the office to be clean
- staff to be seated at their desks
- no eating or drinking at desks
- clear, neat desks
- telephones to be answered quickly
- no radios or loud background noise
- staff who are not serving to be working (not gossiping with each other).

3.3 Teamwork

When a team works well the team members will experience job satisfaction and a sense of well-being – however team working can also present difficulties. You will be able to recall projects where friction has arisen with colleagues because someone has not done their fair share of the work.

All work in the travel sector involves teamwork at some stage. If a team works well, it is more likely to provide an excellent service. Imagine arriving in your holiday resort and finding that someone in the resort team had not told the transfer rep that the flight was going to be early!

A good team will:

- be motivated to achieve the same goals
- have a leader who delegates tasks appropriately
- know the lines of authority
- understand their own and others' team roles

- be confident and have self-esteem
- communicate well with each other
- make clear decisions
- pay attention to detail
- respect and trust each other
- have clear roles and responsibilities
- support each other
- have a 'can do' approach.

All travel and tourism organisations will try to ensure that their staff are working well as a team. As well as contributing to a positive image of the company, a happy staff team is more likely to be efficient. Companies spend huge amounts of money on staff training to help teams work well together.

You will look at teamwork in more detail in Unit 6 (see pages 174–175).

3.4 Business skills

Completion of documentation

Keeping appropriate records and documents is an important aspect of providing excellent customer service. You will need to record information in the following situations:

- taking an enquiry for a holiday (establishing customers' needs)
- dealing with a complaint
- taking payment
- booking an excursion
- taking a telephone message
- dealing with a problem (with a colleague, customer or your manager).

In many situations pro forma (that is, forms to fill in) are provided. One example is an enquiry form which prompts the travel consultant to ask specific questions such as dates of travel, number of adults and children, preferred resort, preferred departure airport, length of stay. Another example is a customer report form used in resorts. A resort representative will need to use this to write a factual report if a complaint is received. The report will then be sent to their head office.

Here are some general guidelines for all paperwork:

- write in block capitals in black ink
- make sure all copies are clear and can be read easily
- fill in all sections – if they are not applicable write 'n/a', don't leave them blank
- don't use jargon or foreign words (or your own abbreviations)
- check the form once it is complete
- make sure you are using the correct form – if unsure ask
- state facts not opinions.

Use of IT

Using IT is an integral part of most people's working lives. This is no different in the travel and tourism sector.

For most roles you will need generic IT skills (such as word processing, use of databases, spreadsheets and email systems) as well as skills specific to a role. For example, people working in an airline reservation team will receive training on the use of computer reservation systems such as Galileo or Amadeus. In a tourist information centre you would need to be able to access the sites and use the software that provide timetables and local information.

In most job roles you will have access to the internet and will need to be able to use it effectively.

Think about it

Many of the large travel agency chains always use standard letters and all use pro forma to gather information from customers. What are the advantages and disadvantages of this?

3.5 Handling complaints

Working in an environment with such a high level of person-to-person contact means that complaints are inevitable. Problems such as lost luggage, delays or stolen goods do not initially reflect badly on the company. Indeed, some of the problems may in fact be the customer's own fault. Examples of problems include the customer who has:

- lost their passport
- forgotten their ticket
- left a case at the airport
- broken a leg
- flight delay
- problems with accommodation.

Did you know?

Seven out of ten customers will do business with you again if you resolve the complaint in their favour.

Even the most successful travel companies receive complaints. Sometimes these may be justified and sometimes not. Whichever the case, knowledge of procedures will help you to deal with the situation calmly without taking the complaint personally. It is important to view a complaint as an opportunity to 'turn a customer around', that is, to change a complaining customer into a satisfied customer. This is challenging, but it will ensure repeat business and customer loyalty as well as giving you job satisfaction.

Figure 4.6: Dealing with complaints

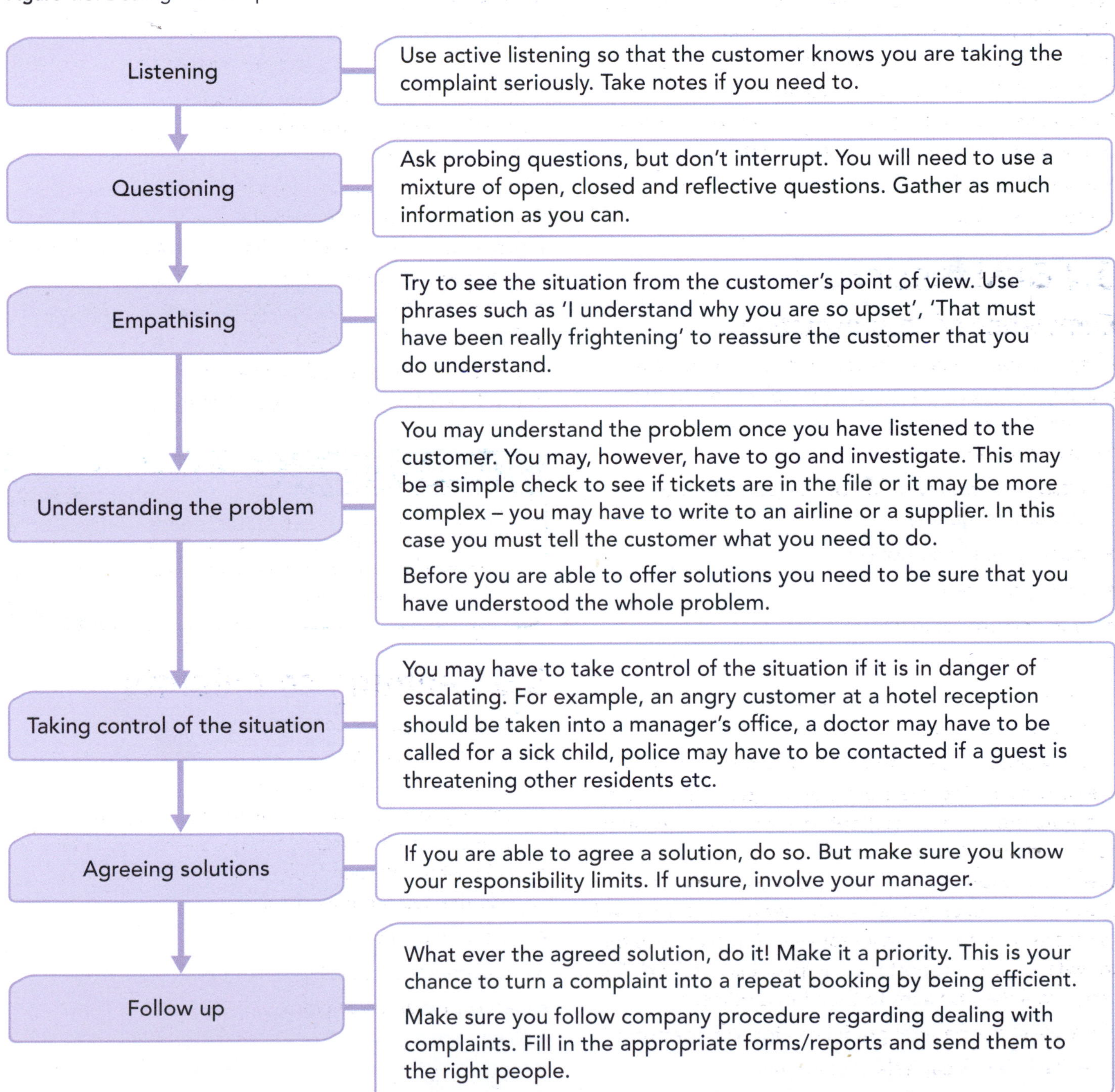

3.6 Selling skills

Selling is just one of the many customer service situations that you may be involved in when working in the travel and tourism sector. It may be an important part of your job, or just a small aspect of it. For most travel and tourism organisations, sales are a fundamental activity as the number of sales determines profit levels and the ultimate success of the organisation.

Much selling still takes place face-to-face, such as in a travel agency The telephone and internet are also key sales tools for many tour operators and airlines.

Whether you are selling face-to-face, on the phone, by letter or email, the same skills are needed and the same process is followed.

Building rapport

The first stage of the sales process is to build a good rapport with the customer. Customers must feel positive and relaxed and under no pressure to buy. They must trust the salesperson and be confident in their ability to find the right product to meet their needs. The environment in which you are working, your tone of voice, body language and what you say to your customer will all contribute towards the rapport.

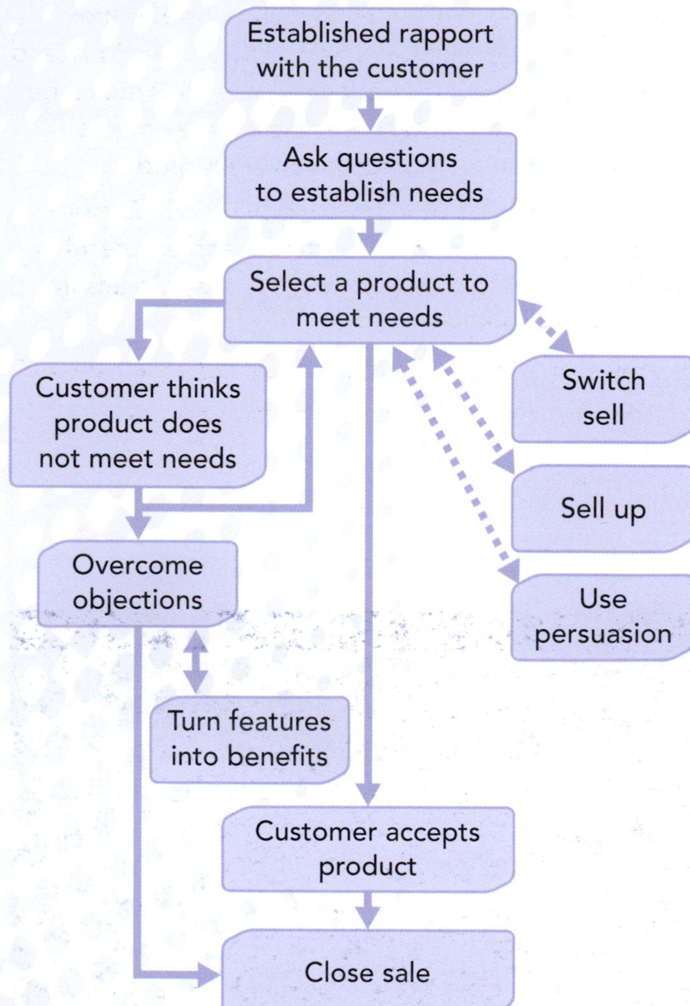

Figure 4.7: The stages of selling

As a salesperson you will also establish rapport by:

- first impressions – smiling and greeting your customer warmly
- your appearance – clean, tidy, neat hair and minimal jewellery
- offering customers a seat
- making good eye contact
- positive body language
- not being distracted by other people or the telephone.

Establishing needs and expectations

Once you have established rapport, find out the customers' needs and expectations. This is perhaps the most difficult part of the sales process, as customers may not know what they need themselves. Through careful questioning and listening you will have to work out what it is they really want. You have already seen that there is a huge range of customers, all of whom have different needs. Remember that your customers may also have unstated needs which they do not tell you about.

First ask questions to establish factual information, gather information about the stated needs and try and pick up on any implied needs. For example, if selling a holiday, you can ask questions to establish how many people are going, when they want to go and for how long. Customers may also be able to tell you what type of accommodation they would like and their preferred destination. Other customers may need you to guide them. Some customers will know only that they want a holiday and expect you to find the perfect holiday to meet their requirements. Careful questioning will be required!

Ask open questions to make sure you get all the information you need. Open questions begin with *what, why, who, how, when, which* or *where*. They will perhaps give you more information than you require, but this may help you discover the underlying expectations and guide a customer to a particular type of product.

To establish customer needs you must:

- ask open questions
- listen actively
- use reflective questions to check understanding – 'So you think Greece was too hot for you in August last year?'
- maintain a positive rapport through good eye contact and positive body language
- keep asking questions and discussing options until you have established customer needs.

Product knowledge

Once you know the customer's needs, you must find a product to match them. If the enquiry is straightforward – the customer knows exactly what they want – this can be done quite easily. However, if customer needs are less clear, it is your product knowledge that may determine whether you can meet them. For example, a customer may want to arrange a trip for a special occasion, but not know which destination or venue meets their needs.

Features and benefits

When presenting the product it is important that you identify the three or four things that are most important to the customer and describe how this product matches these needs – that is, you will introduce the **features** of the holiday and turn them into the **benefits** for the customer.

For example, 'I have just found this holiday in The Gambia. It is available for when you want to travel. I know you want some sun and the temperatures there will be high at that time of year. There is five-star accommodation available and it has a pool, which you particularly requested.'

Key terms

Feature – a particular aspect of a product, for example location of hotel, excursions included, local pick-up, etc.

Benefit – what the customer gains from a feature.

Activity: Features and benefits

Work in pairs. Use brochures to select a holiday destination. Write down ten possible features of the destination. Take it in turns to convert your partner's features into benefits.

Overcoming objections

Customers may not agree with you that the holiday you have selected for them matches their requirements. This may be because you have misunderstood their needs, or simply have not asked enough questions (and so you don't know their underlying needs). If this is the case you must ask probing questions to re-establish their requirements and select a different product.

However, it may be that the customer requires more reassurance. They may be hesitating and unsure what to do. You should establish what it is they are unsure about. For example:

- You: 'What is it about the holiday you are unsure of?'
- Your customer: 'The hotel isn't very close to the beach.'

Table 4.4: Examples of benefit statements

Feature of holiday	Your benefit statement
The hotel has a large swimming pool and a children's pool	'This hotel has a really large pool. There will be plenty of room for you to swim and you won't be disturbed by children's games.'
The hotel is isolated	'It is a wonderfully quiet location – no neighbouring hotels to share the beach with. You will also have great views from all rooms.'
The hotel is in the middle of a town	'You will be right in the middle of things. You can stroll out each evening and really get involved in local life.'
Excursions included	'You have two excursions included in the price, both of which are guided, so you will certainly get a lot of local information.'
Representative available	'A representative will be on hand if you have any queries while you are in the resort. They will be able to advise you where to go and can arrange local excursions and car hire if you decide to explore while on holiday.'

- You: 'That's true. But it's only five minutes' walk and you are right in the middle of town, so it will be great for the nightlife you wanted.'

Overcoming objections is really like turning features into benefits. You need to first establish what the objection (feature) is and then turn it into something that the customer can view as a benefit. You are persuading the customer that this holiday really does meet their requirements.

Activity: Overcoming objections

In pairs, each write down five objections that a customer might make when buying a holiday. Take it in turns to listen to each other's statements, and reply in a way that attempts to overcome the objection.

Closing the sale

Once you have overcome objections you must look out for buying signals. These may be things that are said (verbal signals) or simply body language (visual signals). Examples include a customer:

- nodding to their partner
- looking in their bag for their cheque book or cards
- asking you to reconfirm the total price
- checking flight details again.

It is important that you never rush a customer. Some people are happy to make quick decisions, while many are indecisive. You must look out for these verbal and visual signals. If they are strong and it is clear the customer wants to book, then you could say 'Would you like me to book this for you, before it goes?' Other customers will clearly ask you to book it, for example saying 'Let's get it booked, then!'

In these cases, the sale is closed and you need to reconfirm holiday and payment details with the client, complete the paperwork and take payment.

Assessment activity 4.2

P3 BTEC

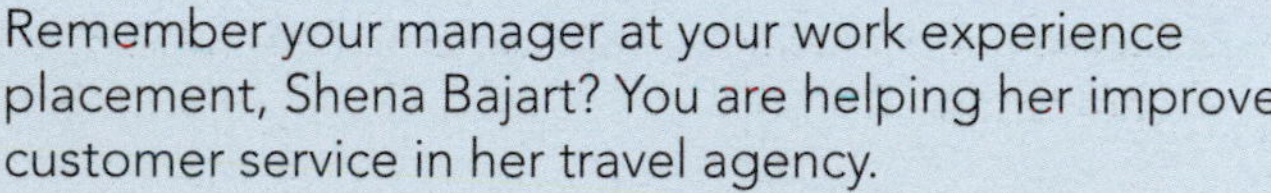

Remember your manager at your work experience placement, Shena Bajart? You are helping her improve customer service in her travel agency.

Shena now wants you to develop a leaflet to give to staff which describes the customer service skills required in travel and tourism. You should include information on:

- communication skills
- presentation
- teamwork
- business skills
- selling skills
- skills needed to handle complaints.

Grading tips

P3 Make sure you include relevant travel and tourism examples rather than general customer service examples.

PLTS

As you organise your time and resources to produce the leaflet to the deadline, you will be practising your skills as a **self-manager**.

Functional skills

When you prepare your leaflet, you will be practising your **ICT** skills of entering, developing and formatting information.

4 Apply customer service and selling skills in travel and tourism situations

4.1 Customer service

Practise applying your skills with the situations in the following activities. Some are face-to-face, some are electronic or by telephone. Some are simple and some more complex.

Activities

Activity: Providing information and advice

- Mrs Smith calls you at the retail agency where you work. She wants to fly from Gatwick to Brussels tomorrow morning to get to an afternoon meeting. She also wants to know the price of a taxi into the city centre from the airport. Find out possible flight times and prices and phone her back with the information.
- Suzanna Fisher is taking a gap year before university. She has booked a world ticket with you. She will be spending part of her year away in Australia and will be visiting Thailand. She is hoping to work in Australia and needs advice about visas. She is in your office so you need to find out and tell her straight away. Tell her also about any immunisations she might need for Thailand.

Activity: Providing assistance

- You work in customer service at the airport. A customer in a wheelchair has arrived but doesn't know what the procedure is for booking assistance to the aircraft. Explain the procedure to the customer and how you will be able to help
- You work for British Airways in reservations. You receive a telephone call from a passenger who wants help in deciding whether to upgrade from economy on a flight to New York. He is travelling next week on Wednesday afternoon. Explain the options available and tell him what the prices are.

Activity: Complaints

- You work as ground crew for British Airways. You have to respond to a complaint about a flight delay. The delay is due to severe weather conditions and therefore the delay is not covered by Denied Boarding Regulations.
- Explain to Mrs M. Moran that there is no case for compensation and apologise for the delay. It is a two-hour delay on a flight from Heathrow to Geneva.

Activity: Dealing with problems

- You work as a holiday representative for a tour operator. You receive an email from a customer who has gone home from their holiday in Cyprus, but has left a coat and a pair of shoes in their hotel wardrobe. The housekeeper has put the items in lost property. Email the customer – Mr Gabor – and tell him how he can recover his property.

Activity: Making a sale

- You are approached by an American customer who is visiting your town for the first time. She wants to know where she can visit an attraction that will be typically British. She will book transport through you.
  - **a** Explain the location and directions to your chosen attraction.
  - **b** Explain to her why it will help her understand something of British history or culture.

Activity: After sales advice

- Mrs Owen has booked car hire for her holiday through your travel agency. On return from holiday she emails to ask if she should have been charged an upgraded car – she was given a Megane when she booked a Clio. She didn't pay any extra, but is concerned in case she owes money to the car hire company.
- Send her an email reassuring her and explaining why she was upgraded.

Activity: Product knowledge

- You work for the Brazilian Tourist Board. You receive a call from a UK resident who is thinking of going there in January on holiday. They want to know what the weather is like. Respond to the call.

Assessment activity 4.3

At the travel agency where you are on work experience, all staff need to improve their customer service and selling skills in order to ensure that they do not lose business to their new competitor. Shena asks you to demonstrate good practice to them.

Demonstrate customer service and selling skills to customers in the following situations.

1 Reply to this letter of complaint.

> 48, Hampton Road,
> Liverpool
> L14 3GD
>
> The Bridge Hotel
> Mersey Road
> Liverpool
> L18 3DR
>
> Dear Sir,
>
> My husband and I visited your hotel for an anniversary weekend on 2nd June.
>
> I wish to make a complaint about the standard of service in the hotel.
>
> We had booked the honeymoon suite, but found that we had been allocated a different room. Although this room was very nice with a four poster bed, it was not what we requested.
>
> My husband wished to swim each morning, but the pool was closed for repairs.
>
> The first night we were able to have a lovely aperitif in the bar before dinner. On the second night we had to go straight to the restaurant, the bar was restricted to a private party.
>
> To top it all we were awoken by the fire alarm on Saturday night and had to come down to reception only to be told it was a false alarm.
>
> All in all we were very disappointed.
>
> I look forward to hearing what you intend to do about my complaints.
>
> Yours faithfully
>
> *Stephanie Brown*

2 Respond face-to-face to the following customer enquiry.

- A young couple come into the agency. They are considering Cyprus as a honeymoon destination. Ask them questions to find out more about their budget, dates and the type of resort and hotel they would like. Use selling skills to help them decide on a suitable honeymoon package.
- First find out about excursions in Cyprus on offer to tourists. Ask the couple questions and sell them an appropriate excursion.

3 Respond to the following telephone enquiry.

Mr Phipps is on the phone. He has already booked a holiday to Dubai and knows that he is flying with Emirates. He wants to know how much it would cost for him and his partner to upgrade to first or business class and what extra services he will get.

Research the information to give him. One of your colleagues should play Mr Phipps who has a lot of questions and is a challenging character. Complete a booking form for Mr Phipps. Your tutor may complete an observation sheet.

Grading tips

P4 P5 Ensure you demonstrate customer service skills to customers in three different travel and tourism situations. The situations must cover written communication, face-to-face and telephone. One of these situations must deal with a complaint.

M2 Ensure you work independently and your customer service skills please both your customers and your company.

M3 Ensure your selling skills are effective and meet the needs of differing customer types in differing situations. You must ensure that you close the sale.

D2 You will need to demonstrate excellent customer service and selling skills by:

- demonstrating good product knowledge
- being consistent in the high standard provided throughout all situations.

PLTS

In this assessment you will practise your skills as an **effective participator**. You will discuss issues of concern to others and seek resolution to the problems set. You will propose practical ways forward and negotiate solutions.

Functional skills

By making contributions and effective presentations in the situations given, you will practise your **English** skills of speaking and listening.

WorkSpace

Elizabeth Dale

Holiday homes salesperson

Elizabeth Dale works in Frejus in the south of France. She lives and works on a campsite where she sells holiday homes for the French camping division of a large British tourism company. Not everyone who comes to the campsite owns a holiday home.

What does a typical day look like for you, Elizabeth?

I start work at 10 a.m. The sales office is about 2 minutes from home. In the office I check emails and any documents that have to be completed for pending sales. I might have a meeting with my manager and the rest of the sales team. I make phone calls to potential customers to try and organise visits to our holiday park.

I have to be very sociable on the park because part of my job is finding new customers, so I chat to people on holiday in case they like their holiday so much they want to buy their own holiday home.

The most important part of my job is actually having a sales meeting with customers. Some people come for two or three days for a free mini holiday. I show them around the park and all its facilities. Then I show them the different styles of holiday homes according to their budget. This is where my sales skills are needed. I have to do my best to sell to meet my targets and earn my commission. I usually finish about 7 p.m. Sometimes we have events for our park owners in the evening and I have to go to those, but they are social events.

Do you have a background in tourism?

I spent several summers working as a lifeguard on campsites in France. That was how I got to know the company. I didn't study tourism but I have a degree and sales experience. I speak French, as does everyone who works here.

What do you like best about your job?

I work outside and get to talk to people all day. And I live on the Cote d'Azur. What could be better?

Think about it!

1 What extra skills do you need to work abroad in customer service?

2 How do you think you would cope with working when most people are on holiday?

Just checking

1 Why is it important to attract new customers even when you have a good customer base?
2 What is meant by body language?
3 How can you demonstrate to someone that you are listening?
4 What is meant by 'rapport'?
5 How does product knowledge help you to provide excellent customer service?
6 Give two examples of how excellent customer service is important to the customer.
7 Give two examples of how excellent customer service is important to staff.
8 Describe what is meant by the following terms: competitive advantage; public relations; customer loyalty.
9 Give five words which are used to begin open questions.
10 What is the difference between a feature and a benefit?
11 Give four examples of things you can do to ensure that you give a positive first impression.

Assignment tips

- The Institute of Customer Service is a useful source of general information about customer service – www.instituteofcustomerservice.com
- If you have a part-time job, ask if you can borrow the customer service manual and read it.
- Whenever you are on the receiving end of customer service, make mental notes about how the service might be improved or how you can learn from it.
- Practise all the activities in the last section before you try the assessment.

Credit value: 10

5 Marketing travel and tourism products and services

This unit introduces you to marketing in the context of the travel and tourism sector. Marketing is the whole process of deciding what the customer wants and then tailoring all the business and its systems to meeting that demand with suitable products and services. Once the products and services are developed they must be communicated to the customers so that they want to buy them.

You will learn about the marketing mix – all the elements that contribute to marketing and how it applies in travel and tourism.

There are many factors that influence marketing decisions; sometimes these are factors that an organisation cannot control. You will find out what these are and how companies can react to them.

You will gain some practical skills in marketing by carrying out a marketing research activity and planning a promotional campaign for which you can design some promotional materials.

Learning outcomes

After completing this unit you should:

1 understand the factors influencing marketing in travel and tourism

2 know the marketing mix (the four Ps) of a travel and tourism organisation

3 be able to conduct a marketing research activity for a travel and tourism organisation

4 be able to organise a promotional campaign for a travel and tourism organisation.

Assessment and grading criteria

This table shows you what you must do in order to achieve a **pass**, **merit** or **distinction** grade and where you can find activities in this book to help you.

To achieve a **pass** grade the evidence must show that you are able to:	To achieve a **merit** grade the evidence must show that, in addition to the pass criteria, you are able to:	To achieve a **distinction** grade the evidence must show that, in addition to the pass and merit criteria, you are able to:
P1 outline the background and concepts of marketing **See Assessment activity 5.1, page 128**	**M1** explain how factors have influenced marketing decisions in relation to a selected travel and tourism organisation **See Assessment activity 5.2, page 139**	**D1** analyse the marketing decisions within a travel and tourism organisation in relation to the marketing mix and influencing factors **See Assessment activity 5.2, page 139**
P2 review the factors influencing marketing decisions using examples from different travel and tourism organisations **See Assessment activity 5.1, page 128**		
P3 describe the marketing mix of a selected travel and tourism organisation **See Assessment activity 5.2, page 139**	**M2** explain how the four Ps work together as a marketing mix in a travel and tourism organisation **See Assessment activity 5.2, page 139**	
P4 plan, design documentation and conduct a market research activity for a travel and tourism organisation **See Assessment activity 5.3, page 144**	**M3** explain how the plan and the documentation contributed to meeting the market research objectives **See Assessment activity 5.3, page 144**	**D2** analyse the results of the market research activity recommending how these results can benefit the organisation **See Assessment activity 5.3, page 144**
P5 plan a promotional campaign for a selected travel and tourism organisation to achieve stated marketing objectives **See Assessment activity 5.4, page 146**	**M4** explain how the planned promotional campaign would enable the objectives to be met **See Assessment activity 5.4, page 146**	
P6 prepare an item of promotional material as part of a planned promotional campaign for a target market **See Assessment activity 5.4, page 146**		

How you will be assessed

This unit will be assessed by one or more internal assignments that will be designed and marked by your tutor. Your assignments will be subject to sampling internally and externally as part of Edexcel's quality assurance procedures. The assignments are designed to allow you to show your knowledge and understanding related to the unit. The unit outcomes indicate what you should know, understand or be able to do after completing the unit.

Samil, 17-year-old BTEC National learner

I am really keen to study more about marketing after doing this unit. It was interesting to find out about all the different areas within marketing that you can specialise in too.

Most of my group liked the promotional campaign best, but I am not that creative so I preferred carrying out the marketing research. I arranged a focus group at my house. I invited some family friends who often fly and prepared some discussion points to cover. It was really good fun and it wasn't difficult to get them to talk, even though I was nervous. I made sure I recorded the conversation so that I didn't have to take notes and remember everything.

The people I interviewed used various airlines, but our tutor had arranged for a speaker from a locally based airline to come and talk to us. This meant we used all their company information for our assessment. I researched Flybe's advertising and another airline as well for further ideas for my campaign. I also looked at three different company reports to help me analyse the factors influencing marketing.

Over to you!

1 Think about a local airline who might talk to your group about their marketing.

2 What other resources would help you get ideas for promotional campaigns?

3 Find out what further study you might do in marketing following your course.

1 Factors influencing marketing in travel and tourism

Set off

Understanding marketing

Ask ten people what they understand by marketing. Write down what they say and bring your notes for discussion with your colleagues. How many people are close to the definitions given below?

1.1 Marketing background and concepts

Definition of marketing

The Chartered Institute of Marketing (CIM) defines marketing as follows:

> The management process responsible for identifying, anticipating and satisfying customer requirements profitably.
>
> *(Source: www.cim.co.uk)*

Function of marketing

The function of marketing is to encompass the whole process of deciding which products and services the customer will want and how they will be delivered to the customer.

Marketing aims to:

- research customer needs
- produce products and services that meet those needs
- know the market – including competitors
- make sure the whole organisation is marketing orientated
- find and communicate with customers
- manage any threats that affect the marketing process.

In the UK, marketing has been a high-profile aspect of business since the 1970s, and today it would be difficult to find travel and tourism companies that do not acknowledge its importance. Most will have a marketing department or marketing manager.

Marketing mix

The marketing mix describes the key elements that an organisation uses to achieve its objectives and meet the needs of its customers. These elements are commonly known as the 'four Ps':

- **P**roduct
- **P**rice
- **P**lace
- **P**romotion.

The four Ps give us the core of a company's marketing strategy.

Although a company develops strategies for each of the four Ps, remember that they are interdependent. For example, if a price is discounted, this will impact on the promotional strategy as the discount must be communicated to the market.

Before any travel and tourism organisation can determine its marketing mix it needs to plan. Plans may be short-term, perhaps for a year, or longer-term, up to five years and beyond. The organisation must have an idea or vision of where it wants to be in its market in the future. You will study the marketing mix in detail later in this unit.

Marketing segmentation – classifying consumers

In order to market their products effectively, travel and tourism companies may segment their market. The market is divided into groups of people with similar characteristics, each group making up one segment. The segments at which the company directs its marketing activity are the target markets.

Market segmentation can be done in various ways. Most companies choose to use not just one but a combination of methods.

Key terms

Market segmentation – identifying different groups of customers for a product. The members of each group will share similar characteristics.

Demographics – the study of the structure/make-up of the human population.

Demographic segmentation

Demographics is the study of the make-up of the population. Demographic trends illustrate how the population is changing. Factors that affect the make-up of the population include the birth rate and life expectancy.

When demographic segmentation is used, consumers are grouped according to:

- age
- gender
- ethnic grouping.

Socio-economic segmentation

In this method of segmentation the population is divided according to socio-economic grouping. These groupings are based on occupation, not income. The classifications are used extensively by advertising media to describe their readership.

Table 5.1: Socio-economic segmentation

A	Upper middle class	Higher managerial, administrative or professional
B	Middle class	Intermediate managerial, administrative or professional
C1	Lower middle class	Supervisory or clerical, and junior managerial, administrative or professional
C2	Skilled working class	Skilled manual workers
D	Working class	Semi-skilled and unskilled manual workers
E	Those at lowest level of subsistence	State pensioners, casual or lowest-grade workers

Geographic segmentation

The marketing data company CACI has produced a classification called ACORN (A Classification of Residential Neighbourhoods) based on postcodes. Every street in the UK is included and categorised into 56 typical neighbourhood categories. Streets which have broadly similar residents are categorised together. The classification is arrived at using information drawn from the census and from market research data.

Travel and tourism companies can easily find out the geographic location of their customers as they usually have access to addresses on their databases. The geographic area from which the customers are drawn is known as the 'catchment area'. The catchment area is very important for tourist attractions as they need to draw customers from as wide an area as possible. Organisations such as VisitBritain need to know from which countries incoming tourists originate in order to target their marketing activities.

Activity: What is your profile?

Go to the website www.upmystreet.com. Enter your postcode and then click on ACORN profile. Find out what your profile is. You can get a detailed profile if you wish.

Psychographic segmentation

With this type of segmentation, consumers are categorised according to personality types, lifestyle and motivation. When it is done well, it is very effective in determining targets, but it is difficult to do accurately. It is very relevant to travel and tourism. For example, environmentally aware people will be interested in sustainable tourism products.

Marketing communication methods

The element of the marketing mix, often called promotion, is also known as marketing communication. You will examine this area in more detail later in the unit (pages 144–146). It is important to recognise that marketing communication can extend to all areas of the organisation – the same marketing message can be presented in all areas of marketing, for example, through branding and logo, as well as promotional messages.

E-marketing

The consistency of marketing message must also extend to e-marketing. E-marketing means using digital technology, usually the internet, to market products and services. As more people become confident about buying over the internet, e-marketing becomes more common. In travel and tourism it usually complements other types of marketing.

The functions of marketing remain the same for e-marketing, although the marketing mix may be applied differently, for example promoting the product to the customer might take different forms such as email.

1.2 Factors

Company ethos

By company ethos we mean the set of values and beliefs that define a company. These can be expressed in a vision or mission statement (see page 94).

These statements are usually published in company literature, on websites and in the reception areas of company offices. The statement is useful to customers as it tells them what to expect in terms of product or service. It is also useful to employees as it gives them a focus for what the company wants to achieve.

It would be surprising to find a mission statement that says the company wants to make a lot of money, even if we think companies do. It is likely that the emphasis will be on service. Here is an example of what could be a vision statement for an airline:

> Our vision is to be the number one choice for air passengers

This seems like a worthy ambition, but the airline needs to determine how they might achieve this. They might do this by establishing broad strategies affecting the following areas:

- stringent safety procedures
- provision of an excellent route network
- provision of excellent customer service
- maximising profit margins.

The company then develops these strategies, forming shorter-term objectives to meet each one.

Activity: Vision or mission statements

1. Choose one of the strategic areas and devise four shorter-term objectives for the airline to work towards. For example, ensure all cabin crew undergo customer service training at least once a year.
2. Find three examples of vision or mission statements for travel and tourism organisations which express the company ethos. For each example, try to identify at least three facts about that company from the statement. List the facts and discuss them with your group.

Social responsibility

The tourism sector depends heavily on the natural environment and therefore has a moral obligation to protect that environment. The Stock Exchange has a series of criteria to benchmark socially responsible companies known as FTSE4Good. Companies that meet the criteria can be listed. This indicates to customers and stakeholders that the company has appropriate policies for **corporate social responsibility (CSR)**.

Companies promote their CSR policies very strongly as a a good CSR policy enhances their public image and helps to sell products.

Key term

Corporate social responsibility (CSR) – the way that companies manage their business to try and have a positive impact on society.

Consumer protection

Consumer protection refers to legislation, standards and codes of practice that are put in place to protect the consumer from unfair trading. Adherence to these consumer protection tools impacts on a company's marketing activities. For example, legislation affects what can be stated in advertisements and brochures.

Legislation

The Consumer Protection Act 1987 makes it an offence to give customers a misleading price indication about goods and services. It lays down rules about the use of terms such as 'reduced' and 'bargain'. Price indications given verbally are also covered. In travel and tourism, this legislation has most relevance to brochures and advertising.

The Trade Descriptions Act 1968 is one of the most important pieces of consumer legislation and section 14 is its most relevant part for travel and tourism. This section deals with the supply of goods and services. It states that it is an offence to make a statement that is known to be false or to recklessly make a statement which is false. This applies to the provision of services, facilities and accommodation and the location of amenities for any accommodation. An offence can be committed even when there is no intention to deceive the customer.

The Unfair Terms in Consumer Contracts Regulations 1999 apply to all contracts. When you book a holiday, a hotel room or a flight you enter into a contract with the seller. The seller will publish terms and conditions associated with that contract – you can read these in any holiday brochure.

These regulations protect consumers against unfair terms in contracts. Sometimes attempts are made to introduce terms and conditions that may reduce the consumer's statutory rights or may impose unfair burdens on the consumer over and above the obligations of the ordinary rules of law.

The Data Protection Act 1998 provides rights for those who have information held about them in 'relevant filing systems'. This may be on computer or in paper files. The act also requires those who record and use personal information to follow sound practice.

An individual can have access to information held about them and, if necessary, have it corrected or deleted. People must have the opportunity to consent to the collection and processing of their data. Personal data must be kept secure, up-to-date and not for longer than necessary.

The Information Commissioner's Office (ICO) administers this act. If you want to have access to information about yourself, you must make a written request to the holder of the information. Travel and tourism companies hold a lot of customer information, which must be revealed if a customer asks for it.

Standards of practice

Codes of practice

The British Code of Advertising, Sales Promotion and Direct Marketing has the following main general principles.

- All advertisements should be legal, decent, honest and truthful.
- All advertisements should be prepared with a sense of responsibility to consumers and society.
- All advertisements should respect the principles of fair competition generally accepted in business.
- No advertisements should bring advertising into disrepute.
- Marketing communications must conform with the code. Primary responsibility for observing the code falls on marketers. Others involved in preparing and publishing marketing communications such as agencies, publishers and other service suppliers also accept an obligation to abide by the code.
- Any unreasonable delay in responding to the Advertising Standards Authority's (ASA) enquiries may be considered a breach of the code.

The Advertising Standards Authority is an independent body set up by the advertising industry to police the rules for advertising, sales promotion and direct marketing. The system is one of self-regulation aiming to protect consumers and maintain the integrity of marketing communications.

The ASA continually checks a sample of advertisements, but also relies on the public to complain about advertisements which do not comply with the code. The ASA can ask for an offending advertisement to be withdrawn or changed. Of course, some complaints are judged to be unfounded.

Travel and tourism organisations are subject to legislation. However, these laws differ internationally. Tour operators in particular have an obligation to ensure the health and safety of their customers on holiday and should have extensive procedures in place for this.

Political, economic, social and technological factors (PEST)

Travel and tourism companies need to be aware of the external factors that influence the operation of their businesses. An analysis of these factors is described as a **PEST analysis**, because the factors involved are categorised as:

- **P**olitical
- **E**conomic
- **S**ocial
- **T**echnological.

A PEST analysis should take place at regular intervals as part of a review of marketing activities. Management should be constantly aware of topical issues which may impact on business, even when a formal analysis is not taking place.

Companies also need to undertake a thorough analysis of internal factors affecting operations. This is known as a **SWOT analysis**, looking at the company's:

- **S**trengths
- **W**eaknesses
- **O**pportunities
- **T**hreats.

You need to know how to carry out these types of analyses and how the information gathered influences marketing decisions.

Key terms

PEST analysis – an analysis that helps an organisation to take stock of the external factors affecting its business, identifying political, economic, social and technological factors. The PEST analysis helps with the SWOT analysis as it can point to opportunities and threats.

SWOT analysis – a means of measuring internal factors (**S**trengths and **W**eaknesses) and external factors (**O**pportunities and **T**hreats) that influence the marketing and operation of a business.

The following are some of the external (PEST) factors which currently affect travel and tourism companies.

Political factors

These often relate to changes in legislation introduced by government. These may be general changes, for example changes to employment law which companies must respect, or changes which directly impact on travel and tourism.

In 2010 the European Package Holiday Regulations were reviewed. All businesses in the travel and tourism sector would be mindful of changes and their impact.

Activity: Package holiday regulations

Find out what changes were made to EU package holiday regulations in 2010 (if any). What would be the influence on marketing activity of any changes?

Tour operators have to be aware of the political situation in the destinations they offer. Some places can become very dangerous to visit. Situations might change rapidly, but tourists will avoid places where there have recently been serious incidences of unrest or terrorism.

Such occurrences cause problems to tour operators as they are unexpected and cannot be planned for. If the situation in a country becomes dangerous tour operators may have to repatriate holidaymakers and switch destinations for those who have booked to go there. The British Foreign & Comonwealth Office (FCO) website (www.fco.gov.uk) gives the current situation on safety in countries all over the world. Tour operators have to try to reassure holidaymakers through their marketing that they will be safe in the destinations they use and that if an incident occurs the tour operator will be able to get them home safely.

Economic factors

Changes in taxes affect tourism as they raise costs. Passengers on airlines have become used to paying air passenger duty, just as they are used to paying road tax. When taxes are raised or newly introduced they become contentious as our case study shows.

Another important economic factor is interest rates. If rates rise it can affect a business's ability to repay loans.

The exchange rate can also dramatically affect a company's costs and will impact on a tour operator's pricing strategy. For example, a tour operator with contracted accommodation in Spain will pay in euros. A weak pound will buy fewer euros and will bring increased costs to the tour operator.

Sixteen European countries have adopted the euro, and although the UK has retained sterling (the British pound) and is not a member of the euro zone, travel and tourism businesses in the UK are still affected by the euro. Customers who come from the continent may expect to use euros in the UK and in fact some hotels and shops will accept them, giving change in sterling. Accepting euros can give businesses a competitive edge.

Social factors

Travel and tourism businesses operate in a rapidly changing market. It is important that marketers take notice of social changes affecting their customers.

People in the UK today generally live longer and are healthier. They have more money to spend than previous generations and time to spend it. Older people make up a vital market for travel and tourism

Case study: Air Passenger Duty increases

Read this extract from an article on the Travelmole website in 2009.

Air Passenger Duty hikes create discontent amongst public and airlines

As Air Passenger Duty is set to rise next week, a new survey reveals that most people believe it is time to reform the travel tax.

From November 1, the APD bill for a family of four flying to the Caribbean will rise from £160 to £200 and from November 2010 that will rise again to £300.

The tax hike affects both short-haul and long-haul travellers, is worked out according to distance of flight (there are four bands) and is higher still if travelling in premium classes.

A YouGov survey of just under 2000 adults, published today and commissioned by easyJet, highlights the fact that private jets, cargo planes and foreign passengers are exempt from the charge. It also underlines that environmentally, the tax does not work as empty planes that fly are raising less revenue that full ones.

Distance to capital city from London	From Nov 2009 Economy/ Premium	From Nov 2010 Economy/ Premium
Band A (less than 2000 m)	£11/£22	£12/£24
Band B (2001 m – 4000 m)	£45/£90	£60/£120
Band C (4001 m – 6000 m)	£50/£100	£75/£150
Band D (6001 m+)	£55/£110	£85/£170

(Source: Dinah Hatch 30 October 2009 www.travelmole.com)

1 What do you think about the tax? Make notes on the arguments for and against the tax.
2 What difference would it make to tax per plane rather than per passenger?
3 Find out the current rate of APD.
4 How will the APD influence marketing for airlines?

operators, who have lost no time in creating holidays specifically for them in off-peak periods.

The media has a great social influence on our culture. Films make us aware of places and inspire us to visit them. Tourism to New Zealand has increased since the release of the Lord of the Rings trilogy of films which was made there. Many visitors to New Zealand are at least partly motivated by the chance to tour sites shown in the films. Knowing this allows the New Zealand tourist industry to maximise their motivation and increase tourist numbers by emphasising the sites of film sets in their publicity.

Technological factors

Technology is probably the area of greatest change with rapid developments in many areas. Self check-in is becoming more common at airports, including passengers checking-in their own baggage. Scanning systems are developing rapidly to try to mitigate terrorist attacks. It is now possible to hire a car without any personal contact, collecting keys and making payment via a vending machine. These changes represent changes to the product, which encourage more customers.

The internet has revolutionised the way we book our holidays and travel. On-line booking systems are common for all modes of transport and for many holidays. Hotel bookings can also be made on-line, showing a view of the room and the facilities. Travel agents and tour operators are using new technologies to market their products and services rather than depend on traditional channels. New technology allows companies to market via the internet and to carry out advertising via other companies' websites. However, it can have a downside as it means that any holiday-maker can place a review, which means unhappy customers can post very negative reviews which may not tell the whole truth or may end up censored.

Activity: Do your own PEST analysis

You have read many examples of PEST factors that may influence marketing in travel and tourism. Remember that these influences can occur on a local, national or international level.

Work with a partner and choose a tourist facility in your area. This could be a tourist attraction, a tourist office or a hotel. Describe the facility and its location. What is its target market? Identify all the political, economic, social and technological factors that will influence marketing activity.

You may need to do some research to find out what is going on in your local area, for example new housing developments that will bring new customers. Look at what is happening nationally as well.

Present your findings to your group and discuss the variations that occur. Are any of the factors you have identified opportunities or threats?

1.3 Influences

All the factors described in the previous section influence marketing decisions in one way or another. They may mean that companies have to introduce new products or improve products, for example in response to competitive activity.

A company might change its advertising strategy to reach a new target market. An example is the use of Twitter or SMS marketing to reach new markets. Prices can be influenced by economic factors or changes in legislation, for example changes in air passenger duty as described above. Changes in VAT, as occurred in 2009 and January 2011, affect prices.

Assessment activity 5.1

BTEC

You have applied for a job as a marketing assistant. As part of the application process, your potential employer has asked you to compile a report which demonstrates your understanding of marketing.

Your report must:

- outline the background and concepts of marketing
- review factors influencing marketing decisions with examples from different travel and tourism organisations
- use examples that are both recent (within the last 10 years) and relevant.

Make sure that you cover the full range, referring to the content and assessment guidance in the unit specification for the detail required.

Grading tip

P1 Make sure you include a definition of marketing, the function of marketing, marketing mix, marketing segmentation, marketing communication methods, e-marketing.

P2 Consider negative and positive factors which have influenced marketing decisions including company ethos, consumer protection, standards of practice and PEST.

Make sure you give sources of information.

PLTS

Exploring issues, events or problems from the perspective of different organisations will help you develop your skills as an **independent enquirer**.

Functional skills

Presenting information on a complex subject, concisely and clearly, will help you to develop your **English** skills in writing.

2 The marketing mix (the four Ps) of a travel and tourism organisation

The four Ps are the tools that allow the organisation to meet its strategic objectives. We will study each of the four Ps in turn, but always remember that they are interdependent.

2.1 Product

According to Philip Kotler and Gary Armstrong:

> A product is anything that can be offered to a market for attention, acquisition, use or consumption that might satisfy a want or a need. It includes physical objects, services, persons, places, organisations and ideas.
>
> *(Source: Principles of Marketing, Prentice-Hall, 11th edition, 2006)*

This definition shows that a service is also considered to be a product. In travel and tourism, businesses are predominantly concerned with the marketing of services.

The marketing for services may be different from that for a physical product, as it is highly dependent on the people delivering the service.

Nature of the product

Intangible

When you buy a product, it is usually tangible – you can touch it. Buying a travel and tourism service is not like that, because travel and tourism products are rarely tangible. They are intangible. This means that you can't see them or touch them before you buy. You may be able to see pictures and brochure descriptions, but you can't try out the real thing.

Perishable

Travel and tourism products and services are often perishable (like food going off in a supermarket). Once a flight has left the airport it is too late to sell any more seats. They have perished. Airlines have to make sure their flights are as full as possible to make a profit.

Service related

Another challenge for marketers is that the service is inseparable from the person providing it. In a restaurant, the food may be of a consistent quality because of the use of high-quality produce and standard recipes. However, the diner's experience will still be ruined if the waiter is having a bad day.

Activity: Tangible or intangible?

Look at a holiday brochure. Choose a holiday and write down everything that is included in the price. You can include items for which you must pay a supplement if you wish.

Try to decide which aspects are tangible products and which are services. Make a table of your findings and compare it with a colleague's. For example, a free T-shirt is tangible. The services of the rep are intangible.

Characteristics

Another way of looking at products is to examine their features and benefits. The product features represent the core value of the product. For example, the features or core of a package holiday are the accommodation and transport. There will be a whole range of added features, depending on the holiday chosen. These might include food, sports facilities and entertainment.

The features convert into benefits for the consumer, such as relaxation, the opportunity to go sightseeing or to learn a new skill, such as windsurfing.

Companies are always looking for new features to add to their products and services. They want to give further benefits to the customer and maintain competitive advantage. Theme parks introduce new rides each season to attract customers. Cinemas sell a wider range of foods and drinks and offer plusher seats and more leg room.

Branding

The brand is the name and image that go with the product and it aims to suggest something about the product itself. Some brand names such as Thomson or Thomas Cook are well-established and have built up a good reputation. Under these 'family' brand names the company owns other familiar brands. For example, Portland is part of the Thomson group. Thomson itself is part of the TUI group. TUI is not as well known as Thomson in the UK, so when TUI acquired Thomson it wisely decided to retain the original brand names.

Think about it

How many holiday brands can you think of? Do the brand names suggest anything about the companies? What kind of image does each brand try to project?

If a brand is successful, it can build up brand loyalty among consumers, where they begin to prefer it over its competitors.

Unique selling point

The product must have some quality that sets it apart from the competition – this is known as the unique selling point (USP). Every product aims to have a USP.

The USP is very useful in marketing as it can be used as a focus for advertising and linked to the pricing strategy. An example of a USP is that of Responsible Travel – the first dedicated travel agent to responsible holidays. In other words, it considers the impact of the tourist on the environment and society.

Product life cycle

The concept of product life cycle is used to show how a product moves through different stages in its life, until it becomes obsolete. It is a useful concept in marketing as it impacts on how the product is marketed depending on what stage the product is at.

It is also important that a company has products in each stage of the life cycle. If all the products were in the decline stage, the company would soon be heading for bankruptcy.

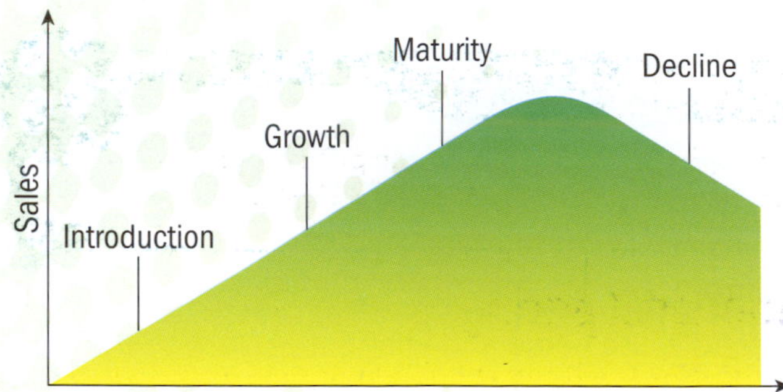

Figure 5.1: The product life cycle

- **Introduction:** The launch of a new product is an exciting, but tense period. A lot of the marketing budget is assigned to advertising and letting customers know it exists. Developing the product will have cost both time and money, so little or no profit is expected in the introduction stage. If the product is accepted by the market then some contribution to costs will be made.

  The people most likely to buy the new product or try out a new service are known as 'innovators'. They are the kind of people who like to be the first to try something new. The price charged at this stage is often high – this appeals to innovators, who do not mind paying for exclusivity – and it helps to repay costs.
- **Growth:** This is the most profitable stage in the product's life cycle and companies are eager to gain these profits while they can. Word-of-mouth promotion is important at this stage, as consumers hear about the new product and want to try it. Competitors will rapidly enter the market, bringing out their own versions of the new idea. Because of this increased competition, it is important for companies to try to build up some brand loyalty. The promotional budget is usually devoted to stressing the product's benefits over competitive products (differentiation).
- **Maturity:** Competition is at its most intense at this stage. Weaker competition will be squeezed out of the market by aggressive marketing strategies. Marketing efforts focus on being competitive, often by promoting low prices. The low-cost airlines are currently in maturity, having had years of unprecedented growth. In spite of this, newcomers are still entering the market, although new entrants are not usually successful at this stage. Maturity is the longest stage of the life cycle.
- **Decline:** Sales and profits start to fall at this point. Marketers must recognise when products are likely to move into this stage, as they must decide whether it is worth staying in the market. An organisation should be diversifying into other markets or products at the beginning of the decline stage (at the latest) to ensure survival. But there are examples of companies who have managed to stay profitable because they are the only player in a market that everyone else has abandoned – in effect they become **niche marketers**.

Key term

Niche marketing – catering for a small, specialist market.

Successful companies have products at each stage of the life cycle. It is difficult to predict how long each stage will last, as many external factors affect the product's life. In travel and tourism, the product life cycle can be applied to products, services and destinations.

Activity: Product life cycle

For this exercise you will need to draw a template of the product life cycle.

Study the list of destinations below and discuss with your colleagues where the destinations are geographically and what they have to offer. Then decide where you think they are in terms of the product life cycle. Put them onto your template.

- Costa Brava
- Costa de la Luz
- Bali
- Kenya
- Prague
- Paris
- Bulgaria
- Barbados
- Haiti.

You will find more information about the development of the product life cycle into the destination life cycle in Unit 7 (pages 205–207).

Repeat the exercise, this time with these travel products and services:

- free meals on flights
- leisure centres in hotels
- internet booking for holidays
- Channel ferries
- spa holidays
- self check-in
- A380 aircraft
- super ships.

Be prepared to justify your decisions and discuss them with your group.

2.2 Price

The second element of the marketing mix is price. Travel and tourism organisations must use pricing as a means of achieving their objectives. If the company doesn't get the price right it will not make a profit.

The simplest approach to pricing is the 'cost plus' method. For this the organisation calculates the cost of producing the product and then adds a percentage to give the return it wants as profit. Although it is simple, it is not the most effective approach to pricing. If sales targets are not met, there won't be a profit. Also, this approach ignores the basic premise of marketing, about identifying customer needs. Every approach to pricing should start with the principle of asking 'What is our customer prepared to pay? Are all the customers going to pay the same price?'

There are many different pricing strategies. A company will determine the strategy to be adopted by considering the stage the product has reached in its life cycle, competitors' activity and the prices of other products offered by the company.

Competitor pricing

This is used in highly competitive markets where companies keenly watch the prices of their competitors and react quickly to any lowering of prices by reducing their own. This happens constantly in airline and tour operation businesses. It also relies on a lack of brand loyalty among customers, as they must be prepared to switch brands to get the best price. It can be a dangerous strategy if prices drop so low that weak companies fail and others lose money.

Odd pricing

This simple approach to pricing can be used in conjunction with any of the others. It assumes that customers will feel that the price is cheaper because it is an odd number rather than the next-highest round number, say £499 rather than £500 – the idea is that psychologically this seems significantly less than £500.

Think about it

Although odd pricing is common practice, no one knows whether it works. What do you think?

Promotional pricing

With this approach the price is linked to a special promotion for a limited period of time. Sometimes the customer has to collect tokens to be eligible for the special price. This draws attention to the product and gains publicity, so is especially useful for new products. Tourist attractions often use this method of pricing.

Differential pricing

With this method, different prices are charged for different groups of people. For example, in museums and cinemas senior citizens and students can expect to pay reduced prices. On trains, the purchase of a Railcard (e.g. family or young person's) gives the holder access to discounted fares.

Discounting

As above, some people receive a discount because they belong to a certain group, for example students. Discounts may be given to avoid losing a sale. For example, although hotels have set rates they are usually flexible. If you are looking for a hotel room and you book on the day, always ask for their 'best rate'. You are sure to get a discounted price because, remember, the hotel room is perishable. If no one takes it, it hasn't made any money.

Seasonal pricing

This is particularly important in the tourism industry. The whole season is divided into three – peak, shoulder and off-peak. Peak season always coincides with school holidays and is when prices are at their highest. This causes problems for parents, who have to pay the highest prices. Some parents take their children out of school to avoid peak-season holidays, but now that they can be fined £100 for doing so according to the Anti-social Behaviour Act 2003. So this is likely to be a less popular option.

It is not just tour operators who charge higher prices at times of high demand. Airlines charge more on Friday afternoons and at the end of weekends, and rail fares cost more during rush hours.

2.3 Place

This is the element of the marketing mix that considers how to get the product or service to the customer. The means of getting the product to the customer is known as the channel, or chain of distribution. In the travel and tourism sector, the channel is complicated by the fact that there is often no tangible product to pass from one to another through the channel.

Physical location and accessibility

Some travel and tourism organisations, such as visitor attractions, have different considerations in terms of the 'place' mix. Customers have to travel to them in order to enjoy what they have to offer. This means the location of the attraction is important, as it must be accessible to customers. Purpose-built attractions such as Disneyland Paris are located near to major road networks. Hotels and ample parking are provided in the vicinity to ease access for visitors and to encourage them to stay longer.

Channels of distribution

As we saw in Unit 1 (page 14) there are many variations on the traditional channel of distribution (also known as a chain of distribution), including use of the internet, telephone call centres, as well as traditional agencies.

The internet has considerably reduced distribution costs for airlines. Most bookings for low-cost airlines are taken via the internet, in line with their business model. This is good news for the airlines and for customers, but it is not so good for travel agents. Travel agents work on a commission basis. They take a small commission from the principal for every product

Case study: Seasonal holiday prices

There have been complaints about 'unfair and unjustified' travel and holiday prices during school holidays. Executives from Britain's biggest tour operators have been asked to explain why prices go up so much at the end of term.

A survey by Travelsupermarket.com in 2009 showed that 31 per cent of parents are prepared to take their child out of school to go on holiday at cheaper times.

July and August are the most expensive times to go away, with prices rising by almost £1000 on a fortnight's holiday in Spain for a family of four.

1. What do you think about the high prices in July and August? Are they justified?
2. Look at some brochures and compare prices from season to season. Work out the percentage increases.
3. What extra costs do you think tour operators have in the peak season?

Make notes on your answers and discuss them with your group.

sold. However, airlines have drastically cut travel agents' commissions and in some cases do not use agents at all. If this trend follows with tour operators, then travel agents will be in a very vulnerable position.

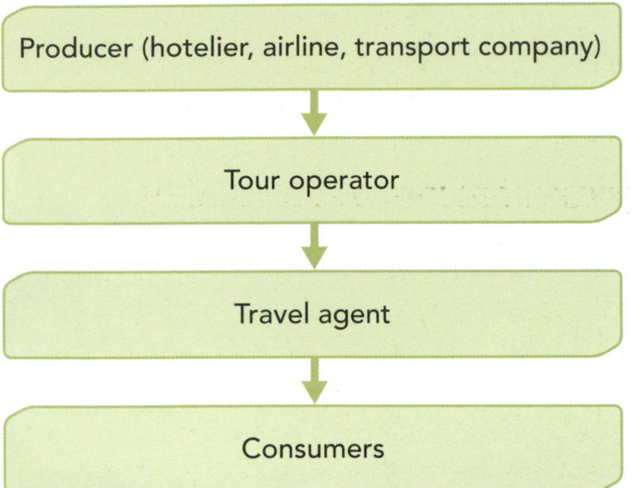

Figure 5.2: Traditional channel of distribution

Another development in distribution is for tour operators to have sales channels on television. For example, the Thomson TV Channel sells holidays, not only from Thomson but from other suppliers too. This means of distribution has been so successful that annual holiday sales through television channels have soared.

However, travel agents still offer a valuable service, particularly for tour operators, some of whom have acquired chains of travel agents (vertical integration) in order to control better their representation to the public. Thomson (TUI) owns its own travel agencies. Thomas Cook has both a tour operation and a travel agency operation.

Figure 5.3 shows the advantages to the tour operator of selling through travel agents.

Some of the disadvantages to tour operators of selling through travel agents are that:

- commission must be paid
- the agent decides how to rack the brochures and may not give prominence to a tour operator's product
- tour operators have little control over the quality or method of selling
- travel agents take add-on sales, for example car hire and insurance.

Some of the advantages of direct selling through a call centre or the internet are having:

- control over how the product is sold
- commission-free products.

Some of the disadvantages of direct selling are that:

- there is no high street presence
- there are high advertising costs to reach potential customers
- there is a need to have call-centre operations, even if only to back up the internet.

2.4 Promotion

In order to achieve their marketing objectives, travel and tourism companies must make both consumers and trade customers aware of their products and services. The tools they use to do this are collectively known as promotion and form part of the marketing mix.

Communication has an important role to play here, and this branch of marketing is often described as 'marketing communications'. The individuals, groups or organisations for whom the promotion is targeted are known as the 'target audience'.

Figure 5.3: Advantages of the tour operator selling through travel agents

Promotional methods

Advertising

The Advertising Association describes advertising as 'messages paid for by those who send them, intended to inform or influence people who receive them'.

Advertising is paid for and is placed in the media. The media is the collective term for television, newspapers, radio, magazines, directories, outdoor sites and advertising on transport. It also includes the internet, although this still tends to be described as 'new media'. New media also includes forms of advertising such as text messaging using Twitter or Facebook.

Television

The British Broadcasting Corporation (BBC), which does not carry advertising and is funded by payment of a licence fee, is probably the most easily recognised organisation in British television. Most television channels are commercial channels – that is, they are funded by the sale of advertising or sponsorship and do not receive any of the licence fee. Examples include all ITV channels.

Advertisers wishing to use television have dozens of commercial channels to choose from. Advertising is sold in 'spots'. One spot is usually 30 seconds long. There is no fixed rate for a spot, as the price varies according to time of day – peak time is 5.30 to 10.30 p.m. when most people are watching. Premium rates will be charged if a particularly popular programme, such as an important football match, is being shown.

Advertisers buy a package of spots. If you watch television for any length of time you will note that the same advertisements are repeated often. This is to ensure that the message reaches as many people as possible. The number of people viewing an advertisement is called the 'reach'.

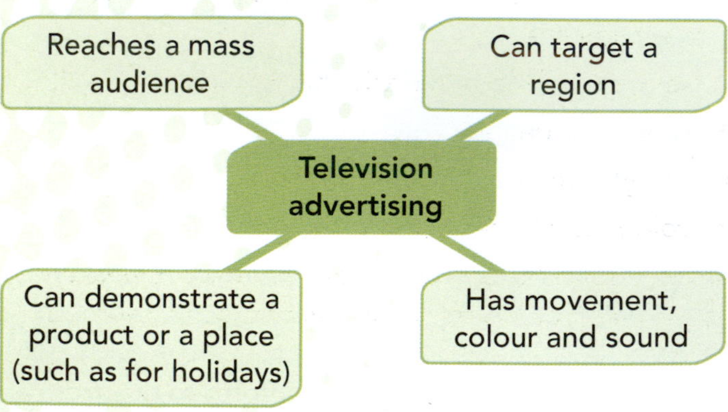

Figure 5.4: Advantages of television advertising

There are many advantages to television advertising (Figure 5.4). It is, however, very expensive. Not only are spots expensive, but there are also the production costs of the advertisement to cover.

Another form of advertising on television is sponsorship. Sponsors pay to be associated with a programme and their logo and product shots appear at the beginning, end and at either side of each commercial break.

> **Activity: TV sponsorship**
>
> Find some examples of television sponsorship. For each example, think about why the sponsor wants to be linked with that programme. Look at travel programmes – are they linked with travel and tourism companies? Discuss your findings with your group.

Radio

As with television, it is the commercial sector of radio that carries advertising. BBC radio stations are funded by the same licence fee as television. There are many local commercial stations and you should note the ones in your locality. There are also some national commercial stations, for example Absolute Radio. You can find out about radio stations by visiting the Radio Advertising Bureau (RAB) website at www.rab.co.uk. This is an independent body that gives information on advertising issues to industry members and the public.

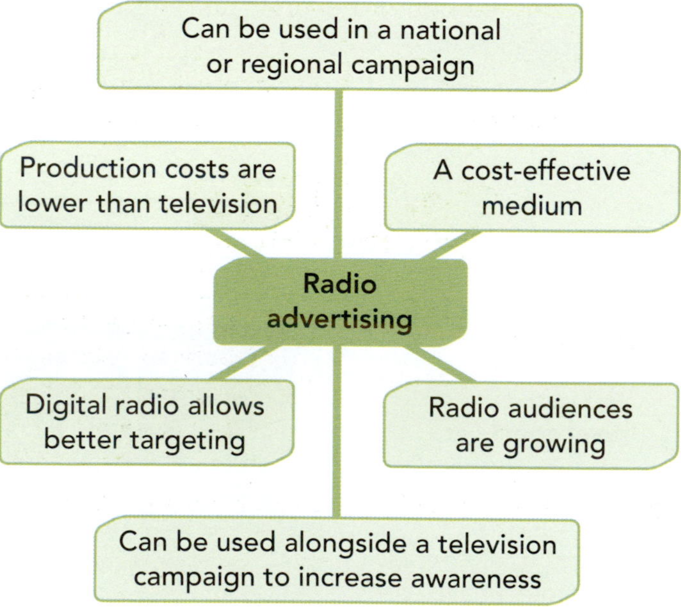

Figure 5.5: Advantages of radio advertising

Spots are sold on radio in the same way as on television, with peak times attracting greater revenue.

Radio advertising is becoming more popular. One of the reasons is the advent of digital radio, which allows greater targeting as the programmes tend to be much more specialised, allowing a company to reach a much more specific segment of the market .

Advertisers who wish to reach the 15–24 age group often use radio as they represent a large part of radio audiences. RAB reported that total commercial reach was 61 per cent of adults in 2009. This meant that 61 per cent of adults in the UK listened to commercial radio.

Press media

The term 'press' refers to newspapers, magazines and directories.

The National Readership Survey is a non-profit-making body that provides estimates of the number and type of people who read the UK's newspapers and magazines. The survey covers about 300 publications. The reader profiles are broken down by age, sex, region and other demographic and lifestyle characteristics. Publishers of press media use these profiles to sell advertising space and advertisers use them to target the correct audience through appropriate media.

Figure 5.6: Advantages of national newspaper advertising

The UK has 12 daily newspapers and 11 Sunday newspapers. *The Sun* has the biggest circulation of all the national dailies and the *News of the World* is the most popular Sunday newspaper.

Advertising is sold by the page, half-page or column. Prices vary according to the position of the advert. The front and back pages are most expensive, as they are most prominent. The newspapers with the highest circulation command the highest rates; therefore *The Sun* is the most expensive.

Activity: Newspaper readership

Find out the latest circulation figures for the UK's newspapers. You can do this by:

- looking at a newspaper's website
- looking at the National Readership Survey website (www.nrs.co.uk/)
- studying the BRAD (British Rates and Data) directory in a library or on line.

Draw up a bar chart comparing the figures.

There are also hundreds of regional newspapers, some of which are free. Some are very highly regarded, such as the *London Evening Standard* and the *Yorkshire Post*. Circulations vary and some circulations are very small, but for a company that wants to advertise its services in a particular locality, they are useful and inexpensive. Classified advertising is more likely to be read in a regional paper than in a national one.

Magazines come in different categories:

- consumer magazines
- business and professional journals.

There are over 3000 titles of consumer magazines in the UK, so the advertiser can be very precise about target audience.

Advantages of magazine advertising include:

- precise targeting
- 'inserts' and regional targeting
- colourful, glossy adverts.

Several travel magazines are aimed at consumers and many aimed at buyers or owners of property abroad.

These can be useful media for transport companies. Women's magazines are also an important category of consumer magazines.

Business and professional publications are aimed at people within particular industries. There are two important ones for travel and tourism, with which you should be familiar. These are *Travel Weekly* and *Travel Trade Gazette*.

A disadvantage of magazine advertising is that the copy must be ready to go to press quite a while before publication, so it is not as flexible as newspaper advertising. It is not suitable for the last-minute discounted offers which are popular in the tourism market.

An advertorial is a promotion that is written in the style of a feature. It looks like the editorial pages, but is promoting a company or a product. Readers will probably assume that it is a feature unless they look closely at the small print, which will state 'advertising feature'.

Cinema

As with any media, marketers look at the audience profile before deciding on a campaign. For cinema, these profiles can be found at www.cinemauk.org.uk.

Advertisers aiming to reach the 15–24 age group may choose cinema advertising as cinema going is the number one leisure activity for this group.

Advantages of cinema advertising include:

- the audience is seated and highly receptive
- advertising can be targeted regionally
- good for reaching the 15–24 age group
- 'still' advertisements are cheap to produce for small local businesses.

Activity: Advertisements in the cinema

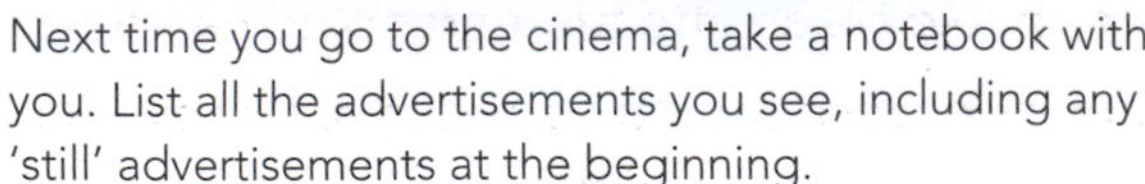

Next time you go to the cinema, take a notebook with you. List all the advertisements you see, including any 'still' advertisements at the beginning.

Try to decide who the target audience is. Is it always the 15–24 age group? Are the advertisements linked to the film in any way? Are any travel and tourism organisations showing advertisements?

Discuss your findings with your group.

Outdoor and transport

Outdoor media usually means advertising billboards. These are placed all over the country in strategic sites, usually on roadsides. Companies which specialise in outdoor advertising sell the space to advertisers. Advertisements can also be placed on taxis, buses, on the London Underground, at railway stations and at bus stops. Large, colourful posters are excellent for the travel and tourism industry, reminding commuters that they can get away to sunnier places.

What advantages do billboards have over other forms of advertising?

Internet

As soon as you connect to the internet you will find advertising messages. These can be linked to searches, so that if you search for low airfares, for example, you will find pop-ups for travel sites such as ebookers.com. The internet advertising spend is growing year-on-year as it becomes more widely used.

Advertisers choose sites which they think their potential customers will visit. They can buy banner advertisements or pop-up advertisements on the host site. These not only advertise, but link to the advertiser's own website. It is even cheaper to buy a text-only link.

Public relations

Public relations is a major part of the promotional mix and very important to those travel and tourism companies that have small marketing budgets. This is because public relations activities are much cheaper than other forms of promotion. Public relations may be carried out in-house or contracted out to a specialist PR agency.

The responsibilities of the public relations department may include the following:

- generating press releases
- media liaison
- organising events
- organising exhibitions
- publication of newsletters
- organising receptions.

A company sets a budget for its public relations work and this is dedicated to the activities listed above. All the activities are designed to present the company in the best possible way in the media or in a community.

Media liaison

This involves dealing with enquiries from the media and issuing press releases. You can find examples of press releases or news items on any tourism company's website. Public relations staff will also ring media contacts if they want to 'place' a story in the press about their company.

Organising events

These may be awards events such as those organised by the travel trade press to celebrate achievements in the sector. Sometimes openings of new retail travel outlets are publicised to encourage customers to attend. There may be incentives such as free gifts or the presence of a celebrity. Cruise ship launches are well publicised events which attract media attention.

Publication of newsletters

The PR department will have responsibility for newsletters. These may be sent to members of loyalty schemes, such as hotel and airline schemes, or to shareholders to make sure they feel involved with company developments.

Organising receptions

Receptions may include lunches and dinners to facilitate networking of personnel.

Sales promotion

Sales promotion includes all those activities which aim to bring about an early or extra purchase of a product and they are found extensively in the travel and tourism industry. A sales promotion is very useful for boosting sales in the short-term, but will run for only a few weeks, otherwise the impact is lost.

Examples of sales promotions are money-off coupons, competitions, buy-one-get-one-free offers and loyalty schemes. Most hotel chains offer incentives such as free nights to regular guests through loyalty schemes. Airlines also operate loyalty schemes, the most famous of which is the AirMiles scheme. This has even been extended to some shops.

Trade promotions are very common in travel and tourism, where call centres and travel agents receive financial or other incentives for sales.

Direct marketing

Direct marketing, as its name suggests, deals directly with the consumer and can take several forms.

The Direct Marketing Association (DMA) has information about direct mail and also other forms of direct marketing such as mobile marketing. Mobile marketing is growing rapidly as, according to the DMA, over a quarter of people in the UK have interacted with it.

Telemarketing is a form of direct marketing where the telephone is used. Cold calling, that is making unsolicited calls, is very unpopular with consumers and is not often used in travel and tourism. However, telemarketing is important in selling holidays and travel to callers who are responding to advertising or other forms of promotion and there are many call centres in travel and tourism businesses.

Materials

Press releases

Press releases are used to place favourable reports about a company in the media or to inform them about a new product. They are extremely cheap to produce and can result in a lot of free publicity.

A good press release should have the following features:

- it should be targeted at the right audience, via appropriate media
- it should be presented in such a way that it can be inserted into a news page or feature with little alteration – this saves work for the receiving editor
- there should be an attention-grabbing headline
- the press release should be dated and show the corporate logo and address
- if an event is being publicised, the venue, date and time must be given
- a photo can be included
- contact details for further information must be given.

Case study: Using a press release

Fabulous Holidays
Trenton Park
Brentwood
BD5 6AG

PRESS RELEASE

21 August 2010

Fabulous Holidays launches cruise brochure

Following the success of the river cruise products offered last year, Fabulous Holidays has secured an exclusive arrangement with Mediterranean cruise specialists, Shipshape. Fabulous Holidays will be the sole distributor of cruises on their new ship, Lollipop.

Fabulous director, Billie Myson says: 'This is an opportunity to expand further into cruising and we look forward to working closely with Shipshape. Their cruise product is unsurpassed and will appeal to a luxury market.'

For further information please contact Billie Myson on 014600 123456 or Joanna Smith on 07777 9876541.

1 Compare the press release with the list of features above. Does it match them all?
2 What is the purpose of the press release?
3 What media are likely to be approached?
4 Why would these media be chosen?

Brochures and leaflets

These are essential promotional tools for tour operators. They are costly to produce, but provide a showcase for the company's products and services.

Getting the brochure out on time is important because if it is not available, when the booking of main holidays begins, sales will be lost. This means that the information in the brochure has to be collated and prices fixed a long time before the season in question. This can cause major headaches for tour operators and may lead to extensive discounting during the season.

Other organisations in the travel and tourism industry produce leaflets, but these are usually smaller and less costly, so it is easier to change them more regularly.

Assessment activity 5.2

Well done! Following your application you have been successful in securing a position of marketing assistant. Your first task is to prepare for a presentation about your companies marketing to a group of marketing undergraduates at Exeter University.

1 Describe the marketing mix at the travel company of your choice: product, price, place and promotion. Explain how the four Ps work together. If you can try to talk to an employee of the organisation and ensure you give specific examples. P3 M2
2 As part of your presentation to the students, you should explain the factors which have influenced marketing decisions at your company. Then detail how each of the factors has influenced marketing decisions. M1
3 Analyse how these marketing decisions bring about changes to the marketing mix:
   - changes in prices of crude oil
   - change in the sterling exchange rate against the dollar
   - reduction in the numbers of business travellers
   - desire to have more environmentally friendly aircraft
   - requirement for qualified/trained staff
   - another factor of your choice.

Present your findings orally to your group with visuals or slides. D1

Grading tips

You could use www.flybe.co.uk to carry out your research. Download the annual report to find out how Flybe has responded to external factors. Research news articles about Flybe as well.

P3 Make sure that you cover the full range, referring to the content and assessment guidance in the unit specification for the detail required.

M1 Consider both factors which have adversely affected marketing and those which have opened up new opportunities. You will need to demonstrate an in depth understanding.

M2 Ensure you explain how the four Ps work together.

D1 You will need to demonstrate a high level of understanding by linking the marketing mix and factors that will have influenced marketing decisions.

PLTS

When you analyse and evaluate information, judging its relevance and value, you are practising your skills as an **independent enquirer**.

Functional skills

When you give your oral presentation, you will present information and ideas clearly to others, using **English** skills of speaking and listening.

3 Conduct a marketing research activity for a travel and tourism organisation

Marketing research is imperative in the marketing process, especially in travel and tourism where not enough is known about why consumers behave as they do. Marketing research enables an organisation to find out about the market, the competition and what consumers want.

Many different methods are used to carry out research, depending on the purpose of the specific research project. Research may be carried out on behalf of a company by a specialist research agency, or it may be done by the company itself, in-house.

3.1 Marketing research activities

Marketing research plan

Identifying objectives

There must be a reason for the research – a set of objectives. What does the organisation want to know?

It could be that an organisation wants to know:

- who is buying the products
- why sales are going up

- why sales are going down
- what people think of the organisation's image
- what new destinations should be introduced.

The range of possibilities for research is endless, but a single piece of research should not try to cover too much ground.

Planning the research methods

Once organisations know what they are trying to find out, they can consider the methodology necessary to find the information. They need to ask themselves:

- who do they want to ask?
- how will they sample?
- how will they reach consumers/what method of data collection should they use?
- where will they do the research?
- who will do the research?
- when will they do the research?

Target group – sampling

It is not usually possible to ask everyone who might be relevant to take part in research. It is more usual to interview a sample of customers. The sample should be representative of the whole body of customers, otherwise the results will be biased.

There are different methods of sampling:

- With random probability sampling, every member of the population has an equal chance of being selected. The company could use its own database as the source of respondents and a percentage of these could be selected at random. When a national survey is undertaken, the electoral register can be used as the source of respondents.
- Quota sampling is a method where not everyone has an equal chance of being selected. The choice of respondents is up to the interviewer, but they have a quota to fulfil based on factors such as age, gender and socio-economic group.
- With stratified sampling the population is divided into groups or strata, according to common characteristics. Then, a random sample is taken from each group.

Collection of data

At this stage the research is carried out and the data are captured either on paper or electronically. Personal interviewers are usually issued with lap-top computers to make the whole process much easier.

Analysis of data

It is possible to analyse data by hand, but it is time-consuming and laborious. Computer analysis is the most common technique and ensures cross-tabulation of data. It is more difficult to analyse qualitative data electronically, because of the diversity of responses.

Evaluation of data

Once the data have been produced and analysed they must be interpreted and conclusions must be drawn from them. Recommendations will be made so that the findings can be acted on. The data, the conclusions and the recommendations should be presented in a report.

Choosing methods and designing research documentation

Types of data

Data are often divided into the categories quantitative and qualitative.

- Quantitative data consists of facts and figures, for example the number of people admitted to a museum in one day.
- Qualitative data are more difficult to collect and to analyse as they are about why people behave as they do and what they think. Sometimes consumers themselves have trouble knowing why they choose to buy certain things.

Data can also be primary or secondary.

- Primary data are data that have been collected for the first time – they didn't already exist somewhere. Collecting these data is sometimes called field research. Researchers do this type of research only when they are sure that the information they require has not been collected elsewhere.
- Secondary data are data that already exist – someone else has collected the information and you access it through your research.

Types of research documentation

Methods of collecting primary data include the following types of surveys:

- questionnaires
- observation
- focus groups
- feedback cards.

Surveys are often interviews carried out with customers. They may be completed by mail, telephone, personal interview or through an internet site. They are usually based on a questionnaire rather than free discussion.

Questionnaires

It has become common practice for tour operators to give their customers questionnaires to complete at the end of their holiday. The response rates are usually good for these types of surveys, particularly if the holidaymakers are travelling by plane. They are a captive audience and the air crew can easily collect the completed questionnaires. The results of these surveys help with planning for the next season and show up faults which the company can then investigate.

When designing a questionnaire, remember the following points.

- Before you write any questions, make a list of what you want to find out.
- Go through the list and discard anything that is not absolutely essential.
- Go through the list again and try to order the information you require in a logical way.
- Write the questionnaire asking general questions first and then more specific questions. Never ask more than one thing in a question.
- Avoid bias in a question.
- Try to use closed questions (yes or no answers) as the responses are easier to analyse.
- Use a limited number of open questions (free answers) if you want to find out the **respondent's** opinion.
- Use a **filter question** if the respondent does not need to answer every question.
- Always put **classification data** at the end. It is not a good idea to start off by asking respondents how old they are and what they do for a living. The exception to this rule is when you need to establish whether the respondent fits a **quota**.

Activity: Design a questionnaire

Using the guidelines given above, design a short questionnaire to be given to your colleagues or friends and family. It could be about where they are going for holidays, or plans for future travel. Make sure it has no more than ten questions and limit the open questions to one. Don't forget to ask for classification data.

- Ask at least ten people to answer your questions and then try to analyse the data according to age/gender groups.
- Explain what kind of travel and tourism organisation would find your questionnaire useful, and how it would produce it.

Key terms

Respondent – the person who is answering the questions.

Filter question – one that allows the respondent to omit certain questions which may not be applicable. For example, 'If you answer no to question 5, go to question 11'.

Classification data – the age, sex and occupation of the respondent. This is used to group respondents into categories.

Quota – the number of people in different age or socio-economic groups to be questioned.

Table 5.2: Advantages and disadvantages of some different survey methods

Method	Advantages	Disadvantages
Personal interview	• Interviewer can explain • Response rate is good • Can use 'prompts' to aid recall	• May introduce bias questions to respondent • Very expensive to administer because of interviewer's time • Difficult to recruit trained interviewers
Telephone interview	• Easy to carry out • Many calls can be carried out in a short time • Response rate is fairly good • Personal contact with respondent	• People find telephone calls intrusive • No visual prompts
Mail questionnaire	• Cheap to administer • Few staff needed	• Very low response rate • Needs an appropriate list of addresses • No explanation of questions to respondents
Internet questionnaire	• Easy to administer • Instant response	• Limited to respondents who access that website, therefore biased • No explanation of questions to respondents

Case study: A holiday questionnaire

Look at the Happiness Holidays questionnaire and answer the following questions:

1 Which questions are examples of open questions?
2 Why is a free holiday on offer?
3 Why does Happiness Holidays ask which newspapers are read by the respondent?
4 Which classification data are asked for?
5 Where could this questionnaire be distributed?
6 What is your opinion of the questionnaire?

Happiness Holidays Questionnaire

Help us and you could win a **FREE** holiday worth up to £1000!

At **Happiness Holidays**, we are committed to making sure that you have the best holiday possible. To help us achieve this, we would like to ask for your help. By providing your views and comments in this questionnaire, you can tell us what you think about your holiday and where you feel there is room for improvement. As a way of saying thank you, you will be entered into our **FREE PRIZE DRAW** to a win a holiday – so don't forget to include your contact details.

SECTION 1 Your holiday booking

Please state your holiday start date: Day ☐ Month ☐ Year ☐

At which resort are you staying? ☐

When did you book your holiday? Month ☐ Year ☐

Is this your first holiday with Happiness Holidays? Yes ☐ No ☐

If no, when was the last occasion? Year ☐ Which resort? ☐

How many Happiness Holidays have you taken in the past five years? ☐

How did you hear about Happiness Holidays?

Television ad	☐	National newspaper ad	☐
Magazine ad	☐	Internet banner ad	☐
Friend's recommendation	☐	Newspaper/magazine article	☐
Internet search engine	☐	Travel agent	☐

How did you book your holiday?

Direct ☐ Through travel agent ☐

Did you use a brochure or the Happiness website to obtain holiday information?

Brochure ☐ Website ☐ Both ☐

SECTION 2 Your holiday satisfaction

How do you rate your holiday overall?

Better than expected ☐ As good as expected ☐
Worse than expected ☐

If worse, please state why:

☐

Was there anything you particularly liked about your Happiness holiday? If so, what?

☐

How do you rate the value for money of your holiday?

Excellent	☐	Very good	☐
Satisfactory	☐	Less than satisfactory	☐

How likely are you to book another holiday or short break with us?

Already booked	☐	Very likely	☐
Quite likely	☐	Not likely	☐

SECTION 3 About you

Please state the age and gender of the person who made the booking.

Male	☐	Female	☐		
18–24	☐	25–34	☐	35–44	☐
45–54	☐	55–64	☐	65+	☐

Please describe the occupation of the principal wage earner in your household

Unskilled worker	☐	Skilled worker	☐
Lower management	☐	Middle management	☐
Senior management	☐	Director	☐
Self-employed	☐	Part-time worker	☐
Homemaker	☐	Retired	☐
Student	☐	Unemployed	☐

Which daily newspapers do you regularly read?

The Sun	☐	The Star	☐	Daily Mirror	☐
Daily Mail	☐	Daily Express	☐	The Times	☐
Daily Telegraph	☐	The Guardian	☐	The Independent	☐
The Financial Times	☐				

Would you be interested in receiving future holiday news and special offers from Happiness Holidays?

Yes ☐ No ☐

Observation

Observation is a very simple and yet effective research method. There are several ways of doing this; in its simplest form, observers can watch consumers, for example at airports, and report on how they behave. Cameras can be used instead of live observers, and the tapes can be analysed at a later date. The observer will use a checklist or take notes to aid later recall.

Mystery shoppers can be used in any sector; for example, staff pose as customers and report on the performance of a travel agency. Journalists in travel and tourism often use this technique and you will see the results regularly in editions of *Travel Trade Gazette*.

Observation is not cheap as you need observers or cameras, and it is time consuming. The observer can also bias the results unless they are completely unobtrusive. The results are also subject to analysis by an observer – who may not be completely objective.

Focus groups

This method of research involves inviting a group of people to participate in a group discussion in someone's home, a hotel or an office. They may be offered an incentive to attend, such as a flight voucher. The objective of the discussion is to find out people's attitudes to a product or service. A group leader, often a psychologist, leads the discussion.

Feedback cards

These are used in retail travel agents quite often and are simply a means of collecting immediate customer feedback. Sometimes they ask for a name and address. If this is the case, the customer will be added to a mailing list.

Secondary research sources

Secondary research is sometimes called desk research as it can be done at a desk, computer or in a library. It collects data that already exist and are available to researchers. These data sometimes have to be paid for and may be internal or external to the organisation. Secondary research is done first – it may lead to primary research if you do not find everything you need to know.

Sources of secondary research that are internal to an organisation include:

- company sales records
- customer database
- costs
- profits
- load factors (airlines)
- productivity.

External sources of secondary data include:

- World Tourism Organization (WTO) – statistics on worldwide tourism
- tourist board websites
- VisitBritain and Star UK websites
- UK International Passenger Survey – statistics on inbound and outbound tourism
- Social Trends and Cultural Trends (Her Majesty's Stationery Office publications)
- Keynotes and Mintel reports – regular reports on everything you can think of; available only to subscribers, but libraries often subscribe
- National Readership Survey figures for newspapers
- Department for Culture, Media and Sport statistics
- travel trade reports
- newspaper surveys and reports.

Activity: Plan a focus group

A local branch of a travel agency wants to find out what kind of travel opportunities students would like in a gap year. They will use the information to source flights and accommodation in various destinations. They have asked you to arrange a focus group with at least six young people who might be taking a gap year and planning to travel.

Prepare a plan for organising the focus group, including details of:

- target group
- when
- where
- who
- means of reporting.

Carry out the focus group and produce a report for the travel agency. Recommend how they could use the results of the market research activity.

Assessment activity 5.3

Your presentation to students at the university was well received. Now you have been entrusted with a further activity at your company where you will demonstrate your marketing research skills.

1 Prepare a plan and documentation for a marketing research activity that will be useful to your chosen company. P4
2 Explain how your plan and documentation will meet your marketing research objectives. M3
3 Conduct the marketing research activity. P4
4 Analyse the results of your marketing research. Recommend how your chosen company could benefit from the results of your marketing research activity. D2

Grading tips

P4 You need to identify the objectives of your research and your target group for the research. Plan an activity for your research that you can design and is feasible for you to carry out. For example, you could test the effectiveness of your chosen company's advertising on your colleagues. You could test awareness of the company's services. You can work in teams to plan and design the research but analysis and evaluation must be individual. You will need to select an appropriate research method and also provide some evidence of using secondary research.

M3 You must explain how the market research method selected and the documentation designed meet the objectives of the market research.

D2 Ensure that your analysis is comprehensive and fully correlated. Record different methods of research. Your recommendations must be fully justified from the results of the market research.

PLTS

When you plan and carry out your research, you will use all the skills of an **independent enquirer**. You will also organise your time and resources, prioritising actions, using your skills as a **self manager**.

Functional skills

When you draw conclusions from your research findings and provide mathematical justifications, you will be developing your functional skills in **Maths**.

4 Organise a promotional campaign for a travel and tourism organisation

4.1 Promotional campaign – the plan

A **promotional plan** forms part of a promotional campaign. It is the detailed schedule of promotional activities that are to be undertaken, where and when they are to be undertaken and the cost.

If this is carried out by an expert, in an advertising agency, for example, then the expert is known as a media planner. A media planner has detailed knowledge of all the different media and their costs and will place the bookings to secure advertisements. They are not responsible for actually creating the promotional materials.

A good promotional plan will give:

- coverage – it will reach a good proportion of the target market
- frequency – there will be opportunities for the message to be repeated throughout the campaign
- good value for the given budget.

Key term

Promotional plan – the detailed schedule of activities that are to be undertaken, where and when they are to be undertaken and the cost.

Objectives of promotion

Remember that promotion is being used with the other elements of the mix to help the organisation achieve its marketing objectives.

The objective may be to:

- inform the public about a new product or service
- inform the public about a change to the product or company
- increase sales
- increase market share
- give reassurance to existing customers
- respond to competitors' promotions
- remind consumers that the company is there
- reinforce the corporate image.

These objectives will be achieved only if the company chooses the right promotional mix – the right medium must be chosen to reach the consumer and the timing must be right.

Promotional methods

A method or combination of methods appropriate to reach the target group must be chosen. Remind yourself of the methods by looking back over the section on promotion in the marketing mix (pages 129–139).

Target market

The entire budget is wasted if the promotional campaign does not reach its intended audience. If advertising needs to be aimed at a mass audience, then television is often the best medium. In the average home in the UK the television is on for more than five hours a day. Of course, that doesn't mean the viewer is watching the advertisement or even that there is a viewer!

Usually the advertiser wishes to reach a particular group of people and will choose a medium where the profile of the audience matches the profile of the intended customer. All the media publish profiles of their audiences – that is, their genders, age groups and socio-economic groups. These profiles help advertisers to select appropriate media.

Activity: Choose the best media

Try this puzzle: match up the products and services on the left with the appropriate choice of promotion media.

- Duty-free perfume
- Palm-top computer
- A cruise
- Travel insurance
- Union Jack beach towels
- Spa holidays
- Cinema listings
- New travel agency opening

- Business travel magazines
- Local newspapers
- National quality newspapers
- Women's magazines
- Local radio
- Sun
- Airline magazines
- Saga magazine

Timings

The right time for promotion is when the purchaser is at the stage of deciding what to buy.

- Hotels will advertise their services when there is a special event in their vicinity, such as a sporting event.
- Theatres send out programme guides at the beginning of each season so that people can book ahead and plan their theatre trips.
- Holiday companies traditionally start their major campaigns just after Christmas. Once the festivities are over, people start to think about their holidays.

Timing is not just about the right time of year; marketers must also consider what day and what time to place advertisements. These decisions will be constrained by their budget.

Budget considerations

Promotional budgets can run into millions. It is easy to see why when you consider that a 30 second spot on national television can cost as much as £25,000. Companies can spend only what they can afford, and it is possible to have a good campaign on a very tight budget by using regional media or by devoting the budget to cheaper public relations activities.

A company will use past experience to set budgets for new campaigns and may set a budget as a percentage of estimated sales to be derived from the campaign.

Procedures for monitoring and evaluating

The process for monitoring a campaign involves evaluating the following.

- Does the campaign reach the target market?

- Have appropriate media been used?
- Does the campaign meet the company objectives?

How is this done?

- All comments/reviews of the campaign are collected.
- Sales are carefully monitored to assess impact, if any.
- Post campaign surveys are carried out to assess recall of the campaign.
- Publicity campaigns that require a telephone response can be allocated individual numbers so that responses can be counted.
- Staff responding to enquiries can be asked where the enquiry came from, pinpointing media that provoked a response.

Activity: Evaluate a promotional campaign

- Choose a current promotional campaign for a travel and tourism company. You can choose a trade or consumer campaign.
- Collect materials from the campaign or make detailed notes on the campaign materials and media schedules.
- Evaluate the campaign by trying to decide what the original objectives were and whether you think it meets them.
- Write a report on your findings suggesting recommendations for improvements.

4.2 Promotional campaign – material

Material you could use in a promotional campaign includes:

- leaflets
- advertisements
- direct marketing letters
- press releases.

For more information on these see pages 133–139.

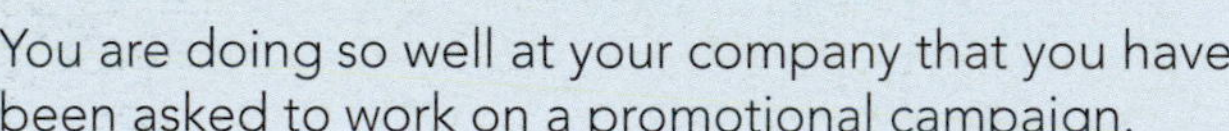

Assessment activity 5.4

P5 P6 M4 BTEC

You are doing so well at your company that you have been asked to work on a promotional campaign.

1 Plan a promotional campaign for your company, giving specific objectives for the campaign. P5

2 Prepare an item of promotional material for use in your campaign, stating the target audience for the material. P6

3 Explain how the planned campaign would meet the objectives set. M4

Grading tip

P5 Include all of the following: the objectives, target market, timings, budget considerations, procedures for monitoring and evaluation and promotional methods to be used.

P6 Ensure the item is attractive and well presented, text should be word processed, spell checked and proof read.

M4 Ensure you explain how your chosen times and media would reach the target audience and how your promotional material would appeal to the target audience.

PLTS

Trying out alternatives or new solutions and following your campaign ideas through will help you develop skills as a **creative thinker**.

Functional skills

When entering, developing and presenting information to meet the target audience you will be practising your skills in **ICT**.

Milena Černý

Marketing assistant for an airline

What does your job involve?

It is a very varied role. I work with the marketing manager and she meets with me every Monday to explain my tasks for the week. This week I have been checking copy for an advertising campaign that will be in the national press. I have to make sure that the fares quoted are actually available – otherwise our advertising would be illegal. I also place the advertisements following a schedule that the manager gives to me.

Some days I am on the phone answering enquiries from the press. We always have to look at our competitors' advertisements to check what prices and deals they are offering.

Recently we decided to sponsor a local football team to improve our public relations. I have been given total responsibility for that.

I arranged for photos to be taken for our website and we are going to have a reception before a match in two weeks, so I am arranging all the food and drink for that and inviting the press along, as well as some local VIPs.

Our department does a lot of research – we have a specialist company to carry out surveys, but we have to analyse which routes are most popular and which have declining numbers. This could be for all sorts of reasons, for example, a destination might become less popular. Routes might be cut or started up on the basis of what we find.

How did you get your job?

My first plan was to join an airline as cabin crew. When I first came to the UK from the Czech Republic, I had to learn English and at the same time I did a cabin crew course. I loved it, but when I finished my parents wanted me to stay at college so I did the BTEC National Travel and Tourism.

After that I got a job with this airline, on check-in. When I saw the marketing job advertised I was already known to be conscientious and reliable. I had studied marketing as part of my course too. I was very lucky as a lot of people applied.

Think about it!

1 What other companies do you know about in travel and tourism that employ marketing assistants?

2 How can you find out what entry requirements are for a post in marketing?

3 What other jobs are available in airlines besides cabin crew or piloting a plane?

Just checking

1 Give a definition of marketing.
2 Explain the following terms as they are used in travel and tourism marketing – 'service related', 'tangible' and 'perishable'.
3 What is meant by social responsibility in marketing?
4 What kind of research methodology does mystery shopping fall into?
5 What are the four elements of the marketing mix?
6 What is a PEST analysis?
7 What is the difference between qualitative and quantitative data?
8 What is the difference between primary and secondary research?
9 Describe some different methods of sampling.
10 What is a mission statement?
11 Describe the stages of the product life cycle.
12 Explain two pricing strategies.
13 What are the different types of press media?

edexcel

Assignment tips

- *Marketing*, *Marketing Week* and *Campaign* magazines often carry reviews of advertising campaigns.
- Take some time to look for examples of advertising campaigns from travel and tourism companies.
- Look at women's and Sunday magazines and find examples of articles or product items placed by public relations departments.
- Find information about marketing from the Chartered Institute of Marketing at www.cim.co.uk

6 Preparing for employment in travel and tourism

This unit gives you the opportunity to prepare for working in the travel and tourism sector. You will already have observed some career opportunities and job roles in travel and tourism when you have been on holiday or visited tourist attractions. In this unit you will investigate those roles, but will also be introduced to other 'behind-the-scenes' opportunities.

You will find out about the different entry requirements, progression routes and training opportunities. You will undertake a personal review focusing on skills, attributes, experience, qualifications and achievements.

You will look at the process of recruitment and selection so that you know what to expect when you find a job to apply for. You will also find some tips on how to complete an application form and get your CV ready.

So you have a better idea of what the working environment is like, you will look at factors that impact on motivation at work and what legislation has to be followed.

Learning outcomes

After completing this unit you should:

1 know about career opportunities in the travel and tourism sector

2 know the stages of recruitment and selection in travel and tourism

3 be able to prepare for application for employment in the travel and tourism sector

4 understand the factors that contribute to an effective workplace.

Assessment and grading criteria

This table shows you what you must do in order to achieve a **pass**, **merit** or **distinction** grade and where you can find activities in this book to help you.

To achieve a **pass** grade the evidence must show that you are able to:	To achieve a **merit** grade the evidence must show that, in addition to the pass criteria, you are able to:	To achieve a **distinction** grade the evidence must show that, in addition to the pass and merit criteria, you are able to:
P1 describe career opportunities within different industries in the tavel and tourism sector **See Assessment activity 6.1, page 158** **P2** describe the roles and responsibilities, entry requirements and progression routes for two jobs in travel and tourism **See Assessment activity 6.1, page 158**	**M1** compare two jobs in the travel and tourism sector **See Assessment activity 6.1, page 158**	
P3 describe the stages of the recruitment and selection process, identifying good practices **P4** produce a personal skills audit in preparation for employment **P5** participate fully in the recruitment and selection process **See Assessment activity 6.2, page 171**	**M2** demonstrate suitability for employment through job application and interview skills during different stages of the recruitment and selection process **See Assessment activity 6.2, page 171**	**D1** consistently present a positive impression in the different stages of the recruitment and selection process **See Assessment activity 6.2, page 171**
P6 explain the factors that contribute to an effective workplace in travel and tourism organisations **See Assessment activity 6.3, page 178**	**M3** review how different travel and tourism organisations motivate staff in the workplace **See Assessment activity 6.3, page 178**	**D2** analyse the factors that contribute to an effective workplace, highlighting good practice from different travel and tourism organisations **See Assessment activity 6.3, page 178**

How you will be assessed

This unit will be assessed by one or more internal assignments that will be designed and marked by your tutor. Your assignments will be subject to sampling internally and externally as part of Edexcel's quality assurance procedures. The assignments are designed to allow you to show your knowledge and understanding related to the unit. The unit outcomes indicate what you should know, understand or be able to do after completing the unit.

Miriam, 18-year-old BTEC National learner

This was one of the most useful units of the course. I already had a CV, but I have updated it using tips from the unit and it looks much more professional.

There are lots of websites mentioned in the unit which I used to find information about jobs. I particularly liked the TUI Travel website, as I found out about a variety of jobs in tour operations that I didn't know about before. It helped me think about my future career and made me realise that there are lots of options.

For my assessment I chose to study the recruitment procedures for First Choice as a lot of information was available on their jobs website www.firstchoice4jobs.co.uk. The local retail agency helped me as well.

Some of my group chose Canvas Holidays to study as we already had a lot of information given in the book, but I wanted to do my own research. I am using the portfolio I built up on careers now as I am applying for a summer job in a resort this year before I go to university.

Over to you!

1 What are your plans after you complete the course?

2 What information can you find about travel and tourism jobs in the public sector?

3 How will you look for jobs at your regional or national tourist board?

1 Career opportunities in the travel and tourism sector

Set off

Canvas Holidays

In this unit, you will find a few examples of how Canvas Holidays manage recruitment and selection, demonstrating good practice. One of the things the company emphasises is that everyone is working as a team and that they should be enjoying their work. Think about this when you are looking for a job.

Find current vacancies at Canvas Holidays on the recruitment pages of www.canvasholidays.co.uk. Look at the case studies about members of the team – note how many of them started their careers as couriers and enjoyed the company so much they never left.

1.1 Roles and entry requirements

Entry requirements differ greatly from job to job. When you are looking for a job, you will study the entry requirements to see if you either have them already, or can acquire them. Later in this unit, you will plan how to improve your personal skills and qualities to prepare for employment.

Entry requirements are categorised into different areas. Personal qualities are those things which are harder to develop as they are often linked to personality, for example, 'outgoing' or 'sociable'. Certain skills will be asked for, for example, 'keyboarding', 'a good listener' or 'driver'. You may not have these skills yet but you can practise them and acquire them. You will also be asked for particular qualifications such as your BTEC National or Maths and English GCSE. Often, particular experience is required, for example 'customer service'. Having a part time job or work placement helps you to get experience.

Retail travel

Many recruits to retail travel agencies are college leavers. They have acquired good background knowledge of the travel and tourism sector and are usually enthusiastic and willing to learn the essential retail travel skills.

Retail travel agents deal with leisure travel, which usually means holiday. If you work in retail travel your prime responsibility is to sell, but you will also have to look after filing systems, take payments and be adept at finding and giving information. The role is examined in detail in Unit 9.

There are opportunities for progression in retail travel. With chains you can progress to area and then to national management. In independents you can reach management level and may then choose to move to a larger company.

Activity: Job advert

Study the job advertisement (below) for a retail travel agent. Comment on the knowledge and skills that would be needed in order to apply for this role.

Sales consultants required

Snow.com is a leading internet-based retailer specialising in the sale of ski and snowboarding holidays. Due to expansion, we have some exciting new opportunities available in our London office for

SKI SALES CONSULTANTS

You will be responsible for booking ski holidays to the European and North American ski resorts.

The ideal candidate will be computer literate, have excellent organisational skills, an eye for detail and preferably telesales experience. You will also be friendly and self-motivated, able to work in a pressurised environment and have a good knowledge of appropriate destinations.

If you want to join a fast-moving, dynamic company and have a genuine passion to deliver the best, we want to hear from you! In return we offer a competitive salary, a free winter holiday, uncapped commission and excellent career prospects.

Please e-mail your CV with covering letter detailing your experience to recruitment@snow.com

Figure 6.1: Advertisement for retail travel sales job

Tour operations

This is one of the most exciting sectors in which to work, as it offers a wide range of opportunities. Unlike retail travel agencies, tour operators are not represented in every town. Tour operator jobs are either at head office or in a resort, often overseas. There is a career structure in each and jobs may be available in any of these departments at head office:

- reservations/sales
- marketing
- accounts
- customer relations
- contracting.

Reservations staff are sometimes based in a call centre. Their role is to handle enquiries by telephone or via the internet. They are set targets of sales to achieve and may be responsible for updating websites. They need very good product knowledge to respond to customer enquiries and they need to be self-motivated to reach targets.

Marketing covers a diverse range of activities. For a tour operator, the functions are the same, but specialist areas include handling the production of publicity material including brochures. Marketing analysts will monitor hits and use of the company's website.

Accounts staff are responsible for ensuring that customers pay deposits and later the balances on their holidays. They are also responsible for payments to suppliers. You need to enjoy maths for this role.

Customer relations include the role of resort representative, discussed below, but tour operators also have a customer relations department at head office to deal with pre- and post-booking enquiries or problems.

Contracting staff are sometimes called the 'Product Manager'. Their role is a very important one of contracting hotels and ground arrangements for holidays or tours. They also source accommodation for new holidays or tours.

Some tour operator positions are open only to graduates. If you are thinking of studying for a degree in the future you might be interested in joining a graduate trainee scheme.

Resort representatives

Many students say being a resort representative is their chosen career and this is not surprising as it gives them an opportunity to meet new people of a similar age and to live in a resort.

Activity: Job hunting

Find some examples of current vacancies for tour operation roles by researching at

- www.prospects4travel.com – click on Vacancies, then Tour Operators
- www.tuitraveljobs.co.uk – click on A World of Opportunities, then Head Office.

Choose a job that appeals to you. Write some notes on the entry requirements for the role and what the opportunities for progression might be.

Some resort representatives are employed all year round, but there are many more positions available in the summer high season. This means there are jobs for students during their holidays. If you do get a permanent job you should expect to move resorts between winter and summer seasons.

The pay is often low, but accommodation is included and it is possible to earn commission and tips.

Activity: Resort reps

Research two resort representative jobs offered on different tour operator websites. Describe the jobs and the qualities and skills needed. Comment on how they are similar to, or different, from each other.

Airports

The types of jobs at airports vary a great deal. Some require very few qualifications, if any. For example, there are many unskilled and relatively poorly paid jobs, such as baggage handlers and catering staff who prepare in-flight catering and bar carts. Other jobs are highly skilled and may be open only to graduates. These include jobs such as air traffic control (based in air traffic control centres such as Swanwick) and operations management.

More than 19,000 people are employed directly on the Manchester Airport site. Some work for Manchester Airports Group, but many work for the other companies at the airport. Even Luton airport, which is smaller than Manchester, provides jobs for over 8000 people working for around 50 different companies.

Remember that public services such as immigration control, customs, police and fire services are all provided at airports, each with its own career structure.

Activity: Jobs at airports

Find out about the types of jobs available in an airport by visiting the interactive guide to Manchester airport at www.u-xplore.com.

Airlines

Airlines employ a variety of personnel such as air crew/flight crew and maintenance staff. Some airlines **contract out** the maintenance and engineering to specialist companies. Most airlines also contract out services like baggage handling and check-in. These services are handled by companies based in airports – for example Swissport and Servisair.

Key term

Contract out – when one business assigns a job to another business.

Travel and tourism learners often express a desire to be air cabin crew, but remember that there are many behind-the-scenes jobs at an airline. There are opportunities for call centre staff dealing with reservations or customer enquiries. As in any company, there are positions in finance, accounts, marketing, human resources and customer relations. In addition, there is usually a yield management department which constantly monitors sales and adjusts pricing according to demand. The operations department looks at routes and determines where new routes should be developed.

The role and responsibilities of air cabin crew are primarily to take care of health and safety. This means if there is an incident on board they have to deal with it in a calm and efficient manner, be able to keep passengers calm and be able to evacuate the aircraft if necessary.

When you travel in an aeroplane, you will see cabin crew giving information, selling goods and serving passengers. Although these tasks form part of the job description, they are not as important as health and safety. Next time you have the opportunity to fly, note how the crew pay attention to health and safety in sometimes small ways: making sure a passenger has their seat belt fastened; telling everyone to be seated in areas of turbulence; checking doors are properly closed.

Here is an example of the kind of entry criteria used for cabin crew:

- minimum age of 19 years
- physically fit to undertake flying duties
- height between 1.60 and 1.89 metres
- a visual acuity of 6/9 with or without glasses
- educated to at least GCSE standard or equivalent
- fluent in spoken and written English
- successful experience within a customer service environment
- an EU country passport holder with the unrestricted right to live and work in the UK and unrestricted entry into other countries.

Many people who take cabin crew jobs move onto something else after a few years, but there are opportunities for progression. Senior cabin crew and cabin managers have a lot of responsibility managing their team and all service on a flight, particularly on a jumbo jet. Cabin crew trainers will have substantial experience of working as cabin crew before being accepted as trainers. Of course, cabin crew might consider moving into other areas of airline operation.

Think about it

Think about the nature of cabin crew work – it has a glamorous image, but is it really glamorous? Think about when you have flown. What were the cabin crew's activities on the flight? What is the effect on their bodies of constant flying? What impact would this lifestyle have on their personal lives?

Accommodation

For a job in the accommodation sector you need to be able to work in a team, work unsocial hours and have initiative.

Many learners look for work in hotels when they complete their BTEC awards because there are opportunities both at home and away and a variety of jobs to choose from. Some young people who are not ready to leave home may look for employment in local hotels. For others finding a job in a hotel in another area of the country provides an opportunity to move away from home.

There are jobs in hotels which do not need qualifications, for example working in the kitchen or in housekeeping. These jobs can be done part time while studying and give you good experience of the hospitality industry. Other jobs in a hotel might need specialist qualifications, such as catering or accountancy.

Hard workers are soon rewarded. You may start as a receptionist but can quickly move into reservations, managing housekeeping, managing events or business activities. For those prepared to travel, the opportunities are even greater as many hotels are part of international chains. You can find out about jobs in this sector by researching on the websites of leading hotel chains and the website www.catereronline.com.

If you want to work in a hotel as soon as you finish your BTEC course, you can apply for a management trainee scheme. An example of the kind of opportunity available is given in the case study.

Visitor attractions

As in every other area of the travel sector, visitor attractions require staff such as marketing, human resources and accounting. These jobs are vital to run any business.

Other jobs available at an attraction will vary according to the type of attraction. For example, engineers are needed at theme parks to design and build the rides.

At stately homes, guides are needed with a detailed knowledge of the history of the house and grounds. Restorers are also needed to work on the fabric of the buildings or on the tapestries and paintings. If a historic property requires a manager they will be looking for someone interested in heritage or conservation work who is able to manage a team of people.

Case study: Concord Hotel Management Trainee Scheme

The Management Training Scheme is designed for students who have completed either a BTEC National Diploma or an NVQ level 2 or 3 in Hospitality and Catering.

Departments covered

- Front office
- Beverage service
- Food service
- Food preparation

Training resume

- Six months are spent in the above departments, each in a different hotel.
- Trainees have the opportunity to gain valuable practical and supervisory experience to enhance the knowledge obtained from their college course.
- A comprehensive training programme endorsed by the Institute of Hospitality, outlining the tasks and areas to be covered in each department, will be issued on joining.
- On successful completion of the two year scheme, a Management Training Certificate will be awarded, leading to a supervisory/management position within the hotel consortium.

Benefits

- Well-known and respected organisation with many years' experience in training young people.
- An opportunity to train in some of the top hotels in England with differing styles, ownership and management.
- Structured training specifically for students who have completed one of the above courses.
- Trainees are fully employed on a practical basis in each department alongside experienced staff.
- Trainees receive regular appraisal from the Group Training Officer and hotel mentor.
- Competitive annual salary paid which includes full board and accommodation.
- Excellent career opportunities within or outside the consortium.

(Source: www.concord-hotels.org.uk)

1 What kind of recruit do you think would be welcomed onto this scheme?

2 Make notes on the qualifications and personal skills and qualities that you think would be required.

3 What qualities and skills do you have that would make you suitable for the traineeship?

Similar categories of jobs are available in other organisations. For example, Disneyland Resort Paris employees are called 'Cast Members'. They do a wide range of jobs, from dancing in the daily parades to welcoming guests on attractions or even taking calls at the central reservations centre. Cast member jobs are often popular with graduates of Performing Arts courses who are looking for work in the theatre eventually. For travel and tourism learners there are training schemes and sometimes internships (work experience) to apply for.

Think about it

Think of a local visitor attraction that you have visited recently. What kinds of jobs did you notice? Think about the obvious ones (shop assistant) and the behind-the-scenes jobs (buyer) and jobs which require special skills (accountant).

Cruises

Cruising is a wonderful way to travel: it is a chance to see the world and get paid for it! There are many different jobs on offer on a cruise ship. Figure 6.2 shows some examples.

When a ship comes into port most of the passengers go ashore, so the crew are allowed time off to go ashore themselves. If you have a long-term contract on a ship you will visit the same ports several times, so you will have a chance to get to know the ports well.

You need to be prepared to work away from home for long periods. You will need qualifications relevant to the post you are applying for, e.g. performing arts for the entertainment team. If you have a second language this would be very useful.

To apply for a cruise ship job:

- apply directly to individual cruise lines
- research the products and services offered by the line
- be specific about the jobs you are interested in
- describe your training, experience, talents and skills.

1.2 Progression

Training and continuing education in travel and tourism

You may want to continue with education or training in the future, so you need to be aware of the opportunities available. There are many different kinds of qualifications and courses, but first you have to determine where you want to do your studying or training.

Full-time education

Travel and tourism courses are available from foundation level to postgraduate degree level in further and higher education. You may already have completed a BTEC Level 2 First Travel and Tourism before starting your current course.

There are hundreds of travel and tourism courses available at universities. Of course, you do not have to study travel and tourism at all – you may choose to study a different subject. Suitable courses include business studies, marketing and event management. All the details of courses are available on university websites. It is worth spending time researching courses as each travel and tourism course differs from the others.

Begin by looking at the UCAS website. This offers various search options, by subject, university or geographic location. Once you have found courses that interest you, go to the relevant university websites for more information.

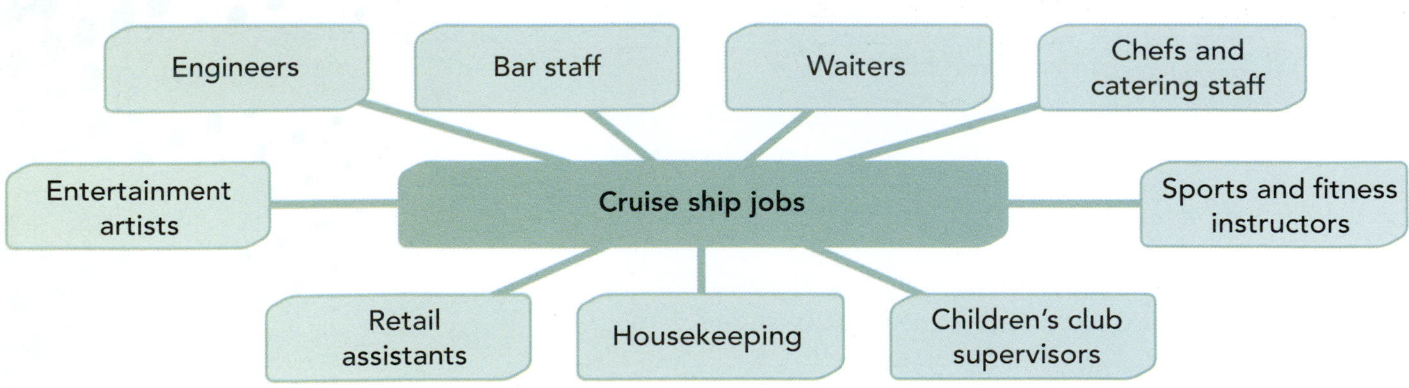

Figure 6.2: Cruise ship jobs

Some young people don't like the idea of going on to higher education straight after their BTEC course. This may be for many reasons: the cost, a desire to get straight into work or having had enough of study. However, after experiencing the realities of working life, many people decide to go to university a year or two later. You can go to university at any time, but only if you have the entry qualifications – so get them now!

Activity: Finding the right course

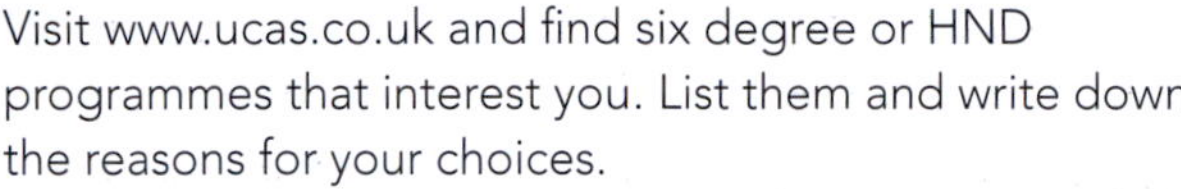

Visit www.ucas.co.uk and find six degree or HND programmes that interest you. List them and write down the reasons for your choices.

Full-time work with on- or off-the-job training

Much of this unit concerns jobs and how to get one, but even when you are employed you will be expected to carry on learning and undergo training. There will be plenty of opportunities open to you. In some industries training is desirable and in others it is essential. For example, if you work as air crew you must attend fire training annually.

If you work in retail travel you will be able to undertake on-line training to learn about products and destinations. You might also study for the Certificate in Travel (Travel Agency). This is the standard examination-based qualification for travel agents, accepted by large organisations and independents. The course is available at Levels 2 and 3.

A similar qualification is available for tour operators, the Certificate in Travel (Tour Operators).

Specialist qualifications are available from BTEC and NCFE for those who choose to be resort representatives.

If you are working in a Tourist Information Centre (or for a tourist board) you will probably train in the 'Welcome Host' and 'Welcome Host Plus' programme. Welcome Host is the official qualification for the tourism industry and it is designed specifically for the service sector (hospitality, retail, transport, library boards, leisure, etc.). Welcome Host is designed to enhance fundamental standards of service by all staff.

Many of these specialist courses can be added on to full-time college programmes or done in the workplace.

1.3. Factors to consider when working in travel and tourism

As you have seen, travel and tourism careers vary within the sector. However, there are some general points about working in travel and tourism:

- the work is often seasonal as it varies with demand from tourists
- shift work is often required
- a lot of the work involves direct contact with customers
- the work is very varied
- travel is not always involved
- some jobs are low paid
- contracts are often temporary or fixed term so that there is little job security
- there are many perks such as cheap travel, seeing new places and of course, dealing with people
- a **Criminal Record Bureau (CRB) check** will be needed for any job that involves working with children or vulnerable adults.

Key term

Criminal Record Bureau (CRB) check – a process for gathering information about someone's criminal convictions and other cautions, reprimands and final warnings given by the police.

Assessment activity 6.1

You are about to start compiling a portfolio of information about career opportunities and specific jobs in travel and tourism. With later assessments in this unit you will add to the portfolio, building up a very useful resource that will help you in the future.

1 Describe a range of career opportunities in the travel and tourism sector. You must describe opportunities from at least three different component industries. P1
2 Choose two job roles in travel and tourism which are of interest to you. Describe each of these roles in detail including: job title, role, main duties and responsibilities, entry requirements and progression opportunities including training, education and specific factors. P2
3 Compare the two jobs you chose for P2, taking into account the entry requirements and opportunities for promotion and progression. M1

Grading tips

P2 Ensure you include: work pattern (for example, seasonal, permanent, full-time, shifts); pay and conditions; qualifications required; skills required; personal attributes required; entry levels, for example school leaver/BTEC National/A level/graduate; progression.

M1 Make sure you say how the jobs are similar and how they are different.

PLTS

When you carry out your research into careers and jobs you will be practising your **independent enquirer** skills.

Functional skills

By using a variety of web resources independently to find information about careers and jobs, you will be developing your functional skills in **ICT**.

2 The stages of recruitment and selection in travel and tourism

2.1 Organisation

Human resources departments usually handle the recruitment and selection process for organisations. It is vital to the success of any organisation that the best staff available are employed in the right positions. A system is needed so that recruitment and selection represent good practice and the employment of staff is not left to chance.

The procedure varies from organisation to organisation, depending on the size and nature of the business, but it is possible to identify the essential stages.

Identifying company needs

Every company should have a staffing plan, giving ideal numbers of staff in each capacity within the organisation. When a vacancy arises, for whatever reason, the impact of the vacancy is considered against the staffing plan. Maybe the post is no longer required, or the nature of the post should change. There may be an opportunity to move staff into different positions better suited to company needs.

Sometimes major restructuring takes place without a vacancy having arisen, due to changes in the business or economic circumstances of the company, for example a takeover of another company or a major economic downturn.

Canvas Holidays looks at courier staffing numbers every year and sets a courier/unit ratio of about 1:10 (a unit is a mobile home or tent). This can vary according to the site and whether it is used as a long-stay or overnight stop. Once numbers are established, a staffing budget can be decided for the year. The courier service is deemed to be really important as it directly impacts on the customer's enjoyment of the holiday.

JOB DESCRIPTION – CANVAS HOLIDAYS	
Job title:	Campsite Courier
Reports to:	Team Leader/Senior Courier/Site Supervisor/Site Manager/Area Manager
Department:	Operations
Role purpose:	To ensure that every aspect of our customers' holiday is of the highest standard possible by providing excellent customer service during the season.

Key tasks and responsibilities:

- Participate in montage and demontage as and when required.
- Montage clean and prepare units, prior to customer arrival, ensuring that they hold a complete inventory.
- Cultivate and maintain good working relationships with the camp proprietor and campsite staff.
- Clean and maintain all units on-site throughout the season, ensuring that they are clean and tidy at all times.
- Reflect appropriate Company Image at all times, ensuring correct uniform is worn at correct times and that guidelines regarding corporate identity, dress and alcohol code are rigorously upheld.
- Ensure that local information in the Information Book and on the notice board is kept up-to-date and that information is added, where possible, to enhance the level of customer service.
- Provide each customer with a personal welcome on arrival and ensure a high level of customer satisfaction through provision of immaculate accommodation, the organisation of customer get-togethers, providing information, problem-solving and regular daily visits.
- Monitor the quality of campsite facilities, as laid out in Health and Safety Guidelines.
- Complete all necessary paperwork promptly.
- Work in a flexible manner in order to achieve the overall objectives of the Company.

Figure 6.3: Job description from Canvas Holidays (Provided by Canvas Holidays)

Job descriptions

A job description is a general statement explaining the purpose, duties and responsibilities of a job. It should include the following information:

- job title and department
- job purpose – the main duties of the role
- responsibilities – to whom the job holder is responsible and all the responsibilities of the post
- physical conditions – where the work is performed, the hours, any hazards or special conditions
- social conditions – in teams, with clients or alone
- economic conditions – salary range, commissions, bonuses, pension, sick pay
- prospects for promotion and training.

Figure 6.3 shows an edited example of a job description from Canvas Holidays.

Person specifications

A person specification matches the right person to the job. It describes the desirable personal attributes of the job holder. It is usually based on a seven-point plan which includes:

- physical make-up – does the job require any special physical characteristics such as strength, good eyesight or height?
- attainments – what type of education is needed? What special occupational experience or training is required?
- intelligence – how much general intelligence should be evident?
- special aptitudes – is a skill in writing or drawing needed? Does the applicant need to be a car driver or speak a second language?
- disposition – what type of personality is desirable? Does the applicant need to be reliable or hard working?
- circumstances – does the applicant need to be mobile? Does he or she have to travel away from home?
- interests.

The job description and person specification are kept on record together and are used to help the recruitment team find the right person for the job.

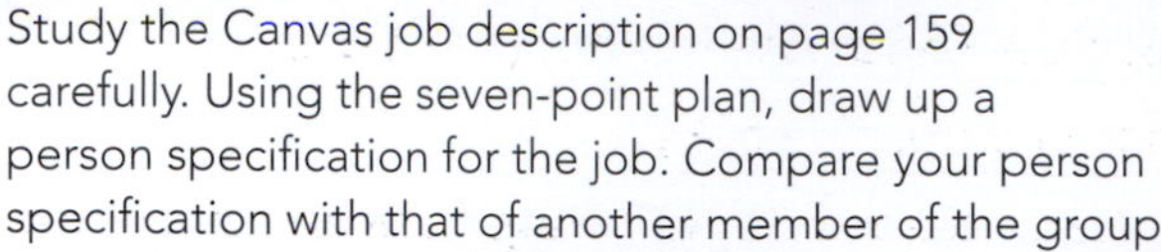

Activity: The right person for the job

Study the Canvas job description on page 159 carefully. Using the seven-point plan, draw up a person specification for the job. Compare your person specification with that of another member of the group.

Advertising

Advertising is used to find suitable candidates. There are many possible locations for placing advertising. It is most important to reach the right people, but cost must also be taken into account.

The following could be used:

- recruitment agencies – general or specialist travel and tourism agencies; to fill a permanent position, the agency charges a percentage of the annual salary for the post, so they are expensive
- job centre – usually used to recruit unskilled or semi-skilled staff; job centres will also pre-interview for the company
- press – local press is ideal for local companies
- radio – frequently used for recruitment; more suitable for local jobs
- 'milk round' – companies visit universities searching for suitable graduate applicants
- internet – on their own websites or through specialist recruitment sites.

Canvas Holidays advertises in many different media. An advertising schedule is prepared and shows all the publications to be used, along with dates and costs. The extract in the following case study shows the publications and websites that Canvas Holidays decided to use in 2009.

Roadshows

When companies send their recruitment teams to venues in major cities to undertake a recruitment drive it is often called a roadshow. They advertise their presence locally, and potential applicants turn up to find out about career opportunities with that company.

'The milk round' is a particular type of roadshow when companies travel to universities in an attempt to recruit students who are about to graduate.

Recruitment agencies

These organisations earn their income by charging fees to companies for undertaking recruitment. Some are specialist companies. An example of a recruitment

Case study: Canvas Holidays – advertising list

Internet

- Canvas recruitment website
- Season Workers
- Anywork Anywhere
- Summerjobs.co.uk
- 247 Recruitment
- Resort Work
- Jobcentre website
- Caravan Jobfinder

Books, magazines, papers

- *Summer Jobs Worldwide*
- *The Gap Year Guidebook*
- *Summer Jobs Abroad*

Other

- recommended by friend/word of mouth
- saw abroad/on-site
- previous customer
- other tour operators.

Study the list of publications and websites used for advertising by Canvas Holidays and answer the following questions.

1. What kind of people do you think Canvas Holidays is trying to attract by advertising in the publications listed?
2. Why do you think previous customers might apply to Canvas Holidays?
3. Where else do you think Canvas Holidays should advertise?

agency specialising in travel and tourism is Holiday Resort Jobs, an on-line resort jobs directory.

Short-listing applications

Organisations select suitable candidates for a job from all the applications received. First, they compare applications to the job specification and person specification, using a list of essential criteria. This may result in many applications being rejected.

They then use an interview checklist to help decide who should be shortlisted. Essential requirements vary according to the position, but for a courier might include availability, a bank account, experience of working with the public, experience of overseas travel or camping. Desirable requirements include a language and experience of working with children to work as a children's' courier.

Interviewing

An interview is a two-way process and can be described as a problem-solving activity to decide whether the interviewee is right for the job and whether the job is right for the interviewee. The interviewer has to direct and control the discussion in order to make an objective decision. Interviews may be carried out individually, in groups or by telephone.

Good practice in interviewing includes careful preparation by:

- reading carefully through applications
- deciding on questions
- considering seating and room layout for the interview.

To establish rapport with the interviewee, the interviewer should:

- smile and maintain good body language
- welcome the candidate
- start by confirming the information in the application.

When questioning, an effective interviewer will:

- start with simple open questions about what the candidate has done
- continue with more difficult, probing questions
- practise **active listening**
- repeat questions or reword them if necessary
- avoid **leading questions**
- avoid answering the question for the interviewee
- to ensure fairness, ask all candidates the same questions
- encourage each interviewee to talk
- ask if the candidate has any questions
- end on a positive note
- tell candidates what will happen next, for example 'We will write to you next week'.

Key terms

Active listening – the process of demonstrating to a speaker both verbally and non-verbally that you are listening and that the information is being received. It is done by maintaining eye contact, nodding and expressing agreement in appropriate places.

Leading questions – those which lead candidates to a specific answer rather than one they have considered themselves, for example: 'We really frown on lateness here. How is your punctuality?'

Canvas Holidays prefer to hold one-to-one interviews. Interviews are held at head office in Dunfermline, as well as in hotels in major cities such as Manchester, London and Bristol. Interviews follow the same format (see Figure 6.4) and interviewers receive both in-house and external training.

Psychometric tests

These are used to test ability or personality. They usually take the form of fairly lengthy questionnaires and the respondent is judged as suitable for a position or not depending on the responses given. The tests are used to support other selection methods rather than as a selection tool that stands alone.

Equal opportunities

Legislation exists to make sure that personnel in employment receive equal opportunities without discrimination. This must be extended to the recruitment process by law and every company should have a policy on fair and just recruitment. You will note this stated on many job advertisements.

Offers of employment

If you are successful at interview you can expect to receive a letter which constitutes an offer of employment (Figure 6.5).

INTERVIEW ASSESSMENT FORM - Courier

Result:

Name:	Date:	Place:
Exact dates:	Position: Courier	Interviewers:

First impressions/reasons for applying:	
Job awareness: CLEANING!!	
Relevant work experience:	
Customer expectations and customer service:	
Problems (real or theoretical):	
Language skills:	
Hobbies:	
Montage/demontage:	
Driving:	
Camping/travel:	
What do they hope to gain from a summer with Canvas?	
What would they do 'to make a difference'?	

Preferred area and why:	Single or team:	Suggested site:

Any additional comments:

Figure 6.4: Interview assessment form

7 May 2010

Stuart Brown
12 Gladstone Park
Cambridge CB14 3RQ

Dear Stuart,

Offer of employment

I am pleased to advise you that you have been successful in attaining the position of Lifegaurd for the coming season. You will be based at La Rochelle (France), commencing employment on 27 June 2010 and finishing on 31 August 2010. You will be required to travel to the site two to three days prior to your start date.

This offer of employment is subject to the receipt of satisfactory references.

There will be a trial period of two weeks, during which time either the employee or employer can give notice to terminate employment.

Your salary will be 1500 euros per month, with deductions for tax and accommodation.

If you wish to take up the offer of employment please return the enclosed form confirming your acceptance and availability within seven days. If you are unable to accept the offer please indicate this on the form and return it. Please note, if we have not received your written acceptance within seven working days we reserve the right to withdraw the offer.

Prior to your departure you will receive a starter pack, containing your travel details and essential packing guide.

Yours sincerely

John Blane

John Blane
Recruitment Team

Figure 6.5: Offer of employment

This is followed by a contract which lays out the terms and conditions of employment. It will include details such as:

- hours of work
- location
- start and finish times/shift times
- holiday entitlement
- rate of pay.

This is quite a lengthy document. You will be required to sign and return the contract, but you will be given a copy to keep for reference.

Once the applicant starts work they will be invited to undertake their first period of training which introduces them to procedures at the company. This is known as induction training (see page 177).

2.2 The applicant

Job applicants also have procedures to follow when looking for work. These procedures include:

- researching opportunities
- producing CVs
- speculative enquiries
- responding to advertisements
- completing application forms
- preparing for inteviews
- attending interviews
- responding to job offers
- references.

You will look at these procedures in detail in the next section, determining best practice.

Think about it

What do you think happens to an application that has spelling mistakes, crossings out or is badly presented?

Activity: Interviews

Arrange to do some practice interviews within your group. Carry out the following activities to prepare.

- Study the job description for Canvas courier.
- Complete an application form, which you can download from the Canvas Holidays website.
- Prepare questions to ask as an interviewer and answers to give as an interviewee.

Alternatively, download job descriptions and applications forms from the internet sites of other companies that interest you.

Take it in turns to play the role of:

- the interviewee
- the interviewer
- the observer.

3 Prepare for application for employment in the travel and tourism sector

3.1 Personal skills audit

You must be realistic about your capabilities, and therefore your options – there is no point in applying for a job for which you have no qualifications. If you are lacking in one or two points only, decide how important they are and whether you should try anyway. Remember that all the things you do in your spare time help develop your personal skills, so include things like membership of clubs and achievements in sports.

It might be useful to carry out an audit of your skills, attributes, experience, qualifications and achievements. This will help you complete a training and development plan as well – you could use the audit on page 165.

3.2 Applying for work

Research

Before you apply for work you will have to carry out research to find suitable jobs. Some relevant sources of information are given throughout this unit, but you will need to find other sources which are appropriate for the type of work you hope to do. These will include:

- newspapers – national and local
- trade magazines such as *Travel Trade Gazette, Travel Weekly, Leisure Opportunities* and *Caterer Online*
- careers specialists
- recruitment agencies
- company websites.

Preparing a curriculum vitae (CV)

Curriculum vitae (CV) literally means an account of your life – it is a summary of your work experience, education and skills. The purpose of your CV is to bring you to the attention of an employer and get you to the interview stage.

You should update your CV constantly. Although you will keep a basic CV on file, you will need to adapt it to fit the particular requirements of each job you apply for. Of course, this doesn't mean changing the facts – it

Activity: Skills audit

Complete the following skills audit. Do this with a partner identifying when you have used these sites.

Skill area	Aspect	Good?	How used?	Qualification held
Communication	Taking notes			
	Spelling			
	Writing letters/reports			
	Oral presentation			
	Interviewing			
Numeracy	Calculating			
	Interpreting statistics			
	Presenting graphs and tables			
IT	Microsoft Word®			
	Microsoft Excel®			
	Internet and email			
Working with others	Contributing to a team			
	Assertiveness			
	Listening			
Improving own learning	Time management and performance			
	Action planning			
	Organisational skills			
Vocational skills in travel and tourism				
Languages				

means altering the emphasis of the CV to make the relevant points stand out.

Your CV should include:

- personal information
- work history
- education
- skills
- references.

Personal information

Give your name, address, telephone numbers and email address. There is no need to give your gender, marital status or number of children, if any. Age need not be mentioned either but, if you are young, it is a good idea to put your date of birth as there may be jobs for which you are not eligible because of your age.

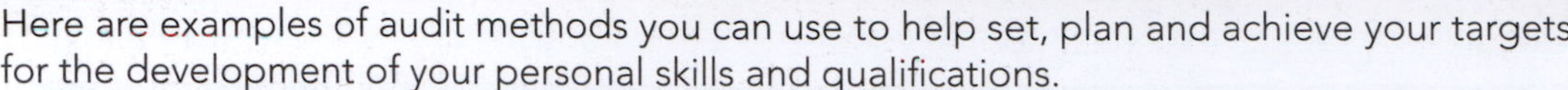

Activity: Setting and developing targets

Here are examples of audit methods you can use to help set, plan and achieve your targets for the development of your personal skills and qualifications.

1 Setting targets

Target	When?
Find an interesting and challenging job	
Gain BTEC qualification with good grades	
Complete final assessments	
Update CV	
Contact tutor about possible jobs	
Carry out research for assessments, prepare CV and covering letter	
Interview practice with tutor, regular reviews of progress with tutor	

2 Development plan

Target	How?	When?	Resources needed
Apply to university	Research courses	Summer holidays	UCAS website, prospectuses, friends at university
	Prepare personal statement	By beginning of October	UCAS instructions
	Complete application on-line	By October	Tutors or careers advisers
	Prepare for interviews	By December	
Improve knowledge of travel and tourism current affairs	Read the travel press regularly – keep a cuttings file	From now	Newspapers, trade press, websites
Improve language skills	Evening class	September	Local college information on language classes
Pass course	Keep to deadlines, prepare timetable of work	By June	

Design a similar target-setting form or development plan and complete it for yourself. You can keep it confidential if you prefer, or you can discuss it with your tutor. If you use the form to show how you will meet your training and development needs, you can use it for your assessment.

Work history

This is where you list all your employment, starting with your current or latest job. If you have never had a job, include any periods of work experience or voluntary work you have done. For each job give the job title, the name of the company and what it does, if it is not well-known. Add a list of your responsibilities in that position. If you can think of particular achievements in that position, list them too.

Education

List your qualifications. As with work history, start with your most recent qualification or course. Include schools from secondary onwards. Do not include GCSEs below 'C' grade. Write the name of the college/school and against it the qualifications you achieved there.

Skills

List any other skills you have. Examples include languages, with an indication of your level, driving licence, First Aid certificate or lifeguard qualifications. Include your key skill and IT qualifications here too. For IT, say which software packages you can use.

References

It is usual to include the names and addresses of two referees. One must be an employer or tutor. Alternatively, you can state that referees are available on request – this gives you time to ask referees for permission to give their contact details.

Profile

Some people choose to start their CV with a brief personal profile. It sums up your skills and experience and gives the employer an instant idea of whether you are suitable for the post. It can easily be adapted to fit a particular post.

CV writing tips

- Keep it brief – two sides of A4 is the maximum.
- Don't try to be funny.
- Don't include visuals, special designs, etc.
- Don't add a passport photo unless specifically asked to do so.
- Tailor the CV to the job in question.
- Don't include anything negative.
- Print it on good quality paper.
- Ask referees for permission before mentioning them.
- Ask someone to check the grammar and spelling.
- Keep a copy of your CV on disk.

An example of a CV is shown in Figure 6.6.

Activity: Write a CV

Follow all the guidelines and the example given above and produce your own CV. Make this a basic CV which can then be adapted to fit a particular job application.

Application forms

Application forms are usually sent out to applicants in hard copy from a company. Some companies prefer application forms to CVs as they then have information in the same format from all candidates and can more easily match it to their criteria. Some companies allow on-line applications, but they often use the on-line form as an initial screening and require a written application from those who manage to get through the screening. You should never apply for a job by email unless expressly invited to do so.

When completing an application form remember to:

- photocopy the form and practise first on the copy so there are no errors on the submitted form
- write clearly – black ink is often preferred as it photocopies better
- answer all questions
- try to give original answers to open-ended questions on customer service, leadership, etc.
- get someone to proofread the form for you

Charlie Richardson
15 St John's Street
Oldham
Lancs OL7 5DH
0161 886 21211
C.Richardson@website.com

Enthusiastic college leaver with Distinction in BTEC Level 3 National Travel and Tourism seeks challenging post in tour operation

Work history

June 2009 - present	Information assistant Oldham Tourist Information Centre Responsibilities include responding to general enquiries, ordering promotional literature, making theatre and accommodation bookings Offered this post following work experience.

Education

Sept 2008 to June 2010 Oldham College	BTEC Level 3 National Travel and Tourism Distinction
Sept 2007 to June 2008 Oldham College	GNVQ Intermediate Leisure and Tourism Distinction
Sept 2002 to June 2007 St Giles High School, Oldham	GCSEs: Maths C French C

Skills	Full, clean driving licence First Aid certificate Basic Spanish IT Key Skill level 3
References	Available on request

Figure 6.6: A sample CV

- ask permission from referees before you include them.

Letters of application

You should never send your CV without a covering letter. Remember, your CV is up to two pages long, and the purpose of your letter is to focus on why you are suitable for the job.

If the letter is poorly presented you will not be selected, so make sure you have studied the section in this unit on writing a business letter (see pages 168–169).

Speculative enquiries

Letters of application may be speculative – this means a letter is sent even if you don't know whether a job

Activity: Matching a CV to a job advertisement

Read this job advertisement.

FRIENDLY TRAVEL

Friendly Travel has been in business successfully for 25 years and has become one of the UK's leading independent travel companies. We pride ourselves on the range of products and the outstanding level of customer service we provide for our clients.

Customer Relations Executive

We are looking for a well-organised, customer-focused person to be responsible for logging in-coming correspondence, acknowledging customer complaints and liaising with other departments to ensure customer complaints are resolved. The post is suitable for a new entrant into the travel trade and training will be given. As much of the correspondence is written, applicants will need excellent letter-writing skills and must also be confident in verbal communication. A knowledge of tour operators and their regulatory practices would be beneficial.

Please forward your CV and letter of application to ...

1. Adapt Charlie's CV so that it is suitable for this position.
   - **a** List the Customer Service and Tour Operations units under the BTEC National qualification.
   - **b** In the profile add 'well-organised'.
   - **c** Under TIC responsibilities add 'dealing with customer complaints'.
   - **d** Make any other changes that you think are appropriate.
2. Now adapt your own CV, drawing on your own experience and skills so that your CV is suitable for this position. If you prefer, you can choose another job advertisement for this task.

vacancy exists. This means it is difficult to tailor the letter as there is no specific job to tailor it too. Instead you must emphasise the skills and knowledge you have that link it with the company's business.

Responding to advertisements

If you are writing in response to a job advertisement, make sure you say which advertisement and give examples of the skills and qualities you have that match the job advertised.

Activity: Letter writing

Write a letter of application for Charlie for the job at Friendly Travel. Use the letter-writing guidance given here and Charlie's CV on page 167 to help you.

Writing a business letter

A business letter is a formal letter. It is often on headed paper, and it is always word-processed. The most common format of a business letter is fully blocked format. This means that everything is aligned to the left.

You should:

- include the name of the recipient if you can, otherwise write to 'Dear Sir/Madam'; never assume a particular gender
- use an ordinary font such as Times New Roman, size 12
- begin a new paragraph for each new point
- if you are responding to a job advertisement, include a reference to the advertisement
- end with 'Yours faithfully' if you started with 'Dear Sir/Madam'
- end with Yours sincerely' if you started with 'Dear [name]'
- print on good white paper
- check everything and then ask someone else to check it again.

Figure 6.7 provides an example for you to follow.

Personal statements

If you are applying for university, you will have to write a personal statement. This is possibly the most important part of your university application as it is your opportunity to explain what is special about you and why the university should select you for your chosen course of study.

Figure 6.7: Writing a business letter

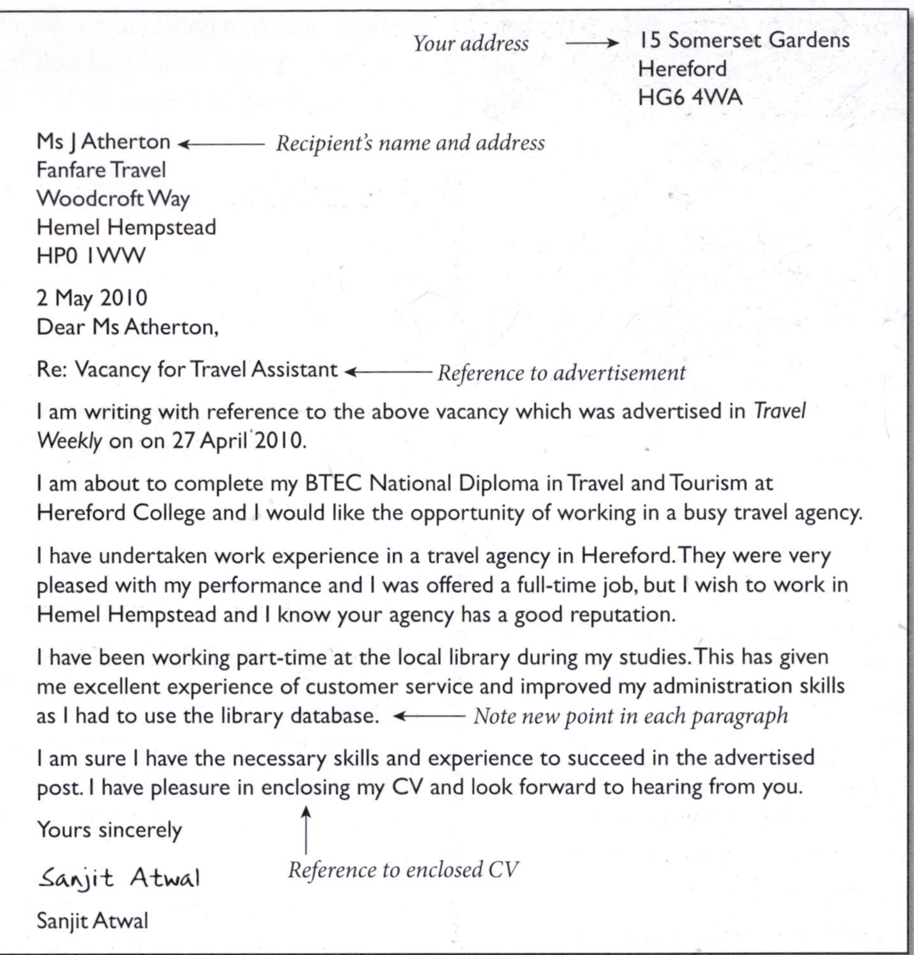

Your address → 15 Somerset Gardens
Hereford
HG6 4WA

Ms J Atherton ← Recipient's name and address
Fanfare Travel
Woodcroft Way
Hemel Hempstead
HP0 1WW

2 May 2010
Dear Ms Atherton,

Re: Vacancy for Travel Assistant ← Reference to advertisement

I am writing with reference to the above vacancy which was advertised in *Travel Weekly* on on 27 April 2010.

I am about to complete my BTEC National Diploma in Travel and Tourism at Hereford College and I would like the opportunity of working in a busy travel agency.

I have undertaken work experience in a travel agency in Hereford. They were very pleased with my performance and I was offered a full-time job, but I wish to work in Hemel Hempstead and I know your agency has a good reputation.

I have been working part-time at the local library during my studies. This has given me excellent experience of customer service and improved my administration skills as I had to use the library database. ← Note new point in each paragraph

I am sure I have the necessary skills and experience to succeed in the advertised post. I have pleasure in enclosing my CV and look forward to hearing from you.

Yours sincerely ↑

Sanjit Atwal Reference to enclosed CV

Sanjit Atwal

Detailed guidance on what should be included in a personal statement is provided along with the UCAS application form. Make sure you read it carefully and practise writing your statement before you complete the final copy or online submission. Don't forget to ask a tutor to check the personal statement with you.

3.3 Interview skills

Advance preparation

If your application succeeds through inital screening and selection, you will be asked to attend an interview. It is most important that you are well prepared. This includes deciding what is appropriate to wear, making sure you know the location of the company, how to get there and how long the journey will take.

It also includes being ready to face all questions likely to be asked during the interview – about yourself, the job and the company.

You may need to prepare a presentation or work towards a short test.

Company knowledge

Make sure you have carried out research into the company, its products and its services. You might be asked about your opinions of the company; if you don't know anything about it you will look foolish. For example, an interviewee may be asked what they thought about the company's new holiday programme for Asia. It would not look good if they replied that they didn't know the company sold holidays to Asia.

Telephone screening

Telephone interviews are quite common when there are a lot of applicants for a job. It can be more stressful for the applicant than a face-to-face interview as the interviewer cannot see your expression or your body language.

A telephone call can be very important; you create an impression even though you cannot be seen. You should prepare for your telephone call just as you would for a face-to-face meeting.

Make a few notes about what you want to say or ask – but don't write a script and read it out, or you will sound very unnatural.

During the call:

- stand up – good body language will affect your voice
- use an appropriate greeting
- introduce yourself – for example, 'Good morning, this is Katy Johnson'
- end the call properly – say thank you and goodbye.

When you are speaking:

- use your voice to make a good impression; vary the pitch, be clear and not too quiet or too loud
- don't ramble, but make your points succinct.

Attending interviews

Interviews may be in groups or individual. If you are invited to a group interview you will be asked to take part in some sort of team activity. Make sure you communicate with the team in a friendly yet clear way, getting your points across. Be careful though not to appear too bossy or loud.

Tests

It is likely that you will be asked to carry out a Maths or English test at the start of your interview, especially if the job you are applying for includes written communication or dealing with money.

Personal presentation

In the travel and tourism industry, staff often have direct contact with the public, so dress code is important. Employers have the right to control their business image, especially when employees are in direct contact with customers, and most travel and tourism companies require their staff to wear a uniform or obey strict dress codes.

Table 6.1: Dress for an interview

Men	Women
Suit – if you don't have one, wear a plain shirt, tie and smart trousers. No T-shirts.	Suit or smart trousers/skirt and top – no mini-skirts. No low-cut tops or thin straps.
Polished dark shoes – no trainers.	Polished dark shoes – no trainers and heels should not be too high.
Hair – freshly washed and tied back if long.	Hair – freshly washed.
	Wear tights with skirts – no bare legs.

When preparing for an interview, dress in a conservative way. This means wearing formal business dress, unless you are specifically told otherwise (see Table 6.1). Make sure every item is clean and free from creases and make sure you too are clean and sweet-smelling.

If you smoke, do not do so just before you enter an interview – it will not give a good impression.

And remember to smile!

Attitude

If you look the part and have done enough preparation you will feel more confident. Paying attention to your body language will also help project a positive image.

- Smile and shake hands when you are introduced to the interviewer (or panel).
- Do not sit down until you are invited to.
- If you cannot answer a question, take a few moments to think before giving an answer, don't leap in.
- Show a positive attitude by listening attentively, showing interest in the information you are being given and asking relevant questions.

Body language

Pay attention to your body language during the interview – try to appear relaxed and open, even if you are feeling nervous. Leaning forward slightly shows you are alert and interested, and maintaining eye contact (without staring) shows you are confident and are engaging with the interviewer.

Responding to and asking questions

Questions are often asked about instances where you have been able to demonstrate your skills. Prepare examples of situations where you have demonstrated particular skills. You should be able to guess the skills that would be appropriate from the job description. For example, think of situations where you had to solve a problem, where you demonstrated leadership or where you showed good customer service skills.

You might be asked:

- Give me an example of when you gave excellent customer service.
- Give me an example of how you handled a difficult customer.
- How have you shown leadership?
- How have you demonstrated initiative?
- Take some care in responding to questions, for example avoid giving Yes/No answers.

At all interviews an opportunity is given for the interviewee to ask questions. Make sure you have some ready. Don't ask about the pay and holidays – you can find out about these later if they haven't already told you. Ask about training and promotion prospects.

If interviewers want to give you a hard time they will start by asking for your questions. Don't be intimidated, take out your pad of prepared questions and fire away!

You may want to do/repeat the activity on interviews on page 164 at this stage.

Time management

Being late does not give a good impression! Plan to arrive 10 minutes before your interview appointment, so that you feel calm and prepared. If possible, do a practice-run of the journey to time it – preferably at the same time of day to allow for traffic conditions.

Evaluation

You may not always be successful in the recruitment process. In fact, you may have to apply for many jobs before you receive an offer of employment. Some companies will give you feedback. If this is the case, listen to the feedback and use the experience to help you positively in your next application or interview. Take this as an opportunity to evaluate your strengths and weaknesses and determine areas for improvement.

Responding to job offers

If you are offered a job, and you wish to accept it, you may receive and accept the offer by telephone, but make sure you formally accept it in writing. You may be offered a job that you don't want. In this case, write a polite letter refusing the offer.

Assessment activity 6.2

You are going to add further sections to the portfolio you are building up about careers and applying for jobs in travel and tourism.

1 Describe the stages of the recruitment and selection process in travel and tourism from the perspective of the employer and applicant, identifying good practice. P3
2 Undertake an audit of your personal skills and attributes in preparation for employment. Ensure you have evidence of any qualifications you claim, for example certificates of attendance at courses. This must include an accurate review of personal qualities, skills, experience, achievements and qualifications and include supporting evidence. Your evidence should include proof of any qualifications, for example certificates of attendance for courses as well as proof of how skills such as customer service skills have been acquired and used. P4
3 Adapt your CV, complete an application form and prepare a letter to accompany your application for a job in travel and tourism. Include in your portfolio an observation record or witness statement which details your performance in an interview for the chosen job. P5

Grading tips

P5 You must have completed all the application documents described and been interviewed for the job. Simulated interviews are permitted.

M2 Demonstrate good practice throughout all the stages of recruitment and selection, showing that even if you still have areas for improvement, you are suitable for employment.

D1 Demonstrate a consistently high level of performance throughout recruitment and selection, with well executed documentation, a professional looking CV and a good performance at interview.

PLTS

- When you carry out your skills audit, identifying achievements and future opportunities, you will demonstrate your **reflective learner** skills.
- The interview process is an opportunity for you to demonstrate your skills as a **self-manager**.

Functional skills

During the interview process you will have to present yourself and your ideas clearly and persuasively. You will demonstrate **English** skills in speaking and listening.

4 Factors that contribute to an effective workplace

4.1 Working environment

Location and working conditions

In travel and tourism, you may be lucky and work at a resort. The holiday atmosphere contributes to a sense of well-being. The sun shines, customers are happy to be on holiday and it is relatively easy to have a positive attitude to work. Contrast this with working in a call centre where you are office bound and have to spend most of the day on the telephone. The organisation has to consider how this poorer environment can be improved so that staff remain motivated.

Hours of work

Hours of work vary tremendously throughout the sector – some people are happy to work unsocial hours because it fits in with their lifestyle or they wish to have time off when everyone else is working. However, the overall number of hours per week should not exceed 40. **Flexible working** is sometimes offered. This means as long as an employee works a set number of hours they can choose when they are – within limitations.

Key term

Flexible working – if employees can work the hours they want, they are better motivated to perform well.

Health and safety

Safety and security factors must be considered in the workplace and legislation such as the Health and Safety at Work Act 1974 must be adhered to. Specific regulations also apply where food is served or where there are chemical hazards, for example in a swimming pool. All these requirements are important.

For some organisations a lapse in safety procedures can mean the collapse of the business and even a prosecution. Companies that organise activity holidays for children, for example, must make health and safety a priority. Health and safety is important for both customers and employees. Employees need to know that they can go about their work in a safe environment and work together to ensure their customers are safe.

Equipment and resources

State-of-the-art equipment and a pleasant environment are important to motivate staff – for example, the latest IT equipment and a comfortable area to take breaks.

Activity: Job improvement

If you have a part-time job, think about the resources you would like to work with. Can you think of areas for improvement that would make your job easier?

Social events

Most companies have a Christmas party or social outings for staff. These are useful events to create a friendly working relationship among staff and to build teams.

Theories of motivation

The motivation and commitment of employees is key to the success of a team and therefore to the company.

Several theorists have come up with models of motivation. We will look at two here, Maslow and Herzberg.

Activity: Motivation

What factors motivate you to go to your job or your course? Think about a member of your family or someone you know who has a good job. What motivates them? Is this motivation different from yours?

Maslow

Abraham Maslow was an American who in the 1940s developed a theory of motivation. The theory is valid still for understanding how people are motivated in the workplace. Employers can use it to provide conditions that fulfil people's needs at the different levels.

Maslow's theory is displayed as a pyramid because employees can only move up the levels once the lower levels are fulfilled. So, an employee cannot achieve at work (level 4) if they are having problems in their personal life or with work colleagues (level 3). Similarly, if they have just been made homeless (level 1) their concern will be finding shelter not performing at work.

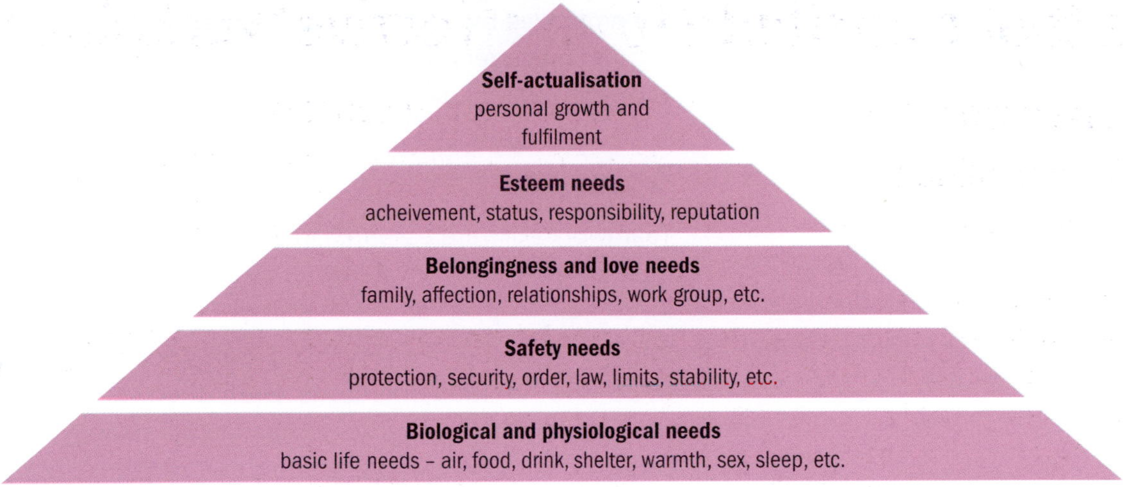

Self-actualisation
personal growth and fulfilment

Esteem needs
acheivement, status, responsibility, reputation

Belongingness and love needs
family, affection, relationships, work group, etc.

Safety needs
protection, security, order, law, limits, stability, etc.

Biological and physiological needs
basic life needs - air, food, drink, shelter, warmth, sex, sleep, etc.

Figure 6.8: Maslow's hierarchy of needs

Think about it

Do you agree with Maslow's hierarchy of needs? Can you think of examples from your own experience?

Herzberg

Herzberg's theory is also known as the 'Hygiene' theory. Herzberg identified characteristics which make people satisfied with their jobs and those which make them dissatisfied: 'satisfiers' and 'dissatisfiers'.

The satisfiers are factors which give people long-term motivation and enable them to enjoy their work:

- the type of work
- promotion prospects
- having responsibility
- sense of achievement
- personal development
- gaining recognition.

The dissatisfiers, or hygiene factors, need to be operating well in an organisation, but according to Herzberg do not ultimately motivate people. However, if they are unsatisfactory then they will de-motivate people. These are:

- salary
- working conditions
- relationships with others – colleagues and managers
- company policy.

Think about it

What are the factors that motivate you to do your course or your part-time job?

4.2 Incentives

Incentives can be used to motivate staff. Here are some examples:

Financial incentives

Remuneration

Remuneration means how much you get paid. You would imagine that this is very important as a motivator. In fact, it is an important factor in attracting people to a company but research shows that it is not the most important incentive.

Bonuses

Bonuses are often based on overall profits and awarded to all employees – usually **performance-related pay**.

Key term

Performance-related pay – the better you perform or the more sales you make, the more money you are paid.

Discounts

Discounts may be given on holidays or travel for those working in the sector. Many who work in travel and tourism receive cheap travel, perhaps by going on standby if they work for an airline or by going on fact-finding trips to a destination if they work for a travel agent.

Incentive schemes

An example of an incentive scheme could be a competition that staff are invited to enter. The competitions may be based on generating new ideas within the company, or how to boost sales, customer satisfaction or commissions on sales.

Pension schemes

You may think you are too young to worry about your pension, but a good pension scheme can act as an incentive for many people who are concerned about security in retirement.

Other incentives

Holiday entitlement

In the UK employees can expect around four weeks' paid holiday per year. In the public sector more holiday is often given, but this may be balanced against lower pay.

Perks

As a perk, employees in the travel and tourism industry may get to travel or live abroad and be paid to live there. They may also be provided with a company car.

Opportunities for promotion and progression

Many employees need a challenge and if they are in the same position, doing a job they find easy, they may become bored and less efficient. So opportunities to move on and face new challenges are important incentives. Opportunities may arise within an organisation and good people are quickly promoted. You may let it be known that you are interested in progression and ask to be sent on relevant training courses and conferences.

4.3 Working relationships

Management style

Management is about motivating people to act in certain ways so that the team can achieve its common goal. A good manager must inform, motivate and develop the team.

People have different styles to achieve this from being very direct about what an employee must do, to a coaching style where the manager tries to encourage the employee by developing and empowering them. A good manager adapts their management style according to a particular situation or the needs of a particular employee.

Teamwork

Teamwork skills are essential in the workplace. You must be able to work with other people in a team even if you don't happen to like them.

A team is a group of people who are working together to achieve common objectives. Even when you are not physically with other members of your team, you can work together by contributing to a sequence of activities with a common aim. For example, a resort representative in Spain may be working in a team with colleagues in head office in the UK.

Team roles

Good teams achieve synergy; that is, together they can achieve more than the members could individually.

More ideas, energy and resources are generated as a group because:

- the team solves problems and makes decisions together
- the team focuses on priorities, with everyone working towards the same aim
- the team provides a sense of belonging and a sense of status
- the team provides a support network.

Not everyone in a team is the same – each person has their own strengths and weaknesses. If each person had the same weaknesses, the team could not work; there needs to be a balance of skills. A method of recognising individuals' strengths and weaknesses is needed in order to build an effective team.

The management expert R. Meredith Belbin has outlined nine team roles necessary for a successful team. One person can represent more than one role, as most people have strengths in more than one area.

Activity: Belbin's team roles

Visit the website www.belbin.com to find out more about Belbin roles. Which of Belbin's roles do you think you fit? You will find a self-perception questionnaire that is used to analyse roles. You are able to complete it, but the analysis itself has to be paid for.

Job roles and lines of responsibility

An organisation chart shows the structure of the company and how the work is divided into different areas. It also shows the lines of responsibility between staff, so that it is apparent who is responsible to whom. An employee studying a chart will find the possible promotion routes.

The chart may show a hierarchical structure or line relationship. This is a very traditional structure and shows a chain of command with each person responsible to the person above them. It is sometimes referred to as a pyramid structure.

Many organisations today would be depicted in a chart with a flatter structure. There are fewer layers of management, and each manager has a broader span of control. Restructuring of organisations often involves getting rid of middle managers, hence the flattened structure.

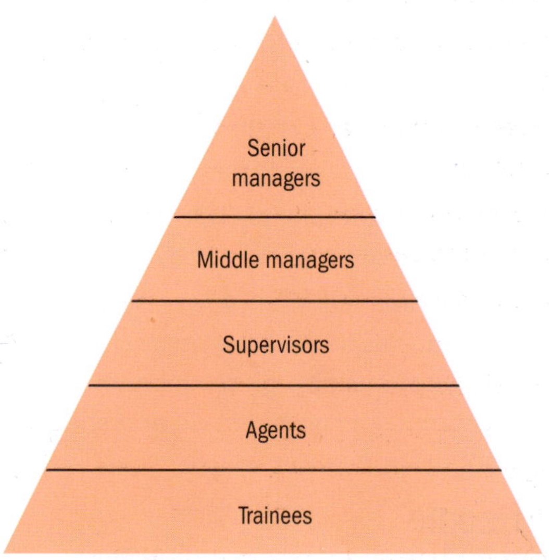

Figure 6.9: Pyramid structure

Channels of communication

Open communication must be encouraged and ideas should be freely expressed in the workplace. There should be trust and support between team members. An effective leader can encourage good communication and shape the way the team works.

Equal opportunities and legislative requirements

Legislation exists to ensure that personnel receive equal opportunities and that there is no discrimination. The Acts of Parliament that you should be aware of are explained below.

Race Relations Act 1976

This Act makes discrimination on racial grounds unlawful in employment, training, education and the provision of goods, facilities and services. The Act defines two main types of discrimination:

- direct discrimination, which occurs when someone is treated less favourably because of their colour, nationality, citizenship or national origin
- indirect discrimination, which occurs when rules that apply to everyone and appear to be fair put a particular racial group at a disadvantage in practice.

Sex Discrimination Act 1975

This Act makes it unlawful to discriminate against someone on the grounds of gender, marital status, gender reassignment or sexual orientation.

The Act was updated in 1986 to remove restrictions on women's hours of work – it allows women to take jobs with flexible hours. The Act not only covers discrimination in the workplace, but in job advertisements and interviews.

Disability Discrimination Act 1995

A person with a disability is anyone who has a physical or mental impairment which has a substantial or long-term adverse effect on their ability to carry on normal day-to-day activities.

This Act makes discrimination against people with disabilities unlawful in respect of employment, education and access to goods, facilities, services and premises.

Employers are required to make reasonable adjustments to accommodate people with disabilities. Examples include providing specially adapted keyboards for arthritis sufferers, facilitating wheelchair access and relocating people with limited mobility to the ground floor.

Equal Pay Act 1970

This Act was introduced to address the problem of women being paid less than men for the same work. It allows employees to claim equal pay for work of equal value in terms of demands made on them, such as effort, skills and decisions made. There is also an EU Directive that states that for the same work, or work of equal value, sex discrimination must be eliminated in all aspects of pay.

Age discrimination

Legislation prohibiting discrimination on the grounds of age was introduced in the UK in 2006. This is in line

Case study: Employment rights

Alison is the manager of a retail travel agency. She went on maternity leave and had a baby. When she went back to work, she realised that she didn't want to work full-time anymore; she wanted to work part-time and have some time with her baby son.

Her employer said she could not work part-time and had to work full-time or not at all.

Alison was going to resign, but got in touch with her union, the Transport Salaried Staffs' Association (TSSA) and explained the situation. An employment rights adviser discussed with her the idea of finding a job-share partner, instead of resigning without trying to find a solution. Alison did manage to find someone who wanted to job share and the TSSA helped them put together a proposal which was accepted by the employer.

1 Find out what the TSSA is and what it does.
2 Was there discrimination in this case, and if so, why?

with a European Employment Directive. This Directive also added sexual orientation and religion to the cases covered by discrimination laws and these are already in place.

Other forms of discrimination

Discrimination at work is a very serious issue and can result in large amounts of compensation being awarded following successful tribunals, not to mention a lot of bad publicity. Employers need to set up policies to ensure that the workplace is free from discrimination.

Measures to be taken include:

- setting up a comprehensive equal opportunities policy covering all aspects of discrimination
- training staff in discrimination legislation and on how to implement the equal opportunities policy
- setting up complaints procedures for instances of discrimination
- ensuring that discriminatory behaviour is never condoned and that action is taken where necessary.

However, discrimination may sometimes be reasonable and is therefore lawful. For example, at airports female security officers are required to search female passengers.

Activity: Equal opportunities

Find out about the equal opportunities policy at your place of work or education. Is provision made for all aspects of discrimination? What happens if someone feels they are being discriminated against? What training is given to staff or students in equal opportunities? Make notes on your findings and discuss them with your group.

Disciplinary and grievance procedures

These must be included in the employee's written statement or contract, or at least there must be a reference to where they can be found.

Disciplinary procedures deal with such matters as warnings to be given before dismissal. Warnings might arise from the following:

- lack of capability or qualifications – although the employer has a responsibility to give training
- misconduct – which includes habitual lateness
- gross misconduct (for example, assault or theft) – this leads to instant or summary dismissal.

Grievance procedures deal with complaints by employees who are not satisfied with aspects of their employment. Employees must be given the name of a person to whom a complaint can be made and should be informed of rights of appeal.

Investors in People

Investors in People is a UK quality standard developed in 1991. Those companies who gain the award have proved that they invest in the training and development of their staff. This is beneficial to employees and also to customers and suppliers.

The standard for Investors in People is based on four key principles:

- commitment from the top to develop all employees
- regular review of training and development needs
- taking relevant action to meet those needs throughout people's careers
- evaluating training and development outcomes for individuals and the organisation in order to continuously improve.

Once the organisation gets the award it is entitled to display the Investors in People logo on company literature.

Activity: Investors in People

What do you think are the benefits to an organisation of gaining the Investors in People Award? Make notes on your ideas. Research a travel and tourism organisation which has been given the award and try to analyse what effect this has had on the organisation.

Mentoring

Mentoring schemes are growing in popularity. They offer employees a one-to-one relationship with a mentor, someone with greater experience and a willingness to listen and advise. The mentor and the mentee meet regularly and discuss aspects of the mentee's job, such as career development.

The mentor does not act as a line manager or superior and is never judgemental, but acts as a sounding board and is able to offer ideas and a different outlook on work issues.

The Hilton hotel chain runs a mentoring scheme for its staff at all levels. Its purpose is to support staff in their career development. Mentors at the Hilton chain are often colleagues of the mentees doing similar jobs, which departs from the traditional model. All of the mentors have had mentoring training.

Other companies have similar, but sometimes less formal schemes, where a new member of staff is given a 'buddy' as a source of information and help.

Job security

Many contracts today are fixed term, especially in areas such as visitor attractions. This means that the period of employment is not indefinite, but lasts for a period of months or a year or two. Such contracts give flexibility for employers – they can lose staff on fixed contracts at the end of the period without penalty. However, such contracts are demotivating for staff as they worry about their future income and job prospects.

4.4 Training

Those employers who wish to ensure an effective workplace will offer ongoing training and development to staff. There are several benefits to organisations and to their workforces. Training can:

- improve individual performance
- improve team performance
- allow staff to be better informed
- equip staff to deal with change and emergencies
- make for a more flexible workforce
- improve morale
- allow managers more time to manage through delegation of other tasks.

Induction training

Employers have to provide instruction and training to ensure health and safety. This is usually a part of induction training. The induction is the first stage of training and is given to new employees; it is important as new employees need to be made welcome and become effective in their work as quickly as possible.

Induction covers:

- the nature of the job
- introduction to the workplace and to staff
- the lines of responsibility
- facilities such as toilets, lockers, canteen
- health and safety basics.

Training opportunities

In-house training

Large companies offer their own in-house training and may even write their own materials. These training courses are very beneficial as they are tailor-made to meet the needs of the company.

External courses

Thousands of external courses are available. These may be specific to travel and tourism or other professional qualifications in areas such as marketing or human resource management. They may be offered by colleges, by travel associations or by private companies.

Companies may allow individuals or groups to attend such courses. Some may be long-term, leading to advanced qualifications, so a great deal of commitment is required on behalf of the individual.

Appraisal

An appraisal is a means of measuring the performance of individual employees. It usually takes place at least once a year and takes the form of an interview with the line manager preceded by some preparatory assessment.

A good appraisal scheme can be a motivating factor for employees if they feel involved in the process and are given constructive feedback.

It is good practice to allow the employee to prepare for their appraisal by providing a questionnaire for them to assess their own performance before the appraisal meeting.

At the appraisal, overall performance is discussed, usually with the line manager. Training needs, future job aspirations and points for improvement are discussed. An action plan should be developed for the individual so that development is encouraged and later monitored.

Assessment activity 6.3

You are ready now to add some more information to your portfolio that will help you with future job search and applications. This time you are adding information from your research into what makes an effective workplace.

1 Explain the factors that contribute to an effective workplace in travel and tourism organisations. You should include information on

Working environment: location; working conditions; hours of work; health and safety; equipment; resources; theorists e.g. Maslow, Herzberg; social events; impact on motivation

Incentives: remuneration; performance-related pay; incentive schemes e.g. commission, bonuses; discounts; holiday entitlement; pension schemes; perks e.g. company cars, free meals, uniform provided; opportunities for promotion and progression; impact on motivation

Working relationships: management style; teamwork e.g. Belbin; job roles and lines of responsibility; channels of communication; equal opportunities e.g. equal pay, legislative requirements; grievance and disciplinary procedures; Investors in People; 'buddies' and mentoring; job security; impact on motivation

Training: induction; training opportunities; appraisals; impact on motivation. P6

2 Review the way two different travel and tourism organisations motivate staff in the workplace. M3

3 Analyse the factors that contribute to an effective workplace, with examples of good practice from different travel and tourism organisations. D2

Grading tips

M3 You can relate your notes to two named organisations.

D2 When thinking about factors contributing to an effective workplace, discuss the relative importance of each factor and give examples of how organisations counter factors which can be negative, such as working split shifts in a restaurant.

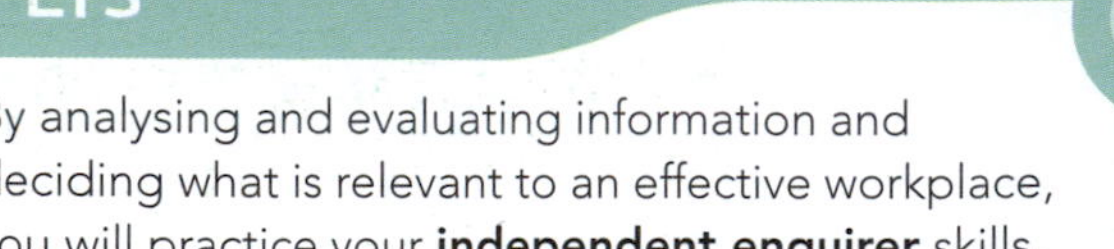

PLTS

By analysing and evaluating information and deciding what is relevant to an effective workplace, you will practice your **independent enquirer** skills.

Functional skills

You will be reading a range of texts and your portfolio of work will show that you understood the main points in the texts. This will demonstrate your **English** skills in reading and writing.

WorkSpace

Bruce Martin

Operations Director, Online Travel Training

Bruce, what does your company do?

Online Travel Training provides training courses for travel professionals – all online. We have over 60 free courses which are open to anyone. Most of our users are travel agents, but learners are welcome to do the courses. All they have to do is register on the website and choose what they want to do.

We offer paid-for courses as well, for example, we offer training in Galileo or Amadeus. This is useful for learners as sometimes companies make GDS qualifications an entry requirement for a job.

Where do the courses come from?

They are designed by travel companies who want agents to be trained in their products or services. We help them to put the course online and they can update it when they need to. The companies pay a fee to set up and then an annual fee to us for marketing to our clients. 13,000 passes were achieved last year.

What's the role of the operations director?

I make sure all aspects of the business run smoothly. Along with my team, we handle the marketing of the company, designing campaigns and making sure we get value for money from companies who carry out the marketing activities on our behalf.

We set up and test new training courses and make sure they function properly. We have added features such as on-line chat so users can ask us for help while they are in the middle of a course.

Your role has a marketing emphasis doesn't it? Has all your work been in travel?

I did spend many years working for an inbound travel company, then I moved into recruitment, eventually to our sister company, New Frontier Recruitment. Most of my work is with travel training now.

Think about it!

How would online training help you prepare for employment?

1 Visit www.onlinetraveltraining.co.uk and find out what training is on offer.

2 Choose a course that you can do in the next week and complete it.

Just checking

1 What does the job role of a resort representative include?
2 Describe the range of jobs in an airport.
3 What kinds of courses can follow a BTEC programme?
4 How would you build up your knowledge of destinations if you worked in a travel agency?
5 What information would be included in a job description?
6 What is the purpose of a person specification?
7 Summarise Maslow's hierarchy of needs.
8 Give five tips for writing a CV.
9 Why is good teamwork important?
10 Give some examples of methods of motivating staff in the workplace.
11 What is the principle of the 1975 Sex Discrimination Act?
12 What is induction training?

Assignment tips

- Many websites are given throughout the unit – use these to help with your research.
- Look at Personnel Today online to find information about effective workplaces – www.personneltoday.com.
- CV writing tips are available on the BBC website www.bbc.co.uk.
- Lots of advice on CVs and interviews at www.monster.co.uk.

7 European destinations

This unit will provide you with the opportunity to study the European travel market. Many sectors in travel and tourism require a sound knowledge of tourism in Europe in terms of locational geography, key destinations and which markets are expanding or declining.

You will use resources to practise locating different countries, gateways and key leisure destinations within Europe. You should be able to locate key destinations and features on a map.

There are many different types of holidays available in Europe, ranging from traditional beach holidays to walking, skiing and city breaks. The choice depends on the motivation of the customer, so we will investigate different motivations and how they can be met.

You will find out what features and factors contribute to the appeal of destinations and appreciate the diversity of tourism products on offer in Europe.

Developing and declining destinations will be studied along with the factors that affect development. Tourists' tastes change and what was once a major destination can easily go into decline. You will find out that some destinations become less popular and why others are increasing in popularity.

Learning outcomes

After completing this unit you should:

1 be able to locate gateways and leisure destinations within the European travel market
2 know the types of holidays available in Europe to meet differing motivations
3 know the factors and features determining the appeal of leisure destinations in the European travel market for UK visitors
4 understand how factors affect the development and decline of the European travel market.

Assessment and grading criteria

The table shows what you must do in order to achieve a **pass, merit** or **distinction** grade and where you can find activities in this unit to help you.

To achieve a **pass** grade the evidence must show that you are able to:	To achieve a **merit** grade the evidence must show that, in addition to the pass criteria, you are able to:	To achieve a **distinction** grade the evidence must show that, in addition to the pass and merit criteria, you are able to:
P1 locate all countries, key gateways and key leisure destinations within the European travel market **See Assessment activity 7.1, page 188**		
P2 select holidays in European destinations to meet specific motivations **See Assessment activity 7.2, page 191**	**M1** explain how selected holidays meet specific motivations **See Assessment activity 7.2, page 191**	
P3 describe factors and features that determine the appeal of two leisure destinations in Europe for different types of visitors **See Assessment activity 7.3, page 203**	**M2** explain how different factors and features of selected European leisure destinations appeal to specific types of UK visitors **See Assessment activity 7.3, page 203**	**D1** give detailed and realistic recommendations for how one European leisure destination could increase its appeal for different types of UK visitors **See Assessment activity 7.3, page 203**
P4 review factors that have contributed to one declining and one developing destination in the European travel market **See Assessment activity 7.4, page 208**	**M3** analyse reasons for the development and decline of selected destinations in the European travel market **See Assessment activity 7.4, page 208**	**D2** justify how current factors could impact on the European travel market in the near future **See Assessment activity 7.4, page 208**

How you will be assessed

This unit will be assessed by one or more internal assignments that will be designed and marked by your tutor. Your assignments will be subject to sampling internally and externally as part of Edexcel's quality assurance procedures. The assignments are designed to allow you to show your knowledge and understanding related to the unit. The unit outcomes indicate what you should know, understand or be able to do after completing the unit.

Carl, 17-year-old BTEC National learner

For my assessment I needed lots of information from atlases, brochures, guide books and travel magazines. I did lots of practice with maps before I did my assessment, so I was quite confident and knew all the European countries, gateways and their locations. I enjoyed doing the maps as I am quite neat and organised and I had fun designing coding systems.

Some of the tasks were focused on the idea of Slovakian students arriving for an exchange. We actually had some Slovakian students arrive whilst we were doing our assessment, so we made posters about European destinations and carried out a seminar about the appeal of destinations. It was interesting to find out that they had different ideas about what to do on holiday than we did. They were much keener on sport activities than us.

My favourite part of the unit was when we were given descriptions of clients and had to find suitable holidays for them and their needs. I spent ages doing research using the internet and brochures and then I had to present my findings to other students who pretended to be those customers. I took my turn at being a customer and asked some very awkward questions.

Over to you!

1. How might you use exchange students to help you with this unit?
2. What resources are available at your college or school to help you with the unit?

1 Locate gateways and leisure destinations within the European travel market

Set off

Visits overseas

According to figures from the Office of National Statistics (ONS), UK residents made 69 million overseas visits in 2008 compared with 18 million in 1980.

Although long-haul travel is growing, most of the journeys made by UK residents are to, and from, countries within Europe. Spain and France are the most popular destinations for UK outbound tourists, with 42 per cent of all journeys, followed by the Irish Republic, the USA, Italy, Greece and the Netherlands.

Visits to many countries fell in 2008, but there were large increases to Romania and Slovakia in Europe and Egypt and Singapore outside Europe.

- Why are most journeys made in Europe rather than long-haul travel?
- What accounts for the popularity of Spain and France?
- Take a small survey of your group. Where were the most popular European destinations for holidays in the last year?

1.1 European travel market

To know the European travel market you need to be able to locate countries, gateways and key leisure destinations within Europe. In this part of the unit we will begin to identify these key locations and you will become familiar with terminology used in defining areas of Europe.

Figure 7.1 shows all the countries of Europe. Some of the countries belong to the **European Union (EU)**. The EU is a partnership between countries which have formed a common market by eliminating trade barriers. It has its own parliament and council of ministers representing the member countries. Over the years membership has gradually grown and there are currently 27 member states.

Key terms

European Union (EU) – the European Union is a partnership in which countries work closely together for the benefit of all their citizens. They work together on issues of common interest, where it is considered that collective action is more effective than individual state action.

Eurozone – the 16 countries that have adopted the euro as their common currency.

The euro, the EU's currency, was launched in world money markets on 1 January 1999; it was adopted by 11 EU states and began use in 2002. Several other countries including Greece and Slovenia have adopted the euro since then.

Countries that have joined the EU are shown in Table 7.1.

Table 7.1 Countries in the EU

Austria	Germany	Netherlands
Belgium	Greece	Poland
Bulgaria	Hungary	Portugal
Cyprus	Ireland	Romania
Czech Republic	Italy	Slovakia
Denmark	Latvia	Slovenia
Estonia	Lithuania	Spain
Finland	Luxembourg	Sweden
France	Malta	UK

Some of these EU countries are part of the **Eurozone**, which means they have adopted the euro as their currency.

In addition, some countries are known as **Schengen countries**. A total of 25 countries have entered into the Schengen agreement including Austria, Belgium,

Denmark, Finland, France, Germany, Greece, Iceland, Italy, Luxembourg, Netherlands, Norway, Portugal, Spain and Sweden. Note that Norway and Iceland are members of the Schengen agreement, but not members of the EU.

Candidate countries are those countries who have expressed a wish to join the EU, but have not yet been accepted.

Activity: Capital cities

Find out the names of the capital cities of the EU countries. Locate them on the map shown in Figure 7.1.

Key term

Schengen countries – Schengen is a small town in Luxembourg where, in 1985, five countries decided to remove border controls and checkpoints between their countries. This is known as the Schengen Agreement. There are now 25 Schengen countries. The removal of controls means that citizens can pass easily between countries to visit or even to work. This also has an impact on tourism: visitors can easily travel between countries without being stopped, or having to show documents and answer questions about their movements.

1.2 Gateways

You know from your study of UK destinations that a gateway is an airport, a seaport or a destination which provides easy access to other destinations. For example, Charles de Gaulle airport in Paris is a gateway to Paris and the transport systems from Paris to other parts of France.

The services through the Channel Tunnel, that is Eurostar and the Shuttle, are gateways between the UK and continental Europe. The Eurostar is the passenger rail service which has terminals at St Pancras in London and Ashford in Kent. The Shuttle service takes cars by train through the tunnel and is accessed at the terminal at Folkestone.

You need to be able to locate key gateways throughout Europe.

Airports

Europe's 30 busiest airports are listed in Table 7.2 with passenger numbers for 2008. Note that London Heathrow is in first position and London Gatwick is in eighth place.

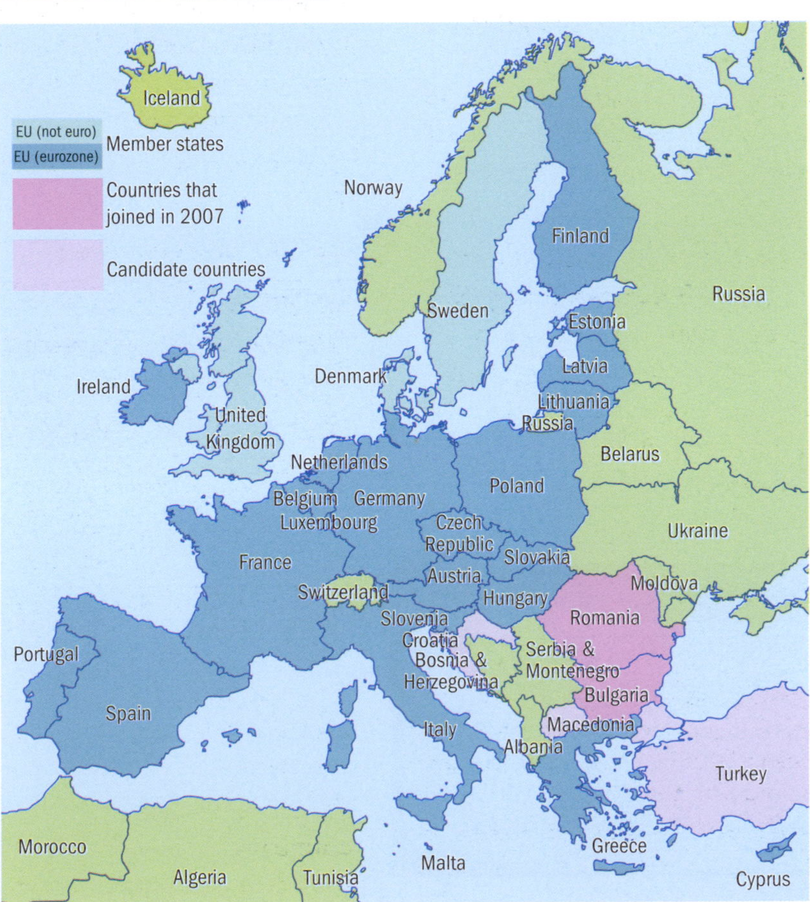

Figure 7.1: Map of Europe showing EU and Eurozone countries

Table 7.2: Top 30 Airports Council International (ACI) airports in Europe by total passenger throughput, January to December 2009

Rank	Airport	Country	Passengers (millions)	Percentage change 2008/9
1	London, Heathrow	UK	66.037	–1.5
2	Paris, Charles de Gaulle	France	57.883	–4.9
3	Frankfurt	Germany	50.932	–4.7
4	Madrid	Spain	48.248	–5.1
5	Amsterdam, Schiphol	Netherlands	43.569	–8.1
6	Rome, Fiumicino	Italy	33.723	–4.0
7	Munich	Germany	32.681	–5.4
8	London, Gatwick	UK	32.401	–5.3
9	Barcelona	Spain	27.301	–9.7
10	Paris, Orly	France	25.101	–4.2
11	Zurich	Switzerland	21.879	–0.8
12	Palma, de Mallorca	Spain	21.197	–7.1
13	Dublin	Ireland	20.504	–12.6
14	London, Stansted	UK	19.957	–10.7
15	Copenhagen	Denmark	19.668	–8.4
16	Manchester	UK	18.840	–12.0
17	Moscow, Domodedovo	Russia	18.674	–8.6
18	Vienna	Austria	18.114	–8.3
19	Oslo	Norway	18.079	–6.6
20	Düsseldorf	Germany	17.793	–2.0
21	Milan, Malpensa	Italy	17.551	–8.7
22	Brussels	Belgium	16.974	–8.2
23	Athens	Greece	16.213	–1.4
24	Stockholm, Arlanda	Sweden	16.098	–11.4
25	Berlin, Tegel	Germany	14.180	–2.1
26	Lisbon	Portugal	13.260	–2.5
27	Helsinki	Finland	12.503	–6.9
28	Hamburg	Germany	12.229	–4.7
29	Prague	Czech Republic	11.643	–7.8
30	Malaga	Spain	11.605	–9.3

(Source: © Airports Council International (ACI))

Activity: Airports

1 Locate all the airports in Table 7.2 on a map of Europe. Find out their three-letter **IATA code**.

2 Find out which airports these codes refer to: AMS, MAD, TOJ, LBG, CDG, ORY, IBZ, PMI, LMZ, AGP. Make some comments about your findings. For what kind of work do you think this knowledge is useful?

Key term

IATA code – an International Air Transport Association (IATA) code is a unique three-letter code assigned to each airport, so there can be no confusion about which airport is which. For example, Manchester airport in the UK has the code MAN and Manchester airport at Boston in New Hampshire USA is MNT.

Eurostar termini

The major Eurostar terminals are located in London St Pancras, Paris Gare du Nord and Brussels Midi. Eurostar also has intermediate stations in Ashford and Lille. There is also a new station, Ebbsfleet International in Kent.

Eurostar trains are able to travel at 186 mph all the way to the Continent, greatly reducing journey times. This is due to High Speed 1, the UK's first high speed line.

Ports

Although we have many ports in the UK, some of them are trading ports for freight traffic rather than passengers. Those that give access to ferry services or cruise ships are of interest to tourists.

We have many crossings from the UK across the Channel to France. The shorter crossings compete with services through the Channel Tunnel. A longer crossing is from Portsmouth to Cherbourg, in France. Because we are an island, we have crossings from many ports to all our neighbours including Ireland, Scandinavian countries, Belgium, Spain and the Netherlands. (See Unit 3 page 63.)

1.3 Leisure destinations

There is a huge variety of leisure destinations in Europe. You need to be able to locate beach resorts, winter sports areas, countryside areas, cities and cruise areas. There are many to choose from, but you can begin by investigating some tour operators' brochures and websites to find out which destinations are popular with UK outbound tourists.

Summer sun brochures will have details of beach resorts such as those in Spain, including Marbella, Benidorm and the Almerian coast. In Portugal, the Algarve is a popular coastal area. Turkish beach resorts and Greek islands will be featured too.

Specialist winter sports brochures have maps and details of main resorts, such as the French Alps, including Chamonix, Meribel and Courchevel. Kitzbuhel and Mayrhofen are popular in Austria and Courmayeur, Claviere and La Thuile in Italy. During winter these are advertised as ski resorts but in summer, these are promoted as destinations suitable for walking and enjoying the countryside.

What other popular beach areas are there in Europe like this one in Corfu, Greece?

Other countryside areas which appeal to tourists are the Italian Lakes, especially Lake Garda and Lake Como. Many package holidays are available to the Lakes. In Germany, the Black Forest is a very beautiful area of highlands and woods. It is said to be haunted by werewolves, sorcerers, witches and the devil.

Specialist city and cruise brochures have details of cities that are popular for both short and long breaks. These are usually capital cities easily accessible by air or train, for example Barcelona, Paris and Prague. Cruise areas are usually in the Mediterranean or Scandinavia, for example the Aegean or the Norwegian fjords.

Activity: Key destinations

For each European country, identify at least three key destinations and state whether they are beach resorts, winter sports resorts, countryside areas, cities or cruise areas. Locate the destinations on a map of Europe, using a colour key to identify different destination types.

Assessment activity 7.1

Your college or school is planning to welcome a group of exchange students from Slovakia. They are also studying travel and tourism and you will be sharing your experiences, skills and knowledge related to the European travel market.

You have decided to hold a series of workshop days where you will present information about outbound travel from the UK to Europe. The Slovakian students will benefit from an increased knowledge of the UK outbound market and develop their map skills and knowledge of European destinations.

You will be preparing a series of maps for the walls. These should be completed on blank outline maps and you may refer to atlases, travel guides, internet reference sites, holiday brochures, textbooks and OAG Gazetteers.

Map 1: Northern Europe, Scandinavia, Iceland, Baltic countries and Russia

Map 2: France, Iberia and Mediterranean Europe

Map 3: Central and Southern Central European and Croatian coast

On each map:

- locate all the countries
- use a key to indicate:
  - EU countries
  - Schengen countries
  - Eurozone countries
- for each country mark:
  - at least one air gateway, with its three-letter IATA code
  - at least one key passenger port (where applicable)
  - Eurostar terminals (where appropriate)
  - at least two key leisure destinations. 

Grading tip

P1: Ensure your evidence as a whole covers all leisure destination types, including beach resorts, winter sports resorts, countryside areas, cities and also cruise areas.

2 The types of holidays available in Europe to meet differing motivations

In travel and tourism it is important to target the right products and services at the right people. This means that different types of holidays are aimed at groups of people who have similar motivations.

Traditionally tour operators separate markets by destination: they produce promotional materials (brochures, websites, etc.) for the USA, Spain, European beach areas, and so on. However, as tourists become more sophisticated, and well-travelled, they are less likely to choose their holiday on destination alone, but also on what they want to do. This is what motivates tourists to travel and to choose a particular destination.

They are likely to choose their holiday based on the leisure experience they desire, for example:

- relaxation – a beach holiday
- family time – a holiday centre, e.g. Center Parcs
- activity – skiing
- desire to learn – city break taking in the culture of museums and architecture
- adventure – rafting
- special interest – maybe a holiday with tango dance lessons
- entertainment – clubbing in Ibiza
- well-being – a spa break
- special occasion – wedding abroad
- sport – a Champions League football match.

Tour operators use this knowledge to their advantage and produce more promotional materials targeting these kinds of leisure experiences.

Table 7.3 shows the type of holiday taken by UK tourists in France, from a Mintel survey of holidays to France published in 2009. It helps us understand the types of holiday people like.

Table 7.3: Types of holiday to France taken, 2007 and 2008

	August 2007 %	November 2008 %	% point change 2007-08
Base: 2007: adults aged 16+ who have ever holidayed in France/2008: internet users aged 16+ who have ever holidayed in France			
City break	32	39	7
Culture/sightseeing holiday	36	30	–6
Touring holiday (i.e. more than two places/cities/regions)	–	24	n/a
Countryside holiday	–	24	n/a
Beach holiday	18	20	2
Theme park visit (e.g. Euro Disney)	16	20	4
Other physical activity (e.g. cycling, hiking, sailing, golf, tennis)	9	7	–2
Skiing holiday	8	7	–1
Wine tasting*	–	6	n/a
Other **	–	14	n/a

* low sub-sample

** 'Other' in 2007 was listed with different options than in 2008, therefore cannot be directly compared.

(Source: Mintel)

Activity: Surveying holidays

Carry out your own survey into types of holidays taken.

- Use a table similar to Table 7.3 and ask a cross-section of people what type of holiday they took last.
- Pool your results with the rest of your group and discuss whether your findings are the same as the Mintel survey on France.

Think about it

A trip, or holiday, may incorporate different leisure activities. Football fans who went to Germany for the World Cup in 2006 might have visited some of the cities and local sites, as well as enjoying the football.

Research Germany and write a list of attractions which might appeal to tourists. You could focus on one of the cities, such as Munich.

The case study on page 191 about Menorca from a Thomson holiday brochure shows that this tour operator is very aware of what people like to do and has provided exactly the information needed. When tourists choose a holiday, they select destinations that offer the type of leisure experience they are looking for, whether it be a sun holiday, an activity holiday, a cruise or tour holiday, or attending a sporting event.

Some destinations have so much to offer that they can provide leisure experiences for all types of people. Paris, one of the top city break destinations, is a good example.

Activity: Travel motivations

1 Study the descriptions of customers below. Assess what their motivations would be and match them with suitable holiday destinations listed on the right.

Descriptions
Joe and Parminder are about to celebrate their first anniversary – Joe is planning a surprise weekend away.
Sarah, a tourism lecturer, is arranging a trip for 20 tourism students.
Paul is very overweight and concerned about his health.
Six lads have been friends since school and spend every weekend out on the town – they want to go away for two weeks together.
Kelly is exhausted after six months looking after her new baby – her mum will babysit for five days so Kelly can go away with her husband for a rest.
Veronica is taking a month out to get some adventure after working in the city for five years.
Moassem and Raj are planning a trip to show their elderly relatives from India around Europe.
Graham and Martin work for an airline so they can take free flights and want to visit some galleries and have a couple of special quiet dinners.

Destinations
Two weeks in Cyprus in Ayia Napa with lots of clubs and bars.
A coach tour of European cities.
Five days on the Costa del Sol, including talks from a holiday representative and clubbing at night.
A week at a detox and yoga centre in the Algarve.
A couple of days in Florence staying in the city centre.
A weekend in Venice including a trip on a gondola.
A few days in a four-star hotel with all facilities on the seafront in Nice.
Diving holiday by the Red Sea.

2 Locate Paris on a map and research access from the UK. Start from your home town and find at least two different routes to get there.

3 Choose two of the travellers mentioned in the table above and research what they could do in Paris and where they could stay. Write up your findings in a brief article suitable for a travel feature. Everything you choose must fit their needs.

For example, if you choose a couple looking for romance, you will need to find:

- a charming hotel with character – and perhaps a four-poster bed in the room
- a quiet restaurant
- a romantic walk along the river
- a boat ride on the river Seine in a *bateau mouche*.

Case study: Destination Menorca

Beaches

Menorca's got over 100 beaches to choose from. In fact, it's got more beaches than Majorca and Ibiza combined. We're talking quiet bays of demerara sands. Sweeps of gold bustling with beach life and watersports. Solitary coves snuggled between cliffs. All lapped by see-through waters. They're pretty much all family-friendly, with feather-soft sands perfect for tiny feet and calm shallows made for little swimmers with L-plates.

Eating out

In lots of harbourside restaurants, you can watch your supper being landed minutes before it hits your plate. Think steaming bowls of still-in-their-shell mussels, tender fillets of tuna and seabass. And topping the lot, Menorca's signature dish of 'caldereta de langosta'. This lobster casserole is slow-cooked with onions, tomatoes, garlic and parsley.

Nightlife

Apart from the bigger resorts, the pace here stays permanently pressed on the go-slow pedal. And that's just how most visitors like it. In most of the smaller seaside villages, evenings start with a 'passeig' – a gentle stroll along the waterfront, eyeing up restaurants on the way. Then it's time to pull up a chair, sip a sangria or two and feast on an al fresco supper.

Shopping

Buy high-quality jackets, bags and belts crafted from the local butter-soft leather. You'll find shops selling gold and silver pieces. Another good place for trinkets is the street markets.

(Source: www.thomson.co.uk/destinations)

1 What motivations do you think this company is trying to meet?

2 What other motivations could Menorca cater for?

Assessment activity 7.2

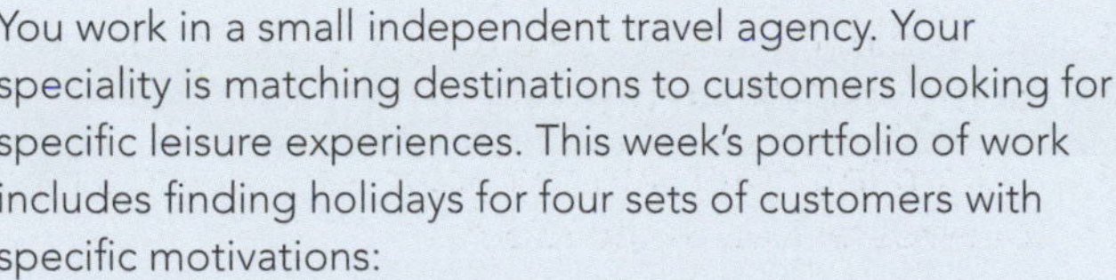

You work in a small independent travel agency. Your speciality is matching destinations to customers looking for specific leisure experiences. This week's portfolio of work includes finding holidays for four sets of customers with specific motivations:

- Sarah and Malik are a couple in their early thirties, are keen mountaineers and are extremely fit and healthy. They are going to take a two week spring break to indulge their hobby.
- Nick has just finished his 'A' levels. He wants to spend a week with seven friends in a lively city to let off steam. They want it all – nightlife, beaches and a bit of culture.
- Jonathan is 45 and divorced. He has recently met a wonderful woman and wants to show how much he cares by taking her on a week's holiday. He knows she likes to relax and be pampered on holiday as she works so hard all year. She also likes culture.
- Elizabeth is going on a hen weekend with five female friends. She would really like to go to somewhere warm in early June. She needs a hotel with spa from Friday to Sunday and her father is paying (money is no object).

1 Find material about holidays in Europe which might meet these motivations.

2 Recommend at least two different destinations from different European countries for each of these customer groups. State why each destination fits that customers' motivation. P2

3 Create a series of information sheets to hand to each set of customers containing brief details of the holidays and destinations. P2

4 Decide which of your recommendations would be most suitable for each set of customers. M1

5 Carry out a presentation to your group and explain why the holiday you have chosen best meets your customers' needs. Use visual aids. M1

Grading tips

P2 You need to select holidays in European destinations which meet the customers' specific motivations.

M1 Ensure you explain how the holidays you have selected meet the customers' specific motivations.

PLTS

Exploring issues from the perspectives of your customers will help you to develop skills as an **independent enquirer**.

Functional skills

Presenting information to your group will develop your **English** writing and speaking skills.

3 The factors and features determining the appeal of leisure destinations in the European travel market for UK visitors

Before we study what gives a destination its appeal, we need to look at the types of visitors who visit Europe from the UK.

3.1 Types of visitors

Here is a summary of the main types of visitor that organisations need to consider providing for, but there are many possible variations.

Solo travellers

Solo travellers may want to join a group, but may prefer the privacy of a single room to sharing and will want to avoid single supplements. Some solo travellers take a holiday in order to meet new people. This is especially true of singles holidays or 18–30 type holidays. Some people combine their love of activity holidays with meeting a new group of people, perhaps by joining a walking or cycling tour.

Couples without children

Couples without children may not want to be anywhere near children and may be looking for romantic locations or adventure and sports activities. They may need relaxation, so they may choose a holiday in the sun or a spa holiday where rest and well-being are emphasised.

Older couples

Older couples may have more time if they are retired and many have money to spend on luxury travel. They are also able to choose when to travel and avoid costly school holiday periods.

Families

Families have different needs depending on the ages of their children. Families with babies and toddlers may be looking for childcare and special meal times. Others may want babysitting, children's clubs, less extreme sports and other children around to play with. Those with older children and teenagers may want suitable activities provided to keep them happy and occupied.

Groups

Groups come together for many different reasons. They may be friends of a similar age who wish to holiday together. They may be a group of people who don't know each other, but have a shared interest, such as studying a language. They may all be travelling together for a special event, such as a test match or a wedding.

A survey by the European Tour Operators Association, investigating the appeal of Europe to tourists, found that the criteria that most influenced their decision to visit a destination were scenery, culture and history.

Activity: Where have you been?

Take some time to think about any destinations you have already visited in Europe. How easy was it to get there? How did you travel within the destinations? What was it you liked about the places? Was it the scenery or the culture and history? Perhaps it was the nightlife and beaches? How do different destinations appeal to you in different ways?

If you have not travelled in Europe yet, make a wish list of places you would like to visit and why.

3.2 Accessibility

Most tourists do not want to travel too far from their country of origin for trips, for reasons of time, cost and convenience. Of course, there are many people who do not choose to fly at all because they are concerned about the impact of emissions on their environment.

UK tourists most commonly take city breaks in Europe, as they can easily access the destination for a short weekend break and still have a full week's work. Tourists will also consider how much further they have to travel to the destination from the gateway airport or port.

Case study: Malta client match

Malta may struggle to shed its image as a package holiday destination for older clientele, but the island has a lot to offer a wide range of customers.

Dave Richardson of the *Trade Travel Gazette* looked at the options in 2006 and they are still valid today.

Families

Not all resorts in Malta have sandy beaches, but of those that do, the best can be found in the north-west.

Mellieha, Ramla Bay, Golden Bay and Ghajn Tuffieha are the most popular among families with young children, and there are a few hotels actually on the beach – Mellieha Bay (exclusive to Thomson) and Radisson SAS Golden Sands at Golden Bay, which opened last summer [2005]. Some 5-star hotels in St Julian's, such as the InterContinental, have their own small beaches.

Belleair Holidays agency sales manager Emma Yorke says: "St Julian's has great facilities, and the hotels are very affordable."

Families with older children tend to head for the neighbouring island of Gozo, which has a good choice of sandy and shingle beaches. Large families often rent one of the island's many converted farmhouses.

Couples

Almost any resort is suitable, and the compact size of Malta means that sightseeing around Valletta is accessible from anywhere.

Holly Gilbert, Thomson product manager for Malta, recommends Bugibba. "It is a developed resort that suits couples of all ages looking for a more lively atmosphere. There is lots on offer in terms of restaurants, bars and nightlife," she says.

Sunspot Tours managing director Martin Bugeja says a hotel favoured by couples is the Fortina in Sliema. "The spa packages there are very attractive. All our clients get deluxe rooms, so it has become a big seller," he explains.

Many couples join together to rent a Gozo farmhouse, as featured by Cosmos. Tracy Young, Cosmos Villas with Pools product manager says: "For 2006 we included a range of higher standard villas which our customers are clearly looking for. They see Gozo as a more specialist product for which they are prepared to upgrade."

Cadogan Holidays marketing manager Jennie Mugridge adds: "For city-lovers, Valletta is popular. The hotels are generally set in quieter areas but close to the city centre, making it easy to explore and then relax at the end of the day."

The tiny island of Comino also attracts couples who value seclusion and opportunities to dive and snorkel.

For the over-55s, spring and autumn are key times to visit Malta, but there is also a long-stay market in winter. They tend to avoid the busier resorts and peak summer, but do a lot of sightseeing.

"Sliema is particularly popular with this age group because it has a beautiful promenade and many opportunities for walking," says Belleair's Emma Yorke. "There is high repeat business and a lot going on, even in winter."

Party animals

Malta is rarely thought of as a party destination, but the neighbouring resorts of St Julian's and Paceville have developed lively nightlife in recent years without compromising the many luxury hotels nearby.

Sunspot's Martin Bugeja says: "Paceville has lots of bars and restaurants, and clubs stay open until four in the morning. Malta may still have a crusty image but this area is amazing, without being vulgar."

Belleair's Emma Yorke agrees that St Julian's is the big draw for clubbers, and says many of them can afford five-star hotels.

Activity lovers

Watersports in general, and diving in particular are popular on the islands, and due to their compact size most resorts make good bases.

Main dive sites include Marsamxett Harbour, where World War II wrecks HMS *Maori* and *Carolita Barge* lie and Dwejra, in Gozo, with the Inland Sea underwater tunnel and Blue Hole.

Thomson's Holly Gilbert says: "For summer 2007 we're looking to promote Gozo as a location for active holidays, due to the quality diving, cliff walks and unspoilt landscapes."

(Source: Trade Travel Gazette, 24 March 2006)

The article on Malta demonstrates how a destination can provide different holiday experiences for different types of people. Read it carefully and then write a similar article for a European destination of your choice.

- Choose four types of customers to consider when matching features of the destination to needs.
- You could include illustrations and make your article large enough to display alongside those of others in your group.

Did you know?

Skiers, in particular, have to consider access to the resort when deciding how to travel. Even if they fly to a gateway airport such as Geneva or Lyon, they will still be faced with a lengthy drive or rail journey into the mountains with all of their skiing equipment.

Transport routes

Without effective transport routes, tourists cannot reach their destinations. Indeed, the transport that is available is usually a factor in choosing a destination.

Figure 7.2 shows that the most popular mode of transport for UK outbound tourists is air, and in fact trips by air accounted for 81 per cent of trips in 2007. Only 12 per cent were by sea and 7 per cent by the Channel Tunnel.

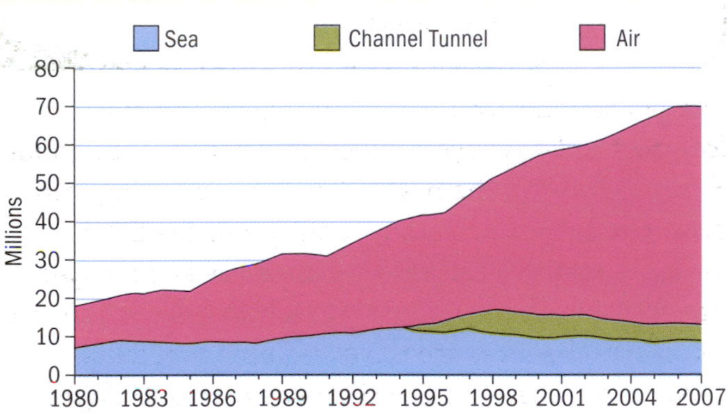

Figure 7.2: Visits by mode of transport

Road and rail

It is straightforward for tourists travelling between the UK and the rest of Europe to make their journey by road. The Channel ports, both sea and rail, give immediate access to motorway networks in France and the UK. From northern France there are excellent motorways connecting with the rest of Europe. These motorways are less congested than those in the UK, so make for less stressful driving. Major roads have been re-classified throughout Europe with 'E' numbers to clarify route planning for motorists.

Traditionally, campers heading for France and Spain travel by road and the ferry costs are included in their camping package. Camping operators provide information about driving abroad and route maps. However, with many low-cost flights available, campers are more often choosing to fly to their destinations. Common practice is for camping tour operators to provide fixed tents, or mobile homes, as camping equipment is too heavy for passengers to carry by air.

The main disadvantage of travelling by road is the length of the journeys, particularly in continental Europe where the speed of coaches is restricted. Eurolines is a well-known international scheduled service coach operator. A typical service is the trip from Birmingham to Paris at a cost of £49 (depending on how far in advance the booking is made). However, the journey takes 11 hours. A similar journey by Eurostar would take about 4 hours.

Eurostar trains from London St Pancras International offer passengers connecting tickets to over 100 other destinations in France, Germany and the Netherlands. This service makes travel by high-speed rail so much easier for UK-originating passengers, as they can book the whole trip through Eurostar and get all the information they need without contacting the rail networks in the countries they wish to travel to.

Some of the destinations served by Eurostar and connecting continental rail services are shown in Figure 7.3. For example:

- Disneyland, Paris – many families take Eurostar from London directly to Disneyland. They can walk to their Disney hotel from the station.
- Paris – you can arrive at the Gare de Nord from London in about the same time it would take to get to Manchester.
- Brussels – the capital of Belgium is said to have the best kitchen in Europe. This makes it a popular destination for lovers of gastronomy.

Figure 7.3: Map showing Eurostar destinations and connecting rail routes

Activity: Comparing journeys

When planning a journey to Paris the main considerations are cost, convenience and comfort.

How long do you think it would take to drive to Paris from the UK? The train through the Channel Tunnel takes less than half an hour, but you need to arrive half an hour before departure. From Calais to Paris it takes about 2½ hours and then you need to add on the time it takes to drive from where you live to Folkestone.

When you calculate costs remember to add petrol costs and motorway charges (in France) to the cost of crossing the Channel.

- Find out how much it would cost to go from where you live to Paris by coach.
- Draw up a chart comparing the coach journey with driving by car, in terms of cost, convenience and comfort.
- Say which one you would choose and why.

Air

As we have seen, air travel is the main form of long-distance travel and the most rapidly expanding transport sector. To cope with increased demand for air travel, many gateway airports have had to expand capacity. For London, Terminal 5 has now opened at Heathrow and Stansted has plans for a second runway. There are over 50 regional airports in the UK, but distances are not so great as to make air travel a preferred option within the UK.

Key terms

Scheduled flights – flights sold on a seat-only basis and run to a timetable, revised for winter and summer schedules.

Charter flights – flights that operate to holiday destinations and according to holiday demand. They do not operate every day to the same destination.

Low-cost airlines – these have developed into major competitors to traditional scheduled airlines in recent years. They offer very few services, such as catering or allocated seats, but do offer low fares. The low fares are not available at peak times or to late bookers.

There are two main categories of air travel: **scheduled** and **charter flights**. Tourists travelling on a package holiday are likely to be travelling on a charter plane, often owned by the tour operator they are travelling with. For example, Thomson is a tour operator and has a sister airline also under the Thomson brand. Charter airlines will sell seat-only deals to fill up their flights and achieve better load factors.

Activity: What's the best route?

The Kidman family is going to the Vendée region in France for a camping holiday. They live in London. They went last year and drove to their campsite, having crossed the Channel using the Shuttle. They are considering flying or rail this year and want to know which route is the best option for them. The family consists of the parents, a boy aged 10 and a girl aged 8. Cost is a consideration, but time and convenience are also important.

1. Draw up a table showing the different routes. (You may first need to locate the Vendée region.)
2. Describe the advantages and disadvantages of the different routes and draw some conclusions about how the features of the routes add to the appeal of the Vendée as a destination.

The airline industry is very competitive and many **low-cost airlines** have entered the market throughout Europe. Some of the new airlines are operating from eastern Europe as the recent entry into the EU of several eastern European countries has encouraged travel to and from this area. Passengers are not always aware whether they are travelling on a scheduled service, low-cost scheduled service or charter flight, as the distinctions between the different airlines have become less obvious.

Sea

Ferry services across the English Channel are surviving despite the building of the Channel Tunnel. P&O operates a service from Dover to Calais, as does Sea France, the only French operator. The journey takes about an hour and a quarter by ship, but the loading and unloading of cars adds another hour. However, some people enjoy the crossing and do not mind the extra time.

The UK is linked by ferry from various ports, not just to France, but to its neighbours in Ireland, Belgium, the Netherlands, Scandinavia and Spain (see Unit 1).

Because of competition from air travel and the Channel Tunnel, operators such as P&O offer many products and services to encourage people to travel by sea. P&O offers shopping, entertainment and city cruises, including two-night cruises from Hull to the Netherlands or Belgium.

Access is not just about transport links. Politics and economics also affect access. Before the fall of the Berlin Wall in 1989 and the liberation of borders, eastern Europeans were not free to travel to their relatives and friends in the west, and vice versa. Even when they received their political freedom with the dissolution of the Soviet Union, the people of Eastern Europe could scarcely afford to travel. This situation has improved dramatically, but it was western Europeans who benefited from visiting new destinations they could easily afford. Prague is a good example, now in the top ten of city breaks from the UK.

Most eastern European countries came late to tourism, so their potential for development is great. There are some airlines operating between the UK and new member states. Some countries, like the Czech Republic, already have a well-developed tourist industry, but there is potential for development outside Prague. Others are just beginning to develop tourism. Air services between Eastern Europe and the UK are provided by some airlines, for example, easyJet, Ryanair and Wizzair.

Activity: Eastern Europe

Choose one of the Eastern European countries that entered the EU since 2004 and whose popularity is increasing with tourists. Find out what is currently provided for tourists in that country, or in one destination within it. Look at transport both to the destination and within it.

1 Describe the accommodation, facilities, attractions and information and identify gaps in provision for tourists.
2 Explain how the different features and factors, described above, influence the appeal of your chosen country for a group of 30 older people (65+) and for a hen party.
3 Make recommendations about how the destination could increase its appeal for older people and for hen parties.

3.3 Climate and weather

Tourists from northern European countries, such as the UK and Germany, tend to travel south for a better climate. There is no need to travel long-haul for the sun in summer.

Poor summer weather in a destination will influence sales for the next season. For example, Brittany in France offers lush countryside and gorgeous beaches. However, it often rains and a rainy summer deters visitors for the next season. Likewise a hot British summer encourages people to stay at home and take domestic holidays the following summer. Similarly, a poor British summer will result in an increase in bookings for holidays abroad the following year.

Ski holidays are dependent on snow and if there are poor snow conditions bookings are seriously affected. In summer months the same mountain areas attract walkers, as the weather is mild and often sunny.

Winter sun holidays are of necessity further afield. Popular destinations in Europe for the winter sun are the Canary Islands which, although Spanish, are located near the coast of Africa.

3.4 Attractions

Natural attractions

The natural attractions of a region can add to its appeal, especially where the geography lends itself to particular activities such as walking, mountaineering or fishing.

Beaches

Beach areas have great appeal to families. The traditional family fortnight by the sea changed in the 1970s from British to Spanish and other Mediterranean resorts. As well as its obvious attractions of sand and swimming, the sea can also provide a variety of tourist activities such as water-skiing, surfing, deep-sea fishing or whale watching.

Popular beach areas include the Italian Adriatic resorts of Rimini, Sirmione and Cavtat. Historical remains, castles and luxury hotels are added attractions.

Turkey has the Mediterranean and Aegean seas to the south and west and the Black Sea to the north. The Aegean coast (also known as the Turquoise coast because of its blue waters) has a number of popular beach resorts.

The Bulgarian part of the Black Sea coast goes from Cape Kartel on the Romanian border to the Turkish border. It includes Golden Sands, a famous Bulgarian beach resort, and Varna, a lively resort with nightlife and casinos.

Spain's resorts, such as those along the Costa Blanca, have attracted package holidaymakers for many years, but that is changing. Tourists are now heading for cities like Barcelona, which offers a variety of activities.

Case study: Effects of weather on bookings

This extract from the Travelmole website shows how weather, as well as cost, affected holiday bookings in 2008.

Rain and cash caution prompt last-minute bookings

Inclement weather and budgetary awareness are driving Brits to book holidays at the eleventh hour, according to online travel agent Lastminute.com.

The website says the rise in costs and the credit crunch has prompted Brits to wait and see if they could really afford a holiday. But now the classic British summer has shown its colours they are booking in droves.

The website reports an increase in its week-on-week trading with traffic of unique visitors searching holidays up 23 per cent over the last week, as the weather declined. It says that European destinations are suffering as Brits look to make their pound stretch further and avoid the costly euro with Turkey and Egypt performing particularly well – both up 14 per cent year-on-year. Bookings to Tunisia are up 95 per cent and Croatia an impressive 150 per cent.

Those looking to stay in the UK on holiday are showing signs of taking a couple of shorter breaks rather than one two-week long holiday. Lastminute says coastal areas are doing a roaring trade, with bookings to Brighton hotels up 70 per cent year-on-year, Bournemouth 20 per cent and Eastbourne 66 per cent. It also reports stronger sales for UK theme parks, attractions, theatre and concert tickets. Breaks including these have gone up 18 per cent year-on-year.

(Source: www.travelmole.com)

1. Explain why people from the UK have been making holiday bookings at the last minute.
2. Why are people from the UK avoiding the Eurozone?
3. What are the reasons for stronger sales for UK theme parks and attractions?
4. What factors would increase travel to Europe again?

There are two groups of Spanish islands: the Balearics, to the east of the mainland in the Mediterranean and the Canaries, off the coast of Africa in the Atlantic.

The Balearics consist of Majorca, Minorca, Ibiza and Formentera. All are suitable for family holidays, but Majorca (Magaluf) and Ibiza (San Antonio and beyond) have also built up reputations as clubbing destinations for young people.

Tourism in the Canaries is concentrated on the four largest islands: Tenerife, Gran Canaria, Lanzarote and Fuerteventura. These mainly volcanic islands are dry with sparse vegetation. Fuerteventura has wide, sandy beaches, but those on Tenerife are less appealing, consisting of black volcanic sand.

Mountains

Ski resorts are obvious examples of destinations in mountainous areas. France is the UK's favourite ski destination with the highest number of visitors to resorts, including Courchevel, Meribel and Belle Plagne. St Moritz is popular in Switzerland. Andorra, sandwiched between France and Spain is a principality with ski resorts.

Mountains are suitable for adventure sports, such as climbing and abseiling, and for other less extreme activities, such as hiking and rambling.

What activities can be undertaken on mountains in places such as Courchavel in the French alps, in Europe?

Case study: The appeal of Spain

There are both scheduled and chartered flights to Spain from all major airports in the UK and from the rest of Western Europe. From the UK there are also ferry services to Bilbao and Santander. The ferry services are useful if travellers are happy with a fairly long sea journey and then a drive to their final destination. There are also good ferry links from Barcelona to the Balearics. Tourists, or immigrants, from Africa travelling to either Spain or France enter Spain via southern Spanish ports like Algeciras.

Many UK visitors drive through France to reach Spain. Most visitors to the Canaries arrive by air, because of the location of the islands.

On the Spanish mainland transport is easy, with good rail and bus links and easily accessible car hire. Spain is also reasonably cheap compared with many other destinations, which contributes to its accessibility.

In Spain, the culture varies enormously from one area or resort to another. In the cities the visitor is more likely to experience authentic Spanish culture with opportunities to see opera, dancing and arts events and try Spanish dishes and tapas. Around Easter there are many religious festivals in all areas.

On the Costa del Sol, in most of the Balearics and the Canaries, the lifestyle is similar to that in the UK and English is widely spoken. In some purpose-built resorts in the Canaries there are no local people. Those that are Spanish have come from other regions of Spain to find work in the tourist industry.

The sun, rather than wanderlust, is the main reason for travelling to Spain, with decades of development having taken place to cater for western European sun-worshippers. Those looking for unspoilt Spain will head away from the costas and islands to the interior or northern coastal areas. Those motivated by the love of culture will travel to the cities of Barcelona to view the architecture of Gaudí or Seville to experience the Easter festivities and religious parades.

Spain has a beautiful coastline (stretching for 4964 kilometres) and mountainous areas such as the Pyrenees and the Sierra Nevada where skiing is popular. The climate is generally mild, with up to 10 hours of sun in the summer and with the highest temperatures in the south.

The Canaries enjoy a temperate climate all year round which attracts those looking for the winter sun.

Each area of Spain has its particular attractions, for example Granada is famous for its beautiful setting and historical palaces and buildings. There are also plenty of attractions offering entertainment for families, such as waterparks and the famous theme park, Portaventura, situated on the east coast near to Barcelona.

1 Mark the following 'costas' on a map of Spain. Identify the gateway airports serving these areas. Find out which are the major resorts in the areas and locate and name them on the map. You can download a map from www.geoexplorer.com or you can use a map from an atlas.
   - Costa Calida
   - Costa del Sol
   - Costa de la Luz
   - Costa Verde
   - Costa Blanca
   - Costa Cantábrica
   - Costa de Almería
   - Costa Dorada
   - Costa Brava

2 Answer the following quiz questions on Spain.
   - **a** In which city is the Prado museum?
   - **b** Which city is famous for Gaudí's architecture?
   - **c** Name the islands that make up the Balearic Islands.
   - **d** Name the islands that make up the Canary Islands.
   - **e** In which city is the Alhambra Palace?
   - **f** Which city hosted the 1992 Olympic Games?
   - **g** Which football team signed David Beckham in 2003?
   - **h** Which country, also famous for tourism, borders Spain to the west?
   - **i** Gibraltar is a territory of which country?
   - **j** What is the native language of Barcelona?

Activity: Mountain ranges

1. Find examples of mountain ranges and ski resorts in Italy, Austria and Scandinavia. For each, locate the area on a map and name the main resorts.
2. Choose one area from each country. Use brochures to compare the ski facilities and costs across the three areas.
3. Recommend a ski resort for a family of four with one grandparent accompanying them, going on their first ever ski holiday.

Inland waterways

Amsterdam and Venice are both famous for their waterways, yet their appeal as city break destinations are quite different. Think of Venice and you think of romance and beautiful palazzos overlooking the Grand Canal and water taxis bustling up and down while gondolas float along at a more leisurely pace. In Amsterdam, the city is vibrant with young people sitting in coffee shops, bars or clubs. There are famous museums alongside designer fashion streets.

For those who like leisurely boating trips, inland waterways like those of the Canal du Midi in France and the waterways of the Netherlands provide a relaxing holiday. River cruises are available along the Rhine and the Danube.

Activity: Weekend break

Draw up detailed profiles of typical weekend break visitors to Venice and Amsterdam. Include, for example, their age ranges, interests and motivations for choosing these destinations.

Case study: Example of a Danube River Cruise

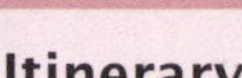

Itinerary

DAY 1	Depart from London Heathrow to Munich and transfer to your ship in Passau for late afternoon embarkation. Sail at 18:00.	DAY 5	Arrive Bratislava, the dynamic capital of Slovakia, at 13:00. There will be an optional city tour. Depart 23:00.
DAY 2	Arrive Melk 08:00. Melk is set amidst Austria's wine growing region. There is an optional visit to Melk Abbey before the ship sails at 12:00.	DAY 6	Arrive Vienna 07:00. Discover this famous city on today's optional sightseeing tour. The ship departs Vienna at midnight.
DAY 3	Arrive Esztergom 07:00. Enjoy an optional excursion to Esztergom and the Danube bend before the ship sails at 12:30. Arrive Budapest 17:00h.	DAY 7	Arrive Durnstein 08:00. There will be an optional walking tour before the ship sails at 12:30.
DAY 4	Discover Budapest at your leisure or join the optional city tour today viewing the highlights of Hungary's capital including the Fishermen's Bastion. The ship sails at 20:00.	DAY 8	Arrive Passau 08:00. Disembark after breakfast and transfer to Munich Airport for the flight to London Heathrow.

(Source: www.cruisingholidays.co.uk)

1. List all the towns visited on the cruise in a table. For each, state which country it is in and what its attractions are.
2. Locate all the towns on a map.
3. Find a similar cruise on the Rhine and repeat the exercise.

Lakes

Italy is famous for its beautiful lakes including Como, Garda and Maggiore. Visitors to Lake Garda can go on walking tours of the area and take boat trips on the lake. The historic city of Verona is nearby where visitors can attend the opera.

In Switzerland the resort of Interlaken allows access to Lakes Thun and Brienz. Bonigen on Lake Brienz is a quiet resort with lakeside walks and pretty chalets.

There are many beautiful countryside areas in eastern Europe with lakes to discover. In Slovenia, Lake Bled is set against a mountain backdrop thick with forests. In Hungary, Lake Balaton is famous for its beauty.

...se study: Lofoten Islands

These islands are located north of the Arctic Circle and are difficult to access. One way of visiting them is to travel first to Norway and then take a 25-minute bumpy flight from the mainland to the town of Svolvaer.

Adventure sports on the islands include snow-shoeing, skiing and whale watching, but in the winter it is dark most of the day so you have to make the most of the few hours of daylight. In the summer, you can try kayaking, boating and fishing in the fjords and at this time of year, there is almost constant light.

1. Locate the Lofoten Islands on a map.
2. Find out how you would get to the Lofoten Islands from the UK and find prices.
3. Find an example of a tour operator offering trips to these islands.
4. Try to find a local website about Lofoten and note what information it offers.
5. What type of tourist would be interested in visiting the Islands?
6. Find out about tourism in Norway. What resorts are popular and why?
7. How dependent is Norway on tourism? What other industries help the economy?
8. What is the Norwegian currency and how do costs relate to those in the UK?
9. Produce a fact sheet with your findings.

The town of Balatonfured is on the north shore and offers health and spa facilities.

Built attractions

Built attractions are developed with the intention of appealing to tourists. They include theme parks, museums, galleries, clubs and theatres. There are several theme parks in Europe, but the most famous is Disneyland, Paris, opened in 1992. Theme parks in the UK mostly appeal to the teenage market, but Disneyland has been targeted to appeal to families. There are fewer thrill-seeking rides and more for the whole family to enjoy together. The Disney theme is followed through into the site's hotels, shops and entertainment.

Museums and galleries in cities are important attractions to visitors. Popular and famous museums include the Uffizi in Florence with paintings by Botticelli, Da Vinci and Michelangelo, the Louvre in Paris where visitors can see the *Mona Lisa* and the Prado in Madrid.

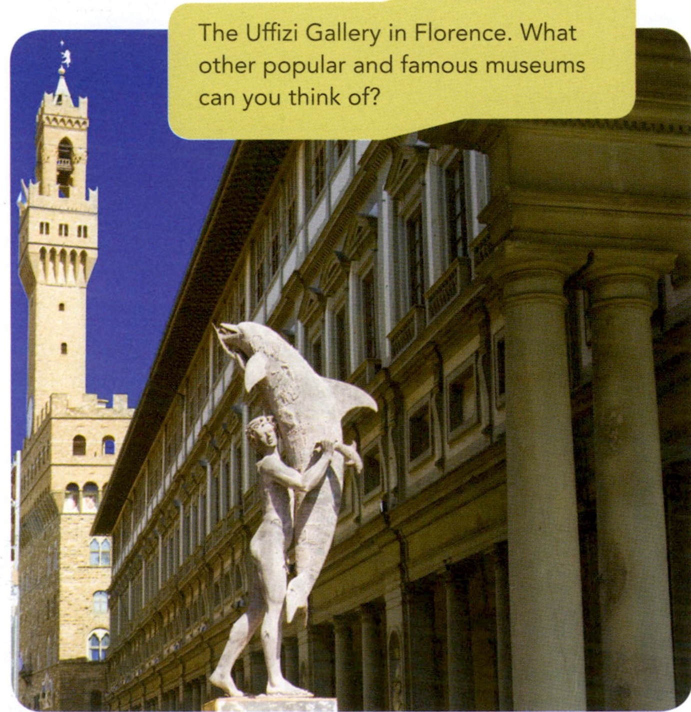

The Uffizi Gallery in Florence. What other popular and famous museums can you think of?

Historic buildings

It is well known that Americans love to see the historic buildings of Europe and although the UK has its share of history, tourists from the UK also find the historic buildings of Europe appealing. Some are well known, like the Eiffel Tower, the Louvre, the Sacré Coeur and the Notre Dame in Paris. In Granada, the Palace of the Alhambra attracts queues of tourists, and Barcelona is famous for its two cathedrals, the Sagrada Família designed by Gaudí and the much older (Gothic) and traditional Santa Eulalia.

Rome is famous for its monuments and visitors flock to St Peter's Basilica, the largest church in the world. Also of interest in Rome are the Sistine chapel, with its famous ceiling painted by Michelangelo, and the Coliseum. There are many examples of historic sites in Italy: Venice built on a series of canals, Florence with its magnificent cathedral and Uffizi museum and, most exciting, the site of Pompeii where visitors can see the remains of the Roman town buried by the lava from the volcano, Vesuvius.

Across Greece and her islands, tourists can hardly avoid seeing historic sites as there are so many, ranging from the Acropolis in Athens which is 2500 years old to temples and the Site of Delphi. In the 6th century BC, Delphi was the centre of Greek religious life and where the oracle of Apollo spoke.

The cities of eastern Europe also have many historic buildings and these are being restored as economies develop and funds permit. In fact, there are several UNESCO World Heritage sites in Eastern Europe, including the museum city of Gjirokastra in Albania with a citadel dating from the 13th century.

Nightlife and entertainment

Many people enjoy some form of nightlife on holiday. It may be music and dancing, a show, a club or a casino. Many cities and resorts appeal to young people on holiday because of the nightlife they offer. Ibiza, Magaluf and Barcelona are examples of Spanish destinations where clubbing is a prime feature. Berlin has a 24-hour clubbing culture which some tourists like.

Casinos are a form of entertainment directed at older groups. On the French Riviera coast there are at least ten casinos. Bulgaria also has casinos.

Fashion and shopping

Some city destinations appeal because of their wonderful shopping opportunities. However, they are usually at the high end of the market and therefore appeal to those with plenty of money. Examples include the designer stores in Milan and Paris. Towns on the Riviera in Monaco and in France, such as Monte Carlo, Cannes and Nice, also have their share of designer shops.

Activity: Museums

Identify at least five museums in Paris. Find out where they are located, whether they are free or charge an entrance fee and what their attraction is to visitors.

Display your information in a table like this:

Name	Location	Free or paying?	Attraction

3.5 Culture

Experiencing local culture is about trying the local food and drink, and being observant about local traditions and codes of behaviour.

It is understood that not all hotels offer a full English breakfast or tea with milk, and that shops may close from lunchtime until 4 p.m. Some tourists love to experience a different culture and lifestyle when on holiday. Some do not! Some hope to find bars and restaurants serving the same food as they get at home and access to their usual daily newspapers. Certain resorts in Spain, for example Torremolinos and Benidorm, cater so well for British, German and Dutch tourists that the Spanish culture is hidden. In contrast, Barcelona is a typically Spanish city, with authentic restaurants and Spanish culture in evidence.

Sometimes tourists need to be made more aware of what to expect from the host country and its culture, so that their behaviour and dress are respectful and do not offend. For example, in many countries, like Turkey, it is acceptable to wear very little on the beach and yet when people leave the beach they must cover up in respect for local custom.

Signature food and drink

Trying traditional food and drink is fun for tourists; at restaurants, local wine will be recommended by waiters and local dishes should be on offer. These vary from region to region, but there are also some national dishes. For example, in France tourists love to try all the cheeses and wines. Pastis, an aniseed-flavoured drink, is often served as an aperitif. In Greece, a similar tasting drink to pastis is ouzo and moussaka is a national dish.

Think about it

- Think of somewhere you have been where you felt you were in a different culture from your own. In what ways did it feel different?
- What would you serve visitors to your region as signature food and drink?

Cultural events

Cultural and sporting events attract tourists, for example the Oberammagau Passion Play in Bavaria, Germany in 2010. Dating back to 1634, these plays are performed just one year in every decade and draw visitors in huge numbers from around the world.

One of the most bizarre and dangerous cultural events occurs annually in Pamplona, Spain. San Fermin, the patron saint of Pamplona, was martyred in Roman times by being dragged through the streets by bulls. This grisly event is commemorated every year with a week-long festival. Each morning some brave, but somewhat foolish, people run for their lives through the streets of Pamplona as bulls are released to chase them.

Case study: Appeal of a European Capital of Culture

Lille is an example of a city destination which is fast rising in popularity. It is situated in northern France near the Belgian border. Two major factors, access and culture, explain its appeal.

For UK tourists, access to Lille is excellent by Eurostar. There are at least 10 trains a day from London St Pancras International and the journey is 1 hour 20 minutes. This is less time than some people spend commuting within the UK! There are also buses from London Victoria, operated by Eurolines. Although not so rapid as the train, this is an inexpensive way to travel.

Lille airport is 10 kilometres from the town, but it is not possible to fly direct to Lille from the UK. To fly to Lille you would need to fly via another hub in France. There are, however, air links from Lille to other French airports and European cities such as Barcelona.

Lille was named European Capital of Culture for 2004. Different cities are nominated every year – Essen in Germany and Istanbul in Turkey were chosen for 2010. The European Commission provides funding to:

- promote diverse cultural activities to a range of people
- increase social cohesion
- create a sustainable cultural heritage.

Lille had over 2000 different exhibitions and performances during 2004, attracting many new tourists. Once in the city, tourists found many other features of Lille to enjoy. There is a medieval town centre, Vieux Lille, with cobbled streets and individual shops. The architecture is interesting, with Gothic churches, and there are good restaurants and bars.

1. Choose one of the current European Capitals of Culture. Describe the following factors and how they contribute to the city's appeal:
   - location of the city
   - access for UK tourists
   - special activities planned for the year
   - other tourist attractions in the city.
2. a. Choose two different types of visitor, for example a family with two teenagers and a group of 18-year-olds. Say what kind of leisure experiences they might find in Lille that would appeal to them.

   b. Compare your findings with a new Capital of Culture in a different European country, using the same customer types. Consider the lifestyle differences between the capital and the UK.

3.6 Economic factors

The cost of a holiday is important to its appeal. This does not necessarily mean that the cheapest holiday is the most appealing. Tourists need to know what quality they are receiving for their money and what is included. An **all-inclusive package holiday** with **full board** might appear more expensive to start with, but once meals and drinks outside of those included in **half board** or **bed and breakfast** have been considered, the all-inclusive price might in the end be better value.

Key terms

Package holidays – holidays that include transport, transfer and accommodation with the following variations:

- **all-inclusive** – also includes all food and local drinks, and sports activities apart from motorised sports
- **full board** – includes breakfast, lunch and dinner
- **half board** – includes breakfast and lunch or dinner
- **bed and breakfast** – includes breakfast

Availability of low-cost travel

Cheap flights are available for those tourists who book their holidays a long time ahead and take advantage of special offers. Booking at the last minute with low-cost carriers is usually expensive, particularly in peak season.

However, the growth of low-cost carriers has opened up routes to several destinations that were previously only served by expensive scheduled flights. For example, Ryanair offers flights to the Italian islands of Sardinia and Sicily: a few years ago these 'chic' islands were difficult to access cheaply. Now there are daily, low-cost flights from London and twice-weekly ones from Liverpool.

Impact of rate of exchange

Tourists have to consider the price of visiting local attractions, entertainment, car hire and eating out when choosing a destination. Tour operators often provide useful comparisons with the UK to help them. However, these comparisons are made at a particular rate of exchange so that the cost to a UK tourist changes as the rate of exchange goes up or down. In 2009 the value of the British pound fell against the euro. The result was that people travelling to Europe from the UK found that things, such as eating out and shopping, were much more expensive.

Perceived value for money

Some destinations such as those developing in Eastern Europe are relatively cheap. Black Sea coastal resorts are good examples. Some city destinations in Eastern Europe are also growing in popularity, as they are 'new' destinations for the UK market and cheap to get to and to stay in. Tourists may think that these destinations represent good value for money, but may find that this is only a perception and the reality is that high standards of accommodation and food and drink are as expensive as they are in Western Europe.

Assessment activity 7.3

BTEC

1 Research the appeal of two leisure destinations in Europe. You could research:
- beach resorts
- countryside areas
- winter sports resorts
- cities

Ensure that you choose different types of destination and in different countries.

2 Create a display about your two destinations with posters and notes or even a film or presentation. Illustrate the factors and features that determine the appeal of your chosen leisure destinations for different types of visitors. These should have information and explanatory notes on:
- accessibility
- cultural factors
- climate
- economic factors **P3**
- attractions

3 Prepare to give a presentation to your class, giving an explanation of how factors and features in each of your two chosen destinations influence the appeal to two different types of UK customers. **M2**

4 Choose one of the destinations. Recommend how the destination could increase its appeal for different types of UK visitor. **D1**

Grading tips

P3 You need to **describe** factors and features that determine the appeal of your chosen leisure destinations for different types of visitor.

M2 You need to **explain** how factors and features that determine the appeal of your chosen leisure destinations for different types of UK visitor.

D1 You need to give detailed and realistic recommendations for how one of your chosen destinations could increase its appeal for different types of UK visitor.

PLTS

Trying out alternatives of destinations and following ideas through will develop your skills as a **creative thinker**.

Functional skills

Selecting and using appropriate sources of ICT-based and other forms of information to find holidays will develop **ICT** skills – find and select information.

4 How factors affect the development and decline of the European travel market

Having looked at the appeal of destinations for tourists and at tourist motivation, it should be obvious that destinations have to change over time to accommodate the changing motivation and needs of tourists.

Developments in transport and access open up new areas of the world which allow them to be developed for tourism. Governments and representatives from interested private sector companies have to work together to plan and develop areas, so that tourism is sustainable and that it evolves without detriment to the interests of local people.

4.1 Factors

Growth of leisure travel

Short breaks

The short breaks leisure market continues to grow. There are several reasons for this:

- availability of low-cost flights
- increased disposable income
- more choice of destinations
- trend to independent travel and booking
- desire to try new activities.

According to Mintel, over 7.5 million short breaks abroad were taken in 2007. The market for short breaks is worth over £2 billion and evidences a trend for a lifestyle with regular holidays for those who can afford it.

The survey showed that the most popular destinations for short breaks were:

- France (e.g. Paris, Bordeaux)
- Spain (e.g. Madrid, Barcelona, Andalucia)
- Italy (e.g. Rome, Venice, Florence)
- Netherlands (e.g. Amsterdam)
- Republic of Ireland (e.g. Dublin)

Those who go on short breaks tend to be people with a high disposable income, a flexible lifestyle and free from domestic responsibility.

Activity holidays

These are a growing market sector as tourists look for holidays where they can indulge in a hobby or learn a new skill. The range is varied, with holidays available to learn languages, to paint, to cook or to learn how to dance.

Most activity holidays are provided by small companies who specialise in particular activities, especially in the UK market. However, many large tour operators have acquired specialist tour operators in order to gain representation in a growing market for activity holidays, particularly overseas holidays.

New products and services

Low-cost airlines

The UK has the largest number of low-cost airlines in Europe and this means that the market opportunities for European travel by UK outbound tourists will continue to be extensive. The increase is particularly marked in the short-breaks market.

New destinations

The development of new destinations in Europe is linked to the provision of low-cost flights. In 2006, direct scheduled flights started up to Bulgaria's Black Sea Coast and Croatia is becoming very popular. Economic factors are also an influence as some of these eastern European countries are much cheaper than the UK. Ryanair and Easyjet offer many flights to eastern European destinations.

Dubrovnik in Croatia. What factors determine the choice of destination for tourists?

Political factors

Accession into the EU of ten new member states in 2004 and two in 2007 meant that travel between these countries was no longer subject to restriction. (Refer to Table 7.1 page 184 to remind yourself who they were.)

In order to attract tourists, individual state governments must invest in the infrastructure, buildings and facilities to develop tourism. They can fund such developments through taxation or by applying for EU funds.

In addition the country needs to adopt legislation and set up a public sector structure to support the development of tourism. Such a structure is very well developed in the UK and you should be familiar with it from Unit 1.

Marketing is also a factor and the developing country will need representation at events such as the World Travel Market in London.

Economic factors

Even in recession, the UK economy is one of the strongest in Europe. The introduction of the euro has had a great impact on tourism within Eurozone countries, as tourists are able to travel without changing currency and can expect less variation in prices as they travel. Even for UK outbound tourists there are advantages: although you have to change pounds into euros, you do not need a whole collection of currencies if you intend to travel throughout Europe.

We have high expectations in terms of travel and tourism and buying a holiday is an important item of expenditure. Most people have travelled abroad, in contrast with previous generations.

Holiday homes

As more people can afford a second home, many choose to buy in Europe. There are many British people with holiday homes in Spain and France and now Croatia has a growing property market. Homeowners need different products from holidaymakers: they do not use hotels, but they do need regular flights and car hire facilities.

4.2 Development and decline

Study of the destination life cycle, developed by R.W. Butler in 1980, helps us to understand how tourist areas develop and evolve. It cannot be applied strictly to all destinations, but is a useful planning guide and shows how destinations can be viewed as resources which have a finite life.

Some communities become dependent on tourism and so if a destination goes into decline their livelihood is put at risk, as are the resources and infrastructure invested in tourism.

Butler identified seven stages of the destination life cycle:

- Stage 1 Exploration
- Stage 2 Involvement
- Stage 3 Development
- Stage 4 Consolidation
- Stage 5 Stagnation
- Stage 6 Decline
- Stage 7 Rejuvenation

Figure 7.4 depicts the destination life cycle. A–E are possible outcomes, from A rejuvenation to E decline. You will note the resemblance to the product life cycle (see Unit 5).

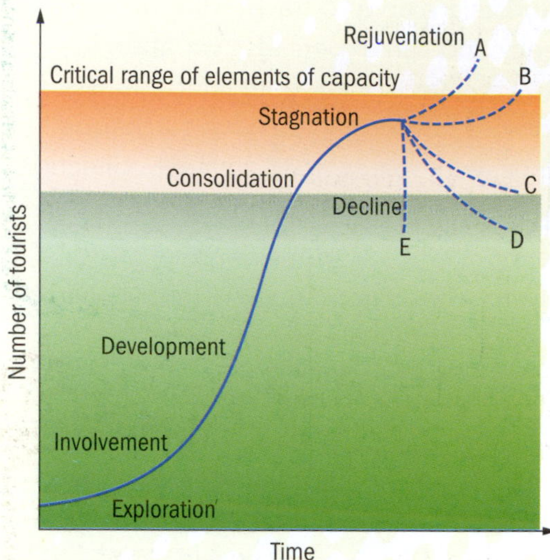

Figure 7.4: The destination life cycle

(Source: R.W. Butler, 'The concept of a tourist area', Canadian Geographer, vol. 24, no. 1 (1980), pp. 5–12)

Stage 1 Exploration

At this stage there are few tourists. Awareness of the destination is very limited. In fact, the few tourists are more likely to be termed 'travellers', as they are the type of people who are looking for adventure and new experiences. They will have found their own independent transport to the destination, as the area will have poor access. There are few facilities and a basic infrastructure. Nothing has been put in place for tourism and as there are so few tourists their impact is negligible. The local culture remains intact and the natural attractions undisturbed, adding to the attraction for the independent traveller.

Think about it

A destination with tourism potential will be located at the start of the destination life cycle in 'exploration' or 'involvement'.

Stage 2 Involvement

The destination begins to develop, travel companies start to organise transport links and there is an increase in tourist numbers. Local people may start to take advantage of the new opportunities opening up to them and build facilities, such as restaurants, and offer accommodation in their homes. The public sector starts to investigate how tourism can be developed and to invest in facilities and infrastructure. There may be some advertising of the destination.

Stage 3 Development

The early 'explorers' will no longer visit this destination. Instead the tourists become more institutionalised and are likely to arrive on organised tours. There is a rapid growth in the number of tourists. The local people start to lose control of development as private companies move in and take control. There will be marked changes in the infrastructure and in the appearance of the destination. There may be massive building projects for accommodation and also of attractions. The public sector's role is very important at this stage if the resident population's interests are to be protected and if tourism is to be sustainable. A tourist season will have emerged and there is heavy advertising to market the destination.

Stage 4 Consolidation

Tourist numbers are still growing, but not so rapidly. The host population has become resentful of the tourists rather than expressing an interest in the visitors. There is extensive marketing to try to extend the season and attract yet more visitors.

Stage 5 Stagnation

This is the stage of mass tourism. Peak numbers have been reached and the types of tourists are those who are looking for much the same experience as at home, possibly with a better climate. The natural environment may have been spoilt or hidden by the man-made attractions and infrastructure in place. The problems and negative impacts of tourism are most evident. The destination is over-commercialised and overcrowded.

Stage 6 Decline

Some of the tourist facilities are closed, or fall into disrepair, as tourist numbers decline and the tourists go elsewhere. The destination may lose tourism altogether.

Stage 7 Rejuvenation

If action is taken, destination managers can avoid the decline and the resort can be rejuvenated. This involves sometimes drastic action and requires redevelopment and the injection of capital.

Think about it

What are the signs of decline?

- physical deterioration of facilities
- shorter average stay
- fewer tourist numbers
- poorer quality of tourist
- poorer quality of tourist product
- fewer overnight stays
- poor infrastructure

Case study: Destination life cycle – Faliraki Greece

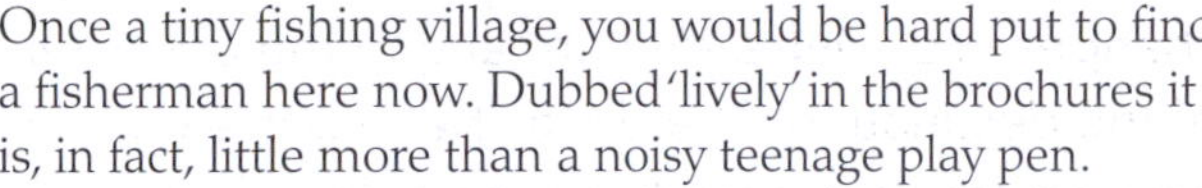

Once a tiny fishing village, you would be hard put to find a fisherman here now. Dubbed 'lively' in the brochures it is, in fact, little more than a noisy teenage play pen.

Jet skiing, go-karting, even bungy jumping, are on offer to the daily influx of frolicky young visitors, whose idea of fun appears to be getting drunk on fizzy beer and making as much noise as they possibly can. And noise there is, brain-addling at night as the bars and clubs wind up to full power. The din is in evidence several kilometres away.

Drinks cost up to six times supermarket prices and street touts for the clubs and bars can be persistent and aggressive. Beaches are a grey, gritty sand and packed with holidaymakers from dawn to well after dusk. Food here is as plastic as you would expect and the only good meal to be had is snapped up by millions of mosquitoes homing in from the nearby lowland to gorge on the bare teenage flesh.

Perversely, recent hotel complexes have adopted a Cycladic village theme for those wishing to enjoy the 'Greek experience'. If you have a two-watt bulb for a brain and an ever-open wallet you will feel very much at home with the majority of visitors in this Greek version of the Spanish costas.

(Source: www.greekisland.co.uk)

1. At what stage of the destination life cycle is Faliraki?
2. What factors contributed to the development of Faliraki as a tourist destination?
3. In your opinion does it have any future tourism potential? Consider what measures can be taken to attract tourists to Faliraki. Make some notes and discuss your ideas with your group.

Assessment activity 7.4

Choose one developing and one declining destination in the European travel market and write an article about each.

1 In your article you should review:
- the features of development or decline (for example, tourist arrival numbers are going up or down)
- why it is developing or declining (for example, money has been spent on refurbishment or there have been terrorist attacks)
- its position in Butler's cycle. P4

2 Analyse the reasons for the development or decline of your destinations. For example, a low-cost airline may have started a route to the destination, so this will mean increased numbers of tourists. M3

3 Justify how current factors could impact on the European travel market in the near future. For example, further terrorist activity in Egypt will deter tourists from visiting tourist resorts. D2

Grading tips

P4 You need to **review** factors that have contributed to one declining and one developing destination in the European travel market.

M3 You need to **analyse** reasons for the development and decline of your selected destinations in the European Travel Market.

D2 You need to **justify** how current factors could impact on the the European travel marketr in the near future.

PLTS

Planning and carrying out your research on developing and declining destinations will develop your skills as an **independent enquirer**.

Functional skills

Working on the style of an article will develop your **English** writing skills.

WorkSpace

Nick Spartacus

Public relations worker in Ibiza

Nick is a graduate from a BTEC National Travel and Tourism programme and has found seasonal work on the Spanish island of Ibiza – a major dance music and clubbing destination. He is working in public relations (PR) for a nightclub.

Nick lives on the island for the entire summer season and his role is to meet with tourists and promote the nightclub he works for and to ensure the club is busy and successful.

What are the main elements to a working week for you?

We have three main nights at the club that I have to promote: Tuesdays, Thursdays and our main night, Saturdays.

In a typical week, I go around the busy areas of town wearing promotional t-shirts and talk to holiday makers telling them about the club and thereby creating interest and awareness. There is a lot of communication with the public so I have to be very friendly and chatty, but I rarely find this difficult as everyone is on holiday and in high spirits.

On the day of the events it is my job to sell the tickets. I walk along the promenade and beaches and, in a friendly manner, ask people their plans for the evening before explaining the offers I have for our nightclub. On the evening of the club nights, I take part in a promotional parade with other members of the PR team and professional dancers. I enjoy the parade the most because everyone is having fun and we get lots attention, which creates a great image for the club.

So what are your plans after this season?

Through the work I have been doing I have made a lot of contacts, which will mean I am guaranteed the same sort of job next year and even a good possibility of gaining a managerial role. I have also managed to make contacts, which have offered me winter work for nightclubs back in the UK or in other winter tourism destinations.

Think about it!

1. How would you find a job abroad?
2. What preparations would you need to make before you went?
3. What particular problems might be associated with working away from home?

Just checking

1 Name the countries which joined the EU in 2004 and 2007.
2 What is the Schengen agreement?
3 What is Eurostar?
4 What is the appeal of road travel?
5 What is the appeal of air travel?
6 What is the common feature of Venice and Amsterdam?
7 Where are the Loften Islands located?
8 Which Spanish resorts offer nightlife to young people?
9 What are the stages of the destination life cycle?
10 Define disposable income.

Assignment tips

Collect as many resources as you can and share them as a group. Ask your tutor for a storage place.

- Practise locating countries and destinations many times before your assessment.
- Put maps on the walls to remind you of locations of countries and destinations.
- Be really neat when you complete maps.
- Look at lots of holiday brochures and try to work out what motivations they are appealing to.
- Keep on top of what's going on in the sector by reading travel trade journals and the national press. This will help you know which destinations are developing or declining.
- Use statistics from the WTO (www.world-tourism.org) to find out which European destinations are developing or declining.

Credit value: 10

8 Long-haul travel destinations

The popularity of long-haul travel with UK outbound tourists has increased in recent years. This has been a very exciting development for tourists, who can now fairly easily reach far-flung beautiful beaches or even go for a long weekend to the opera in Sydney.

In many areas of travel and tourism, knowledge of long-haul destinations is not only desirable, but essential. You need to know what types of destinations are available – from cities to beaches – and what makes them attractive to tourists from the UK. You will explore different types of holidays, so that you understand how they appeal to the varying motivations of different types of visitors.

You will also explore external factors, such as travelling times, restrictions and how current events can impact on long-haul travel. You will use different reference sources to help you locate destinations and gateways.

Learning outcomes

After completing this unit you should:

1. be able to locate major long-haul destinations of the world
2. know the types of holidays offered within long-haul destinations that meet different visitor motivations
3. understand how factors can affect travel to long-haul destinations
4. know the features and facilities that contribute to the appeal of long-haul destinations for different types of visitors
5. be able to plan a long-haul tour.

Assessment and grading criteria

The table shows what you must do in order to achieve a **pass**, **merit** or **distinction** grade and where you can find activities in this unit to help you.

To achieve a **pass** grade the evidence must show that you are able to:	To achieve a **merit** grade the evidence must show that, in addition to the pass criteria, you are able to:	To achieve a **distinction** grade the evidence must show that, in addition to the pass and merit criteria, you are able to:
P1 locate major long-haul tourist destinations in different continents **See Assessment activity 8.1, page 216** **P2** outline different types of holidays available in long-haul destinations that meet specific UK visitor motivations **See Assessment activity 8.2, page 224**		
P3 explain how factors affect travel to long-haul destinations **See Assessment activity 8.3, page 228**	**M1** review how travel factors affect travel to selected long-haul destinations **See Assessment activity 8.3, page 228**	**D1** analyse the impact of travel factors on selected long-haul destinations **See Assessment activity 8.3, page 228**
P4 describe features and facilities that contribute to the appeal of a selected long-haul destination for different types of visitors from the UK **See Assessment activity 8.4, page 236**	**M2** assess the significance of different features and facilities on the appeal of a selected long-haul destination for different types of visitors from the UK **See Assessment activity 8.4, page 236**	**D2** evaluate how the selected destination has capitalised on its features and developed its facilities to attract different types of visitors from the UK **See Assessment activity 8.4, page 236**
P5 plan a multi-centre long-haul tour to meet a given UK visitor profile, showing sources used **See Assessment activity 8.5, page 240**	**M3** independently plan a detailed multi-centre tour, clearly justifying selections for the specified visitor profile **See Assessment activity 8.5, page 240**	

How you will be assessed

This unit will be assessed by one or more internal assignments that will be designed and marked by your tutor. Your assignments will be subject to sampling internally and externally as part of Edexcel's quality assurance procedures. The assignments are designed to allow you to show your knowledge and understanding related to the unit. The unit outcomes indicate what you should know, understand or be able to do after completing the unit.

Karen, 18-year-old BTEC National learner

This unit is quite demanding. There are such a lot of places to learn about. I bought a very good atlas as I found I needed it so often. The only long-haul holiday I had been on was to Florida. I was tempted to use this for my assessment, but on reflection I decided I wanted to find out more about places I hadn't visited.

One of our group had a very good idea for the tour. She asked a friend who was planning a gap year if she could plan the trip for them. She really enjoyed it, because it was real. For mine, I planned a month's tour around South America for my parents, as they have always wanted to go there. They are not really going though.

We had already got used to reading travel journals and newspapers for our other units, so we carried on doing that, taking it in turns to report every week on a current issue. For this unit we were looking for factors that affected travel to long-haul destinations. I also subscribed to www.travelmole.com. It was free and now I get email updates about travel and tourism news.

Over to you!

1 What long-haul destinations have you/people in your group visited?

2 What resources could you use to help you with this unit?

3 What long-haul destinations do you think would be most difficult to visit?

1 Locate major long-haul destinations of the world

Set off

World Tourism

Go to the website www.unwto.org. Find the United Nations World Tourism Organization's (UNWTO) report *Tourism 2020 Vision* in the facts and figures section.

- Where are the top three **tourism receiving** regions expected to be by 2020?
- What will world international **tourist arrivals** be by 2020?

Download the report *Tourism Highlights:*

- Find out the latest figure for world international tourism arrivals.
- What was the 1990 figure?
- What is the percentage change?
- Find the same figures for **tourist receipts**.
- What is the difference between receipts and arrivals (latest figures)? What does this mean?
- Why are receipts shown in US dollars?
- Find the top ten world tourism destinations (arrivals and receipts). Are they the same? Explain any differences.

Ask your tutor to check your work.

1.1 Reference sources

In Unit 3 you were introduced to a range of reference sources. You will need these again for this unit. In addition, you will need the following:

Up-to-date country guides, area guides, resort and city guides

The *World Travel Guide* is probably the best-known directory for the travel trade. It contains factual information on every country including transport, accommodation, visa requirements, health and a social profile.

Manuals

OAG produces a comprehensive series of guides for air and rail. The travel trade commonly uses these. Some are quite complex to follow and demand a knowledge of time zones and airline codes.

Specialist brochures

Most tour operators produce specialist long-haul brochures and it will be useful for you to collect a selection of these as you work through this unit.

Remember that some tour operators now produce electronic brochures, which you can download from their websites.

The internet

You have already been using the internet for your research, but now you need to look at specific long-haul destination websites.

- Useful examples are www.geographia.com (destination information) and www.worldatlas.com (maps and country information and it has some map tests).
- You will also find tour operator websites and websites from the tourist boards of countries which will interest you.

Key terms

Tourism receiver – a country that tourists choose to visit. The US is a major receiver.

Tourist arrivals – numbers of tourists visiting a country expressed in the numbers of visits.

Tourist receipts – the amount of money spent in a country by tourists.

- Many travel guides are available online. Examples include www.fodors.com and www.lonelyplanet.com
- The UNWTO is a useful source of statistics on visitor numbers to destinations. You might find the printed version in your library, but it is also available on-line (see page 214, Set off). You will find some excellent information freely available on this site, but detailed reports are available only to subscribers.
- The Foreign & Commonwealth Office (FCO) website is also a good source of information on travel factors.

1.2 Destination type and range

A long-haul destination is one with a flight time from the UK of over six hours. All European, North African and Asian countries bordering the Mediterranean are therefore excluded.

A destination can be a town or city, a coastal area, a tourist island or island group, a countryside (natural) area or a purpose-built resort area. It could be a cultural or an historical area. Examples of destinations include the Gold Coast in Australia, Hong Kong, the Maldives, the Canadian Rockies and Disney World in Florida.

The range of long-haul destinations available to UK outbound travellers has increased dramatically in recent years. We can visit cities, such as New York and Sydney, and experience their unique culture. Destinations like Florida offer beaches and exciting visitor attractions that suit all members of the family. Far-flung countries like Vietnam, Cambodia and China are now accessible. Knowing about these long-haul destinations is important for working effectively in travel and tourism and in this unit you will be able to develop locational skills and knowledge.

You need to know the location of major long-haul tourist destinations, particularly the most popular and those which you choose to study in depth. The following activity is designed to revise or kick-start your geographical knowledge.

Major tourist receiving areas

Some of the areas you have located are known as 'major tourist receiving areas'. This means they attract tourists in great numbers and usually from many areas of the world. These areas include the Caribbean islands, popular for island holidays and cruising, and south-east Asia.

Activity: Where in the world?

For this activity you will need a world map. Download a map from www.geoexplorer.co.uk or use an outline map from your world atlas.

1 Locate and name the following on the map:
   - the equator
   - the northern hemisphere
   - the southern hemisphere
   - the continents of Asia, North America, South America, Africa, Australasia, Europe
   - the Atlantic, Pacific and Indian oceans.

   Use an atlas to help you complete your map and ask your tutor to check your work.

2 Study Figure 8.1 and then locate the regions on a world map. For each region identify five main tourist destinations and locate them on your map. Decide what type of destinations they are, for example city or coastal. Use a key to identify the type.

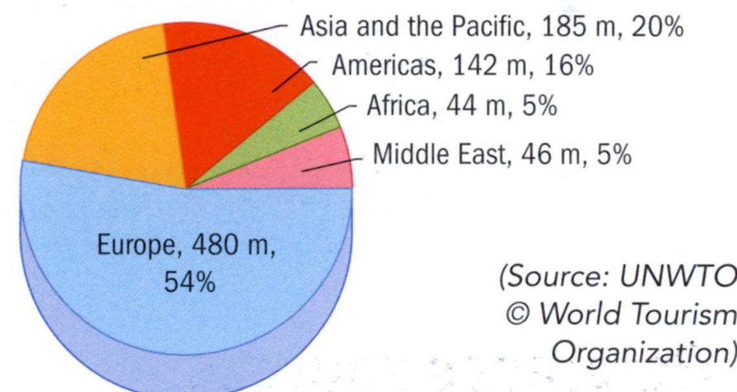

(Source: UNWTO © World Tourism Organization)

Figure 8.1: International arrivals by world region, 2008

3 In an earlier activity you looked at the UNWTO website and found out which countries had the most tourism arrivals. Locate these countries on the world map. Find out the name of the capital city for each country and locate these also.

4 The statistics for regions and countries you have looked at so far have come from international statistics – so they tell us which regions and countries are most popular with all tourists, not just UK tourists.

   Kuoni Travel listed the following as their top ten destinations for bookings in 2009: **Maldives Sri Lanka China and Hong Kong Thailand Dubai Malaysia USA Singapore Australia Egypt** Locate all these destinations on a world map.

You should be able to locate other areas that are diverse in appeal, some well known and others less so. Destinations range across continents so you must be able to locate all the continents.

Case study: Lower prices bring long-haul destinations within reach

Long-haul holiday destinations such as the USA, Australia and South Africa are now more accessible than they have ever been thanks to consistent reductions in airfares, according to ABTA – The Travel Association.

Sean Tipton, a spokesman for the travel association, said the cost of flying has come down "drastically" in the last 40 years, meaning long-haul holidays are no longer the preserve of the affluent.

He went on to point out that the Americas are the most popular long-haul destination of all for UK travellers and described Florida, which sees around a million visitors from Britain every year, as 'very affordable'.

Mr Tipton added "We are a very well-travelled nation, people are very well-travelled and we have been going abroad in large numbers for 40 years now. People like to try out new destinations and increasingly that means long-haul destinations out of Europe and further afield."

According to the latest holiday costs report from the Post Office, Thailand is the most affordable long-haul destination for Brits this year, followed by South Africa and Malaysia.

(Source: www.justtheflight.co.uk/news)

1 What are the reasons for the rise in popularity of long-haul destinations?

2 Why is Florida particularly appealing? Think of other reasons besides affordability.

3 What other types of holidays are available in the USA? Give examples.

Assessment activity 8.1

You work as an assistant for the training officer of a long-haul tour operator. You need to ensure the agents know the location of long-haul destinations and understand how to meet customer needs by selecting appropriate products. To help them do this, prepare a series of world and continent maps.

- Locate and label the continents of Asia, North America, South America, Africa, Australasia on a blank outline map of the world.
- On a blank outline map for each continent, accurately locate and label five examples of destinations that attract UK tourists. Use a key to distinguish different destination types.
- For each continent, ensure your five examples cover the different destination types: cities, coastal or beach resorts, purpose-built and natural attractions and historical/cultural areas.

Grading tips

P1 Ensure that you are as neat as you can and use colours/a key for clarity.

Activity: Locations worldwide

Locate the following on a world map and provide a brief description of each location:

- **The Gold Coast** (Australia) – popular for its miles of surf beach, lush green rainforest, good hotels and theme parks
- **Patagonia** (Argentina and Chile) – once a remote backpacking destination, but now attracts cruise passengers, adventure and activity holidaymakers
- **Uluru-Kata Tjuta National Park** – a World Heritage Site in the centre of Australia
- **Walt Disney World** in Florida and California, USA.

2 The types of holidays offered within long-haul destinations that meet different customer motivations

There has been a change in the perception of long-haul travel with UK tourists. A few years ago long-haul travel was considered to be out of reach of most people, reserved for the rich and famous. It has become more popular from the UK in recent years as air fares have become cheaper and air travel more accessible. Having become used to regular travel and holidays throughout Europe, people are looking for new experiences and want to visit new places.

2.1 Destinations

Cities

Cities may be visited as part of a tour or for short breaks. The most popular long-haul cities visited are New York, Sydney and Bangkok.

Coastal or beach resorts

Stunning beaches may be a reason for visiting a destination. However, remember that there are many beautiful beaches in Europe so climate is an important factor. In winter, customers have to travel long-haul to take a beach holiday.

What types of holiday might be available in New York?

Purpose built

All the attractions in Orlando, Florida, have been purpose-built to attract tourists to the area. Although Disney World was the first theme park in the area this was followed by Universal Studios, Seaworld and several water parks. Destinations like Las Vegas have also been built solely for tourism.

Natural

Natural destinations include mountain ranges, rainforests and deserts and they offer a wide range of opportunities for tourists. These also include Safari parks, the Grand Canyon and the Great Barrier Reef (i.e. destinations which are natural).

Historical or cultural areas

Sometimes the history and culture of a region are so interesting that the whole tourist industry is based on that culture. The 'Inca trail' has developed as a result of the tourist fascination with Peru's Inca history. See the case study on Machu Picchu on page 235.

2.2 Holiday types

When people are considering booking a long-haul holiday they are most likely to be thinking first about the type of holiday they would like. Of course, different types of customers look for different types of holidays.

To make choices even more complex, we are all motivated by different sets of factors. For example, a couple who have worked hard all year may want to relax at a beach destination and not be disturbed by children. Another couple might prefer to relax by indulging in watersports. If tourists are looking for a skiing holiday they have to go to a mountain area; for a diving holiday they will be looking for a coastal area with specialist facilities, clear waters and with lots of marine life to see.

Many long-haul holidays are offered as packages. People are less likely to travel long distances independently because low-cost flights from companies like easyJet are not available to these destinations, so customers are not as likely to save money by booking flights. However, the trend for independent travel is on the increase. Tailor-made holidays are available, for example safari holidays are popular.

Short breaks

Long-haul short breaks appear to be a contradiction in terms, but are becoming more popular. New York is a top destination, as are Bangkok and Dubai. The people who take long-haul short breaks are usually couples without children. They have money to spend and they can fit in the breaks around their busy jobs. They may be going shopping or for a weekend in the sun, but the common factor is a desire to do something different.

Low-cost flights and flexibility on air routes have made long-haul air travel easier and hotels are often cheaper than in the UK. Arriving back at work and saying you have been to Hong Kong for the weekend is exciting. In fact, Hong Kong has become a popular short break destination offering shopping and sightseeing. Other exotic weekend destinations include Havana, Buenos Aires and Rio de Janeiro.

Single-centre holidays

These are usually hotel-based. They are convenient as once the tourists arrive, they can unpack and relax and enjoy their environment. Staying in one place does mean that the opportunities for sightseeing are limited and therefore the visitor might miss some aspects of history or culture.

The case study (page 219) describes a single-centre holiday in the Maldives. The resort has many facilities, so that guests do not need to leave at all.

Twin or multi-centre

A multi-centre holiday takes in a number of destinations. Customers spend a few days or a week in each location and then move on to another centre, often by air travel.

Touring

Tours may be fly/drive, rail or coach. They can be organised, or travellers can hire a car and do their own planning. Tours may take in natural attractions, coastal areas and built attractions, such as museums or galleries.

Multi-centre tours are very popular with long-haul tourists – once they have travelled a long way to arrive at a destination, they want to see as much of the area or country as possible.

Those wanting to tour will have to consider the options for local transport very carefully, making sure it suits their needs.

Stopovers

Many travellers opt to stop over on long journeys to break the tedium of a lengthy flight. This provides an opportunity to see another place and its culture en route. Traditional stopovers on the way to Australia are Singapore and Hong Kong, both ideal for two or three days' stay before continuing on.

When considering whether a destination has appeal as a stopover, travellers will consider distance (it's obviously best if it's about halfway), cost and the facilities available. Generally, people on stopovers want short transfers from the airport to their hotel and they usually prefer to avoid complex excursions or activities. They are most likely to enjoy some shopping and local sightseeing.

Cruising

For those with lots of time to spare, cruising is an option. Usually a holiday in itself, it is also a means of travelling to a destination. A popular holiday for UK travellers is crossing the Atlantic on a liner, spending a few days in New York and then returning by air.

All the major cruise lines offer 'fly cruises' to destinations such as the Caribbean and Far East. That means that the prices quoted usually include the flight and all the arrangements are made for the passenger. Flights may be charter, where the ship is large enough to warrant charters arriving from various departure airports, or they may be scheduled. The more expensive cruises often use scheduled flights because of the extra flexibility and the perception of luxury. Also included in the price are the accommodation, meals, activities and entertainment on board and usually room service.

World cruises appeal to a lot of people, but not many can usually afford the time or the money to do them. Prices start at around £11,000 per person and can be two or three times that depending on choice of accommodation. Also, it obviously takes some time to sail around the world so work commitments might get in the way. The customer profile tends to be older retired people – with plenty of money!

Case study: Single-centre holidays

KUONI

MALDIVES › INDIAN OCEAN 39

****

Reethi Beach Resort

ALL INCLUSIVE OPTION

Filled with casual charm and friendly faces, the Reethi Beach holds true to the relaxed Maldivian way of life. There are stunning swathes of beach to tempt you into utter relaxation and great sports facilities for the more energetic.

LOCATION › In the unspoilt Baa atoll, approx. 35 minutes north of Malé by Trans Maldivian Airways seaplane. **FEATURES ›** Main buffet restaurant, coffee shop over the spectacular lagoon, choice of bars and speciality restaurants. Squash, tennis, badminton, tropical spa offering treatments, airconditioned fitness centre (all payable locally) and swimming pool. Catamaran sailing, canoeing, parasailing, kitesurfing, waterskiing, glass bottom boat and diving school (all payable locally) are available. There is also occasional evening entertainment. **ACCOMMODATION ›** 100 villas (30 overwater), each with airconditioning, ceiling fan, minibar, television, telephone, and terrace. Standard rooms have partially open-air bathroom with shower. Deluxe villas with sitting area, bath and Maldivian swing. Water villas in pairs on stilts over the water, a few minutes from the beach, with CD player, tea and coffee making facilities, bath and balcony. **MEALS PER NIGHT FROM ›** HB £23, FB £39, ALL £62. **NB ›** Reethi Beach Resort is closing May15-Jul31 2010.

KUONI PLUS

NO SINGLE SUPPLEMENT › (Standard and Water bungalows) valid Apr27-Jul19. **HONEYMOON / 25TH ANNIVERSARY ›** Fruit basket, flowers, special candlelit dinner with bottle of wine. **EARLYBIRD SAVER ›** All stays of minimum 7 nights booked by Feb28 2010 for stays Apr27-Dec20 receive a discount of up to £65 per person per week. **RENEWAL OF VOWS ›** This romantic ceremony is available at Reethi Beach, please ask for details and see our Wedding brochure.

KUONI EXCLUSIVE

All Kuoni holidays to the Maldives on scheduled flights (SriLankan, British Airways and Emirates, not Monarch) include access to the VIP Lounge in Malé Airport on your departure.
All offers apply to 2010. Call or see online for 2011 offers.

ALL INCLUSIVE OPTION

› All meals taken in the main restaurant, selected drinks, house wine by the glass from the main bar › 2 half day excursions › Free windsurfing equipment › Free use of fitness centre, squash, badminton, use of tennis courts (tennis balls at extra cost) › 1 free introductory dive per stay.

PRICES IN £ PER PERSON AT TIME OF GOING TO PRESS BASED ON MONARCH AIRLINES CHARTER FLIGHTS EX LONDON GATWICK AND ON SRILANKAN AIRLINES SCHEDULED FLIGHTS EX HEATHROW FOR THE PERIOD 01 NOV 10-31 MAR 11. TRANSFERS INCLUDED

FOR UP TO DATE PRICES & GREAT OFFERS, SEE YOUR TRAVEL AGENT OR WWW.KUONI.CO.UK

Ref No.	Holiday	Room Grade	Meal Plan	No. of Nights	Holiday Prices 01Jan 31Jan	01Feb 29Apr	30Apr 30Jun	01Jul 11Jul	12Jul 15Aug	16Aug 31Aug	01Sep 30Sep	01Oct 31Oct	01Nov 31Dec	01Jan 31Jan	01Feb 31Mar	Extra Nights From	Single Supp Per Night From
I00198	Meeru Island Resort	Garden Room	FB	7	-	-	969	1079	1135	1049	1039	1069	1365	1379	1399	42	30
I00150	Meeru Island Resort	Superior Room	FB	7	1265	1299	999	1099	1159	1135	1069	1099	1399	1415	1435	47	32
I00151	Meeru Island Resort	Jacuzzi Beach Villa	FB	7	1485	1525	1145	1265	1315	1289	1215	1255	1629	1655	1679	67	47
I00152	Meeru Island Resort	Water Villa	FB	7	1595	1635	1225	1345	1399	1375	1299	1335	1725	1775	1799	79	55
I00153	Meeru Island Resort	Jacuzzi Water Villa	FB	7	1895	1929	1589	1719	1769	1745	1665	1719	1999	2045	2079	131	92
I00156	Reethi Beach	Standard	RB	7	1265	1289	975	995	1149	1125	1075	1099	1355	1395	1419	24	-
I00157	Reethi Beach	Deluxe Villa	RB	7	1435	1479	1099	1135	1315	1289	1239	1279	1549	1589	1599	43	16
I00158	Reethi Beach	Water Villa	RB	7	1515	1549	1195	1225	1399	1375	1335	1375	1639	1669	1685	55	-

UPGRADES › Never has premium flying been better value for money. See p460-465 for upgrades available along with supplements.

COMPLETE FLEXIBILITY › Your thoughts, our know-how. Together we can tailor make your perfect holiday.

FLIGHTS › For full details of flight schedules, including regional options, please see p460-465.

FLIGHT SUPPLEMENTS › Ex UK: 2010: 08-14Feb £69, 22Mar-04Apr £69, 07-20Dec £269, 21-27Dec £45.
Ex Maldives: 2010/11: 01-08Jan £95.

HOTEL SUPPLEMENTS › See relevant hotel page for extra night costs and appropriate supplements. Peak season supplement per room per night: MEERU ISLAND RESORT from £8. REETHI BEACH RESORT from £52.

MEAL PLAN › RO no meals › RB breakfast › HB breakfast and dinner › FB breakfast, lunch and dinner › ALL All Inclusive › MMP mixed meal plan as detailed.

KUONI PLUS › For full conditions see p466-471.

IMPORTANT HOLIDAY INFORMATION › Please read p466-471 before you book your holiday. The price we confirm at the time of booking is the price we guarantee. This includes any increases or reductions to the above prices at that time. Holidays which do not fall completely within the date bands specified may be subject to a reduction or increase. See www.kuoni.co.uk for the best available price.

1 Draw up a detailed profile of the customer best suited to the holiday illustrated. What would their motivation be? Illustrate your profile if you wish.

2 Using brochures, find an example of a single-centre holiday suitable for a family wanting relaxation and activities. Explain why your choice is suitable for the family.

2.3 Visitor motivation

Why do people travel? Why do people go on holiday? A great deal of research has been done into motivation for travel, but consumer behaviour is a difficult area to research, as sometimes we ourselves don't know exactly why we do something. There are probably as many reasons for going away as there are tourists who go. Tourists on holiday together at the same resort do not necessarily have the same motivation for being there.

Case study: 'Explorism is the new tourism'

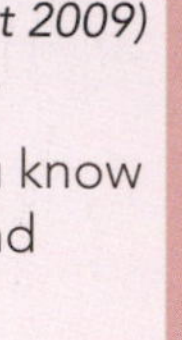

The tour operator Kuoni has coined a new phrase: 'Explorism is the new tourism'. In research the company reported, in 2009, that today's travellers are looking for more than a mere two-week holiday. They are looking for personal fulfilment. Their research aimed to find out not just where people travel, but why.

Nick Hughes, former managing director at Kuoni, said: "Travel is no longer just a holiday choice. It impacts our lifestyle, stimulates our well-being and influences our fashion, design and food choices. Kuoni customers really want to delve deeply under the skin of their destination, to explore further and experience more. We call this growing trend Explorism and we believe it is the new tourism."

(Source: www.kuoni.co.uk, Long-haul report 2009)

1 Hold a group discussion around Nick Hughes' statement. Try to find examples of people you know using their holidays to explore destinations and have new experiences.

2 Decide whether you agree with Nick Hughes.

Types of visitor motivation include the following.

Relaxation

Tourists may be motivated by the need for rest and relaxation, having worked hard all year. This motive could manifest itself in the choice of a simple beach holiday for relaxation in the sun. It might be reflected in the choice of a spa holiday where rest and well-being are emphasised.

Special occasion

The natural attractions of a destination are usually what make it suitable for a special occasion, such as a wedding. Many take place in beach resorts. Facilities such as catering and accommodation will be carefully considered, especially if there are guests and everyone wants to stay in the same hotel.

According to a Mintel survey, one in 10 couples get married abroad. This amounts to 35,000 weddings a year; many of these are long-haul. This amounts to huge potential business for tour operators. Since 1998, the number of people choosing to marry abroad has risen by more than 50 per cent. One of the many reasons for people choosing to have their wedding abroad is cost. The average cost of marrying abroad is £3000–£4000, including the honeymoon, compared with £15,000 for an average UK wedding.

Think about it

Think about other reasons for getting married in a long-haul destination. Discuss the advantages and disadvantages with your group.

Couples wanting a wedding abroad in a beautiful beach setting with hot sunny weather must be aware of climate information for the destination and time of year they are considering.

Although popular, beach weddings are not the only option. Tour operators are coming up with new ideas for weddings abroad all the time to try and get a larger share of this lucrative market. All major long-haul tour operators offer wedding packages. Here are some ideas:

- Virgin offers a wedding ceremony on the 55th floor of the Empire State building in New York.
- Las Vegas is popular – couples can get married in one of the wedding chapels on Sunset Strip and the bride can even get an Elvis look-alike to give her away.
- Kuoni offers the possibility of marrying in Sydney on a sunset harbour cruise or outside the famous opera house.
- Most of the beautiful Caribbean islands are geared up for weddings on perfect sandy beaches.

Some tour operators have a wedding list service where family and friends can contribute to the cost of the

Activity: Lots of holidays

For this activity you are in the fortunate position of going on lots of holidays!

1 Imagine you are taking the holidays in the table.

- For each one, find a suitable long-haul destination that suits *you*.
- Repeat the activity and imagine that you are finding destinations for the same holiday for your grandparents or a much older couple.
- Use brochures and websites to help you and make sure you can locate each of the destinations.
- When you have finished, compare your choices with someone else's and discuss their differences and similarities.

2 Think about your last trip away somewhere long-haul. What motivated you to travel? Was it to visit friends or relatives? In that case your motivation might have been a desire to reinforce friendship or family bonds. Perhaps you were motivated by a sense of duty to visit an elderly family member? Discuss your thoughts with your group.

Holiday	You	Older couple
Short break		
Multi-centre tour		
Stopover to Australia		
Hotel-based holidays		
Special occasion (wedding)		
Activity-based holidays		
Visiting friends and relatives		
Cruising		
Touring and sightseeing		

wedding in lieu of a wedding gift. Or they can buy add-ons to the holiday, for example a yacht trip, a helicopter ride or a special dinner for two.

Activity: Wedding planning

Plan a wedding holiday abroad for a special client – you or someone you know well.

- Think of all the features you would like the holiday to have and select several possible destinations. Use the climate information in Figure 8.2.
- Take a blank world map and label all the destinations with notes about the features of each one.
- Make a poster of your wish list and the holiday you would choose.

Activities

Customers may choose their destination because it allows them to pursue a particular interest or hobby. They may choose an activity such as cycling, diving or trekking.

Serious cyclists can take their own cycles by air and carry their gear when they reach the destination. All specialist cycling operators will provide bikes if wanted and most offer a range of different cycling holidays ranging from extremely taxing mountain bike tours to gentle rides through the countryside. A good example is Cycle Cuba, where people can combine a holiday, while the same time raising money for charity through sponsorship.

Climate is an important consideration for customers taking a cycling holiday. If it is too hot then the cycling is uncomfortable and too taxing. The landscape of the destination must be carefully considered to suit the cycling ability of the group.

Attractions and entertainment

Many families are motivated by the desire to enjoy some form of entertainment on holiday. This could take the form of visiting theme parks or just choosing a resort where evening entertainment and children's clubs are provided.

Some people look forward to gambling on a holiday, even if it just to try it once. Las Vegas is the prime example of a destination geared up to fulfil this motivation.

Culture and history

Those who visit a destination to study the historic architecture, arts and music are motivated by a desire to experience culture. In its wider sense many tourists want to experience the language, lifestyle and food and drink offered by another culture. We often describe those who like to travel further and further afield in search of new experiences as having 'wanderlust'.

Gap-year students often express a wish 'to travel' and what they usually mean is that they want to meet new people, see places and enjoy new experiences. Typical travel destinations on a student tour will be Australian cities, Thailand, Fiji and the USA.

ESSENTIAL FACTS FOR WEDDINGS AND HONEYMOONS

HOW'S THE WEATHER?

Bali: tropical climate with a dry season during our summer and a rainy season in our winter; year-round showers. Average temperature 30°C.

Caribbean: sunny and warm all the time, but beware the hurricane season from June to November. Temperatures between 25°C and 30°C.

Cyprus: very hot in the summer, mild the rest of the year; lots of sunshine. Temperatures between 15°C and 35°C.

Florida: sunny all-year-round, very hot and humid in the summer, but can be chilly in mid-winter, particularly in Orlando. Temperatures between 15°C and 40°C.

Greece: very hot in the summer, mild in winter, year-round sunshine. Temperatures between 5°C and 30°C.

Kenya: year-round warmth, with a dry season in our winter and a rainy season in our summer. Temperatures between 25°C and 30°C.

Las Vegas: sunny all-year-round, extremely hot in the summer and cold in the winter. Temperatures between –5°C and 40°C.

Mauritius: year-round tropical warmth. Temperatures between 25°C and 30°C.

Maldives: warm all year, with a rainy season during our summer. Temperatures between 30°C and 35°C.

New York: very cold and snowy from November to March, steaming hot in mid-summer. Temperatures between –5°C and 35°C.

Sri Lanka: hot and humid all-year-round with two distinct monsoon seasons from May to July and December to January. Average temperature 30°C.

Sydney: seasons opposite to the UK, so warm in our winter and cooler, though never really cold, in our summer; can rain in winter, but consistently sunny in the summer. Temperatures between 12°C and 25°C.

Figure 8.2: Information for people planning to get married abroad

What types of holiday motivation could Las Vegas fulfil?

Natural world

People often go on holiday to escape from their busy lives and experience a totally different environment. This need to escape may be fulfilled by visiting an eco resort or by taking up activities in a natural environment, such as skiing or mountain climbing. Another example of experiencing the natural world is taking a safari, where animals are viewed in their natural habitat. Tanzania is a popular safari destination and offers adventure too, being a developing African country.

Media influences

A popular film attracts fans and film lovers to its location. The *Lord of the Rings* film locations are famous tourist locations in New Zealand.

Health tourism

This is a popular trend, particularly for non-essential treatments such as cosmetic surgery and dental treatment. Tourists book treatments in hospitals abroad because they are offered more cheaply than those in the UK. Companies offer packages which include the treatment, transport and accommodation. Others have travelled to India where private hospitals offer surgeries such as hip replacements at cheaper prices than in the UK, even when transport costs are added.

Education

Many tourists visit other countries in order to take language courses and many language schools have opened up in all major cities to cater for them. South America is popular for those who want to learn Spanish and want to travel further afield than Spain. Many UK students undertake educational trips abroad as part of their courses, including learning a language.

Activity: Away from it all

Find three examples of long-haul holidays that meet the motivation of someone who needs to be alone and escape the hurly-burly of life. Choose one and say why it might appeal to you.

New Zealand is just one location which has benefitted from the film industry. Can you think of any others?

Assessment activity 8.2

This assessment relates to the same scenario introduced in Assessment activity 8.1 where you are helping the training officer of a long-haul tour operator.

Select one long-haul destination from each of the following categories, ensuring that each of your examples is from a different continent:

- cities
- coastal or beach resorts
- purpose-built
- natural attractions
- historical or cultural areas.

For each of your chosen destinations produce an information sheet giving a short outline of the types of holidays offered to meet different types of UK visitor motivations.

Include brief details of holidays you have found with named operators. Say which motivations the holiday appeals to, for example a short break to New York with Virgin Holidays might meet motivations of shopping and culture.

Make sure you have included all the different holiday types in your information sheet at least once.

You must cover:

- short break
- single-centre
- twin or multi-centre
- cruise
- tour.

You should cover each type of visitor motivation at least once:

- relaxation
- special occasion
- activities
- attractions/entertainment
- culture and history
- entertainment
- natural world
- other, e.g. media, shopping, education, visiting friends or relations (VFR).

Grading tips

P2 When you **outline** different types of holiday available in long-haul destinations, make sure to include all the different holiday types and each type of UK visitor motivation at least once. Remember each holiday type can meet several motivations.

PLTS

Planning and carrying out research into different types of holidays and motivations will help to develop your skills as an **independent enquirer**.

Functional skills

Using a style suitable for information sheets will help to develop your **English** writing skills.

3 How factors can affect travel to long-haul destinations

When people are planning long-haul holidays there are several factors that affect their choice of destination. In this section you will look at these factors and assess their relative significance in customer choice.

3.1 Travel factors and their effects

Time zones

As you travel round the world you pass through different time zones – regions where the local time is set in relation to a world standard time. The term usually used for this world standard time is **Greenwich Mean Time (GMT)**. GMT is also known as Zulu, or more commonly Coordinated Universal Time (UTC).

Daylight-saving time (DST) has been adopted in most regions of the world, so that the hours when people are working or studying match the period of available daylight. In the UK it is known as **British Summer Time** (end of March to end of October). Other countries may introduce daylight-saving time on different dates.

When travelling, people must ensure that time changes are included in time calculations.

Key terms

Greenwich Mean Time (GMT) – a term used for world standard time. Each time zone to the east of Greenwich time zone is ahead of GMT, that is +1 hour, +2 hours, etc. Each time zone to the west is behind GMT, that is –1 hour, –2 hours, etc. Going eastwards you add hours to GMT and going westwards you subtract hours from GMT.

Daylight-saving time (DST) – seasonal time changes to maximise daylight hours when people are at work.

British Summer Time – daylight saving time in the UK. At 1:00 a.m. GMT on the last Sunday in March the clocks go forward by one hour and on the last Sunday in October they revert to GMT.

Activity: Time zones

You are going to New York for Christmas shopping at the beginning of December. Your flight leaves the UK at 9:30 a.m. and the flight takes 7 hours. What time is it in New York on arrival?

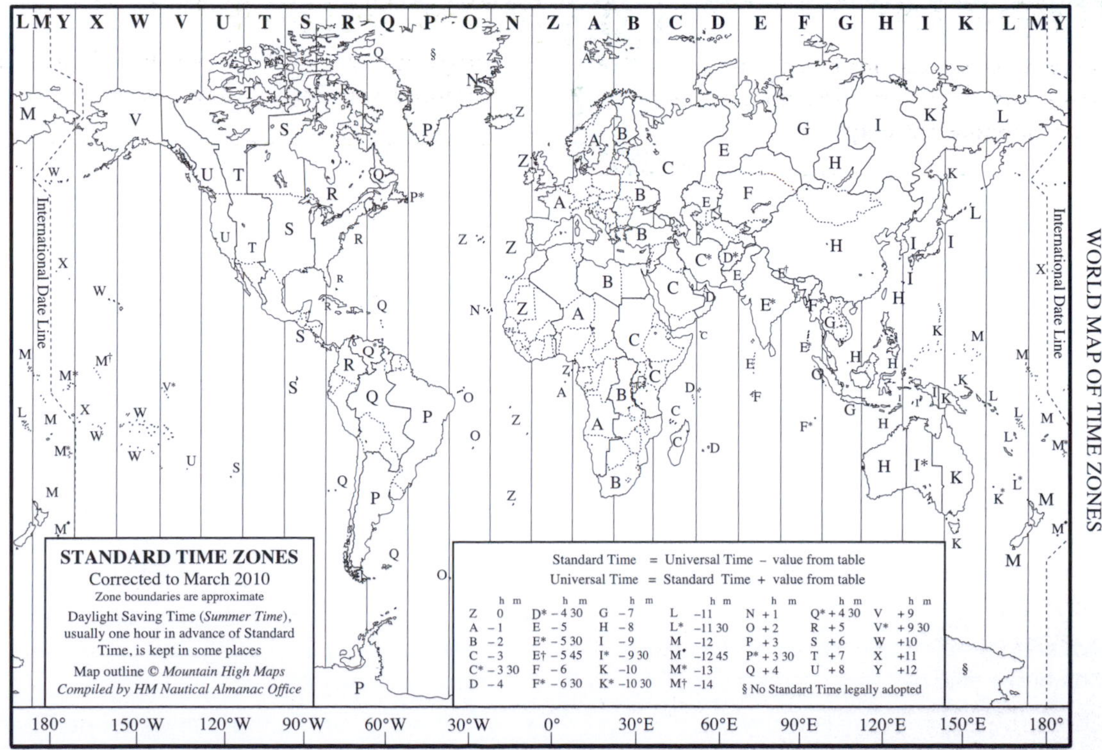

Figure 8.3: Time zone map *(Source: HM Nautical Almanac Office, © Council for the Central Laboratory of the Research Councils)*

International Date Line

The International Date Line is the imaginary line on the Earth that separates two consecutive calendar days. Travelling east across the line takes the traveller back one day; travelling west takes the traveller forward one day. Cruise passengers crossing the Pacific will be affected by the date line.

On a map it is shown as 180° away from the meridian that goes through Greenwich, on the line of longitude.

Jet lag

A severe effect of crossing time zones and the International Date Line can be jet lag.

People who travel regularly will understand that it is possible to mitigate the effects of jet lag and some journeys produce fewer problems than others. If you travel to Cape Town, for example, the time difference is minimal even though the flight is quite long. Travelling east means you can take a night flight from the UK, yet still arrive in Singapore before sunset and experience a lovely evening.

Activity: Jet lag

New Zealand has one time zone, which is 12 hours ahead of GMT. DST is in effect from mid-October until mid-March. The clocks advance by one hour for DST.

Crossing time zones can cause 'jet lag' – usually going east is worse than going west, because inbuilt bodily rhythms are disturbed and it can take a few days for the body to re-adjust to the new time zone. The 12-hour difference in New Zealand could mean it takes several days to return to normal. Travellers may find that they are falling asleep during the day and staying awake at night.

- Find out what can be done to alleviate jet lag.
- Produce a short information sheet that could be given to air passengers before their flight.
- Find out what other health problems may occur or be aggravated through flying.
- What health advice is generally given to travellers by tour operators and airlines? Collect some examples and discuss.

Deep vein thrombosis

Deep vein thrombosis (DVT) is a clotting of the blood in any of the deep veins – usually in the leg. It can be fatal if the clot breaks off and makes its way to the lungs, where it can then affect the lung's ability to take in oxygen.

It is thought that being immobile for a long period of time is a risk factor and that is why any kind of travel – not just flying – can increase risk. Airlines are very aware of the risks and offer advice to passengers about DVT prevention. They give suggestions for exercises to do while seated and recommend that passengers walk about when possible.

Most people are unaffected by the possibility of DVT and are unworried by it. However, certain people may

Case study: Hurricane Katrina

Ernesto became the first hurricane of the Atlantic season yesterday with winds of 75 m.p.h. Forecasters said it would strengthen as it headed toward the Gulf of Mexico, where it could menace a wide stretch of coastline, including New Orleans.

The storm could grow into a category three hurricane with winds of at least 111 m.p.h. by Thursday, said the US National Hurricane Centre in Miami. Category 3 Hurricane Katrina struck the city a year ago tomorrow.

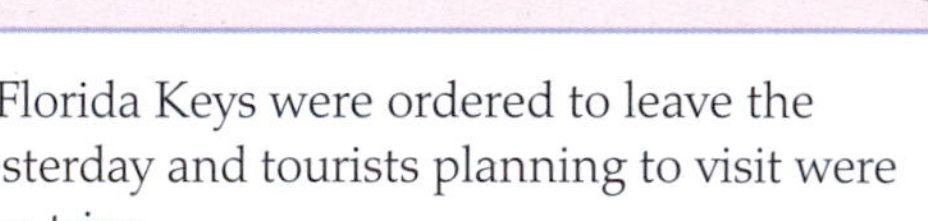

Visitors to the Florida Keys were ordered to leave the island chain yesterday and tourists planning to visit were told to postpone trips.

Emergency officials claimed the New Orleans levée system was ready for another major hurricane. "I think we're in good shape," said Don Powell, coordinator of Gulf Coast rebuilding. "There's no question in my mind, we're ready."

(Source: www.travelindustryreview.com Travel Industry Review 28 August 2006)

New Orleans was devastated by Hurricane Katrina in the summer of 2005.

- Find out how the region fares today and how much renovation and repair has been carried out.
- How open is the city to tourists today?
- Produce a short newspaper article on your findings.
- Research figures for tourism in New Orleans and make a comparison of figures before and after Hurricane Katrina.
- What is the current trend in visitor numbers?

be at more risk and may decide not to travel on long journeys. Those with increased risk are those who have other risk factors, such as varicose veins or obesity.

Climate and seasons

Tourists need to be aware of climate zones and seasonal variations when arranging trips. This sounds obvious, but many tourists arrive in Thailand, for example, and find it is the monsoon season and they didn't check first. The problem of encountering poor weather, unexpected by the tourist, has increased as people have ventured further afield.

Hurricanes are common in the Caribbean region in our autumn period. In 2008, Cuba and the Florida Keys were evacuated as Hurricane Ike struck. In 2004 Hurricane Ivan devastated Grenada and some hotels are still in the process of being re-built.

The effect of such extreme climatic conditions is that the economy of the affected region suffers as tourists are not able to visit until the danger has passed and any repairs are carried out.

Seasonality

Planning long-haul trips means thinking about time and season differences. For example, is the best time to visit Australia in our summer or in their summer? Visitors need to be aware of the hemisphere in which their destination is located.

Entry requirements

Depending on destination tourists may require various documents, including visas and vaccination certificates. These can take time to acquire and therefore will prevent tourists choosing some destinations at the last minute. In addition, visas or vaccinations can add an extra cost to the holiday.

Travel restrictions

Travel restrictions are put in place by the government when it is unwise for tourists to visit a destination, usually because of a dangerous political situation or an outbreak of disease. You can find about any current restrictions on outbound travel from the UK from the Foreign and Commonwealth Office website at www.fco.gov.uk. Restrictions vary in severity from a total restriction on travel to advice on dangerous areas which should be avoided.

If tourists have already booked a holiday when restrictions are levied then a tour operator will offer an alternative holiday or a refund. With independent travel the situation can be more serious – even if a tourist has travel insurance, it is very unlikely to provide cover for an outbreak of war or terrorist activity.

Safety

Visitors' safety can be compromised for different reasons. Many parts of the world are affected by terrorist activity at different times and of course, it is difficult to know where attacks might occur. The FCO is only able to say where risk is heightened. Other places might be deemed unsafe because of local events. In 2010, Jamaica was the location of several shootings as police tried to arrest a local gangster. Events spiralled and tourists were encouraged to stay well away from the capital, Kingston.

Health

Health restrictions usually relate to the requirement for vaccinations. Some countries will not permit entry without typhoid and yellow fever vaccinations, for example, and a certificate must be shown to prove they have been done. Occasionally outbreaks of disease prevent people travelling. The swine flu outbreak in 2009 deterred travellers to Mexico for some time. HIV is prevalent in some countries and advice is given to travellers to avoid sexual contact to prevent contracting the condition.

Travellers should be aware of differences in culture and levels of poverty when travelling and avoid displays of comparative wealth.

Think about it

At the time of writing, the FCO advises against all travel to Gaza, Samoa and Somalia. Do you know why? Go to the FCO website to find out whether the advice remains the same.

Social situations

When considering where to go on holiday, tourists may well decide against travel to a certain area for ethical reasons. For example, it is hard to enjoy a luxurious holiday in a resort when you know that people nearby are living in extreme poverty. This might occur in, for example, the Gambia or parts of India. Of course, the opposing view is that your money can help to alleviate poverty.

Effects on travel

Some of the factors discussed decrease our motivation to travel to a destination. High levels of crime dissuade tourists. Reports of terrorism may put an end to tourism in an area for a period of time. Pollution or natural disasters, such as floods or earthquakes, also decrease motivation to travel to a destination.

Activity: Factors affecting travel

Choose three of the travel factors from the last section. For each, report on the effect on travel for UK visitors. Consider whether they would travel at all and what precautions they might take if they decide to travel.

Assessment activity 8.3

1 Produce an information sheet which explains how travel factors can affect travel to long-haul destinations. Make sure you include all these factors:

- time zones
- climate and seasons
- travel restrictions
- health issues
- safety
- social situations
- entry requirements.

For each factor you need to say what the effect would be and give at least one long-haul example. For example, a UK visitor going to Australia would need a passport and a visa. Both are expensive and add to the cost of the trip. If the visitor forgot to get the documents they would not be allowed to travel. P3

2 Produce another information sheet which reviews how travel factors affect travel to selected destinations. (You could use the destinations from Assessment activity 8.2 on page 224). The same destination can be used for different factors.

- Research newspapers and trade magazines to get up-to-date information. M1
- Include a section which analyses at least two different travel factors and their impact on at least two long-haul destinations within the last five years. For example the impact of hurricanes on travel to the Caribbean and swine flu on travel to Mexico. D1

Grading tips

P3 Ensure you give one relevant long-haul example for each of the factors explained above.

M1 Ensure you use news reports and articles to **review** how factors affect travel to your selected destination.

D1 Ensure you **analyse** two different travel factors from the last five years, and their impact on two different long-haul destinations.

PLTS

Analysing and evaluating information to determine the impact of travel factors will help you develop skills as an **independent enquirer**.

Functional skills

Using a style suitable for an information sheet will help you to develop **English** writing skills.

4 Features and facilities that contribute to the appeal of long-haul destinations for different types of visitors

In this section, you will explore the features of long-haul destinations, how they are suitable for different types of holidays and how destinations appeal to different customer types. Remember that people may look for varying types of holiday to fulfil their needs at different times of the year. For example, a couple with children may take a family holiday in the summer, a skiing holiday at spring half-term and a short break, without the children, for shopping in New York before Christmas.

4.1 Types of visitors

You need to know the types of visitors from the UK that particular destinations appeal to. First, remind yourself of the different visitor types. Leisure travellers include families, young and old couples, backpackers, those seeking adventure and retirees. Remember too those visiting friends and relatives (VFR), business travellers and those travelling for medical or educational reasons.

For VFR travellers, their destination is determined by where their friends or relatives live. Similarly, business travellers' destinations are determined by the location of a meeting or conference. The business traveller looks particularly at access, in terms of convenience, and at the facilities available in the destination, such as easy transport, accommodation and food. The VFR traveller will also be considering accessibility, but may not require accommodation at all. People travelling for education will go the place that offers suitable programmes at prices they can afford.

Gap-year travellers are not just between school and university, although that is where the term came from. There is a growing trend for older people to take a sabbatical (a break from work) later in life. These people are sometimes known as 'SKIs' (Spending the Kids Inheritance)! A further group in their late twenties, having finally paid off their student debts, take a year out before settling down and having families. These are known as 'QLCs' (Quarter Life Crisis). Many gap-year travellers use the opportunity to undertake voluntary work.

According to Mintel (*Independent Travel UK* 2006), by 2010 there will be around 2 million gap-year travellers around the world. Mintel calls older travellers 'career gappers' and even older ones 'denture venturers'!

Think about it

How would the needs of gappers like SKIs, QLCs or denture venturers differ from traditional gap-year travellers? When do you think is the best time to take a gap year?

All of these visitor types have their own particular motivations, which affect the type of holiday they want. They will consider the specific features and facilities at a destination to make their choice. These include accessibility, attractions, destination facilities and climate.

4.2 Accessibility

Methods of transport

Routes by air

Most long-haul travel is by air for reasons of time and convenience. More direct flights are now available too.

Airline routes are very complex. Each airline has its own routes, but enters into different types of partnership with other airlines to extend its networks. British Airways (BA) is one of the world's major airlines, so it serves as a good example.

BA flies to many destinations worldwide. Most long-haul flights are from Gatwick and Heathrow, but regional airports are beginning to offer long-haul flights, for example Bristol and Doncaster. This is good news for people who may have had to travel from regions to a London airport and then change to a direct flight.

Even if a tourist decides to travel by air there are still decisions to be made about which class to travel. Scheduled flights offer business and first class, although airlines use different names for their services. Even charter flights, such as Thomson Airways, offer premium class for those who are prepared to pay a bit more.

Premium class

You can fly premium to all Thomson Airways long-haul destinations.

What's included? You get more space than Standard seats with at least 36′ seat pitch, your own 9′ seatback TV, free drinks (not including champagne), a four-course meal, plus a snack before landing, a luxury pamper pack and much more besides.

(Source: www.flights.thomson.co.uk)

Availability and frequency

Tourists will be influenced by the availability of flights from regional airports although not that many offer long-haul flights (exceptions to this include Bristol airport). Frequency of services is also important, some routes are offered daily or weekly, others such as flights to New York several times a day.

Cruise

Cruising is very suitable for long-haul travel. Passengers can opt to join a ship in the UK, for example at Southampton, and sail to their cruise area. Those with less time to spare will fly to a port, for example Miami, where they can join their cruise ship. This is often the most popular option.

Travelling time and cost

Most tourists do not want to travel too far from their country of origin for trips, for reasons of time, cost and convenience. Tourists choosing to travel long distances, for example to Australia from the UK, make that trip infrequently and tend to go for a longer period of time. The Caribbean is more popular with US tourists than those from the UK as the flight times, and therefore costs, are lower. However, developments in air travel routes have led to an increase in long-haul travel – if your special interest lies in seeing elephants in their natural habitat then you will travel to do it.

Travellers will also consider how much further they have to travel to the destination having arrived at the gateway airport or port. Until a few years ago tourists visiting Tobago had to change to a local flight in Port of Spain, Trinidad, as the runway could not accommodate large jets. Since the runway was extended, the provision of direct flights to Tobago has brought about an increase in tourism. In general, access to worldwide destinations has become easier and cheaper.

Suitability for the traveller

In the same way that planes have different classes, ships offer larger cabins with more facilities: these are correspondingly more expensive. Each customer has to decide how much they are prepared to spend, what facilities are essential and which are merely desirable. Basic accommodation is towards the bottom of the ship without windows and little space. At the other end of the spectrum, passengers can have suites with plenty of room, large windows and balconies.

Convenience

Some destinations are inconvenient to visit because of inaccessibility, perhaps requiring flight changes or boat trips to reach them. Travellers who are short of time may prefer to go to places that are easily reached by direct flights. Inconvenience may also include difficulties with language or currency.

Activity: New York

Imagine you are going shopping with friends to New York for four days. You are flying with Virgin Atlantic. Visit its website and find out how much extra per person it will cost to fly in premium economy or upper class. What extras do you get for this money? Is it worth it?

4.3 Attractions

Attractions add value to a destination and add to the appeal. They can sometimes be the sole reason for visiting a destination. Here are some examples of the types of attractions to be found in long-haul destinations (see pages 217–224):

- natural attractions, e.g. mountain ranges, rainforests, deserts, national parks and beaches
- purpose-built attractions, e.g. theme parks and museums
- events, e.g. carnivals, sports and music
- shopping
- culture, e.g. festivals, events, arts, local customs.

4.4 Destination facilities

By facilities, we mean the following:

- local transport

Case study: Mount Kinablu

borneo

land beneath the wind

ORIGINAL

BSC TRIP CODE

PHYSICAL
CULTURE SHOCK

- Discover the myths of the mountain at a Dusun village
- Trek up Mt Kinabalu for sunrise
- Watch giant green turtles coming ashore
- Spot Sabah's exotic jungle wildlife

13 days, ex Kota Kinabalu

Departs every Saturday

DEPARTURE GUARANTEED

ITINERARY... Day 1 Kota Kinabalu Experience the frontier charm of Kota Kinabalu, a city sandwiched between palm oil plantations and the sultry South China Sea. **Day 2 Village Stay** Learn about the spiritual and social ties that the Dusun have with the imposing Mt Kinabalu at a village homestay. **Days 3-4 Mt Kinabalu** Fuelled by fresh mountain air and stunning views begin the climb of Mt Kinabalu. It's a challenging trek but take time and enjoy the region's remarkable array of flora and fauna. **Days 5-6 Poring Hot Springs** Wake early to catch sunrise at the summit - the final ascent is tough, but the view from the top is awe-inspiring. Scramble down to Poring for a well-deserved soak in the hot springs. **Days 7-8 Kinabatangan Jungle Camp/ Homestay** Enter the steamy rainforest of Kinabatangan and see how the locals contribute to its conservation. Spend a night in the jungle amid hornbills, macaques and proboscis monkeys. Stay in a traditional Malay village to get a privileged view of their culture. **Day 9 Sandakan** Explore this busy commercial centre, home to historic Chinese temples and an island-studded bay. **Day 10 Turtle Island** Be touched by the sight of giant green turtles coming ashore to lay their eggs. **Day 11 Sepilok Orangutan Reserve** The soulful eyes of Borneo's 'wild men' will melt hearts on a visit to the Sepilok Orangutan Rehabilitation Centre. **Days 12-13 Kota Kinabalu** Appreciate the impressive collection of tribal and historical artefacts at the Sabah Museum or marvel at a fine example of Islamic architecture at the State Mosque.

Photography Competition 2007, Baby of the forest, Malaysia - David Lazaar

ACCOMMODATION Hotels/guesthouses (6 nts), bed and breakfast (1 nt) national park lodges (2 nts), tribal village (1 nt), homestay (1 nt), camping (1 nt) **TRANSPORT** Plane, minibus, speedboat, longboat, local bus, walking **GROUP SIZE** Max 12 **MEALS** 5 Breakfasts, 1 Lunch, 3 Dinners **BUDGET** Allow US$250 for meals not included **DEPARTS** Every Sat & selected Mon **GUARANTEE** Departure guaranteed **CARBON EMISSIONS OFFSET** 139 kg **NOTES** 1. You are required to arrange and purchase internal flights before travel. Please see Trip Notes (Important Notes) for details. 2. Most accommodation has shared bathing facilities and cold water only **TRAVELLER RATING** 4.78 out of 5

borneo unearthed

ORIGINAL

BSY TRIP CODE

PHYSICAL
CULTURE SHOCK

- Go wild in the jungles of Borneo
- Come face to face with an orangutan
- Follow the ancient Headhunters' Trail
- Walk in colossal caves

Kinabatangan Jungle Camp/ Homestay
Mt Kinabalu
Kota Kinabalu
Miri
Kuching
Sepilok Orangutan Reserve
Iban Longhouse
Mulu N.P.
BORNEO

19 days, Miri to Kota Kinabalu

DEPARTURE GUARANTEED

ITINERARY... Day 1 Miri Watch the locals haggle at the fish market or simply kick back with an icy-cold beer. **Days 2-5 Mulu National Park** Follow the old Headhunters' Trail on a walking safari through unspoilt wilderness and past limestone peaks. Wander into Clearwater Cave, home to Asia's longest underground river, and the enormous Deer Cave. **Day 6 Kuching** Get an urban fix while soaking up the sights of this graceful city, once ruled by the infamous White Raja of Sarawak. **Days 7-8 Iban Longhouse** Cruise river rapids to a village homestay and learn about the Iban hosts' culture and traditions. **Day 9 Kuching** There's time to explore the waterfront or discover the origins of the city's name at the Cat Museum. **Day 10 Kota Kinabalu** Swim, snorkel or simply relax on a seaside escape in Kota Kinabalu. **Day 11 Sepilok Orangutan Reserve** Visit Sepilok, where orphaned and injured orangutans are rehabilitated and returned to forest life. Stretch legs on one of many walking trails into the forest or head into Sandakan for some excellent seafood and a waterfront sunset. **Days 12-13 Kinabatangan Jungle Camp/Homestay** Spend a night in the wilderness of Borneo, home to wild elephants and crocodiles. A village homestay gives a first-hand experience of traditional Malay culture. **Days 14-16 Mt Kinabalu** It's hard work climbing South-East Asia's highest peak, but the views over Borneo's jungles are truly rewarding. **Days 17-19 Kota Kinabalu** Enjoy beachside fun, and a much deserved rest, while staying at a guesthouse in Kinarut, just outside bustling Kota Kinabalu.

Photography Competition 2009, Heading into the jungle, Borneo - Johanna Aldred

ACCOMMODATION Hotels/guesthouses (7 nts), bed and breakfast (1 nt), national park lodges (4 nts), camping (3 nts), homestay (3 nts) **TRANSPORT** Plane, minibus, express boat, speedboat, longboat, local bus, taxi, walking **GROUP SIZE** Max 12 **MEALS** 10 Breakfasts, 4 Lunches, 6 Dinners **BUDGET** Allow US$300 for meals not included **DEPARTS** Selected Thu **GUARANTEE** Departure guaranteed **CARBON EMISSIONS OFFSET** 203 kg **NOTES** 1. You are required to arrange and purchase internal flights before travel. 2. Combination trip. Please see Trip Notes (Important Notes) for more details **TRAVELLER RATING** 4.78 out of 5

Start	Finish						
2010		13 May	31 May	07 Oct	25 Oct	24 Feb	14 Mar
07 Jan	25 Jan	27 May	14 Jun	14 Oct	01 Nov	03 Mar	21 Mar
21 Jan	08 Feb	03 Jun	21 Jun	28 Oct	15 Nov	17 Mar	04 Apr
04 Feb	22 Feb	17 Jun	05 Jul	04 Nov	22 Nov	31 Mar	18 Apr
18 Feb	08 Mar	24 Jun	12 Jul	18 Nov	06 Dec	14 Apr	02 May
25 Feb	15 Mar	08 Jul	26 Jul	25 Nov	13 Dec	28 Apr	16 May
04 Mar	22 Mar	15 Jul	02 Aug	09 Dec	27 Dec	12 May	30 May
18 Mar	05 Apr	22 Jul	09 Aug	23 Dec	10 Jan	19 May	06 Jun
25 Mar	12 Apr	05 Aug	23 Aug	**2011**		26 May	13 Jun
01 Apr	19 Apr	19 Aug	06 Sep	06 Jan	24 Jan	09 Jun	27 Jun
15 Apr	03 May	02 Sep	20 Sep	20 Jan	07 Feb		
29 Apr	17 May	16 Sep	04 Oct	03 Feb	21 Feb		
		30 Sep	18 Oct	10 Feb	28 Feb		

additional information about this destination is available at **intrepidtravel.com**

47

(Source: Intrepid Travel)

1 Locate all the destinations mentioned above on a world map.

2 Choose one of the treks and do some research to find out more about it.

Describe the features and facilities of the destination and explain why those features make the destination suitable for a group of adventurous young people.

Consider climate, landscape, transport routes and accessibility, accommodation, local services, attractions, local culture and facilities.

Present your work in the form of an advertising storyboard which includes all this information and can be used to promote the destination.

- accommodation range and cost
- sport and entertainment
- food and drink

Most destinations will offer all these facilities, unless very remote and under-developed. However, they may be offered to varying standards from very basic to ultra luxurious in one destination. Different types of visitors demand different grades of accommodation and other facilities.

For example, a group of students visiting Thailand might take long bus rides to travel around the country and use bikes or **tuc tucs** locally. They could stay in a very basic hut right on the beach and go to full moon parties for their entertainment.

An older, wealthier couple might fly to travel within the country and take private taxis. They might choose a four- or five-star hotel with a pool, simple entertainment and fine dining.

Key term

Tuc tuc – a motorised rickshaw or three-wheeled cart operated by a driver, commonly used in Asian countries and in some African countries.

4.5 Climate

UK tourists often want to escape the British climate, hence the sale of winter sun holidays. The Caribbean is a great choice for winter sun as it has a hot climate all year and in winter the hurricane season is over.

Long-haul destinations may also be chosen for skiing because of the probability of good snow and the wish of UK visitors to try a non-European resort. Examples are Whistler in Canada and the Blue Mountains in Australia.

Of course, extreme weather conditions can be a deterrent, as we saw on page 226.

4.6 Examples of features and facilities

Natural attractions

One way of experiencing natural attractions is to go on foot. Trekking is a popular activity to undertake on holiday as it offers adventure, yet can be tailored to the ability and wishes of different groups of travellers. Families can trek together in destinations, such as the Himalayas. Experienced climbers can visit steep and tricky mountains, such as the Karakoram range in Pakistan or the sheer-sided Mount Roraima in Venezuela. Billed as the ultimate wildlife experience, a trek to the gorilla sanctuary in the Parc du Volcan rainforest in Rwanda offers excitement and helps ensure the survival of the gorillas.

Trekking is a popular adventure holiday. It is a good idea to book with a reputable operator if you are inexperienced, as they will provide a local guide and will ensure that no risks are taken with health and safety. An example of a trekking operator is Exodus Travel, which has over 35 years' experience and organises travel to Europe, Africa, Asia, South America, North America, Australasia and the Antarctic.

How does Havana in Cuba appeal to tourists?

Activity: Havana

Use brochures to find an example of a short-break to Havana. Describe the features of Havana in detail, including facilities, accessibility and culture, saying why it is suitable for a short-break and what type of customer it would appeal to. Draw up a fact sheet of your findings of not more than one side of A4.

An independent trek might work out cheaper but could be difficult to organise, as a guide would have to be located and transport in remote areas might be difficult to find.

Built attractions

Havana, the capital city of Cuba, is located in the Caribbean. Cuba's natural attractions include long stretches of beautiful beaches, but the appeal of Havana lies in its architecture and history.

The city is in the process of restoration and is a World Heritage Site. There are plenty of museums, including the famous Museum of the Revolution. The climate is hot all-year-round, but subject to hurricanes in the late summer. Local transport is difficult for tourists, as there is little public transport, but taxis are widely available.

Case study: Boston – getting around

Public transport

The *Massachusetts Bay Transport Authority (MBTA)* operates four subway lines (blue, green, red, orange), which spread out from a central point at Park Street Station, at the northeast corner of Boston Common. The 'T', as the system is known, began in 1897 and is the oldest in the USA. The lines run Monday–Saturday 05:00–01:00 and Sunday 05:20–00:45.

MBTA also runs 13 commuter rail lines, three boat services and 185 bus routes. The public buses are cheaper and have many more stops than the subway, but can be more difficult to orientate.

A single fare costs US$1.25 on the subway and US$0.90 on buses. The fare is US$1.55 for travel in three zones and express buses cost from US$2.20-3.45. Passes (*Boston Visitor's Passport*) for one day (US$7.50), three days (US$18) and seven days (US$35) are valid on both. Route maps are available at all stations.

Driving in the city

Boston is not on a simple grid plan, curving as it does to accommodate both the Charles River, running more or less west–east, and the coastline, running more or less north–south. Though the 'Big Dig,' the most expensive tunnel re-building project in America's history, has been completed, traffic in the city is still very congested. Parking can be confusing with many areas having local residents' rules and public parking lots being expensive.

A car is only necessary for locations outside the city. Much of the central part of Boston was built before cars and so lends itself to exploration on foot and public transport in and around Boston is good and inexpensive.

Taxis

Taxis are plentiful and can be hailed on the street or reserved by telephone, but they are not cheap. All rides within the city are metered at US$1.75 for the first quarter-mile, then at US$0.30 for each subsequent eighth-mile. There is a US$5 extra charge for a station wagon or van request.

Water taxis

An interesting way to get to know the inner city area is to use the water taxis, which run throughout the year both as commuter taxis and as ordinary water buses. *City Water Taxi* operates 10 waterfront stops (Monday–Saturday 07:00–22:00, Sunday 07:00–20:00), with tickets starting at US$10. Shuttles run to Logan International Airport with *Harbor* Express, Hull and Quincy Shipyard for US$12. From Quincy to Boston or Hull to Boston the one-way fare is US$6.

Limousines

Limousines are available from many companies. Basic hourly rates start at US$50 not including extras, such as toll fees and a 20 per cent tip for the driver.

Car hire

Hire cars are available from several companies. Most car hire companies require drivers to be over 25 years of age or impose hefty surcharges. Basic daily rates begin at US$43 plus tax per day and weekly rates at US$210 plus tax. There is an additional fee of US$.0.60, plus taxes can be up to 23 per cent on top depending from which location the vehicle is rented.

Bicycle hire

Cycling on the city streets of Boston is not for the fainthearted. Only brave locals do so. There are scenic cycle paths, however, along the Charles River. Day rates are US$35 and helmet and lock are included.

(Source: Travel Trade Gazette, 23 November 2007)

Several types of local travel are featured in this article. For each one, discuss what type of customer it is most suitable for and say why. Make an oral presentation to your group on your findings.

Case study: Beach to their own – Thailand

Thailand is the Far East's premier beach destination for UK holidaymakers, with resorts ranging from the brash and breezy to romantic hideaways. Howard Carr outlines the resorts' attractions and suggests which would suit what type of customer.

Phuket

A one-hour flight from Bangkok, Phuket is a large island rather than just one resort. Its mixture of busy beaches and secluded bays makes it one of the most popular destinations in Thailand, with something for most types of holidaymaker.

The main holiday playground is lively Patong, with plenty of shops, night markets, bars and clubs. Phuket Town is also worth visiting for its temples and Chinese heritage.

"Phuket attracts all types of clients from backpackers to millionaires," says Travel 2 Far East product manager Kerry Towers.

Ko Samui

Thailand's third-largest island is about two-thirds the size of the Isle of Wight. Its position on southern Thailand's east coast means its climate differs to west coast resorts such as Phuket. The rainy season is from October to January, as opposed to May to November on the other coast.

Hotel development on Ko Samui has been heavy over the past few years, particularly since the 2004 tsunami when many holidaymakers switched to the east coast from resorts damaged in the disaster.

The main beaches of Chaweng and Lamai are within easy reach of the island's airport. Lined by luxury hotels, they can get quite crowded in the peak season. Beaches on the south and west coasts are more remote and therefore quieter.

Away from the beaches, Ko Samui's beautiful scenery is one of its great attractions. Highlights include lush mountain jungle, waterfalls, coconut plantations and traditional villages.

"Ko Samui is for those who prefer to stay in a smaller hotel on an island which still has a paradise feel," says David Carlaw, Premier Holidays' head of Faraway product.

Flight time to Ko Samui from Bangkok is one hour 20 minutes.

Hua Hin/Cha-Am

About a three-hour drive from Bangkok, Hua Hin is the oldest beach resort in Thailand. It is home to the Thai royal family's summer palace.

Hua Hin has a good range of beachfront hotels, shops and restaurants, but its royal connections help to give it a more relaxed and genteel atmosphere than other resorts such as Phuket.

"Hua Hin appeals to those who are more price-driven and looking for an easy beach extension from Bangkok without extra air travel," says David Kevan, Western and Oriental group head of product.

Krabi

The southern Thai province of Krabi is about a one-hour flight from Bangkok and a two-and-a-half-hour drive from Phuket. It is renowned for its beautiful beaches backed by dramatic limestone cliffs and caves and for scores of tiny islands including Phi Phi, a location for films including *The Beach and The Man with the Golden Gun.*

Clients wanting a choice of nightlife on their doorstep should opt for hotels in Ao Nang itself, while those seeking greater tranquillity should consider the many options nearby on Phang Nga Bay.

Boat trips offer the chance to explore Krabi's secluded coves and islands. Other popular activities include scuba diving, snorkelling, kayaking, rock-climbing and jungle treks.

Jetset product manager Jonathan Ditte recommends Krabi for couples and honeymooners. "It offers an authentic taste of Thailand. It's the place to relax and do very little," he says.

(Source: A guide to Thailand's beach resorts, Travel Trade Gazette 15 May 2009)

1 Which resort, or resorts, would best appeal to families?

2 Evaluate the suitability of each of the resorts listed for a group of 19-year-old college leavers.

3 Carry out some research into the tourist arrival figures for Thailand. What is the trend?

Accommodation in Havana is available at a range of budgets from basic *casas particulares* (B&B) to five-star hotels. There are several recently restored boutique hotels, small, and individually themed, rather than part of a chain.

The city is renowned for its salsa music and this can be heard in many bars and on the streets. Havana can be visited as a short break, but many tourists take a couple of days out of a longer holiday in Cuba to visit the capital.

Local transport

It is important that tourists can access information about local transport so that they can easily get around. Boston is a good example of a city that has a wide range of transport for tourists.

Accommodation and costs

When people are planning their long-haul trip they will have a type of accommodation and associated cost in mind. This might range from a sophisticated 5-star hotel to a simple guest house where they might experience local culture. When accommodation is booked, the tourist will make choices about food and drink ranging from all inclusive to board only which allows people to choose local restaurants to dine in.

The Far East evokes images of saffron-robed Buddhist monks, golden temples and idyllic islands. In Thailand, you'll find chic designer beach hotels, sumptuous spa resorts and luxurious villas perfect for chilled out holidays. Cambodia and Vietnam are less travelled, so visitors are welcomed with open arms. Many wartime scars are now sobering tourist experiences, but the joyful nature of the people shines through.

Retrace history at the gigantic temple of Angkor Wat in Cambodia, with its grand towers shaped like lotus buds. Further east, we can take you through Japan, visiting Tokyo, Hiroshima and Kyoto, riding a Bullet Train and taking your own photo of Mount Fuji. The Terracotta Army, Great Wall and Yangtze River – see them all during a China tour.

(Source: Kuoni Worldwide, September 2009)

Case study: Machu Picchu

Hiram Bingham, an American explorer, first discovered Machu Picchu in 1911. It is an Inca city located 120 kilometres North West of Cusco in Peru and before discovery it was hidden by dense jungle on the mountains where it is located, 2430 metres above sea level.

The city's stone constructions are spread over a narrow and uneven mountain top, bordering a sheer 400-metre drop over the Urubamba River canyon. Because of the fascinating architecture the site has been designated a UNESCO World Heritage Site and has become one of South America's major travel destinations.

Many adventure holiday companies offer tours there and local operators sell day tours from Cusco. The only means of transport is a train from Cusco to Aguas Calientes, the nearest town to Machu Picchu. Then there is a 20-minute bus journey up the mountain to the ruins.

The popularity of the site has led to problems – it is in danger of being destroyed because of the large number of visitors. In the late 1990s visitors were restricted to 500 per day to protect the site. UNESCO is considering a further restriction to 100 visitors per day.

1. Find out more about Machu Picchu by researching on the internet and in other resources. Report your findings.
2. Present the arguments for and against restricting visitor numbers. You could use your ideas for a debate in your group.
3. Find out about three more long-haul destinations that are based on a historical or cultural attraction.

Produce a brief fact sheet for each one, illustrating the appeal of the destination.

Choose one of these destinations and evaluate how it could capitalise on its facilities to influence future development.

Culture

Many tourists hope to experience local culture when they are on holiday and, of course, this is one of the benefits of travel. Destinations may have cultural attractions built for other purposes, such as the Taj Mahal in India or ancient temples such as those in Sri Lanka. The cultural experience may be provided by local events or festivals, demonstrating the music and dance of a destination.

It is important that tourists show respect for the local culture and tour operators can help with this by giving information to holidaymakers before they travel.

Some destinations offer a cultural experience along with the possibility of seeing wonderful natural attractions and beautiful coastlines.

The following extract from the Kuoni Worldwide brochure demonstrates the diversity of experience available in the Far East.

Events

Tourists may visit a region to participate in an event, for example carnival in Rio de Janiero, a wine festival in California, or the World Cup.

Shopping

Shopping facilities are essential for tourists on holiday. They often provide a source for local souvenirs, but visitors may also go to New York specifically for the shopping

Assessment activity 8.4

BTEC

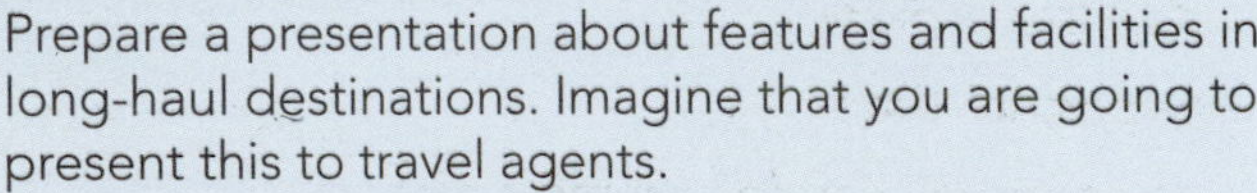

Prepare a presentation about features and facilities in long-haul destinations. Imagine that you are going to present this to travel agents.

1 Choose a long-haul destination and describe all the features and facilities of the destination in detail. You should include at least all of the following:
   - accessibility (methods of transport, their frequency, costs and facilities)
   - attractions (natural. built, events, shopping, cultural)
   - destination facilities (local transport, accommodation range and cost, other facilities such as sport, food and drink)
   - positive and negative climate features
   - appeal to different types of visitors (e.g. leisure, business and other types).

   Make sure that you link the features and facilities to the different types of UK visitor. P4

2 Write a report, to accompany your presentation, which identifies and assesses the significance of the different features and facilities on the appeal of your chosen destination, for different types of visitor from the UK.
   - Consider why these are significant for its popularity and look at visitor numbers. For example, have these increased since a new attraction or event was introduced? M2
   - Include a section in your report which evaluates these features and facilities, showing how the destination has capitalised on its features and developed its facilities to appeal to different types of visitor. D2

Grading tips

P4 Choose your destination carefully. Make sure you can access lots of information about it. You need to show how it appeals to different types of visitors.

M2 You need to assess how the destination appeals to different types of visitor, considering how developments may have affected its appeal.

D2 Consider choosing a destination which has had massive planned development undertaken as this will provide greater scope for evaluation. Ensure you clearly evaluate the features and facilities.

PLTS

Organising your time and resources, and prioritising actions will help you to develop skills as a **self-manager**.

Functional skills

Writing in report style with accurate punctuation, grammar and spelling will help to develop your **English** writing skills.

5 Plan a long-haul tour

When you plan a long-haul tour you will be considering all the factors discussed so far in this unit to determine what to include in the tour.

5.1 Before you start

Visitor needs

First, establish what kind of customer you are dealing with and establish their needs by questioning. You will need to find out:

- who is travelling
- their budget, for example economy or luxury
- their motivation – are they looking for relaxation, culture or adventure?
- restrictions in terms of time they can travel, length of tour and any special needs.

Travel

Once you have established the customer's needs think about the transport options and what will suit them. Decide on:

- the mode of travel – air, rail, self-drive
- the distance to travel and journey times – to get to the starting point and then from place to place on the tour
- the classes of travel – depending on facilities required and budget
- the provider.

Accommodation

Consider your customer's preference for:

- motels
- hotels
- campervans
- ship/boat
- camping
- facilities needed, for example catered or self-catering.

Use appropriate reference sources to find all the relevant information for the tour.

5.2 Putting together the itinerary

At its most basic, the **itinerary** gives details of the journey to be undertaken, in order to arrive at and return from the destination. However, for a multi-centre holiday the itinerary may be much more complex, as it must give details of times and accommodation in each centre.

An itinerary for a tour must have departure times and details of journeys and activities for each day of the tour.

Key term

Itinerary – a detailed plan for a journey which is clear, chronological and accurate.

A basic itinerary for a journey to a destination includes:

- passenger details
- departure date
- departure time
- departure point, for example airport
- mode of transport, for example airline
- arrival point
- arrival time
- contact details in case of enquiry.

An itinerary for a tour must include more detail:

- client details
- check-in details
- flight (service) numbers
- transport operator, type and class
- tour operator, if used
- departure and arrival in local time
- intermediate stops
- transfer details
- additional services, for example trips booked, car hire
- accommodation details, for example room type, level of service, extras, address
- passport, visa and health requirements
- activities planned (and other activities available)
- procedure for enquiries or amendments.

Ms Gillian Dale is flying on:

Thursday 07 December
London Gatwick to New York JFK; Fledgling flight 12:23 dep. Thursday 07 December 14:15; arr. Thursday 07 December 17:20

Check-in opens Thursday 07 December 11:15; Closes Thursday 07 December 13:15

Sunday 10 December
New York JFK to London Gatwick; Fledgling flight 12:24 dep. Sunday 10 December 18:45; arr. Monday 11 December 06.15

Check-in opens Sunday 10 December 13:45; Closes Sunday 10 December 15:45

Hold baggage and sports equipment
One hold bag per passenger only. The one passenger on this booking may only check-in a total of one bag. If you need to take more, please add the revelant charges to your booking.

Passport and ID
Approved photographic ID is required on all flights, including domestic services.

Pack safely!
Take care when you pack your bags. No dangerous goods may be taken in baggage and some other items may only be carried in certain parts of the aircraft. Security measures in the UK and at other European airports also strictly limit what you can carry in your hand baggage; these limitations are currently subject to change at short notice. Please ensure you check our on-line travel update for the latest information before flying.

Baggage allowance
Each paying passenger may take one standard piece of hand baggage, dimensions 45 × 35 × 16 cm and one piece of standard checked-in hold baggage weighing no more than 20 kg. Additional charges apply if you exceed this allowance.

Figure 8.4: Basic itinerary for a flight

Case study: Tour itinerary

west coast

great western safari

OVERLAND

POP TRIP CODE

●●●●○○ PHYSICAL
●●●●○ CULTURE SHOCK

- Relax on a Perth beach
- Traverse the gorges of Karijini
- Encounter dolphins in Monkey Mia
- See the bizarre Pinnacles Desert
- Drift over the amazing Ningaloo Reef
- Chill out on Cable Beach
- Traverse the bumpy Gibb River Road
- Experience the beauty of El Questro
- Explore the mysterious Bungle Bungle Ranges
- Enjoy a yarn over an icy-cold beer in Darwin

22 days, Perth to Darwin

ITINERARY... Day 1 Perth Relax on the beach or at the football. **Day 2 Kalbarri National Park** Explore surreal moonscapes in the Pinnacles Desert. Spend a relaxing evening around the campfire on a riverside ranch. **Days 3-4 Monkey Mia** Encounter dolphins up close and discover the magnificent sights of Gathaagudu (Shark Bay) through Indigenous eyes. **Days 5-6 Coral Bay** Snorkel, scuba or swim on the amazing Ningaloo Reef. Keep an eye out for manta rays and turtles, or get close to the ocean's largest fish, the whale shark. **Days 7-8 Karijini National Park** Explore red gorges and stunning wildflowers. Cool off in idyllic Karijini waterholes then once the sun sets, tell tall tales by starlight. **Day 9 Eighty Mile Beach** Camp near these sweeping shores and take in panoramic Indian Ocean views, just a short walk from camp. **Days 10-12 Broome** Shop for pearls, take a sunset camel ride or chill out with a cocktail on Cable Beach. Explore Broome's cultural diversity on an optional afternoon tour of the town. Sample local mangoes, beers, seafood and bush tucker, capped off with a sunset beach barbecue. **Day 13 Windjana Gorge** Travel off the beaten track in the Kimberley Ranges. Explore amazing underground caves at Tunnel Creek and spy crocodiles basking in the afternoon sun at Windjana Gorge. **Days 14-15 Gibb River Road** The rugged Gibb River Road snakes through the King Leopold Ranges and some outstanding gorges. Cool off in tranquil rockpools and camp in the Kimberley bush. **Days 16-17 El Questro** This sprawling Outback cattle station can be explored by land, water or air. Ride horses, take a river cruise or fly over the property by helicopter to experience the Never Never's vast, desolate beauty. **Days 18-19 Purnululu National Park (Bungle Bungle Ranges)** Tackle a rough, dusty dirt road to reach the Bungle Bungle 'beehives', created by erosion and river flows over 20 million years. Until recently the region was only known to locals. **Day 20 Timber Creek** Travel across Gregory National Park and over the border into Timber Creek, reputedly Australia's best barramundi fishing spot. **Days 21-22 Darwin** Take a refreshing dip at Edith Falls en route to Darwin, the tropical Northern Territory capital.

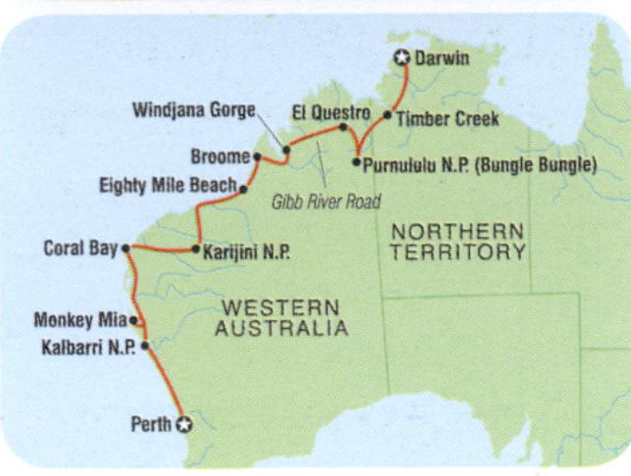

Above: Windjana Gorge National Park, Western Australia - Tourism WA
Below: Photo Competition 2009, Camel ride, Cable Beach, Western Australia - Kathryn Buder

ACCOMMODATION Hotel (2 nts), lodges (2 nts), camping with facilities (10 nts), bush camping (6 nts), farmstay (1 nt) **TRANSPORT** Safari vehicle, 4x4 safari vehicle, walking **GROUP SIZE** Max 18 **MEALS** 19 Breakfasts, 11 Lunches, 17 Dinners **BUDGET** Allow AU$200 for meals not included **DEPARTS** Selected days from Apr - Oct **GUARANTEE** Subject to min 6 **NOTES** This trip also operates in reverse, see Trip Code PON **TRAVELLER RATING** 5.00 out of 5

Start	Finish	Start	Finish	Start	Finish	Start	Finish
2010		18 Jun	09 Jul	11 Oct	01 Nov	17 Jun	08 Jul
10 Apr	01 May	11 Jul	01 Aug	**2011**			
03 May	24 May	03 Aug	24 Aug	09 Apr	30 Apr		
26 May	16 Jun	26 Aug	16 Sep	02 May	23 May		
		18 Sep	09 Oct	25 May	15 Jun		

22

for trip notes, availability and more, enter the trip code at **intrepidtravel.com**

(Source: Great Western Safari from Intrepid Travel Holidays Jan 2009 – April 2010)

1 Using the itinerary checklist, make notes of what extra information the customer would need.

2 Produce a new itinerary with all the extra information included. You will have to research suitable flights.

3 Describe the type of visitor this tour is suitable for and explain why.

Assessment activity 8.5

Read the following scenario and produce an exemplar itinerary.

Two couples in their mid-20s wish to arrange a multi-centre holiday together. They are Marsha and Frederik and Carla and Pedro. They all work in London. Frederik and Pedro are archaeology graduates, although they now both work in the city. Marsha and Carla are lecturers at a college of further education. Marsha lectures in communications and Carla in art.

The four want to visit South America. All have busy lives and need to incorporate some relaxation and rest into their holiday, but they also want to visit different places of interest. They are high earners so can afford luxurious surroundings. They want the opportunity to visit historical sites and the men would like to pursue their interest in archaeology. Carla would like to look at local arts and crafts and may want to buy some pieces to bring home.

All want some time to rest on a beach in the sun and to wine and dine in the evenings, but it is also important that they get to know the local culture. They can travel in March or April (around Easter time) for two or three weeks.

1 Produce an itinerary for this multi-centre tour.
   - Your tour must contain at least four centres, transport arrangements from the UK and between the centres, including journey times, distances and options available.
   - It should also include accommodation to be used en route and at each centre, as well as the attractions/events available to the visitor at each centre. Include also any pre-booked excursions.
   - You must devise the tour yourself and note reference sources used including both electronic and printed sources. P5
2 Add notes to the itinerary, justifying how the tour meets the needs of the two couples. M3

Grading tips

P5 Make sure you construct your own tour and it is not copied from a brochure. Provide evidence of your individual research by showing the sources you used. Use a wide variety of reference sources. Remember to compile a bibliography.

M3 Consider cost and particularly the choice of appropriate accommodation and transport when you justify your choices.

PLTS

Exploring issues from the perspective of others by producing an itinerary suitable for your customer needs will help you to develop skills as an **independent enquirer**.

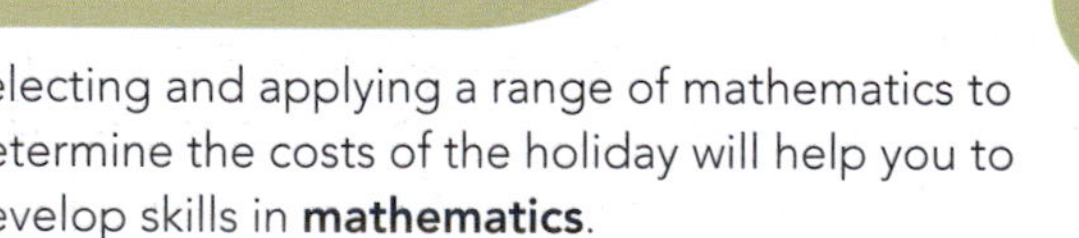

Functional skills

Selecting and applying a range of mathematics to determine the costs of the holiday will help you to develop skills in **mathematics**.

WorkSpace

Andy McQueen

Travel Advisor

Andy works for a long-haul Travel Company, which was established 20 years ago and specialises in travel for students and young people. One of their main areas of expertise is long-haul adventure travel. It is Andy's job to research and develop tours for the company to sell. "I love this job because I'm able to offer people a real experience and in turn experience it myself."

Andy, please tell us more about your role and the skills and qualifications you need.

I work in a local branch and it's my job to listen to a customer's needs and wishes regarding their travel and customise a tour for them.

Some clients are what we call 'free spirits' and prefer just the minimum from us. They are more in it for the journey experience, so I would just sell them their flights and possibly the first night's accommodation. Others may be more complex and what we call in business 'inertia breakers'. They want their whole trip structured for them, in which case I will have to contact airlines and hotels and tours in order to tailor-make a holiday experience the client will enjoy.

Every customer is different and I have to customise a trip for their individual needs. In order to do this efficiently I had to complete a six week basic training from the company on top of my BTEC Travel and Tourism National Diploma. Also, actual experience of travelling has been really beneficial and people skills in listening and enthusiasm are crucial.

Where do you think the experience in this job will take you in the future?

I would like to move up the ladder with the company as they offer great bonus incentives and free holidays. I hope to move into the head office in the next few years and continue to work within the company. The experience and skills I've picked up within the branch will help me to progress within the company or even at another travel agent if I preferred to move in future.

Think about it!

1 Explain what is meant by 'inertia breaker'.

2 Why is experience of travelling important for this role?

3 How does this company differ from other travel agents?

Just checking

1 Name three useful reference sources for long-haul travel information.
2 Explain the difference between tourist arrivals and receipts.
3 Why is Australia a popular long-haul destination for people travelling from the UK?
4 Why is Florida suitable for families?
5 Why are people travelling so far now for short breaks?
6 Give two examples of cities suitable for long-haul short breaks from the UK.
7 How does education motivate people to travel?
8 What is Greenwich Mean Time?
9 How can jet lag be alleviated?
10 Why might the government put travel restrictions in place?
11 Give an example of how looking for a certain type of holiday affects customer choice.

Assignment tips

Collect lots of different long-haul brochures for this unit.

- When choosing destinations for assessment purposes, make sure visitor information is available.
- Remember to use the United Nations World Tourism Organization (UNWTO) statistics to find out visitor numbers.
- Remember to look at spending as well (tourist receipts)
- Look for articles in newspapers about factors that affect travel to specific destinations.
- Look out for articles that are about development in a destination and think about why it has happened

Credit value: 10

9 Retail travel operations

When you finish your studies you may opt to work in the retail travel industry. This component of travel and tourism has faced substantial change in the last few years and is still changing in order to meet customer needs. With the correct skills and knowledge, you can forge a great career in retail travel. There are travel agencies in all localities so it is a flexible option in terms of location. You will have the opportunity to practise your customer service skills at first hand with people who are excited about booking travel or holidays. There are plenty of incentives for staff who work hard, including educational trips to holiday destinations.

In this unit you will find out how retail travel agencies operate, how travel agents are linked with other businesses in travel and tourism and how they co-operate or compete with one another.

You will examine the impact of advances in technology on the sector and how retail agents fight to have competitive advantage.

You will learn how to select different products and services to meet customer needs and how to select leisure holidays to meet customer needs.

Learning outcomes

After completing this unit you should:

1 know the retail travel environment

2 know retail travel operational practices

3 understand how retail travel organisations seek to gain a competitive advantage

4 be able to select, cost and provide information for leisure holidays to meet the needs of customers.

Assessment and grading criteria

This table shows you what you must do in order to achieve a **pass**, **merit** or **distinction** grade, and where you can find activities in this book to help you.

To achieve a **pass** grade the evidence must show that you are able to:	To achieve a **merit** grade the evidence must show that, in addition to the pass criteria, you are able to:	To achieve a **distinction** grade the evidence must show that, in addition to the pass and merit criteria, you are able to:
P1 describe the retail travel environment **See Assessment activity 9.1, page 253**	**M1** explain the importance of links and relationships within the retail travel environment **See Assessment activity 9.1, page 253**	**D1** analyse how the use of technology has impacted on the retail travel environment and retail operational practices **See Assessment activity 9.1, page 253**
P2 describe retail travel operational practices **See Assessment activity 9.1, page 253**	**M2** compare the effectiveness of the operational practices of two retail agents **See Assessment activity 9.1, page 253**	
P3 explain how different retail travel organisations use techniques to seek to gain competitive advantage **See Assessment activity 9.2, page 256**	**M3** compare the effectiveness of the techniques used by two retail agents to gain a competitive advantage **See Assessment activity 9.2, page 256**	**D2** recommend the use of alternative techniques to gain further competitive advantage for two retail travel agents **See Assessment activity 9.2, page 256**
P4 use appropriate resources to select, cost and provide information on packages holidays that meet specific customer needs **See Assessment activity 9.3, page 258**		
P5 use appropriate resources to select, cost and provide information on tailor-made holidays that meet specific customer needs **See Assessment activity 9.3, page 258**		

How you will be assessed

This unit will be assessed by one or more internal assignments that will be designed and marked by your tutor. Your assignments will be subject to sampling internally and externally as part of Edexcel's quality assurance procedures. The assignments are designed to allow you to show your knowledge and understanding related to the unit. The unit outcomes indicate what you should know, understand or be able to do after completing the unit.

Jenny, 18-year-old BTEC National learner

I was looking forward to this unit as I have had a work placement in a retail travel agency and I collected lots of information about their procedures which I knew would help me. Even so, there were quite a lot of new things to learn.

I had a lot of the information I needed for my first assignment, but I still had to find out more about the different types of agent and the technology they used. My placement was at a small independent agency, so I visited a First Choice shop with one of my group to find out how a chain differed. The manager agreed to talk to us and showed us how their systems worked. I also looked at some websites on consortia to find out more about them.

We all enjoyed finding holidays for customers in Assignment 2. We practised a lot before the assessment. Our tutor suggested that we practised in threes. One would be the agent, one the customer and the third was an observer using the checklist on page 258 to feedback to the agent.

I am not sure if this is the career for me as I really want to travel – a lot – but it was really useful to know so much about how this industry works.

Over to you!

1. What local retail travel agents can you think of? What information can you get from them?
2. How might your group work as a team to gather information so that you don't all approach the same organisations?
3. What kind of travel do you think retail agents get to do?

1 The retail travel environment

Set off

Local travel agents

Get to know your local travel agents. You can visit and collect brochures. Have a look at their procedures – discreetly. Look at the environment.

- What kind of displays can you see?
- Is there an effort to create a holiday atmosphere?
- Do you feel welcome?

Report back on your impressions to your group.

1.1 Retail agencies

ABTA – The Travel Association defines a retail travel business as follows:

> Retail business is business transacted in the capacity of a travel agent, i.e. a person carrying on business, in whole or in part, as agent for a principal remunerated by commission or otherwise, in respect of the sale or offer for sale of travel arrangements. Retail businesses are not in contract with the client.
>
> *(Source: www.abta.com)*

Role of a retail travel agent

A retail travel agent acts as an intermediary (middleman) between the customer and the **supplier**. The retail agent does not buy the products or services of the supplier and sell them on; rather, retail agents work on a **commission** basis. The commission is variable between suppliers. Charges for a retail agent's services are becoming more common and acceptable to customers.

Key terms

Supplier – for a retail travel agent, a supplier can be a hotel, transport company, tour operator, insurance company, etc.

Commission – a percentage of the value of the sale, paid by the supplier to the agent who made the sale.

Types of retail agencies

Retail agencies specialise in leisure travel – that is, mostly holidays – but some do cater for business customers. There are different types of retail travel agent.

Multiples

Multiples are chains of more than 100 branches – some are on almost every high street. They are usually public limited companies who prefer, and can afford, prime locations. TUI and Thomas Cook are the major brands and control just over a quarter of high street retail travel agents between them.

Independents

An independent retail travel agency is often owned by a family or partnership. These outlets are more likely to be found in smaller towns as it is difficult for them to afford the high rents of prime locations. Many independents have been bought out by multiple chains, but those that remain have a reputation for good personal service.

Activity: Northenden Travel

Northenden Travel (www.northendentravel.co.uk) is an example of a family independent. It is a sizeable business employing over 40 people, but is nowhere near the scale of the multiples.

- Find out about family owned and managed Northenden Travel.
- How does the company's independence allow them to offer a better service?

E-agents

Many major tour operators are on-line. They recognise that internet access and use are growing and that they need this element to their business. There are also companies that trade as on-line travel agencies without any retail shop presence. They sell packages, flights or accommodation. Examples include Expedia and Lastminute.com.

Home workers

Many people enjoy the flexibility of working from home, especially those with family commitments. There are several companies operating in this market with a network of home workers. Examples include Travel Counsellors and Future Travel (part of Co-operative Travel).

Call centres

Some companies have dedicated call centres. Many of them are tour operators and flight agents. However, some are operated by travel agents, for example STA. It is not appropriate for call centres for the travel market to operate in developing countries, which are cheaper to run, as operators must have knowledge of the UK outbound market and destinations.

Think about it

Virtual call centres now exist where the agents are located in their homes with calls going to a central number. Calls are distributed to agents depending on availability and their specialist knowledge. What are the benefits for the home-based travel agents in a virtual call centre?

Holiday hypermarkets

These are very large retail travel agencies with staff who specialise in particular holiday types. They tend to be located in large shopping centres where there is a lot of passing trade. They have many promotions, but are expected to hit high sales targets. First Choice was the first company to introduce this type of retail travel agent and they have over 30 outlets, many situated in retail parks.

Miniples

Miniples are chains, but they tend to be smaller and less powerful than the multiples. They are usually located in one region where they may be well-known and have developed a good reputation. Premier Travel based in Cambridge is an example, with more than 20 outlets.

Consortia for independent agents

Independent travel agents usually seek to maintain control of their own businesses, yet they can lose out on the buying power of a large group and find it difficult to compete against the big tour operators. Joining a consortium can help them with this problem.

Consortia allow the travel agents to gain the benefits of being in a group, yet retain their independence. Some consortia give the agents the option of using the consortium brand name, which gives the benefit of recognition by the public. Examples of consortia in the UK are Freedom Travel, Advantage and Global.

Benefits include:

- the consortium negotiating deals with suppliers
- recognised brand name
- use of technology systems and bonding schemes.

Disadvantages include:

- cost, although it varies a lot between consortia
- control – a consortium like Global operates as a franchise, so the agent is not completely in control of the business.

Activity: Franchises

If you were setting up your own travel agency you might decide to start as a **franchise** to reduce risk. Visit the website of a franchise, for example www.freedomtravelgroup.com and detail how belonging to the franchise reduces risk, for example offering ABTA – The Travel Association membership. Make some notes on your findings.

Key term

Franchise – buying the right to sell a company's products or services under a brand name.

1.2 Products and services

The travel agent provides a range of products and services including:

- information on holidays and travel
- booking of traditional package holidays
- tailor-made and dynamic packages
- booking of travel, for example scheduled and charter flights
- accommodation
- ancillary sales, for example parking or excursions, insurance
- scheduled and charter flights
- currency exchange.

Travel agents traditionally sell package holidays and historically this has provided the most revenue in commissions. To boost that revenue, agents will try to add on **auxiliary sales** including transport to the airport, insurance and excursions on holiday.

There is a current trend for customers to use travel agents for advice and brochures, but book their holiday on-line at home. To compete, agents have become much smarter at putting together tailor-made holidays – or **dynamic packaging**. We may also see agents charging for providing advice and information.

Key terms

Auxillary sales – selling additional products and services that add value to the basic holiday or travel arrangements.

Dynamic packaging – industry jargon for tailor-making a package suited to the needs of a particular customer.

Activity: Buying insurance

Is it cheaper to buy insurance from a travel agent or from an insurance company? Find out the cost of insurance for a two week holiday for two adults to Spain from a travel agent. Compare with the same deal from an insurance company.

- Which is cheaper?
- What is the percentage difference?

Links with other organisations

Because travel agents work on a commission basis, the relationships they have with other companies are very important. These relationships may take the form of trading agreements or they may be part of the same trading group, for example Thomson travel agents belong to TUI UK.

The sectors that travel agents deal with are:

- hotels and other accommodation providers
- transport providers
- ancillary providers such as insurance companies
- car hire companies
- tour operators.

1.3 Relationships

Vertical integration

The principle of vertical integration was explained in Unit 1 (see page 15). It occurs forwards or backwards in the chain of distribution when an organisation takes over another company or role in the chain. It gives the advantages of control and of economies of scale. The major multiple travel agents in the UK are owned by vertically integrated companies.

The integration of companies into one group allows the tour operators to control the distribution of their products. Although all agencies sell each other's products, they give preference to their own brands. For example, they will display more brochures for their own-branded products. Agents also receive larger commissions when they sell their own products.

Think about it

A policy of promoting own brands is known as 'directional selling'. Critics say that it means customers are not given a full choice.

Horizontal integration

This occurs when companies are bought out or merged at the same level in the chain of distribution. For example, one travel agent buys another.

Activity: Making links

Figure 9.1: Links with the trade press

Figure 9.1 shows how Manchester airport cements its relationship with the travel trade by thanking them for voting for the airport in the TTG Travel Awards. The Travel Awards themselves bring together different components of the travel and tourism sector. Other companies attract the interest of travel agents by offering training or competitions.

You will notice that there is a trade support contact on the advertisement.

Discuss with your group what kind of support the airport might offer to travel agents.

Activity: All change!

It is very difficult to keep up with changes in the ownership of travel agents. Look in the trade press for recent changes. Look for examples of:

- a travel agent taking over another
- a travel agent being bought by a tour operator
- a travel agent going out of business
- the opening of e-agents.

Make a display of your findings. Specify whether your examples are of horizontal or vertical integration.

Agency agreements

Travel agents work on behalf of principals or tour operators. If both travel agent and tour operator are members of ABTA – The Travel Association they will be bound by the ABTA Code of Conduct.

This lays out the responsibilities of an agent to customers, tour operators and other suppliers.

An agency agreement will lay out the terms and conditions of the contract, including commissions. If a travel agent stocks a tour operator's brochure and sells from it, there is an implied contract between them, even if there is no written agreement. ABTA – The Travel Association provides a model contract for its members to use with their suppliers. Preferred agents will be discussed later.

2 Retail operational practices

2.1 Working practices

Front-and back-office systems

Front-office procedures are to do with selling products to customers. Back-office procedures are to do with suppliers of the products and the running of the office: following up bookings, making payments, banking, ordering brochures, stationery and currency, etc. These procedures do not involve the customer.

Travel agents use a number of systems:

- Viewdata – the interactive screen system that travel agents use to access the tour operators' reservation systems
- Computer Reservation System (CRS) – each tour operator, airline, cruise line, etc. has a computer reservation system accessible by the Viewdata system. These have been superseded by GDS systems
- Global Distribution Systems (GDS) – more sophisticated developments of the computer reservation services. They might combine several computer reservation systems from different suppliers and offer other travel services also. Examples include Amadeus, Galileo, Sabre and Worldspan.

The current GDS systems offer:

- real-time availability
- 24-hour access to the system
- multi-operator searches.

Activity: GDS

What would the agent need to know when searching for a holiday for a customer? Make a checklist of the details the agent needs to search their GDS system. Compare your list with others to make sure it is correct.

Procedures and documentation for selling travel services

The procedures and documentation for selling vary between travel agencies and according to whether the agent is selling a package holiday or different components. Galileo is an example of a common system used for looking for package holidays, but for individual components such as accommodation the agent will log in to a supplier's trade to check availability and prices.

The basic procedure for a travel agent is as follows.

- Establish a rapport with the customer.
- Identify exactly what their needs are.
- Establish if they will be booking today or looking for information on cost.
- If a booking is made, complete a booking form and ask the customer to sign it.
- Take the payment (either in full or a deposit), enter the details of the payment into the system and give the customer a receipt.
- Ensure that the customer has insurance – this is a sales opportunity and chance to earn further commission.
- Consider what other add-on sales can be made, for example excursions or currency.
- Enter all details into the system, make copies of all paperwork completed and file it.
- Post or email tickets to the customer, or set them aside to be collected.
- Reconcile all payments against the banking printout that lists all transactions and is generated from the computer at the end of a day.

Merchandising and displays

It is important that the agency and the window display appeal to passers-by. Late deals are a common merchandising tool to attract people and these are often displayed on cards in the window. These are compiled by staff who search for the offers on their systems.

Racking policies and preferred operators

Racking refers to the practice of displaying brochures on shelves for customers to browse. Vertically integrated travel agents give prominence to their own products. Independent travel agents select the range of products and services they want to offer based on the quality of the offering and customer demand. Preferred operators are those who work closely with the agency, perhaps providing staff training posters and better commissions. Their brochures will be more prominently displayed.

How is racking used in a travel agency?

Commission level

Commission is paid monthly and depends on bookings made. The commission differs with each product or company.

Airline commissions can be as much as 10 per cent, for airlines like Emirates, or zero for the low-cost airlines. Some travel suppliers operate a tiered system where agents are categorised. Top agents (those who do a lot of business for the supplier) can negotiate high commissions.

Sales targets

A sales target for each branch is set by head office. The target is divided between individuals, with more experienced staff expected to sell more and part-time staff having smaller targets. Bonuses may be paid when staff reach their targets. For multiples, targets may be set by suppliers which is often implemented at branch level.

Switch selling

Switch selling is when a customer intends to buy a certain product, but is sold a different one by the agent. If it occurs because the agent is listening to the needs of customers and wishes to recommend a product better matching their needs, then it is acceptable. It is contentious to switch sell in order to attain a better commission or other incentive.

2.2 Technology

Using technology

You have already seen how technology is used in the daily working practice of a travel agent. It is also used in training. Agents can log onto websites provided by tour operators or tourist boards and carry out on-line training.

Independent agents may find replacing hardware and introducing new applications very expensive and the retail travel industry is not renowned for embracing new technology. However, there are some very useful applications available. An example is the Carbon Tracker tool introduced by Travelport. The technology enables the carbon footprint for travel by air, rail and car hire to be calculated for journeys of under two-and-a-half hours.

Impacts of technology

As travel agents invest in new technology they should in return get an increased volume of sales. Bookings should be made more quickly with the new systems and it should be possible to have up-to-date information on availability. Agents have greater awareness of new products and services available from principals. Administration procedures are less susceptible to human error and procedures are less time-consuming than manual methods.

Figure 9.2 shows how people use the internet to look for travel products and services.

There are those who think that retailers will disappear from our high streets and that we will all book over the internet and others who think that retailers have a future.

Many industry experts think that those retail travel agencies which do survive will have to offer a personal service (dynamic packages) with expert knowledge of destinations and products, booking components separately to give the customer exactly the holiday they want.

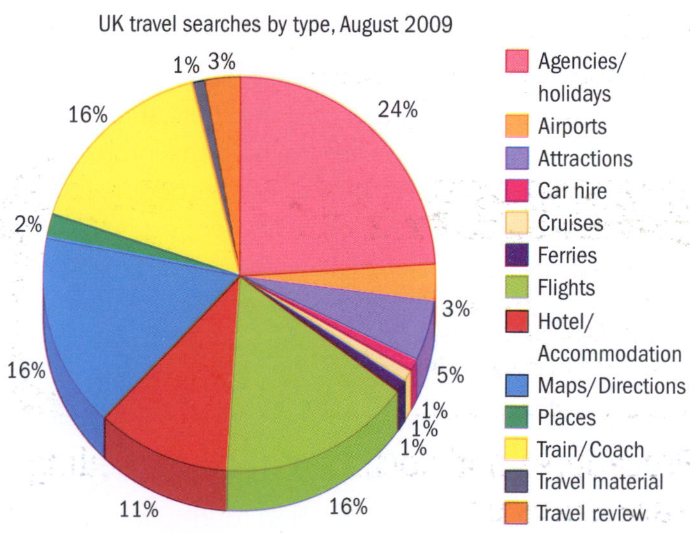

Figure 9.2: How do people search for travel?

(Source: weblogs.hitwise.com)

There will always be some people without internet access and people who demand personal service or just can't cope with booking their own holiday arrangements. Where travel agents are booking products which do not carry a commission, such as low-cost flights, some are charging service fees. Where a fee is charged the service offered has to be excellent or customers will go elsewhere – it cannot be just a booking service.

Think about it

A typical service charge is £20–25 and if the customer makes the booking then the charge can be credited against it. Why do people choose to pay more money when they could book it themselves for less? Would you pay for service in a travel agency?

2.3 Legislation

When travel agents tailor-make packages for customers, they act as tour operators and therefore must be aware of and abide by all the relevant legislation.

The Package Travel, Package Holidays and Package Tours Regulations 1992

These regulations impact on retail travel agents as they cover not only the organisation of package holidays, but also the selling of them.

Travel agents need to understand and adhere to these regulations when they sell and also when they tailor-make packages for clients. The regulations are aimed primarily at tour operators.

Data Protection Act 1998

This legislation provides rights for people who have information held about them in 'relevant filing systems'. A travel agent's files are held on computers and on paper. The Act requires those who hold the information to follow sound practice. This means that people must have access to the information if they request it and have it corrected or deleted if necessary. They must also consent to the collection and processing of their data. Personal data must be kept secure and up to date and not kept for longer than necessary.

Consumer protection

There are many laws in place to protect consumers. These are not specific to travel and tourism or travel agents but apply generally across all industries. However, it is important that travel agents are aware of them and ensure they abide by them.

Acts in place to protect consumers include:

- Trade Descriptions Act 1968 (see page 125)
- Supply of Goods and Services Act 1982 (the section of this Act which is important is the one relating to a contract being carried out with 'reasonable care and skill'. Travel agents must ensure that they carry out the bookings correctly.)
- Unfair Terms in Consumer Contracts Regulations 1999 (see page 125).

Contract law

When a customer books a holiday with a travel agent they enter into a legally binding contract with the tour operator offering the holiday. Travel agents ask the customer to read and accept the tour operator's conditions before booking, but do not enter into a contract with the customer themselves. They may ask the client to sign a document allowing the travel agent to act on their behalf.

Activity: Reading the small print

Do you think people read the booking conditions when they book a holiday? Do you read them?

Make a list of the details you think are covered in booking conditions. Compare your list with that of a colleague and the actual booking conditions given in a brochure or on a flight booking.

2.4 Trade associations and memberships

ABTA – The Travel Association

ABTA is the UK's best-known trade association for tour operators and travel agents. Of foreign package holidays sold in the UK, 90 per cent are sold through ABTA members. In 2008 ABTA merged with the Federation of Tour Operators (FTO), reinforcing its role as the leading travel association and increasing benefits for both ABTA and FTO members.

ABTA represents over 5000 travel agencies and 900 tour operators in the UK.

It is important for agents to join, as the public will look for an ABTA travel agent when booking travel and holidays. The main benefit to consumers of booking through an ABTA travel agent is that, in the event of the agent or tour operator going bankrupt, ABTA will ensure that people can continue their holiday arrangements if an agent fails or have a refund if a tour operator fails. It gives them a sense of security, knowing that the travel agency follows ABTA's code of conduct and is bonded. However, membership is not compulsory for travel agents.

Air Travel Organiser's Licensing (ATOL)

ATOL is the government's licensing and bonding scheme for tour operators selling holiday packages that include flights, and flight specialists selling charter and discounted scheduled airline tickets. If a business fails, the Civil Aviation Authority (CAA) will protect customers overseas and provide a full refund to those unable to travel.

Travel agents who sell only package holidays would not require an ATOL bond. However, as travel agents are increasingly offering dynamic packaging, they need to apply for an ATOL bond to protect themselves and their customers.

Association of Train Operating Companies (ATOC)

ATOC represents the interests of train operating companies to the government, regulatory bodies and the media on transport policy issues. The organisation is also responsible for licensing travel agents to sell rail tickets and other rail products.

International Air Transport Association (IATA)

Travel agents who want to sell or issue international airline tickets must be accredited by IATA. There are detailed criteria for accreditation. You can look at these on the IATA website (www.iata.co.uk).

Assessment activity 9.1

BTEC

You are an assistant in the offices of ABTA – The Travel Association. Your department deals with travel agency support and is preparing for a conference entitled 'The Future of the British Travel Agent – Strategies for Survival'.

The conference will help members stay up to date with developments in, or affecting, the retail travel sector and show them how they can remain competitive in a rapidly changing environment.

You will carry out the research for the ABTA presentations. Your findings should be clearly presented with suitable headings, sub-headings and illustrations. Ensure you:

- Describe the retail travel environment of today, including a description of **all** types of retail agents along with a named example and the products and services they offer. P1
- Produce a diagram with descriptive notes, showing the different links and relationships between retail agents and tour operators, accommodation providers, transport providers and ancillary providers giving named examples. Include examples of integration and other links. P1
- Explain the importance of links and relationships between travel agents and other organisations in travel and tourism environment in the diagram. Give examples. M1
- Describe the operational practices of two different types of retail agent. Give specific examples of working practices, technology, legislation, trade associations and licensing. P2
- Compare the effectiveness of the operational practices of retail travel agents described above. M2
- Building on all your research and evidence so far, analyse how the use of technology has impacted on the retail travel environment and on operational practice. D1

Grading tips

P1 Ensure you describe the roles of all the following with examples of each:

- independents
- multiples
- e-agents
- home workers
- call centres
- holiday hypermarkets
- miniples
- consortia.

P1 Describe the range of products and services that the retail agents provide with specific examples and include traditional package holidays; tailor-made holiday; ancillary sales; scheduled flights; charter flights and accommodation.

P2 Choose your agencies carefully to allow you to progress to M2.

M1 Consider why the links and relationships have developed and how they affect the organisations concerned.

M2 Look at the similarities and differences in operational practices and comment on which are more effective.

D1 Ensure you demonstrate a clear understanding of the retail travel environment and retail operational practices. Focus on how technology has changed the way retail travel agents operate.

PLTS

By analysing and evaluating information and judging its relevance, you will be practising your skills as an **independent enquirer**.

Functional skills

As you evaluate the application of ICT tools and facilities used to present information to retail travel agents, you will be developing your **ICT** skills.

3 How retail travel organisations seek to gain a competitive advantage

3.1 Techniques to gain competitive advantage

Whatever the type of agent, multiple or independent, a travel agent has constantly to develop and be innovative in order to gain competitive advantage over other retailers.

Level of service

This is of the utmost importance. When customers book on-line, face-to-face service is missing. If travel agents can make sure that customers receive superb service in their retail outlets, that becomes a reason to use the agent rather than book direct.

Staff training

Training employees well is the best means of being competitive. Through training, agents develop their selling skills and destination knowledge and are thus able to provide personal service to customers. There are different types of training, ranging from induction for new staff, to ongoing training to update skills and knowledge and weekly sessions given by the manager for all staff.

Promotional activities

Promotional activities include any activity that encourages customers to buy. Competitions can be held in agencies so that customers want to come in. The prize may be a voucher towards a holiday – in a competition promoted by another organisation. This can lead to good publicity. Alternatively a recent promotion at First Choice involved using aroma technology to attract customers: customers walked into the travel agency and smelt ice cream to evoke a holiday feeling.

How can travel agents promote holidays to Australia?

Discounting

Large chains may run a discount promotion to encourage sales in times of poor trade. Some travel agents ensure competitiveness by constantly checking offers in their competitors' shops and matching the prices. Others offer low deposits for a limited period to entice people to book immediately.

Activity: Promoting holidays

In small teams, think up two ideas for promoting holidays to Australia and produce the materials for them. Make the promotions into a display for others to see.

Developing the range of products and services

Travel agents can develop their range of products and services by introducing those from tour operators and promoting them. Sometimes they branch out into different areas. For example, one travel agent now sells a range of luggage. Some agents specialise in specific markets to become experts in the area, e.g. cruise, adventure travel, and long-haul.

Think about it

The CCS call centre (encompassing P&O cruises, Princess cruises, Cunard and Ocean Village brands) is now to open on Sundays. How does this help them to gain a competitive advantage?

Add-on sales

Add-on sales are a vital part of a travel agent's business. They include all the extras such as travel insurance, parking, currency exchange, excursions and entertainment. Staff are trained to make these add-on sales.

Dynamic packaging

Dynamic packaging (see page 248) is perhaps the most significant in terms of competitive advantage as it offers a personal service to customers and saves them the time and effort of doing it themselves.

Integrated organisations

Integrated companies are so large and powerful that they are able to adapt to a changing market by developing different means of distributing their products and services. Besides having retail outlets, they have call centres and websites and they sell on television, some via their own television channels. Their size can give them a pricing advantage as it allows the ability to discount and offer special deals with certain suppliers.

Activity: Travel distribution

Travel Update News

A re-structure has recently taken place at Fabulous Travel following its merger with Sea and Sand Holidays. A new director, Nick Ford, has been appointed to manage the integration of systems with a particular focus on distribution.

His first task is to introduce a web-based selling system that can be used for all the company brands. At the moment each company uses a different system, resulting in different services being offered to customers depending on which website they use or whether they book through a retail agent.

The aim is for a seamless, consistent product and service offering via the same selling system – whether a customer books on-line, by phone or in a retail agency.

It is estimated that a combined total of 60% of sales come via the two company websites and about 40% through retail agents.

- Describe the different methods of distribution used by Fabulous Travel.
- Explain why these methods of distribution are used and why changes might have occurred in percentage of sales from different types of distribution.

Assessment activity 9.2

Remember that you are helping prepare for ABTA – The Travel Association's conference on 'The Future of the British Travel Agent – strategies for survival'. A workshop is planned on competitive advantage. You are to prepare material for the workshop in the form of discussion notes.

1 Explain how three or more different types of retail travel organisations use techniques to gain competitive advantage. Make sure you cover:
   - level of service
   - staff training
   - promotional activities
   - the range of products and services on offer
   - add-on sales
   - ancillary products and services
   - dynamic packaging
   - integrated organisations. 

2 Compare the effectiveness of the techniques used by two retail travel organisations to gain a competitive advantage. Consider the similarities and differences and highlight which are most effective. M3

3 Recommend the use of alternative techniques for the organisations to improve competitiveness. D2

Grading tips

M3 Ensure your evidence is specific and that you include specific up-to-date examples. Use the travel trade press to help you keep aware of new developments.

D3 Justify your recommendation providing examples to support your suggestions. You will find it useful to focus on the same two travel agents you used for M3.

PLTS

When you recommend new techniques to improve competitiveness, you will be practising your skills as a **creative thinker**.

Functional skills

By writing discussion notes which can be used to communicate information effectively and persuasively, you will be developing your skills in **English**.

4 Select, cost and provide information for leisure holidays to meet specific customer needs

Traditionally, the role of travel agents has been to sell package holidays on behalf of tour operators. But this role is changing. Although travel agents must still know how to select and cost a package holiday, there is a greater emphasis on arranging tailor-made holidays to meet different customer needs.

4.1 Customer needs

The selected holiday should accommodate the individual needs of the customer. All customers have basic needs: transport, accommodation and food.

In addition they have needs relating to their special requirements. They also might require particular facilities such as five-star accommodation, or alternative activities for different members of the party.

The travel agent will start by finding out about the type of customer and their needs. They will ask about the number in the party and who they are. They will need basic facts such as departure date and point of departure. They will ask about the destination and what type of accommodation and board is required. Once this basic brief is ascertained, the agent will ask more questions to find out specific needs and start their search.

Activity: Details and requirements

Make up some customer details and requirements that you can present to another member of your group. These should be for customers who are looking for a UK domestic holiday in the summer. In turn, accept a customer profile and requirements and put together a suitable domestic holiday.

4.2 Packaged holidays

The range of package holidays on offer is endless, with a full range offered by the major operators such as Thomas Cook and TUI UK. As a travel agent you would need to be familiar with the range of brochures offered by every tour operator selling package holidays, these could include packages by air, coach, self-drive and cruise. Tour operators help agents (and promote their products) by providing training packs or training sessions for agency staff.

Brochures may be general (for example, Summer Sun) or related to any kind of specialism (such a specific destination). Holidays offered may be **short-haul** or **long-haul**.

Key terms

Short-haul – a flight of two to three hours.

Long-haul – a flight of more than six hours.

The brochure is a selling tool for the tour operator. There is always a description of the resort, details of available accommodation and facilities offered, price charts according to season and costs of supplements, for example, to have a single room or an extra person in a room. Supplements are added for flights in case of upgrades, there may be under-occupancy supplements or child discounts.

4.3 Tailor-made holidays

These are more exacting for the travel agent as they have to know where to find all the information for the different components of a holiday, whereas if they book a package the tour operator has done the ground work for them.

Some booking systems now bring together databases of accommodation, flights and transfers and help them research and book tailor-made packages. The agent can book using airline websites and accommodation websites directly, but in this case they would add a **mark-up** for the service.

Key term

Mark-up – an additional price increase/cost.

Activity: Lapland

You work in a travel agency and have a customer who wants to take her children to Lapland in December to meet Father Christmas. She will be travelling with two children, aged six and nine. They want to go for two nights from any London airport and on any dates in December. The parent wants meals included as far as possible. Tailor-make a holiday for the trio and present the details.

4.4 Information

A travel agent also needs to be able to give the customer information about passports, visas and vaccinations. It is usual for travel agents to provide a passport and visa application service which the customer will pay for.

They will have to provide an itinerary with check-in details, flight numbers, times, accommodation details and baggage allowances. You must know where to find this information.

Activity: Questions

Here are some typical questions overheard in a day's work at a travel agency. Can you answer them? You might have to do some research.

- What do I do if my baggage is overweight at the airline check-in?
- Can I get a visa on entry to Kilimanjaro?
- What is different about going first class on Eurostar?
- I am leaving Heathrow at 10:00 a.m. I want to take the airport bus from Stansted. What time should I take the bus?
- Can you take hand luggage and a handbag on a plane?

Assessment activity 9.3

ABTA – The Travel Association was very happy with your work preparing for their conference. They decide to send you to a retail agent to support them for a few weeks whilst they are short of staff.

You are to deal with customers and sell products and services. You must select cost and provide information on both package and tailor-made holidays that meet the needs of the customers.

Use package holiday brochures for briefs 1 and 2.

Package holidays

1 **Mr and Mrs Fremantle** are retired and in their sixties and live in Kent. They wish to spend a week in a hotel in Bruges for a Christmas break. They want a hotel with at least half board, a heated pool and some entertainment. They would prefer a superior room and will pay extra for it. Cost is not an issue. They want the package to include transport but they do not want to fly.

2 **The Geary family** needs a relaxing Easter holiday. They want to go somewhere with their 6-year-old twins that is warm, has beaches and is not full of young clubbers. They think the Caribbean would be perfect. They want all facilities to be close at hand as they do not wish to hire a car. They are looking for a hotel with half board and a children's club. The budget for the holiday is £5000 and they would like a child discount. This must cover any supplements (but not spending money). They want to fly from Manchester even if there is a supplement.

Use varied resources for briefs 3 and 4, including brochures and the internet.

Tailor-made holidays

3 **Sayid** wants to arrange a surprise for his fiancée's 30th birthday. He is very concerned that you don't contact her about arrangements or send any documents to their address. He wants to go to Paris on Eurostar and stay in a 'posh' hotel for two nights at a weekend on B and B basis. They live in Norwich so he wants you to arrange transport to London St Pancras and the transfer from Gare du Nord in Paris to the hotel. He has asked for bed and breakfast and flowers to be in the room on arrival with a message from him. You must also book a trip on a bateau mouche (river boat) for the couple. The birthday is in six weeks' time. Sayid has told you he can spend up to £1000.

4 **Jenny Horrocks** is looking for a special holiday to celebrate an anniversary. She wants to take her husband back to the place where they first met, on the slopes of Kilimanjaro while on a climbing expedition. They have no wish to climb any more, but want to go on safari in Tanzania for a week followed by a week in a luxury hotel on the island of Zanzibar. They want you to arrange the whole trip including transfers. The holiday will take place for two weeks in April or May next year. They want to fly from Heathrow and want full-board accommodation.

Once you have found holidays that fulfil the needs of your customers, produce a full written breakdown of the holidays, you must include:

- your calculations
- marked up relevant brochure pages
- check-in details
- transport times
- accommodation details
- flight numbers and timings (where relevant)
- baggage allowance (where relevant)
- passport, visa and vaccination requirements (where relevant)
- a day-to-day breakdown (where relevant).

Present the holidays to your customers explaining why it fits their needs. P4 P5

Grading tips

P4 Support your breakdown with relevant brochure pages, print outs and screen shots.

P5 Make sure at least one of your components for each customer is from a brochure and at least one from the internet.

PLTS

As you carry out research, exploring possibilities from the perspective of your customer, you will be practising your **independent enquirer** skills.

Functional skills

You will have to determine the mathematical methods needed to carry out your price calculations and apply them, gaining functional skills in **Maths**.

Jo Quincey

Assistant team leader

I sell flights and holidays to customers either face-to-face or on the phone. We don't have a call centre, so if someone phones having looked at our website the call is re-routed to one of our shops. We call people who have emailed the website as well.

The skill in selling is to build a rapport with the customer. For them it should feel like a friendly conversation. We have ongoing training to ask very specific questions about their trip. Customers have often done research before they call, so it gives me more clues about what they are looking for and what the obstacles are for them.

I also deal with complaints and I look after new staff. It costs about £5,000 to train someone before the even start in store, so we want to keep them.

What qualifications and skills did you need to get this job?

I have a degree in Tourism, but not everyone has – you do need some background in travel and tourism as well as sales and customer service experience. Organisational skills are really important – I found organising course work for college helped with this. You do need knowledge of geography and it helps if you have travelled yourself. Enthusiasm is essential. In terms of development I have been on leadership courses and had Gallileo training.

Are there any perks?

Yes, I have been to Australia on a familiarity trip, there are discounted rates on holidays and flights for agents. About once a month we get a night out in London, sponsored by a different travel company each time. My company throws a summer ball and a Christmas ball.

What next?

It's a great company for moving up as they like to recruit from the inside when possible. There are opportunities in head office as well as being a team leader in a branch. You need at least a year on the retail side and then you can expect to move up.

Think about it!

1. Consider three aspects of Jo's job that you think you would be really good at and explain why.
2. What kid of job do you think Jo could progress to?
3. What is Galileo training?

Just checking

1 Identify the different categories of retail travel agents.
2 What is meant by 'racking policy'?
3 How does ABTA – The Travel Association help travel agents?
4 What are the benefits to a travel agent of joining a consortium?
5 What are add-on sales?
6 Identify three types of promotional activity a travel agent might use.
7 Give an example of a reservation system.
8 What is a Global Distribution Service?
9 What is dynamic packaging?

Assignment tips

- Every time you pass a travel agency, think about what type it is, who owns it and how effective its displays are.
- Collect current brochures to help you know the products on offer.
- See if you can meet some ex-students who now work in travel agencies.
- Read *Travel Weekly* and *Travel Trade Gazette* – these are trade magazines aimed at travel professionals.
- Spend some time looking at e-agents' websites.
- Try to get some experience in a travel agency, even if it is a day shadowing staff.

Credit value: 10

10 Business travel operations

Business travel is a career in its own right. The Guild of Travel Management Companies (GTMC) has even created a qualification, the Certificate in Business Travel, for those who want to specialise. If you aspire to a career in business travel, you must understand how business travel organisations operate and how they meet the needs of their customers.

In this unit, you will learn about the different types of business travel agents and the products and services they provide. You will find out about their day-to-day operations, what legislation is important to business travel and what licences they need to hold.

Business travel is as dynamic as the rest of the travel and tourism sector and you will explore the factors, both national and global, that impact on business travel.

Finally, you will practise your skills in selecting, costing and providing information for business customers.

Learning outcomes

After completing this unit you should:

1. know the business travel environment
2. know business travel operational practices
3. understand the factors affecting business travel
4. be able to select, cost and provide information for business trips.

Assessment and grading criteria

This table shows you what you must do in order to achieve a **pass**, **merit** or **distinction** grade, and where you can find activities in this book to help you.

To achieve a **pass** grade the evidence must show that you are able to:	To achieve a **merit** grade the evidence must show that, in addition to the pass criteria, you are able to:	To achieve a **distinction** grade the evidence must show that, in addition to the pass and merit criteria, you are able to:
P1 describe the current business travel environment **See Assessment activity 10.1 page 272**	**M1** explain how factors are currently affecting the business travel environment and operational practices **See Assessment activity 10.1 page 272**	**D1** discuss the current business travel environment and how business travel agents are responding to current challenges **See Assessment activity 10.1 page 272**
P2 describe business travel working practices **See Assessment activity 10.1 page 272**		
P3 summarise business travel legislation, trade associations and licensing requirements **See Assessment activity 10.1 page 272**		
P4 review the current factors affecting business travel **See Assessment activity 10.1 page 272**		
P5 use appropriate resources to select, accurately cost and provide information for two business itineraries **See Assessment activity 10.2, page 274**	**M2** justify how the costs, the itineraries and information provided fully meets the customer brief **See Assessment activity 10.2, page 274**	

How you will be assessed

This unit will be assessed by one or more internal assignments that will be designed and marked by your tutor. Your assignments will be subject to sampling internally and externally as part of Edexcel's quality assurance procedures. The assignments are designed to allow you to show your knowledge and understanding related to the unit. The unit outcomes indicate what you should know, understand or be able to do after completing the unit.

Katja, 19-year-old BTEC National learner

Once we had completed the Retail Travel unit, I thought that this unit would be very similar. There were areas of overlap between the two units, for example, in legislation. However, there were whole sectors of business travel that were completely new.

We learnt about incentive travel and the conference market and visited a travel exhibition to see how it was organised. For my assignment, I did most of my research on the internet looking at what business travel agents offered as services. This was the best way to do it as we don't have any major business travel agents in my area. I also looked at some reports on business travel. This wasn't that easy, as some of the reports I found at first were out of date and some were American. Then I found an on-line magazine called *Business Traveller* which was really useful to find out about products and services offered for business travellers. I got some information from a website called Eye for Travel as well. This one had links to some reports.

I enjoyed the second assignment for this unit as once we had done our research we role-played the results, presenting our itineraries to each other. I had to do quite a lot of maths to get my costings right.

Over to you!

1 Think about where you will find resources for this unit.
2 How will they differ from those you used for retail travel?
3 Can you think of local business travel agents who might help your group?

1 The business travel environment

Set off

What is business travel?

These days business travel agents are more likely to be known as Travel Management Companies (TMCs), reflecting the complexity of the business. Business travel agents do not just book one-off flights or hotels, but manage all the business travel requirements of large corporations.

About 15 per cent of trips, both overseas and domestic, are for business. Although this percentage seems small compared with leisure travel, business travellers spend more: domestic business trips generate 21 per cent of the total spend on business travel (according to a Mintel report).

For overseas trips the spend is even greater. Four out of five overseas business trips are to Europe, yet these trips account for only 57 per cent of expenditure.

1 What kind of business trips do you think domestic business travellers are making?
2 If so many business travellers go to Europe, why don't these trips account for more of the expenditure?

1.1 Types of business travel

Travelling on business can take many forms. Individuals may be travelling to meetings, to exhibitions or to make sales calls to customers.

There are also many occasions when large groups of people travel individually, or together, to take part in a conference or corporate event. Companies that organise business travel are operating in a different market to those who organise conferences and events and are usually different companies. However, overlap does occur, for example Kuoni is a well known tour operator, yet has an arm of its company which specialises in event management.

Incentive travel

This is the term used when companies offer travel and entertainment to employees as rewards for good performance. For example, a successful sales team may be taken away for a weekend's leisure to celebrate their success or motivate them for the future. The aim is usually enjoyment and relaxation rather than work, as the trip is a reward for work already done.

Some travel companies have started divisions to organise incentive travel events, conferences and large meetings, as we saw with Kuoni.

Exhibitions and trade fairs

There are exhibitions and trade fairs for just about every type of product. Business people attend trade fairs to keep up-to-date on the latest developments in their industry, find suppliers for products and services and to network with colleagues.

There are two aspects to the organisation of fairs and exhibitions. Firstly, there are companies who organise the exhibitions and sell stands to exhibitors. An example is Reed Exhibitions. They have a division, Reed Travel Exhibitions, who focus on travel events. Secondly, there is a lot of business to be gained in organising travel to the exhibitions and accommodation for attendees.

Think about it

You can find out about all the exhibitions in the UK by looking at www.exhibitions.co.uk. An important annual travel exhibition is the World Travel Market.

Did you know?

There is an annual Business Travel Show held at Earls Court in London each February as part of the Business Travel Week.

Conferences and meetings

The Meetings Industry Associationn (MIA) is the largest association for the meetings industry for the UK and Ireland, providing support for venues and suppliers in the meetings industry. A company wishing to organise a large meeting, or conference, could approach the MIA to find out about companies who can make the arrangements for them.

Each year a survey (the UK Events Market Survey) is carried out to measure the key characteristics of the UK events and conferences market. It is based on data supplied by over 500 venues. The latest survey (at the time of publication) showed the events and conference market to be worth about 7 billion in 2009, although this had declined from 2008.

Organising a conference or large meeting is a complex process and could take up to a year. Most annual event organisers start the next year's planning as soon as one event is finished. Conference attendees will require hotel bookings, transfers, information electronically and by post. There may be additional tours and social events to plan.

Corporate events

Corporate events may take several forms. Examples are award ceremonies, product launches and hospitality events.

Corporate hospitality is the provision of entertainment to clients by a business. It is similar to incentive travel, but is for customers rather than employees. A company specialising in corporate hospitality will be able to acquire tickets for major events such as rock concerts and sporting events like Wimbledon. It will also provide catering and transport if required and offer executive boxes or restaurants, where guests can be entertained. The aim of corporate hospitality is to build up a good relationship with customers so that they are more likely to buy the products and services of their host.

The market leader in corporate hospitality in the UK is Keith Prowse. The company is owned by Compass, a catering company that provides food services for sporting, social and corporate events. Note that this company does not specialise in business travel and this market is quite different.

What types of place offer corporate hospitality?

Activity: Keith Prowse

Visit the Keith Prowse website at www.keithprowse.co.uk. Find a sporting event to which you would be interested in taking six very special clients. Find out what would be offered on the trip and cost it for seven people (including you).

1.2 Business agencies

Role

The role of business travel agents is to book accommodation and travel for business travellers. There is little leisure travel to be arranged, however business travellers may ask for leisure travel, such as flights and hotels to be organised for accompanying partners.

Although the role is similar to that of a leisure travel agent, the hotels booked are likely to be in cities and offer business services. Flights are likely to be scheduled rather than chartered, as business travellers are looking for convenient times and departure points. Some companies may specialise in organising corporate events and incentive travel rather than travel bookings for individuals.

Independent agencies

Business travel agents are often independent agents who have chosen to specialise in the business market. They are frequently located in business parks so that they can capture local business. As they are independent they are able to offer a very flexible service and meet individual requirements. This flexibility and personal service enables them to compete with the large corporate agents like American Express.

National agencies

National business travel agents operate from one country. For example, Flight Centre Business Travel is the UK travel management subsidiary of Flight Centre Limited, Australia's largest retail travel company. It targets small and medium enterprises (SMEs) and has many branches in the UK.

Global agencies

Global business travel companies operate throughout the world. Major players in the global business travel market are HRG, Carlson Wagonlit and American Express Business Travel. Another large company is BCD which operates from over 30 locations in the UK. This is a Dutch-based business built around the acquisition of TQ3 Travel Solutions and purchasing of a stake in The Travel Company.

These large businesses offer booking services, consultancy services on travel management and supplier negotiation – that is negotiating favourable prices with airlines and hotels. They offer these services both on-line and through agencies.

Implants

Implants are agents operating within a business premises, so that they are on hand to look after travel requirements as needed. The agent may often work alone and is employed by a business travel agency, not by the company in whose premises they are based.

E-agents

As in leisure travel, there is a huge demand for on-line business travel services. You may be familiar with the website offering travel services, Expedia. Expedia claims that its corporate travel business, launched in 2002, is the fifth largest by turnover worldwide.

In 2008, the company re-branded its business travel under the Egencia brand. It was thought that a specific brand for business travel would help challenge the market leaders.

Activity: Job opportunity

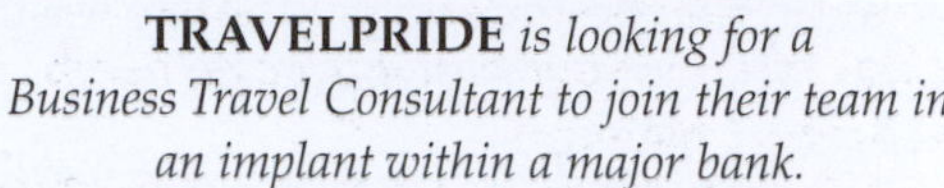

TRAVELPRIDE *is looking for a Business Travel Consultant to join their team in an implant within a major bank.*

You will be expected to plan first class and business class itineraries for this important customer. Excellent customer service is a given. You need to have very good knowledge and experience of using Galileo. A knowledge of fares and ticketing types is desirable.

If this was the kind of job you wanted to apply for, how would you gain the experience needed for this role?

1.3 Products and services

Remember that business travel agents may be dealing with small companies sending individuals on business trips to corporate clients who want all of their business travel managed.

Basic services will always include:

- accommodation bookings
- flight bookings – either scheduled or low-cost, business, first or economy
- transfers
- car hire or rail tickets (surface transportation)
- ancillary sales, such as car parking or insurance.

Figure 10.1 gives an idea of the services offered by business travel companies.

The agency will book accommodation for customers, arrange travel such as flight bookings, transfers and ancillary services such as insurance and parking.

Flight bookings range from low-cost flights to full-service scheduled flights in first or business class, depending on the travel policy of the traveller's company and budget available.

An on-line travel management business like Travelocity offers a very sophisticated range of products and services. They build up close relationships with corporate customers to offer excellent service. The customer will be allocated an account manager who is their point of contact. The on-line capacity is supplemented by call centres so that customers can speak to a consultant. Such call centres are accessible 24-hours a day.

ELITE TRAVEL SERVICES

We look after all your business travel needs

Dedicated Account Manager
Our dedicated account managers tailor products and services to meet your needs.

Fully inclusive travel solutions
We offer a complete range of travel services ranging from air, land & sea to passport, visa & insurance requirements.

24 Hour Emergency Assistance
Any day, all day. One number to call in case of missed connections, lost documents or any emergency.

Worldwide Hotels
We have negotiated rates with some of the world's best and extensive hotel chains. Prices are competitive and include executive rooms.

Leisure Services
We can provide a range of leisure products and services for your company employees. Many are offered at discounts.

Flexible Payment Options
Credit accounts are available depending on value of business. All major debit and credit cards are accepted.

Management Analysis and reporting
We offer full analysis of travel arrangements, hotels and other services to meet your needs and achieve efficient costings.

Meeting and Conference Services
Our specialist team is able to offer special group discounted fares, venue sourcing and conference arrangements.

Figure 10.1: An example of products which might be supplied by business travel companies

Management of a customer's travel expenditures

This means analysing data so that a corporation knows exactly what is being spent on business travel and where. The travel management company manage the data and make it available to the customer 24-hours a day in a spreadsheet or database.

Negotiation with suppliers

The agent negotiates terms on the customer's behalf with airlines, car hire companies and hotels.

Activity: Comparing agencies

Visit the services page of www.cambridgebusinesstravel.co.uk, the website of Cambridge Business Travel, an independent travel agency. Find out what products and services it offers.

Compare the services offered with those of a major travel management company such as Travelocity or HRG. Think about what type of customers would use each agency. Present your findings in a table.

Case study: Virgin Atlantic Airways

Virgin Atlantic Airways offers a fast-track security channel for business passengers. Airline passengers can opt to travel in upper class with all the luxury that provides. They also offer travel services to business customers.

This extract from the Virgin website explains the travel service that Virgin offers to business customers.

Finding and booking business travel and business class flights is simple with Virgin Atlantic. We offer a high-quality business travel service to companies of all sizes. Small- and medium-sized companies benefit from Virgin Atlantic's business travel service, just as much as large multinational corporations.

We've won many awards for service, like the Business Travel World Award for best long-haul business airline. But winning such accolades doesn't make us complacent. If anything, it makes us strive even harder for excellence.

We make every effort to ensure our business class flights are the very best value. We also make sure all of our business travel passengers get the high-quality service they expect from Virgin on every single flight.

We offer a range of services for business travel clients. For example, Flyingco is our innovative loyalty scheme designed to reward both the individual traveller and the organisation they work for.

(Source: www.virgin.com)

1 Go to, either, the British Airways website or the Virgin website, and find out what the differences and similarities are between first or upper class and economy.

2 What factors would determine whether a business traveller went in first class or economy?

Products and services provided by suppliers

All hotels and airlines want to tap in to the lucrative business travel market and constantly bring out new products and services to entice business travellers.

Hotels offer Wi-fi and business centres as a matter of course. Business customers may choose executive rooms. Even cheaper hotels, such as the Premier Inn chain, offer wireless internet and meeting rooms. Hilton hotels and Novotel host many conferences and meetings and provide many services to help the organisers of these meetings. They have dedicated conference staff who look after events and are on hand during events, conferences and meetings.

2 Business travel operational practices

2.1 Working practices

Procedures and documentation for selling products and services

For individual passengers, the business travel agent works in much the same way as the retail agent, although they will be buying individual components such as flights rather than packages. When dealing with corporate business, procedures are rather different.

The business travel agent hopes to win large accounts and manage them, resulting in long-term repeated business. Large accounts have a dedicated account manager who is responsible for managing all their business travel.

The first stage is, as in retail, to listen to requirements, but also to understand the business objectives of the customer. A large corporation looking for a business travel agent will expect current travel patterns to be analysed and improvements, in terms of cost cutting or better service to be offered.

Once the account is set up, individuals from the company can contact the agency and make travel arrangements in accordance with the policy agreed. The account manager should review the services provided at regular intervals, suggesting improvements if needed.

Global distribution systems

You were introduced to global distribution systems (GDS) in Unit 9 Retail travel (page 250). The systems are of even greater importance to business travel. Journeys are often very complex, not just point-to-point. The business traveller may have a meeting in one city and have to transfer, with minimum connecting time, to another. If different airlines are used, the agent can use GDS to book efficiently the necessary segments of the journey, mixing airlines on one ticket and making sure connecting times work out.

Did you know?

There is a GDS just for rail. Known as Evolvi, it has been designed just for travel management companies to book rail journeys for their customers. Find out more at www.evolvi.co.uk.

Commission levels and sales targets

These are closely linked. Agents receive commission from suppliers (that is, from airlines and hotels) for bookings. As suppliers try to cut costs, commission levels fall. Agents have to compensate for cuts in commission levels by charging customers for their services, as do retail agents. Agents are set sales targets by their organisation and will receive a bonus payment if they reach those targets.

Cost-saving techniques

We saw earlier that the business travel agent studies travel patterns and looks for cost-cutting possibilities for their clients. For example, they may be able to negotiate deals with a hotel chain for cheaper rooms through bulk purchase and then recommend that hotel to their customer. This may apply to airline seats as well.

Promotional schemes

In the case study on page 267 you were introduced to Flyingco, the Virgin frequent flyer loyalty scheme for business travellers. Flyingco is targeted at smaller businesses and offers cost savings for the company and personal frequent flyer benefits for the business traveller.

Activity: Loyalty schemes

Find out about two different loyalty schemes aimed at business travellers and compare them. Decide which one is more appealing to the business traveller.

Design your own promotional scheme for business travellers using a hotel chain.

Present it to your colleagues. Start your research at www.businesstraveller.com/loyalty.

Service level agreements

It is part of the account manager's role to ensure that agreed service levels between the business agency and the customer are adhered to. Examples of items in the agreement are turnaround time on booking requests, services such as 24-hour phone contact availability and adherence to company travel policy.

Working to the company and passenger profile

The business travel agent keeps details of a company's regular passengers. This saves time and errors when making bookings on their behalf as information is on file. In addition, the agency must be aware of the company's policy on travel so that they make bookings that conform to policy. For example, the company might stipulate that employees only travel in economy, or that they stay within a budget for accommodation.

2.2 Related legislation

The legislation applicable to business travel is the same as for retail travel. Refer to page 252 to find out more. The Data Protection Act does not apply to corporate information, but to individuals' data. Policy will be stated in an agent's terms and conditions.

2.3 Trade associations and licensing

Guild of Travel Management Companies

The Guild of Travel and Management Companies (GTMC) was started in 1967 by a group of six business travel agents. Its name then was the Guild of Business Travel Agents.

The aim of the GTMC is stated as:

- to be a committed and respected organisation representing the interests and requirements of the business travel market
- to be recognised as delivering the best standard of service, quality and value to the business traveller.

The services it offers members include:

- lobbying for members within industry and with government
- providing training and qualifications for business travel agency operatives
- running a technology working party
- lobbying on pan-European issues through The Guild of European Business Travel Agents (GEBTA).

Civil Aviation Authority

The Civil Aviation Authority (CAA) is responsible for regulating the UK aviation industry (www.caa.org.uk). It is funded by the aviation industry, not by the government.

The CAA runs the ATOL financial protection scheme, relevant to business travel agents (see page 253). Most holiday companies who sell air travel or packages in the UK are required by law to hold this licence. It is granted once the CAA has checked the ability of the company to contribute to a travel protection fund. If the company fails then the fund is used to ensure that customers do not lose their money.

If a business travel agent is organising packages for customers they will need the ATOL bond. If they are booking through other tour operators or airlines they should check that these suppliers hold ATOLs.

Association of Train Operating Companies

The Association of Train Operating Companies (ATOC) is the trade body for the companies which run scheduled passenger trains on the rail network managed by Network Rail. The ATOC provides services specific to business and retail travel agents to help them give a better service and promote rail services with the agents.

Travel agents need to be licensed by the ATOC in order to sell rail tickets. To be licensed the agent applies and pays an initial fee. Once licensed, the agent receives 5 per cent commission on ticket sales.

International Air Transport Association

The International Air Transport Association (IATA) is the international trade body representing airlines. It represents about 230 airlines which carry about 93 per cent of scheduled airline traffic.

Travel agents apply to be accredited by IATA so that they are able to sell airline tickets. Business travel agents gain access to airline members' inventory and ticketing worldwide and are able to access and use IATA's billing and settlement plan. This is a system whereby travel agents can issue just one sales report and payment to a central point, rather than paying airlines individually Sales can also be reported electronically.

IATA run several courses of interest to business travel agents. You may be familiar with their Fares and Ticketing programmes, but they also run more advanced courses for complex bookings, for example Advanced Airline Sales Strategies.

3 Factors affecting business travel

3.1 Factors and their effects

Changes in the global economy

Strong economic growth and healthy overseas trade activity lead to a growth in business travel. When strong economic conditions prevail, companies may extend their business to new international markets, which necessitates more travelling for employees. Emerging economies in the Far East, for example China and India, have resulted in more travel to these areas. According to a Mintel report, in the last period of general growth between 2006 and 2007 business travel increased by 3.1 per cent (partly due to the growth in Far Eastern economies).

There are several factors which result in cuts in business travel budgets. These factors include recession when there is less trade, increases in fuel charges which make flying more expensive and the devaluation of the pound against the euro and other currencies. The effects of these cuts are that:

- business travellers switch to economy flights, particularly on short-haul flights
- on long-haul flights, business travellers may opt for premium economy rather than first class (according to the CAA UK international scheduled business travel at major London airports fell by 6 per cent between 2007 and 2008)
- use of executive jets fall
- travellers switch to standard rail fares rather than first class
- business is conducted by a day trip rather than overnight stays
- cheaper hotel rooms are sought.

However, some businesses do extremely well when others become more cost conscious. Low-cost airlines, like Ryanair and easyJet, win customers from more expensive airlines, although they still suffer in a prolonged recession. Cheaper hotel chains, like Premier Inn and Travelodge, do well with increased bookings, while premium brands have to offer rooms at cheaper rates to keep their occupancy figures buoyant.

Although business travellers might not opt for first class rail, they do switch to rail travel from car hire. According to the GTMC survey, between 2007 and 2008 rail travel increased by 13 per cent, while car hire decreased by the same.

Technology

It has been possible for a long time to hold meetings via video conferencing, **telephone conferencing** and **web conferencing** (**e-meeting**). When these technologies were first introduced it was anticipated that they would have a significant impact on business travel. However, this was not proved to be the case, although their use might rise in times of recession. Some companies may choose to host **web seminars**.

Most companies consider that holding face-to-face meetings and networking are crucial to business success, even though they incur expense in travel.

Key terms

Telephone conference – participants dial in to a pre-distributed telephone number and are all able to hear each other and speak. As some voices sound similar, it is good practice to state your name each time you contribute to the conference.

Web conference – this takes place over the Internet and can incorporate sound and cameras or at its most basic, live messaging.

E-meeting – another term for a web conference, that is, a meeting using web-based software, allowing people to communicate over the Internet.

Web seminar – a tutor and delegates are online at the same time and delegates follow the resources online. The seminar can incorporate sound and cameras.

Activity: Web conferencing

Do you know how a web meeting works? Visit webex.com and watch the video of how it works. What do you think are the drawbacks?

Terrorism

Terrorism acts tend to have a short-term impact on travel, estimated at 4–6 months before travel behaviour returns to normal levels. Lastminute.com reported that the London bombings of 7 July 2005, and the failed attacks two weeks later, affected bookings to the capital for only a short period.

Key term

CSR (corporate social responsibility) – how an organisation manages its business activities to produce an overall positive impact on society.

Research carried out in the US in 2001, following the terrorist attacks on the World Trade Centre, found that organisations were planning to use technology to limit the need for face-to-face meetings and travel. A similar pattern emerged following the embargo on air travel caused by volcanic ash in 2010. Video conferencing provided a useful alternative to face-to-face meetings.

Health epidemics

Outbreaks of Severe Acute Respiratory Syndrome (SARs) and swine flu have affected travel over the last few years. Health epidemics always result in temporary restrictions on travel.

For example, when SARS first broke out in 2003 the World Health Organisation (WHO) issued a travel advisory against all travel to Hong Kong and Guangdong. As epidemics spread, travellers become vulnerable to infection wherever they travel to.

In 2009, there was flu pandemic, known as swine flu. This is the advice about pandemic flu issued by the Department of Health relating to travel (see page 272):

Case study: The future of business travel

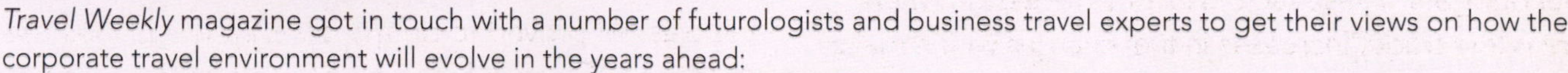

Travel Weekly magazine got in touch with a number of futurologists and business travel experts to get their views on how the corporate travel environment will evolve in the years ahead:

Prepare for a leaner travel diet: It is all about trading down – premium economy instead of business; conferences at a local, less smart hotel; the five-star hotel giving way to a three-star hotel. The glamour of business travel could evaporate quicker than people think.

Expect more scrutiny: As a result of factors, such as better technology and reporting, increasingly we will see all business costs being scrutinised. Unless a TMC can add value and go the extra mile, the client will feel they can do it themselves and save money in the process.

Corporate social responsibility (CSR): Concerns over the environment and CSR will drill down into all elements of the procurement process. With more data and greater compliancy, even small- and medium-sized enterprises will get in on the act.

Finding new income streams: As the sector continues to become more streamlined and cost conscious, TMCs will have to identify new sources of revenue and use their resources, experience and relationships to add value.

Technology is power: Databases, GDSs, search engines, mobile internet, location-based services – expect more. Peter Deane, vice-president of sales for technology firm Handy Group, said: "The question you need to ask is 'Are you embracing them in a way which will enable you to provide added value to the business traveller?'"

It's all about time: The future is about handing back to employees the most valuable commodity in today's business environment: time. Potentially the train can get you there quicker while you work remotely or sit in on a video conference instead of boarding that transatlantic flight.

(Source:www.travelweekly.co.uk)

1 Interview someone who travels regularly for business.
2 Assess how glamorous their travel is.
3 Find out how their pattern of travelling has changed over the last two years. Have they taken different modes or classes of travel or hotel? Do they travel more or less?
4 Do they use a travel management company or book themselves?
5 What steps do they take to consider the impact of their travel on the environment?

Produce an article similar to the one above with your findings.

The Government is not planning to restrict travel within the UK during a pandemic unless it becomes necessary for public health reasons. Any restrictions which are considered are likely to be on an advisory basis. Scientific modelling shows that internal travel restrictions would have little impact on the total number of people infected by flu. The public will be advised to reduce non-essential travel where possible.

With regards to international travel, the evidence on the benefits and disadvantages of various approaches for border closures is being kept under review. UK nationals may be advised against all but essential travel to certain countries or areas during a pandemic through the usual FCO Travel Advice process.

Source: www.dh.gov)

Political unrest

Political problems in a country may erupt into violent demonstrations and dangers when travelling. If a country is known to be unstable the UK government will advise against travel to the area. You can find out which countries are restricted by looking at the Foreign & Commonwealth Office (FCO) travel website.

It is more difficult to reach countries where there is unrest as airlines will limit or pull out their services. For example, it is quite difficult to travel to parts of West Africa because of limited air services.

Assessment activity 10.1

BTEC

Crystal Travel is a retail travel agency operating in a town in the South East of England. Business has been poor over the last two years and the owners have decided to focus on business travel rather than retail.

They have been receiving a lot of ad hoc business from local companies and think that they can bid for corporate business from the many companies with premises on an expanding Science Park in the area.

As a consultant with expertise in business travel, you have been asked to produce a manual which will help current staff understand the business travel environment and how their working practice might be different.

For both parts of this assessment activity, make sure that you cover the full range, referring to the content and assessment guidance in the unit specification for the detail required.

Part 1

Produce a manual with the following sections:

- a description of the current business travel environment with a description of the role of different business agents and different types of business travel. **P1**
- a glossary of useful terms **P1**
- a description of the working practices of different types of business travel agents **P2**
- a summary of the relevant legislation, trade associations and licensing requirements that business travel agents need to adhere to **P3**
- a review of current factors affecting the business travel environment.

Part 2

Your manual was very useful and you have been asked to expand on your review of current factors affecting the business travel environment by preparing a presentation for your colleagues which explains:

- how three of the factors you discussed in the manual affect the business environment and impact on operational practice **M1**
- how business travel agents are responding to current challenges in their business environment **D1**

Grading tips

P1 Demonstrate that not all business travel agents deal with all types of business travel, but may specialise.

P2 Make sure you cover all of procedures and documentation for selling products and services, GDS, commission levels and sales targets, cost-saving techniques, promotional schemes, service level agreements and working to profiles.

P3 Include the Data Protection Act, Package Travel Regulations, GTMC, CAA, ATOL, ATC, IATA.

P4 Identify all effects associated with each factor.

M1 You can develop the information you used for **P4**. Remember to include industry examples of the effects of working practices, related legislation and licensing requirements.

D1 Include statistics and other published information.

PLTS

Planning and carrying out the appropriate research in assessment activity 10.1 will help to develop your skills as an **independent enquirer**.

Functional skills

Making an effective presentation in assessment activity 10.1 will help you develop your **English** skills in speaking and listening.

4 Select, cost and provide information for business trips

4.1 Customer brief

What does the customer want?

The business agent must find out the following about the customer:

- who is travelling
- party size
- dates
- class of travel required
- departure point
- accommodation required
- board basis
- surface transport needed, for example car hire.

The agent may need to know the status of who is travelling, for example, is it the managing director or a salesperson? This can affect the class of travel. The company travel policy must be known and adhered to. It is possible that people with higher status in the company travel first class. Some companies may insist that all employees, whatever their role, travel in economy or with low-cost flights.

The travel policy may also affect the class of accommodation booked, for example single rooms are usually smaller and less comfortable, some policies state that 'double rooms for single use' should be provided.

Surface transfers are unlikely to mean the local bus service. People travelling on business usually expect taxis to be booked on their behalf. A managing director may be entitled to a chauffeur driven car. As long as the agent is aware of company travel policy, they should be able to make suitable arrangements.

How much will it cost?

Unlike leisure travel, packages are not available for business trips, so the agent is likely to book all the components separately from different suppliers. They should, as business agents, be able to negotiate preferential rates for their customers

The agent will have to produce a costing for the customer and this may involve converting currencies back to GBP (£ sterling), adding on their commission and working out the full cost to the customer.

Bookings for accommodation in particular, may be made in different currencies. A customer would not expect to see a costing with several currencies in it, so the agent must convert everything to the preferred currency for the customer.

The costing should also show net rates with VAT shown separately. This is because companies will be able to claim back the VAT paid on travel and therefore, need the exact amount.

Commission can be earned in two ways. On some bookings, it will be paid by the supplier (for example an airline or hotel) to the agency. Some suppliers (for example some low-cost airlines) do not pay commission to agents. It is usual for a business travel agent to charge the customer for their services, especially when there is a high level of personal service.

Once the information has been found and costed, the agent will produce an itinerary for the customer.

4.2 Itineraries

An itinerary (page 237) should include client details, check-in details, flight numbers, departure and arrival times, details of accommodation, baggage allowances, **elapsed flying time**, **reconfirmation** procedures and any additional services booked.

Key terms

Elapsed flying time – actual time you have been in the air.

Reconfirmation – requirement to confirm that you will be on a flight you have booked.

Activity: Basic journey itinerary

Produce a basic journey itinerary for Julian Selzer and Christian Murray, who will be travelling from Gatwick to Brussels for a business meeting. They are travelling on Monday morning next week and returning on Wednesday morning.

- Find suitable flights from Gatwick and write out an itinerary for the pair.
- Find a city centre hotel for two nights.

4.3 Information

The business travel agency must be able to give the customer information about passports, visas and vaccinations. The customer may require insurance, but it is more usual for a company to have a travel insurance policy covering all its employees.

The agent may need to explain procedures for altering bookings and any business protocols.

Assessment activity 10.2

You work for Sensational Business Travel and have some clients to help.

1 Benjamin Sims has to arrange a business trip to Paris and London. He is currently in Stockholm. He has asked you to arrange the following:
   - an airport hotel in Stockholm for Monday night
   - a morning flight next Tuesday from Stockholm to Paris
   - car hire from the airport in Paris for three days – make sure pick-up and drop-off are at the right airports
   - flight to London some time on Friday
   - return flight from London to Stockholm on Saturday
   - hotel for the stay in Paris and London – at least four-star with gym and business centre.

Benjamin wants to travel business class on the flights. You need to know that he is vegetarian, has a British passport and wants to know if there is any visa or health information he should be aware of.

Note: At least one of the components for Benjamin's journey must be booked from a brochure. P5

2 Rohan Bhalinder is travelling to Sydney to speak at a medical conference.

   You know the following:
   - he will be travelling from London on a Saturday and returning two weeks later
   - he wants to spend one night in Singapore on the way
   - he requires a hotel in Singapore and one in Sydney (five-star).
   - Rohan will travel in business class
   - Rohan has an Indian passport
   - he will need a taxi in Singapore to get to the hotel and back
   - Rohan is diabetic.

For each customer produce a detailed itinerary. Ensure that it is clearly presented. Include any additional information your customers will need. Produce a full costing, converting all currencies to GBP. Add 5 per cent commission to any net costs. Include any screen shots or brochure pages supporting your bookings. The itineraries must be chronological and accurate. P5

Justify how the suggested selected components of your itinerary meet your briefs. M2

Grading tip

M2 Explain why you selected your components in relation to time, convenience and cost.

PLTS

Exploring issues from the perspective of your customer will help develop your skills as an **independent enquirer**.

Functional skills

By identifying the mathematical methods needed to do your costing, applying them and using appropriate checking procedures you will be practising your skills in **Maths**.

WorkSpace

Matthew Davies

Business travel consultant – music industry

What made you decide to specailise in business travel?

I work in London as a business travel consultant. After my BTEC, I worked in a retail travel agency in my home town, but I wanted to move to London. My friends were there so my social life at home had dropped off. I thought I would earn more money, even though I would pay higher rent.

I saw my current job advertised and I was thrilled when I got it. It was a tough interview and I had to demonstrate that I had sufficient experience of business travel. Fortunately, I had been responsible in my previous agency for any business enquiries that came in.

Tell us about your job

I work only on music accounts. That means all my customers are in the music business. Our customers are top bands and singers and we also look after some *X-Factor* competitors, which means that discretion is vital for my job.

We offer a personal service, so I have met some very famous people! I have to organise some complex itineraries for groups of people going on tour. I organise their flights, hotels, transfers and make sure all their luggage gets there. Pop stars have a lot of equipment and clothes to take with them.

I love my job, but the stressful part is that tour managers or customers often make changes at the last minute. I have to stay calm and deal with their requests and make amendments to bookings. Last week one singer asked for a rowing machine to be available in her hotel room.

Think about it!

1 Analyse what skills and knowledge would be needed for this role.
2 Assess yourself in relation to the role.
3 Make a table listing what skills and knowledge you would need to develop in order to apply for this job and say how you can develop them.

Just checking

1 What is meant by incentive travel?

2 Why does it take a long time to organise a conference?

3 What is an implant?

4 Why do business travel agents review the travel policy of a company?

5 What is 'Evolvi'?

6 What is a loyalty scheme?

7 Give two examples of factors which result in cuts in business travel budgets.

8 Why might a budget hotel chain benefit from a recession?

9 Describe the role of the Civil Aviation Authority (CAA).

Assignment tips

- Try these websites for your research:
  www.eyefortravel.com
  www.businesstraveller.com
  www.thebusinesstravelmag.com
- Look at the business travel sections in the travel trade press, such as *Travel Trade Gazette.*
- There are often articles about business travel in the press – especially papers like the *Financial Times* (see www.ft.com/business-travel).
- Try to find a business travel agency in your area who might be prepared to send someone to talk to your group.
- Remember that VisitBritain reports on business travel and not just on leisure travel.

Credit value: 10

12 Responsible tourism

This unit introduces the principles of responsible tourism – that is, tourism which takes into consideration its impact on a destination's environment and the lives of its people.

You will learn how tourism can have both positive and negative effects on the destinations it serves. You will find out how tourism organisations can maximise the positive effects and minimise the negative by adopting strategies which embrace the principles of responsible tourism in planning and management.

The roles and objectives of the different agents involved in tourism development are examined and you will see how the private, public and voluntary sectors all play a different part in development in destinations.

You will use your research skills to study recent and current developments in responsible tourism and you will use your knowledge and skills to plan a holiday for a specific client that is based on the principles of responsible tourism.

Learning outcomes

After completing this unit you should:

1 know positive and negative impacts of tourism on destinations

2 understand roles and objectives of agents of tourism development

3 understand strategies used to manage responsible tourism in destinations

4 be able to plan holidays incorporating principles of responsible tourism.

Assessment and grading criteria

This table shows you what you must do in order to achieve a **pass**, **merit** or **distinction** grade and where you can find activities in this book to help you.

To achieve a **pass** grade the evidence must show that you are able to:	To achieve a **merit** grade the evidence must show that, in addition to the pass criteria, you are able to:	To achieve a **distinction** grade the evidence must show that, in addition to the pass and merit criteria, you are able to:
P1 describe economic, environmental, and socio-cultural impacts of tourism on destinations **See Assessment activity 12.1, page 287**		
P2 compare roles and objectives of different agents of tourism development **See Assessment activity 12.2, page 298**	**M1** explain the consequences of differing roles and objectives of tourism development agents in a selected destination **See Assessment activity 12.2, page 298**	**D1** recommend solutions to conflicting interests between different agents of tourism development **See Assessment activity 12.2, page 298**
P3 examine strategies used to manage responsible tourism in destinations **See Assessment activity 12.3, page 302**	**M2** assess the effectiveness of strategies used to manage responsible tourism in a selected destination **See Assessment activity 12.3, page 302**	**D2** suggest improvements to strategies used to manage responsible tourism in a selected destination **See Assessment activity 12.3, page 302**
P4 plan a holiday incorporating principles of responsible tourism to meet a specific client brief **See Assessment activity 12.4, page 304**	**M3** justify the extent to which the planned holiday meets specific principles of responsible tourism **See Assessment activity 12.4, page 304**	

How you will be assessed

This unit will be assessed by one or more internal assignments that will be designed and marked by your tutor. Your assignments will be subject to sampling internally and externally as part of Edexcel's quality assurance procedures. The assignments are designed to allow you to show your knowledge and understanding related to the unit. The unit outcomes indicate what you should know, understand or be able to do after completing the unit.

Tamara, 18-year-old BTEC National learner

When I started this unit I was thinking about responsible tourism in terms of far away countries, of protecting coral reef and turtles and looking after the environment.

However, the first thing we did was have a visit from tourism planners at our local authority. We learnt how important tourism is to our local economy and yet it has to be managed so that tourists and residents can use facilities without causing too much disruption.

The planner also talked a lot about traffic management in our city. We talked about where coaches were allowed to park and why, how park and ride has helped the city centre and why car parks are so expensive. He even asked for our ideas on how to encourage people to use public transport. I am noticing tourists, and what they are up to, much more now when I am around the city centre.

I decided to do part of my assignment on the city centre and found that all the plans were available on-line.

I had to choose a developing destination for my assessment as well and I decided to choose Cuba as I had been there on holiday and I had collected some information when I was there. It was harder to find information on the internet, but my tutor helped me find some suitable websites.

Over to you!

1 What do you know about tourism management in your town? How can you find out?
2 What destinations are important to you in terms of investigating responsible tourism? For example, are you interested in people getting jobs or in preserving the environment?

1 The positive and negative impacts of tourism on destinations

Set off

Are you a responsible tourist?

Similar terms used to describe variations on **responsible tourism** are fair trade tourism, green tourism, sustainable tourism, ecotourism and alternative tourism. These all follow the same basic principles:

- minimise negative economic, environmental and socio-cultural impacts
- create economic benefits for local people and improve their quality of life
- promote the conservation of natural and cultural heritage
- promote respect between tourists and local people.

1 Think about your last holiday or trip. What impacts do you think your visit had on your destination? For example, if you ate out you provided work for local waiters (positive), but a rowdy group may have caused noise pollution (negative).

2 Write your thoughts on a big piece of paper. Include the type of holiday and destination and two columns: positive impacts and negative impacts.

3 Share and discuss your thoughts with the group.

Key terms

Responsible tourism – recognises the impacts of tourism on a destination and seeks to maximise the positive impacts and minimise the negative impacts.

MEDW countries – countries in the more economically developed world.

LEDW countries – countries in the less economically developed world.

1.1 Destinations

No matter what kind of destination a tourist visits – be it in developed or developing countries (**MEDW** or **LEDW countries**) – their activity will have some impact.

In a historic city, important buildings need to be protected from crowds of visitors, while the income from tourism can pay for preservation. At the seaside, tourists bring much needed spending to areas with little economic activity, yet stag and hen parties can be noisy and behave badly in town centres. In the countryside, tourists might undertake activities such as motor scrambling which interrupt the peace. Such impacts can be even more evident in developing countries.

In this first section we will examine the different impacts of tourism on destinations.

1.2 Positive economic impact

Increased domestic income and foreign currency earnings

Tourism development brings economic benefits in terms of increased expenditure in an economy. This may come from domestic or inbound tourism.

Inbound tourism brings with it increased earnings from foreign currency exchange. In developing countries, investment from foreign companies helps build the infrastructure and the facilities needed for tourism.

In countries like the UK, the government also benefits from increased revenue as it receives taxes from businesses earning revenue from tourism and in VAT from goods and services bought by tourists.

The multiplier effect

Direct tourism expenditure has a wider impact on the economy. If a tourist visits a destination and stays in a hotel, the hotel then spends money on local services and provisions to run the business and provide food and facilities for guests. Staff working at the hotel receive wages which are then used to buy further goods and services. Thus, the impact of the initial spend is 'multiplied' throughout the economy. This is **the multiplier effect.**

Key term

The multiplier effect – the additional revenue, income or employment created in an area as a result of tourism expenditure.

The multiplier is expressed as a ratio. For example, if there were an injection of spending into a local economy because of tourism expenditure at a new attraction, this would lead to further indirect spending in local shops, on transport and so on. If the attraction led to £100 million revenue and the additional revenue in the area was £250,000, this would give a multiplier effect of 1.25.

It can also be applied to jobs: the building of the hotel leads to direct employment in the hotel, but also to extra employment in the construction and service industries.

The World Travel and Tourism Council estimates that tourism generates an indirect spend equal to 100 per cent of direct tourism spend.

Increased employment

Tourism is not a statutory duty for local authorities – they don't have to spend money on it, but they do. Tourism was worth £115.4 billion to the UK economy in 2009 and provided around 2.7 million jobs either directly or indirectly.

Education and training

Jobs in tourism are generally desirable in developing destinations. Employees may be able to undertake professional training to improve their job prospects. The quantity and quality of training naturally varies across countries and companies. In areas of good practice, line staff may receive weekly training and support for higher education programmes.

Improved infrastructure

Development may bring about improved infrastructure which tourists and local people can both use. For example, improvements in roads allow people to travel more easily – this brings more tourists to remote areas and improves transport for local people. Or there may be improvements in the infrascructure providing clean water supplies.

Case study: Eurostar train services

In 2007, Eurostar train services moved from Waterloo Station to the newly completed St Pancras International Station in London. This is part of the plan developing the new high-speed line between London and the Channel Tunnel.

Eurostar prefers St Pancras for its operations because it has more underground lines and direct rail links to the Midlands and the north of England and Scotland. It is hoped that these links will encourage travellers from those areas to use Eurostar and increase custom. Eurostar also operates services from two stations in Kent: Ebbsfleet in North Kent and Ashford in the southern part of the county. South Eastern operates operates a domestic high-speed service which connects with Eurostar at St Pancras and Ebbsfleet from Stratford in East London and Ebbsfleet in Dartford, Kent. Stratford is placed to bring people to the Olympic Village ready for 2012.

The high-speed line cuts the journey time from London to Paris to 2 hours 15 minutes and the journey to Brussels from London takes 1 hour 51 minutes.

1. Discuss how these improvements in journey time and infrastructure can provide economic benefits in the UK.
2. Are there any negative impacts you can think of?
3. Find out what other partners are involved in the high-speed train link development. How will the 2012 Olympics aid the development?

1.3 Negative economic impact

Leakage

Economic benefits can be lost if goods and services used in the tourism industry are imported rather than local goods and services used. For example, food and drink for hotels may be imported, or materials and workers could be brought in from outside the area for construction projects. These are examples of **leakage**, where the local economy does not benefit.

> **Key terms**
>
> **Leakage** – the amount of money for supplies and services paid for outside a region: money that does not, therefore, benefit the local economy.
>
> **Enclave tourism** – occurs when tourists spend the whole holiday in their hotel resort or when on a cruise ship all the activities and meals take place on board. In these circumstances, the local population does not benefit from the tourists being there.

Leakage can be prevented by sourcing local materials, using local produce, allowing people to sell crafts in resorts and employing more local people. However, if tourists spend all their time in a hotel resort, for example (**enclave tourism**) they will not benefit the local economy.

Decline of traditional employment

Traditional industry can be penalised by tourism if workers choose to leave their employment in search of jobs in the tourist industry. This often occurs in developing countries where the jobs in tourism may initially provide more pay.

Seasonal unemployment

Although seasonal employment affects the local economy, it also has a social impact as those who find themselves out of work for part of the year must find some other form of employment. They may turn to a black-market economy to find work.

Increased living costs for the local community

When tourists arrive in an area, particularly a developing area, they can have an impact on costs. Restaurateurs find that tourists are able to pay higher prices than locals and so can put prices up. Taxi drivers can charge tourists more. Retailers can sell more expensive goods. In the worst cases this can produce a two-tier economy.

When tourists buy second homes in a locality there is often an impact on house prices, which means that local people can no longer afford to buy houses in their own area.

Overdependence on tourism

Economic distortion can occur when one region of a country is highly developed for tourism and other areas have none. This occurs to an extent in the UK where the south east and London receive far more tourists than other regions. It is a greater problem in countries where there is little other industry.

Overdependence on tourism is a potential problem. Tourists are fickle and fashions change quickly. An economy dependent on tourism will suffer if tourists leave or if a natural disaster occurs, like the hurricane that devastated New Orleans in 2005.

1.4 Positive environmental impact

Environmental education

Visitor centres are usually a source of information for tourists and school groups. Such education helps the tourists understand the reasons for conservation and encourages them to respect the environment. It also allows children and students to learn about the environment in a practical way. Some national parks provide information and fact sheets for schoolchildren that they can download from the internet.

Conservation of natural and built environment

Sites and properties are protected and preserved for the enjoyment of visitors and to conserve the heritage. Tourism contributes enormously to this conservation in several ways:

- the fact that a site is a tourist attraction means it is recognised as warranting preservation
- National Parks, and other conservation bodies, provide information and education for tourists, thus helping tourists' environmental awareness
- revenue from entrance fees to attractions pays for conservation activities
- conservation holidays are a growing market sector as offered by BTCV and the National Trust.

Regeneration of derelict areas

Both the built and natural environment benefit from upgrading and regeneration when a tourist opportunity is uncovered by local and national government. Examples include the Liverpool and Salford dock areas. Salford has a theatre and museum beside new residential and shopping developments.

1.5 Negative environmental impacts

Congestion

Within the UK, most day visitors and domestic holiday-makers travel by car, causing traffic congestion and pollution at destinations and attractions. Some villages in Yorkshire and in the Lake District are now closed to traffic, while large car parks have been built on the outskirts to accommodate the visiting coaches and cars.

Pollution

In coastal resorts, jet skis and motor boats cause noise pollution and air pollution from the petrol fumes produced. The noise causes distress to wildlife and the petrol fumes can destroy marine life.

Another pollution problem is the disposal of sewage, particularly in developing destinations where sewage plants either do not exist or are not able to cope with the extra waste. The cruise sector is booming, but cruise ships produce tonnes of waste. Sewage pollutes seas and rivers, damages wildlife and encourages the growth of algae which in turn damages coral reefs.

Coral suffers damage in many ways, including trampling by snorkellers and divers, destruction by anchors from boats and in some instances mining for building materials.

As resorts grow, the building of hotels can obscure the existing features and visual appeal of an area.

Loss of natural habitats

Some countryside areas can be targets for tourism development. Without careful planning and controls, the clearing of land for tourist facilities can deprive wildlife of natural habitat.

The countryside is a key element of tourism in Tynedale, Northumberland. In the Tynedale Core Strategy, the council states: "It is accepted that tourist accommodation and facilities often need to be outside of towns and villages and it is intended to continue to allow for small scale new tourism development in the open countryside. In terms of tourist accommodation this means camping, caravan and chalet development". The intention of the Core Strategy is to prevent new permanent buildings being constructed in the open countryside for tourism accommodation, lest they later default to being general residential houses which would be unsustainable. Hence the policy to limit new tourism accommodation in the open countryside to caravans, chalets and campsites. On the other hand, in order to facilitate tourism, an important part of the economy, other buildings can be allowed for tourism use if there is no alternative within a settlement – e.g. if the tourist attraction itself is away from villages.

Activity: Save the turtles

What is more important – preserving the countryside or allowing such development? The presence of tourists can be detrimental to wildlife, which can be frightened away from its natural habitat by noise and disturbance.

The Greek island Zakynthos is the home of the loggerhead turtle. The female turtles come back each year to the beaches to nest and lay eggs in the same place where they themselves hatched. The males stay in the sea. The species is under threat because Zakynthos is also a vibrant tourist destination. The turtles are prevented from coming onto the beach by the noise from nightclubs and from beach parties. The eggs that do get laid may be inadvertently smashed by tourists. Those babies who do manage to hatch get confused by the bright lights and, instead of heading for the sea and moonlight, go the wrong way. The World Wildlife Fund (WWF) has launched a campaign to help protect the turtles.

What do you think the Greek government could do to protect the loggerhead turtles without losing their tourism business? Discuss your ideas with your group.

Erosion of resources

A problem in many destinations is that the influx of tourists puts pressure on scarce resources. Water is a scarce resource in many places and tourists tend to use up more than local people. Where there are golf courses and gardens, for example, even more water is used for watering grass and flowerbeds.

Land is taken for the development of hotels, airports and roads consequently causing loss of natural habitats. Soil is eroded for development, resulting in a change in the landscape. Forests are cleared for ski-resort development.

Case study: Valley of the Kings

VALLEY OF THE KINGS COULD BE RUINED BY TOURISTS

Officials are concerned about the impact of tourists visiting the Valley of the Kings in Egypt. The tombs of the Pharaohs, including that of King Tutankhamen, are likely to be destroyed in 50 to 150 years if they remain open to tourists. The problem is the humidity and fungus caused by the breath of thousands of tourists each day. Preventative measures include restricting the numbers of visitors and installing ventilation systems to protect the carvings and painted decorations in the tombs.

(Source: Adapted from The Times *19 August 2009)*

1 Why do you think this situation has been allowed to develop?
2 What other measures could be taken to protect the tombs, while still allowing tourists access?
3 Find another example of erosion caused by tourists and explain it to your group.

What damage are tourists doing to the Valley of the Kings?

Trampling occurs on well-trodden trails spoiling the countryside that people have come to see. Walkers are encouraged to stay on paths in order to reduce the erosion.

1.6 Positive socio-cultural impacts

Community facilities and public services

Roads and rail networks may be introduced to cater for tourists, but are also of benefit to locals. Sport and leisure facilities may be introduced and the standard of living for the host community may generally improve.

Improved standards of living

Regular wages, clean water, effective sewage systems and road and rail networks improve quality of life for local people, as well as providing facilities for tourists.

Improved social status

The status of local people can be improved when tourists recognise and respect the culture of the community they are visiting. Also, gaining a job in tourism can lead to enhanced status in the community.

Preservation of customs and crafts

Traditional crafts, such as lace making in Malta, can be revived because the tourist trade makes them viable again. In some destinations, hotels have now adopted a policy of inviting local people into their complex on a particular evening each week to sell their crafts to the tourists staying there.

Harlequin Hotels & Resorts is committed to being a responsible and considerate community partner by having a positive economic impact and supporting community goals, both within and outside its resorts. Across all its resorts it is important to Harlequin to engage local communities and make them an integral part of our experience. It applies fairness in the workplace and respects the national and local laws of countries where it has resorts.

Harlequin wants to encourage the local community to use its sporting facilities as well, providing a means for children to be engaged in new sports with the use of the site's facilities through schools or local clubs.

Think about it

What is better? To bring the crafts into the resort environment for guests to see and buy, or to encourage the guests to go out and visit local businesses?

Revival of festivals and ceremonies

In the same way that crafts are preserved, sometimes festivals and events are kept going because of tourist interest. Traditional dances and ceremonies may be staged for the benefit of tourists.

How can tourism benefit local culture?

Cultural education

Travelling to new places can bring about a better understanding of different cultures. In the best case scenario, tourists learn about the food and traditions of their destination and the hosts learn about their visitors. Having visitors interested in the host culture can reinforce the cultural identity of the nation as they proudly show it to visitors.

1.7 Negative socio-cultural impacts

Crime

Increases in tourism numbers are often accompanied by a rise in levels of crime. Tourists may carry cameras, mobile phones and ipods and wear expensive clothes and jewellery, so they become targets for criminals.

Resorts may be built in enclaves next to poor areas and tourists may become afraid to leave the resort for fear of crime. The host population then becomes resentful of tourists who do not mix with their society or spend their money in the community. General resentment may be expressed by rudeness towards tourists and even hostility.

This was a particular problem in Jamaica and in Florida several years ago, but education programmes for tourists in the form of advice brochures given out before arrival have helped improve safety.

Sex tourism

Tourism has encouraged the growth of prostitution in destinations as young women are willing, or persuaded, to sell their bodies to provide an income.

There are several organisations that are fighting against sex tourism. One is ECPAT (End Child Prostitution, Child Pornography and Trafficking of Children for Sexual Purposes) which is a network of organisations and individuals working together to eliminate the commercial sexual exploitation of children. ECPAT provides training to the travel and tourism industry on developing policy and practical measures to protect children from sexual exploitation. Training is available to hotels, tour operators, travel agents and others interested in ethical and sustainable tourism.

It is not only men who engage in sex tourism. Many middle-aged white women visit Jamaica to be entertained by young local men. Commonly known as 'milk bottles' they are willing to spend money on the men in return for nights out and sex.

Conflict

Western tourists visiting developing countries represent an entirely different and sometimes unknown society. Members of the host community may try to copy western behaviour or dress, resulting in changes to their traditional way of life or causing conflict between the hosts and the visitors.

Tourists sometimes fail to respect the customs and traditions of the host country, causing irritation. The host population may feel resentful about the wealth of the incoming tourists. Even though the tourists may not be wealthy in western terms, they have a lot more disposable income than the people in the developing destination. This resentment can lead to crime.

The term 'lager louts' mainly originated in Spain and the Balearic islands. It was used disparagingly about British male tourists who, after drinking copious amounts of cheap drink, behaved irresponsibly, annoying the local population. Such behaviour has given British holidaymakers a poor reputation in some areas.

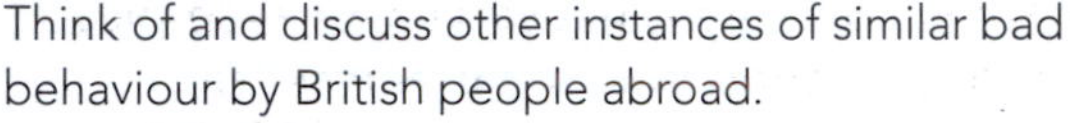

Think about it

Think of and discuss other instances of similar bad behaviour by British people abroad.

Displacement

When tourism is regionalised in a country, people may leave their homes and communities to take up jobs in tourism. More serious displacement occurs when whole communities are moved on to make room for tourism development. Recently, there was contention as hundreds of people were displaced from Chattisgarh in India to make room for a National Park aimed at bringing tourism to the area.

In the late 1980s, people were evicted from the Mkomazi Game Reserve in Tanzania. Tourists are allowed in to view the wildlife, but the indigenous people are confined to a narrow strip of land along the Pangani River. This has happened in several locations in East Africa in the name of conservation. Tourism Concern runs campaigns to help such displaced people.

Loss of cultural identity

As it becomes easier, faster and cheaper to travel the world, so each destination begins to look something like another. For example, McDonalds burger restaurants can be found almost anywhere, including Eastern Europe and Africa. Some tourists want to live exactly as they do at home – but with sunshine. In many resorts in Spain you can see English pubs and food advertised for sale. This kind of development results in a loss of the destination's cultural identity.

In the southern resorts of Tenerife, in the Canary Islands, there are beautiful hotels with excellent facilities and good food, but there isn't anything remotely Canarian. Even the hotel workers are from mainland Spain. You have to hire a car and travel away from the purpose-built resorts to find the Canarian culture.

Staged authenticity

In contrast to the view that tourism preserves national dance and ritual, critics sometimes believe that traditional events and dances are degraded by being put on specifically for the entertainment of tourists.

Case study: Tourism in Libya

Libya has introduced a 20-year plan for tourism and hopes to entice developers to Libya by giving them free land and tax incentives. Investors would need to improve the infrastructure, as well as build new hotels. The existing hotels need updating to bring them up to western standards. Many small tour operators have started up and hope to offer tourist packages.

The country has great potential. There are old towns to explore, deserts to cross and beaches to lie on. In addition, there is the attraction of the ruins of a lost Roman empire.

One problem for tourists is that the signs are all in Arabic and an entry visa is needed. Also, it is not envisaged that alcohol will be served anywhere but within enclosed resorts, as it is important the Islamic culture is maintained.

1. Check the location of Libya and name its capital city.
2. Find out why there has been no tourism to Libya for the past 20 years.
3. Discuss the potential positive and negative impacts of western tourism on Libya.
4. Put all your information together in an information sheet.

Assessment activity 12.1

For some of the assessments in this unit you will be working for The Travel Foundation, a charity set up to respond to concerns over the sustainability of travel and tourism. The Foundation aims to protect and enhance the environment and improve the well-being of destination countries, as well as the holiday experience for customers.

You can find out more about The Travel Foundation at www.thetravelfoundation.org.uk and in the case study on page 302.

The Foundation provides support and information for travel and tourism organisations and for travellers. In this assessment you will be contributing to a booklet to be targeted at businesses and travellers.

The Travel Foundation wishes to issue an informative booklet which highlights the impacts of tourism in destinations. You must carry out research and produce a booklet which can be distributed to organisations in travel and tourism.

Your booklet must include a description of:

- economic impacts – at least three positive and three negative examples
- environmental impacts – at least three positive and three negative examples
- socio-cultural impacts – at least three positive and three negative examples.

Grading tips

P1 Consider a variety of tourism activities, for example cruising, skiing, new developments and regeneration. Make sure that you cover examples of towns, cities, countryside areas and seaside resorts from countries in the LEDW and MEDW.

Try to find your own examples through research and note your sources.

PLTS

As you present your ideas and experiences in inventive ways in your booklet you will develop skills as a **creative thinker**.

Functional skills

By entering, developing and formatting information to make your booklet, you will be developing your **ICT** skills.

2 The roles and objectives of agents of tourism development

Tourism development can be defined as the process of providing facilities and services for visitors to a destination in order to gain economic and other benefits. Although it occurs throughout the world, it does not occur at the same rate. In some countries and destinations tourism development is in its early stages, while in other destinations it is well established.

Tourism development is complex. It may mean a local area opening up to visitors, the development of a specific resort or hotel, or a country setting up policies and tourist board structures to promote tourism. On a national level, tourism development is driven by governments setting a policy for tourism and creating a structure that promotes tourism.

In this part of the unit you will learn about the many different kinds of organisations and agencies involved in tourism development. You will learn about their role and their reasons for being involved in tourism development. These organisations represent the,

private, **public** and **voluntary sectors**. They are sometimes described as 'stakeholders'.

Roles vary from providing travel and tourism resources, products and services, to providing funding or marketing. Many agents are involved in conservation. We will consider the varying roles as we study each type of agent.

Key terms

Private sector – owned by shareholders or individuals rather than the state. They are commercial companies and usually aim to make a profit.

Public sector – public sector organisations are owned by the state and receive their funds from local or central government and usually aim to provide a service. Their policy will be directed by national or local government.

Voluntary sector – voluntary organisations are often charities or pressure groups. They do not always make a profit, but put funds into the company activities, for example, conservation.

2.1 Private sector agents

Landowners

Landowners and owners of stately homes are not always cash rich and seek to develop their properties and land to benefit from tourism. Most British stately homes are open to visitors for some part of the year. Many welcome film crews to their parks and houses and then benefit from increased tourism as the films gain publicity.

In developing countries, land owned by local people is often bought up cheaply by developers. If local authorities are powerful enough they can prevent this happening and ensure that local people are involved in development. Where locals own the land they can make money from tourism and stop the arrival of large hotel chains.

In Tobago there are very few large hotels as local people own the land – and want to keep it. They welcome tourists and cater for them with local produce. Some of the hotels are all inclusive and these

Case study: Beach policy in Barbados

In Barbados, all beaches are public. Everyone is entitled to access. However, access to beaches has become an issue of contention in recent years because:

- there is a lack of vacant coastal land
- when land is available it is very expensive
- landowners want properties which reach to the sea to have boundaries which prevent access
- new beach land with disputed ownership has appeared through coastal works.

The declared policy is that all citizens and visitors alike must have access to all beaches, including, where possible, windows to the sea.
In a Special Report prepared in 1999, the Ombudsman of Barbados said that "if the need for windows to the sea was pressing in 1980, it is immensely more necessary in 2000, to provide Barbadians with a continual view of their most precious natural asset. It seems to me that the retention and creation of windows to the sea is a clear must."

1 Do you think the policy should be changed? What would be the benefits and disadvantages to tourists, landowners and local people of changing the policy?

2 Draw up a chart illustrating your findings.

are not so beneficial to the economy, as tourists have all their needs catered for in the hotel.

Property developers

Property developers may be individuals who decide to open a hotel, or major international companies responsible for developing whole resorts. Property developers are in business to make money out of their developments and are often in conflict with host communities who do not want to lose their land or see over-development. The public sector has to take responsibility for overseeing development and ensuring that community needs are met and that development is sustainable. The Bahamas provides a good example.

The government policy is to extend the economic benefits derived from tourism and to have a hotel sector that is private sector led. In the UK, it is the norm for hotels to be privately owned, but in 1992, 20 per cent of hotels in the Bahamas were government owned. Now, less than 5 per cent are in public ownership. Many hotels were bought and refurbished by international investors and developers. New hotels have also been built and re-development of resorts has taken place.

A consortium of US, UK and South African investors bought four hotels on Paradise Island and re-developed them at a cost of over $250 million. The government gave exemptions from property tax and customs duty for companies investing in hotel and resort development. The purpose was to inject capital investment from the private sector into development, rather than the government providing capital from taxes.

Travel and tourism organisations

Tour operators, travel agents and airlines have a major role to play in tourism development. They are instrumental in introducing large numbers of people to destinations when they organise flights, accommodation and package tours. Their decisions to operate in new destinations can have a tremendous impact. Many are very aware of responsible tourism and have policies demonstrating their good practice.

One way that a tour operator can try to practise responsible tourism is by joining the Tour Operators' Initiative. This is an organisation of like-minded tour operators whose aim is explained on the organisation's website (www.toinitiative.org). Note that tour operators are in the private sector, yet this initiative is voluntary, non-profit making and open to all tour operators. With this initiative, tour operators are moving towards sustainable tourism by committing themselves to the concepts of sustainable development as the core of their business activity and to work together to promote methods and practices compatible with sustainable development.

Entertainment companies

Entertainment companies usually enter into a development in the later stages and choose a location where they will benefit from the advent of tourism. Examples include cinemas, casinos and leisure centres. Like hotels, they can aim to use renewable resources.

Activity: Your last holiday

Think about the last holiday you went on. What were the leisure and entertainment centres in your resort? Did they add to or detract from your holiday experience? Why? Discuss your ideas with your group.

2.2 Public sector agents

The public sector role is of utmost importance as it is responsible for setting policy on tourism and for putting in place the legislation needed to implement policy.

In a developed country like the UK, the public sector structure is well established and works in harmony with the private sector to develop and monitor tourism. In countries where the tourism industry is in its infancy, the government may have less control over development than private enterprises and has to begin the process of establishing national tourism organisation networks.

National government

The structure of public sector tourism in the UK is shown in Figure 12.1.

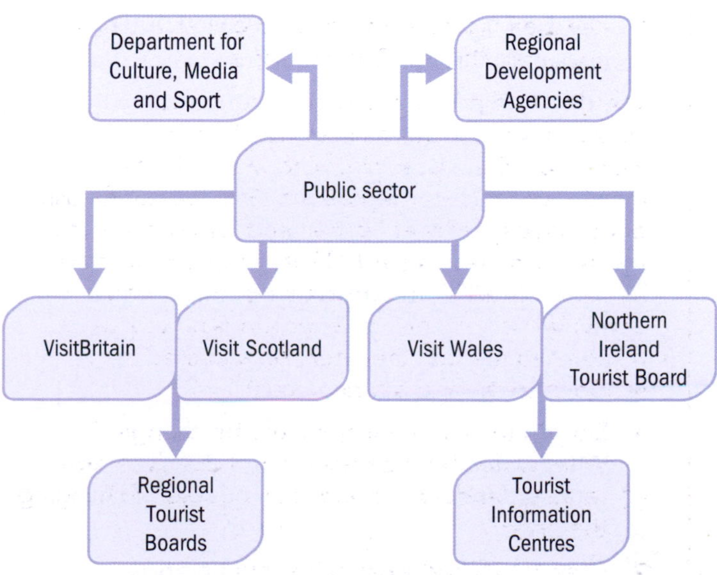

Figure 12.1: Public sector tourism in the UK

Case study: Tourism strategy

Winning: A Tourism Strategy for 2012 and Beyond

This report was published by the DCMS in readiness for the 2012 Olympics, laying out the strategies to maximise the benefits of hosting the Olympics.

The key strategies are:

- engage all UK tourism businesses in a national campaign
- improve international perceptions of Britain
- deliver a first class welcome to all visitors
- improve the skills of the workforce
- drive up quality in accommodation
- maximise the opportunities for increasing business visits and events
- spread the benefits across the UK
- improve sustainability.

In pairs take one of the key strategies. Look at the report on the DCMS website for more detail (www.culture.gov.uk).

1. Research three pieces of evidence to demonstrate that your selected strategy is being achieved.
2. Suggest one thing that might be done that is not yet happening.

The Department for Culture, Media and Sport (DCMS) states its role on its website "We work with the industry and the public sector to improve the reputation of the UK at home and abroad as a world class destination."

National and Regional Tourist Boards

VisitBritain and the other national tourist offices are responsible for implementing government policy nationally and the Regional Tourist Boards are responsible for implementing it in their regions, alongside the Regional Development Agencies (RDAs). These bodies are all **quangos**. Note that the government is currently seeking to replace RDAs with Local Economic Partnerships (LEPs). It looks like this will happen by March 2012, with the LEPs set to cover small areas than the RDAs.

Local authorities play an important role in supporting the tourism sector through their statutory duties and because they recognise that tourism is a major contributor towards the economy. Local authorities have tourism departments and plans.

Key term

Quango – an acronym which stands for Quasi Autonomous Non-Governmental Organisation, otherwise known as a non-departmental public body. Quangos are set up by government with government funding, but they work independently of government.

You can read about the structure and roles of public sector tourism in Unit 1.

Think about it

Examples of quangos include the Regional Development Agencies (RDAs). Can you think of and name any other quangos? How do you think their role might change as budget cuts and policy changes are implemented?

Local authorities

Local authorities provide the infrastructure for tourism. This includes roads, lighting, water and sewerage, public transport systems and signs. These facilities need to be well-managed to ensure an area is fit for tourists.

Local authorities own visitor attractions such as museums, art galleries, swimming pools, parks and gardens. Public spaces must be clean and attractive to attract tourists.

Many local authorities carry out marketing activities and provide visitor information through Tourist Information Centres (TICs) and other bodies.

Activity: Local authority role

Find out what your local authority role is with regard to tourism. Make a poster outlining its role and include a diagram showing how the local authority relates to other agents of tourism.

Case study: Sustainable tourism development in Wales

Visit Wales is the Welsh Assembly's tourism team, within the Department for Heritage. Visit Wales principal role is to provide leadership and strategic direction to the tourism industry in Wales. Its strategies define a vision for tourism, establish priorities for partnership action and sets targets for growth.

In addition, four Regional Tourism Partnerships (RTPs) were set up in 2002 to cover north, mid, south-west and south-east Wales. Their principal role is to lead the implementation of four regional tourism strategies which seek to improve the competitive performance of tourism, so that it makes a better contribution to the economic and social prosperity of Wales. The RTPs work in partnership with Visit Wales, local authorities, tourism businesses and with other organisations to undertake a range of marketing, product investment and business support activities on behalf of the tourism industry.

The Wales Tourism Alliance (WTA) is widely recognised as the voice of the tourism industry in Wales.

The WTA, via its member organisations, represents some 7000 tourism businesses, covering all the major sectors of the industry. WTA member organisations include pan-UK, pan-Wales and regional bodies.

The role of the WTA is to inform and convey the views and needs of the tourism community to the Welsh Assembly Government, the Minister for Heritage (whose portfolio includes tourism) and to Westminster (on non-devolved issues).

The WTA works closely with the industry, the Welsh Assembly, Visit Wales and VisitBritain on UK matters. It aims to link sectors and raise main policy matters with politicians and Visit Wales.

There are around 60 Tourist Information Centres (TICs) in Wales. There are 22 local authorities in Wales. All local authorities in Wales support tourism with dedicated budgets and staff, with some able to offer small-scale grant aid as well as coordinating marketing activity.

(Source: new.wales.gov.uk)

1. Describe the roles of agents involved in tourism development in Wales. You will need to do some further research to find out about the different bodies.
2. Explain how the agents involved in tourism development in Wales could have conflicting objectives.
3. Explain how responsible tourism has been considered by agents of tourist development in the Welsh public sector.

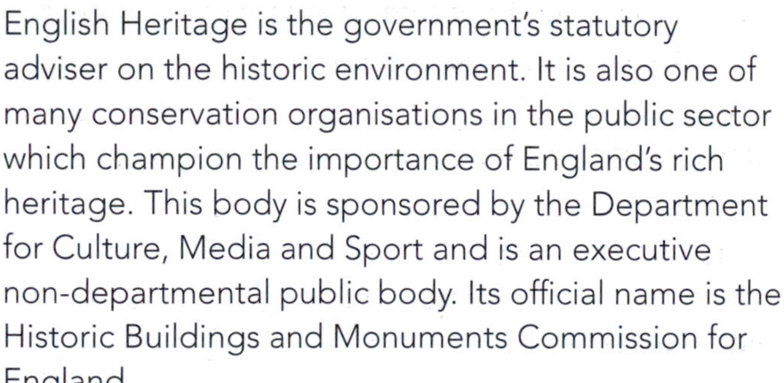

Conservation organisations

English Heritage is the government's statutory adviser on the historic environment. It is also one of many conservation organisations in the public sector which champion the importance of England's rich heritage. This body is sponsored by the Department for Culture, Media and Sport and is an executive non-departmental public body. Its official name is the Historic Buildings and Monuments Commission for England.

The organisation also works with other government departments whose work also affects heritage, such as the Department for Environment, Food and Rural Affairs (DEFRA), which takes care of policy on rural issues, and the Department for Community and Local Government. The government provides funding for English Heritage which supplements it by earning revenue from the historic properties under its care.

Organisations like English Heritage aim to encourage everyone to enjoy and participate in the historic environment. The role of English Heritage is described on its website: 'Our role is to champion and care for the historic environment which we do by:

- improving understanding of the past through research and study
- providing conservation grants, advisory and education services
- identifying and helping to protect buildings and archaeological sites of national importance
- maintaining over 400 historic properties and making them accessible to the broadest possible public audience
- maintaining the National Monuments Record as the central publicly accessible archive for the historic environment in England.'

(Source: www.english-heritage.org.uk)

The heritage sector contributes immensely to tourism. According to new study, one third of foreign visitors cited heritage as the main reason for coming to Britain. The economic benefits derived from heritage assets to the community or region can be measured in terms of jobs, visitor spending in retail shop at and near the destination, or increased revenue.

Activity: English Heritage

Find out more about heritage conservation at English Heritage. What partners does the organisation work with? How does it fund projects? You might choose a particular project to report on. Write up notes on your findings.

2.3 Voluntary sector agents

Many voluntary sector organisations are charities and pressure groups. Probably the best known in tourism is the National Trust. However, there are several voluntary organisations related to sustainable tourism development.

Registered charities

The purpose of charities in travel and tourism is to promote responsible and sustainable tourism. They may do this through education programmes which raise awareness, by advising businesses on how to practise responsible tourism or by lobbying government to change policies.

Community groups

Community groups may be formed specifically to deal with proposed tourism (or other) developments or may have been formed for a different purpose, but then become involved in tourism development. Local people wish to be consulted on possible developments to protect their personal and community interests. Community groups can also act as pressure groups.

Pressure groups

These organisations work to lobby government and change policies. Many of them are concerned with protecting the environment and wildlife. Examples include the Wildlife Trust which is a conservation charity dedicated to wildlife and Tourism Concern whose role is described in our case study.

Case study: Tourism Concern

Tourism Concern campaigns against exploitation in tourism and for fairly traded and ethical forms of tourism.

Unregulated tourism development is continuing to devastate environments, degrade cultures and destroy traditional livelihoods. We work to address these in our projects and campaigns as well as through the production of reports, research and educational resources.

The issues

Displacement, exploitation, environmental damage – find out about all the key issues in our quick interactive guide.

Projects

We support the work of non-governmental organisations (NGOs) and communities who are finding their own solutions for tourism related poverty and exploitation.

Campaigns

Campaigning is our core activity. We respond to requests for help from individuals, communities and groups from all over the world who are challenging the damage to their interests caused by the development of tourism.

(Source: www.tourismconcern.org.uk)

1. Visit the Tourism Concern website and choose one current campaign. What is the role of Tourism Concern in this campaign?
2. Do the objectives of Tourism Concern in your chosen campaign conflict with those of government or developers?
3. Explain either the potential conflict or the way that different stakeholders work together.

Activity: Conservation

Choose one of the following organisations involved in responsible tourism:

- Tourism Concern
- Green Hotels Association
- Wildlife Trust
- CERT (Centre for Environmentally Responsible Tourism)
- Earthwatch
- Kathmandu Environmental Education Project

Work with a partner. Research the chosen organisation. Prepare a presentation which covers:

- the objectives of the organisation
- an example of a current project
- how to support the organisation.

The rest of this section details the various objectives agents might have. Although these objectives are categorised here, remember that in most cases objectives are a mix of political, economic and socio-cultural.

2.4 Political objectives

Tourism is related to politics in that it is the government of a country that determines tourism policy. The policy is often to use a national network of tourism organisations to attract greater numbers of tourists to generate revenue or to manage tourism in a sustainable way. There may be other political objectives too.

Enhancing image

How a country is perceived is often related to tourism and the perceptions of visitors. Where a country has suffered conflict and is in the stage of recovery, tourism can be a means of proving to the international community that the country is stable and safe and help to raise the profile of the area.

Croatia provides a good example. As part of the former Yugoslavia the area was a very popular tourist destination. The civil war in the 1990s meant that the tourism industry was devastated. Although a lot of Croatia was unaffected by conflict, tourists naturally stayed away. Now, tourism is an essential part of the country's regeneration.

Creating a national or regional identity

National identity comes from images and experiences within a country, but also from how others perceive the country. How a country is perceived is often related to tourism and based on the perceptions of visitors.

A country may present itself in a certain way in its publicity, and on its website, to promote a particular identity and therefore attract visitors.

For example, what do you think of when you think of the Netherlands? Windmills, bikes and tulips? Cheese? If you look at the banner on the Netherlands website you will find all these traditional images. It reinforces people's perceptions of what the Netherlands is like and what they hope to find if they visit it.

Key term

National identity – the attachment people feel to their country of birth or residence through a set of shared behaviours and characteristics.

Figure 12.2: The website of The Netherlands Board of Tourism uses traditional images of Holland

Activity: National identity

1 Choose three countries. Discuss your perceptions of those countries as a tourist. How do you think tourists see the British? Are these perceptions correct? What gives the UK its national identity?

2 We also have perceptions of people from different regions. Think what your perceptions are of a Londoner, a Glaswegian or someone from Yorkshire. How do regions present a united front to tourists?

Raising the profile of an area

When tourists return from a destination after having good experiences, they tell their friends and family. This word of mouth promotion in conjunction with promotional campaigns is one way of raising the profile of an area.

2.5 Economic objectives

In most cases economic objectives are the aim of tourism development. This is not surprising as worldwide tourist arrivals and receipts are increasing and all countries would like a piece of the action. The World Tourism Organization (WTO) reported that the number of international tourist arrivals recorded worldwide grew by 2 per cent from the previous year and exceeded 900 million in 2007.

The economic objectives of tourism development include:

- employment creation
- revenue generation – the multiplier effect
- increasing foreign currency earnings
- economic regeneration.

Tourism creates jobs, both directly and indirectly. Direct employment occurs in hotels, airports, airlines, tour operators, travel agents and tourist offices.

Employment creation

Indirect employment occurs in industries and businesses that service the travel and tourism industry. For example, construction workers are needed to build the infrastructure that supports tourism such as roads and rail networks, hotels and gas and electricity services. Also, local shops and services benefit from tourist business and will be able to employ more people.

Revenue generation

You read about the multiplier effect on page 281. Revenue is generated by visitors spending directly on tourism, but also on related businesses. It is also generated as it provides income for those employed in tourism.

Increasing foreign currency earnings

Tourism generates foreign exchange earnings. Tourism is an invisible export. This means, if tourists spend their money in the UK, it brings the same benefit to the economy as if they buy goods exported from the UK in their own countries. By the same token, when UK residents travel abroad they spend their money in another country and this equates to buying imported goods in the UK.

Inbound visitors spend money whilst in the UK and some also spend money on travel with UK carriers. The more tourists who come into the UK, the more the spend increases and the more revenue the economy gains.

The impact on the economy of incoming and outbound tourism is recorded in the travel balance, a section of the **balance of payments**. Each sector of the economy is measured in terms of its imports and exports. A happy situation for an economy is where there is a surplus in the balance of payments rather than a deficit: that is, more money coming in than going out.

Key term

Balance of payments – one of the UK's key economic statistics. It measures the economic transactions between the UK and the rest of the world. It indicates the difference between spending on imports and exports.

Case study: Kashgar, China

The ancient Silk Road trading town no longer feels as different as it did.

How is Kashgar losing its identity?

What's the problem?

This fabled old Silk Road oasis city is losing its identity and fast becoming a playground for Chinese and Western tourists. What was once a chaotic, colourful bazaar, in a dusty field on the edge of town, has been moved into a covered market and turned into a sanitised tourist attraction. The livestock market where Kazakh and Uygur traders haggle over horses and sheep is now one giant photo opportunity.

Worst of all, the Uygur culture – a nomadic, Turkic-speaking, Islamic people from Central Asia – is in danger of being overwhelmed as tourism achieves what decades of political suppression has failed to do. The Chinese are travelling in greater numbers than ever and across the country, from Xinjiang to Tibet, local cultures are being marginalised as temples, mosques and villages are given the theme park treatment and turned into tacky, commercialised 'scenic spots'. The ancient Uygur city at the heart of Kashgar is surrounded by six-lane highways and it is starting to resemble any other Chinese city.

What's the solution?

Go now, while the Uygur population is still a majority. Instead of just flying in for the Sunday bazaar, stay a few days, giving you time to get to know the city. Ignore the 'Kashgar Old City Scenic Spot' and instead wander the souq-like lanes of the old town, where veiled women sit outside mud-brick houses and old men with beards and prayer caps bake nan bread in clay ovens on the street.

If you can, go during Ramadan when the streets burst into life with music at dusk and everyone gathers at the night market by the main mosque to eat mutton, noodles and dumplings.

Tony Kelly, travel writer

(Source: www.wanderlust.co.uk)

1 Summarise the problems arising from tourism at this destination.

2 Describe any positive impacts that tourism might have in this destination.

3 What other solutions can you propose other than those suggested in the article?

Economic regeneration

Tourism development is often used as a tool for regeneration both in cites and in coastal resorts in the UK. Dockland areas in Manchester and Liverpool have been regenerated with housing, restaurants and tourist facilities. The Lowry Centre in Salford (near Manchester) is a good example, as the Case study on page 297 shows.

Areas which are in decline, perhaps because traditional industries like mining have closed down, are in need of employment and investment. Tourism can be a means of injecting new life into an area. Grants from RDAs and the EU can help and local authorities will invest funds.

Income from tourism should be reinvested in social and public projects. Tourism taxes are often in place for such purposes. In The Gambia, tourists are subjected to a £5 tax on arrival. This money is earmarked for improving the infrastructure of the country and for training local people to enable them to work in tourism.

2.6 Environmental objectives

Habitat and heritage preservation

Precious natural habitats and heritage sites have to be conserved or they will be lost to future generations. It is often difficult to balance conservation with allowing the public to view or enjoy their heritage and parklands.

National Parks are heavily protected and although people are allowed to enjoy them, there are restrictions on the types of activities that can take place. Historic buildings, such as the colleges in Cambridge and Oxford, are often open to the public, but access is restricted by time and numbers, so that too many tourists are not detrimental to the buildings' structure.

Revenue from tourism can be used to preserve heritage sites. Ironically, the preservation is sometimes necessary because of increased tourism. Tourists wandering around a site cause erosion and litter.

Another means of attempting to control the flow of visitors is through **ecotourism**. The idea is to bring small numbers of people to enjoy the natural resources and culture of a destination without changing the basic culture or ecology.

Key term

Ecotourism – Ecotourism represents the ideal of minimising negative impacts and practising environmentally responsible tourism in relatively undisturbed natural areas.

Environmental education

As we noted earlier (see page 282), education is an important part of achieving environmental objectives. One approach is that taken by the Eden Project in Cornwall. They offer 'green' work placements. The idea is to encourage young people to become environmental champions of the future. The RSPB and the Royal Botanic Gardens of Kew, in London, will also offer placements.

An example of an environmental education programme is given in the case study on page 297.

2.7 Socio-cultural objectives

Development of community facilities

Sometimes planning permission is only given to developers as long as they provide facilities for the host community alongside, or as part of, their development. Examples include leisure facilities or even schools. In addition, the host community has a better standard of living because of the increased revenues from tourism.

Promoting cultural understanding

Welcoming visitors to a country or community can promote mutual understanding. It can also inspire people to learn new languages and to try new foods and experiences.

On a global level such interaction can help promote peaceful societies. This works both ways. Hosts must have a positive attitude to visitors and be encouraged to welcome them and take part in community tourism initiatives. On the other hand, visitors must respect the people and the culture of the destination they are visiting.

Maintaining traditions and beliefs

Traditions may be lost as younger generations lose interest in preserving them. The objective of tourism may be to preserve such traditions and in fact cultural and heritage tourism are rising in popularity. For example, in Mexico, Zapotec weavers from Oaxaca live in a 'craft village' known for specialising in certain textiles. They are able to demonstrate and sell their work to tourists while preserving an ancient craft.

Case study: Salford

The Quays is Greater Manchester's unique waterfront.

The re-development of Salford Quays has created a world-class business, cultural and residential area of great national and regional significance. More people now work at the Quays than in its heyday as a major seaport. The area has also become a popular residential area with a regular tram service to West Salford, Altrincham and Manchester city centre. The development of MediaCityUK will continue to develop the area's vibrant economy, fantastic leisure assets and high-quality residential buildings.

Key milestones such as the opening of The Lowry in 2000, with its theatres, galleries, shops, bars, restaurant and conference facilities, along with the Digital World Centre and the Lowry Outlet mall and leisure development, have marked a major watershed in the sustainable regeneration of the area.

The Quays has established itself as a tourist destination of choice with a wealth of world-class entertainment, sporting, leisure and cultural facilities, including the Salford Triathlon World Cup.

Future plans aim to spread the success and vitality of Salford Quays' regeneration into other parts of Salford. The creation of MediaCityUK, commercial development, the transformation of the river corridor into Irwell City Park, as well as extensive residential developments will help to create a successful business district, international tourism destination and an exciting and vibrant place to live.

(Source: www.salford.gov.uk)

Find out more about regeneration, either in Salford or in your own town if appropriate.

- Find out who are the stakeholders involved in regeneration projects.
- What are their roles in the regeneration?
- How do you think the regeneration will impact on the economy?

Present your findings to your colleagues.

Case study: Discover Coral Reefs School Program

Our award-winning program provides every 4th grade student in the Florida Keys with an introduction to the coral reef. Educator Joel Biddle begins with a video/talk at the Reef Relief Environmental Center (for Lower Keys students) or the John Pennekamp Coral Reef State Park Visitor Center (for Upper Keys students), an excursion to the reef aboard a glassbottom boat, a follow-up slide show entitled 'We All Live Downstream' and use of printed materials including the 'Coral Reef Guide for Kids of All Ages' and 'South Florida's Water Wonderland'. The Reef Relief Teacher Kit enables educators around the world to introduce their students to coral reefs.

(Source: www.reefrelief.org)

Do some research and find out your own example of a coral reef audit or conservation programme. Produce a poster with an explanation of the programme.

Assessment activity 12.2

The Travel Foundation has asked you to carry out further work on their behalf. They want to undertake some case studies to investigate the roles of different agents involved in tourism development and how they work together.

You could find out about your local tourism development plan for your case study. If this is not suitable, you can access the plan on the Isle of Wight Tourism website (nl.islandbreaks.co.uk)

You will present your case studies as an illustrated article (on-line if you wish) for members of The Travel Foundation.

Your case studies must cover:

- a comparison of the roles and objectives of different agents involved in tourism development P2
- an explanation of how differing roles and objectives can cause conflict in a suggested destination M1
- clear suggestions as to how the conflict situations may be resolved backed up with evidence. D1

Grading tips

P2 Ensure you have at least three examples from each of the following sectors: private, public and voluntary. The agents will have varying objectives, so make sure you show how they differ.

M1 Ensure that your case studies cover development of your destination and that the development you investigate is current.

D1 You will need to show that you have considered how the parties might negotiate and compromise with each other. You should also ensure that you have included suggestions of how conflict situations can be resolved and ensure you have evidence to show this. Refer to good practices from elsewhere to support your suggestions.

PLTS

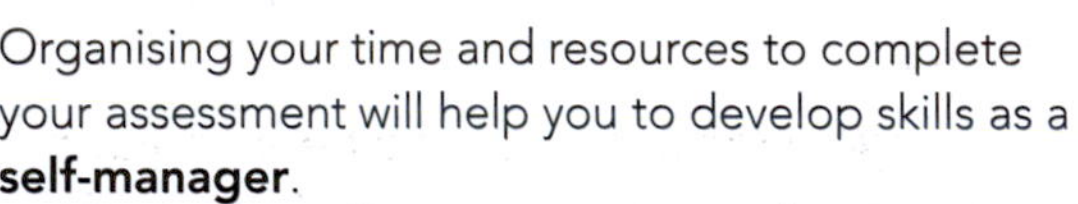

Organising your time and resources to complete your assessment will help you to develop skills as a **self-manager**.

Functional skills

Presenting your work in a style and format suitable for an article will develop your **English** writing skills.

3 Strategies used to manage responsible tourism in destinations

Different strategies are used to maximise the positive impacts of tourism and minimise the negative impacts. This section of the unit examines some of these strategies.

3.1 Maximising positive impacts

Retention of visitor spending

Where tourist facilities are owned by local people, more of the income from tourism is retained in the community. This can be achieved in various ways:

- regulation on ownership of hotels so that they cannot be entirely foreign owned
- encouraging the development of small businesses
- encouraging partnerships between local people
- hotels should be encouraged to buy produce locally wherever possible rather than importing.

This last way may mean that support has to be given to local producers to help them meet the needs of large hotels. Hotels or local government may supply seeds and agrochemicals on credit to producers to help them set up. In some cases hotels have participated in 'adopt a farmer' projects.

Where tourism takes place in particular geographic regions, tours should be set up to other areas to allow other communities to benefit from tourism. A good example of this is 'agro tourism' where local people turn their farmhouses into tourist accommodation or restaurants. The restaurants provide meals serving traditional local delicacies. The aim of these projects is to help local people benefit from tourism, especially when they are no longer able to make their living from agriculture.

Calatonazor in Soria province, Spain. How can agro tourism benefit a destination?

Widening access to facilities

There are many examples of good practice where the proceeds of tourism are used to bring improved facilities and a better standard of living to local people.

Turtle Island is a privately owned resort in Fiji. It has Green Globe status and it has implemented projects to aid local people. There was no secondary school on the island despite the fact there were three primary schools. The resort owners initiated a project to provide a school. It was completed in 2002. Now the school has six teachers and over 50 pupils.

Healthcare in the islands of Yasawa was also basic. There was no resident doctor and a lack of equipment in nursing stations. For many years, the resort has funded eye clinics. At these clinics local people can be issued with glasses, get cataract operations and even corneal transplants. The resort also sponsors other medical clinics throughout the year, but the ultimate goal is for a state of the art medical centre on the island.

Investment of tourism income in community projects

Income from tourism should be reinvested in social and public projects. Tourism taxes are often in place for such purposes. Earlier in the unit (page 296) we saw how in The Gambia tourists are subjected to a £5 tax on arrival to help improve the infrastructure of the country.

Of course, this is not always the case. In 2009 a controversial green tax was proposed in the Maldives. Visitors would be charged up to $3 a day to raise money in local taxes. The fear amongst tour operators is that this tax will deter visitors to the islands. It is not clear how the proposed tax would help climate change projects or even whether it would be designated to do so.

The following extract from the Responsible Travel website explains how a community tourism project in India works.

Responsible Travel provides community-based tourism holidays

We would like to invite you to take in a small part of this great land, on a volunteer project in Bangalore.

There is a huge variety of projects here so your skills will be matched to the project that needs you most. Options include shelters and schools for street children and children from slums, homes for severely handicapped people and schools for deaf and hearing impaired children.

Here are just some examples of the projects you can help at. The street children project is a great stepping-stone into care work. A YMCA shelter supports homeless boys, and you will be giving advice on health, nutrition and family planning. If you are good with your hands, you could also help with carpentry lessons – a valuable trade for street-dwellers. Female volunteers also have the choice of working in a home for disabled women. The project aims to provide occupational skills and you assist with light exercise, English tuition and craftwork.

(Source: www.responsibletravel.com)

Case study: Negril beach resort

Sandals Negril beach resort

Our mission is to offer the ultimate Caribbean vacation experience by innovatively, reliably and consistently providing the safest and highest quality services and facilities to guests, while attaching a premium to our human resources and being among the most environmentally responsible and community friendly groups in the hospitality industry.

Staff awareness: Team members, participation in workshops and seminars conducted by the environmental committee, local government organisations, and also by non-governmental environmental organisations.

Water conservation program: Monitoring of total water use on property (pools, guest rooms, kitchens, dining room and garden areas).

Energy management program: Use of Timers on electrical equipment such as Jacuzzi blowers, steam rooms at the spa, outdoor lighting for walkways, refrigeration equipment in the kitchens, etc.

Waste management program: Waste disposal practices and procedures at the hotel such as recycling of linen and bed spreads, food, office paper and packages.

Control of hazardous substances: Hotels determine the suitability of products before any purchase is made and provide full training for staff whenever new chemicals or equipment are purchased for use in the hotel.

Social and cultural development and interaction: Promoting and selling local tours and attractions with special recognition of 'Green tours' at the tour desks. Inviting local craft vendors to the hotel at least once per week to display and sell their craft items.

(Source: www.sandals.com)

In 1998, Sandals Negril beach resort and spa was the first all-inclusive resort to earn Green Globe Certification, following the resort company's efforts to modify its water systems and energy requirements, adjust its waste management programme and bolster an already-extensive community outreach programme.

Within three years of Sandals Negril's first certification, the remaining 11 Sandals Resorts and all four beaches resorts had also achieved certification.

1 What is the Green Globe Award?
2 What is the Green Globe based on?
3 Find an example of another company awarded Green Globe and explain why.

Training and employment of local people and tourism education

Hotels should employ local people wherever possible. Where local people lack the necessary skills, training programmes should be implemented. Training may take many forms from induction to specific job training.

Some large hotel groups have a good record of doing this. An example is Sandals in the Caribbean, who claim to have compulsory training for 120 hours per year for line staff in their hotels.

The benefits of training staff include a more satisfied staff who are more likely to remain in post. This leads to lower staff costs as turnover is low. If the staff are satisfied with their work this will lead to better customer relations and in turn customers will be more likely to remain loyal.

3.2 Minimising negative impacts

Visitor and traffic management

The objective of tourism is not always to maximise visitors. Where resources and space are limited then the aim is to manage visitors and prevent negative impacts which occur through erosion of paths, buildings and over-development. Examples of such visitor management occur in many historic towns and at historic sites such as Stonehenge.

Case study: Friends of the Lake District

The Friends of the Lake District is a registered charity, established in 1934 and currently supported by about 6700 members and affiliated organisations.

We work to:

- encourage vibrant rural communities, and develop improved links with them, within a living, working and sustainable landscape, especially in the uplands
- demonstrate good practice across the whole range of our work and particularly through land ownership
- improve the Cumbrian landscape through an Environmental Improvement Grants scheme.

(Source: www.fld.org.uk)

1 Explain how tourism in the Lake District can have negative impacts on the region.

2 Explain how the measures suggested in the Friends of the Lake District tourism policy would benefit the local community.

3 Suggest further ways in which the positive impacts of tourism in the Lake District could be maximised and the negative impacts minimised.

Think about it

How many tourists are too many? Some small islands in the Mediterranean have begun to try and reduce tourist numbers in order to minimise the negative effects of tourism. How do you think they still make profits from tourism?

Planning control

Restrictions on the quantity and type of building help prevent a destination becoming over-developed.

In Majorca tourism has become the most important source of revenue to the economy. Parts of the island have become over-developed due to mass tourism. Eventually action had to be taken to try and reverse the decline in the island's image as a cheap destination for low spending, heavy drinking tourists. Building restrictions were imposed on hotels throughout the island and the capital, Palma was restored.

Change as a result of environmental impact assessment and environmental audits

Environmental auditing should begin with an analysis of the environmental resources in the area. Careful planning, a long time in advance of building, can help ensure that environmental resources are protected and conserved during development. **Green building** helps decrease the negative impact of tourism on the environment.

Key term

Green building – building methods that use energy efficient and non-polluting materials for construction.

Examples of environmental auditing include several programmes which aim to protect coral reefs throughout the world. These include monitoring the state of the reefs and education programmes to help conserve them.

Sustainable tourism policies

Private organisations, such as tour operators, working in destinations abroad are in a position to influence responsible tourism and there are many examples of good practice.

In the UK, different tour operators have banded together to develop The Tour Operators' Initiative. Some tour operators, for example Thomson, support The Travel Foundation, a UK charity that claims to help protect the natural environment, traditions and culture.

Find out more about the Tour Operators' Initiative at www.toinitiative.org.

Case study: The Travel Foundation

The Travel Foundation is an independent UK charity that aims to help the outbound travel industry manage tourism more sustainably.

It offers a unique resource to the tourism industry, helping to safeguard resources on which business depends and balancing the need for sustainability with profitability.

The Foundation's focus is on protecting and enhancing the environment and improving the well-being of destination communities, thereby enriching the tourism experience, now and in the future.

The Foundation partners UK travel companies to make tourism a force for good – that minimises negative effects on the environment and uses income from tourism to protect and preserve both precious natural resources and local traditions and culture.

- Consumers get greater quality and an enriched holiday experience, as well as the reassurance that their favourite destinations will be protected for generations to come.
- Businesses are better able to meet the needs of the customer, at the same time as protecting the resources on which their future depends.
- Destination communities receive greater benefit from tourism, with a boost to their local economy and conservation of the natural environment, local traditions and culture.
- Local and national governments have evidence to develop effective tourism policies and support destination communities and environments.

(Source: www.thetravelfoundation.org.uk)

1 Find three ways in which The Travel Foundation helps businesses practise sustainable tourism.

2 How is the Travel Foundation funded?

Assessment activity 12.3

Following the success of your previous article on agents of development, The Travel Foundation has asked you to produce a follow up. In this article you will be examining the strategies used to manage responsible tourism in destinations.

You can produce an illustrated article once again (on-line if you choose). Your article must include:

- descriptions of real strategies used to maximise positive impacts and minimise negative impacts with examples from destinations (where possible) **P3**
- assessment of the effectiveness of the strategies in one destination **M2**
- suggestions for improvements to manage tourism in one destination **D2**

Grading tips

P3 Make sure you use examples from towns or cities, countryside and seaside destinations in both MEDW and LEDW.

M2 Consider both the benefits and limitations of the strategies in place and make clear judgments.

D2 Ensure suggestions are valid and reasonable and backed up with evidence and good practice skills you have already developed. Refer to good practice from elsewhere.

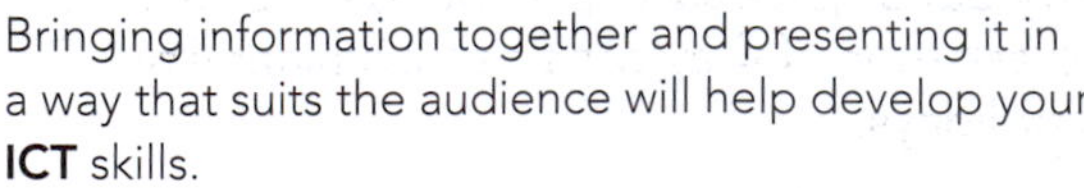

Functional skills

Bringing information together and presenting it in a way that suits the audience will help develop your **ICT** skills.

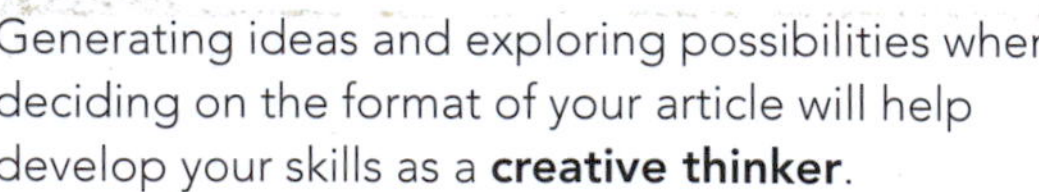

PLTS

Generating ideas and exploring possibilities when deciding on the format of your article will help develop your skills as a **creative thinker**.

4 Be able to plan holidays incorporating principles of responsible tourism

In this section you can develop your skills in putting together a holiday that allows customers to practise responsible tourism, and reassures them that the companies they use are ethical, and take steps to maximise the positive impacts of tourism in destinations.

You need to consider the transport to and within the destination, activities and attractions, as well as the destination itself.

Remind yourself of the principles of responsible tourism by reading back through this unit and by studying examples of policies from various tour operators. There are activities in this section to help you do this.

Activity: Responsible tour operators

1 Choose two well-known tour operator brands. Use their brochures and websites to assess their responsible tourism credentials. Summarise your findings in a table like this:

Name of tour operator and brochure assessed	
Stated policy	
Evidence of interaction with host communities	
Evidence of promotion of conservation	
Other comments (e.g. carbon offsetting for flights)	

2 Decide whether the company would be suitable for customers with very strong principles about responsible tourism.

3 Write some notes for the chosen tour operators explaining how they could improve their approach to responsible tourism.

Case study: First Choice

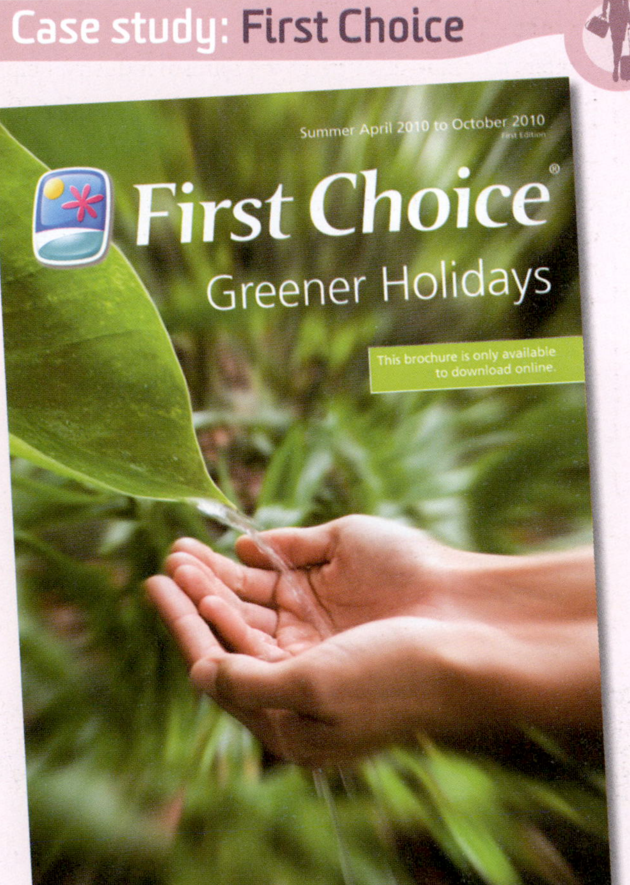

First Choice is an example of a tour operator with a dedicated 'Greener Holidays' brochure. It was introduced for the 2010 summer holiday season. It includes over 41 properties which have received Travelife awards for their environmental and social practice. There are helpful tips for tourists on what they can do on holiday to make a difference to the local community. The company believes, following their own research, that there is a demand for mainstream sustainable holidays.

The green brochure helps agents meet the needs of clients wanting sustainable holiday options.

1 Why do you think there is a need for such a brochure?

2 Explain what a Travelife award is.

3 Carry out a quick survey of friends and relatives and ask them if they consider sustainability on holidays.

Discuss your results.

Activity: Responsible tourism

You work for a tour operator that specialises in producing tailor-made ethical holidays for customers. You receive a telephone call from a customer. They want to go on holiday at the end of May. The party is a family of two parents and three children between 5 and 10 years old. The family does not fly, but will take ferries. They would be happy to take a holiday in the UK.

They want to stay in a hotel and can spend up to £2000 for two weeks. The budget must cover accommodation and transport, but not activities. The parents want to go somewhere that will have activities for their children if the weather is poor. They like to 'do things' rather than lie on beaches.

It is very important to the parents that their holiday adheres to principles of responsible tourism and you will need to explain how their holiday does so.

Work in pairs to produce an itinerary for the family including costs and suggestions for activities.

Assessment activity 12.4

You work for a travel agent that prides itself on selling holidays that adhere to the principles of responsible tourism. Customers approach them because of their reputation and often ask for tailor-made holidays.

Today, you have been approached by David and Julia Bevan. They are both teachers at a secondary school. They don't have children. They can only go away in school holidays and they want a summer holiday which takes up five weeks, from the third week in July until the end of August. Their budget is about £3000. This doesn't include spending money.

At home, they take part in many community activities and pride themselves on their environmentally conscious lifestyle. This means they are keen on recycling, tend to cycle rather than drive, although they do have a car, and they buy their household products and clothes from companies with reputations for ethical trading.

They want a holiday, but at the same time take part in a conservation or community project. They are happy to fly, but will want to take part in a carbon offset scheme. They are very concerned that their trip follows the principles of responsible tourism and you will have to explain how their holiday does so. They want to travel to a developing country rather than Western Europe, but as it will be mid-summer they don't want temperatures too hot, that is not above 40° centigrade.

1. Plan a holiday for the Bevans, including details of transport, accommodation, attractions and activities.
2. Write up the holiday details and then present them to the Bevans. State how it meets the principles of responsible tourism. P4
3. Explain and justify how the holiday meets their needs and how it follows the principles of responsible tourism. M3

Grading tips

P4 Make sure you plan a holiday yourself and do not use a package and give full details including transport and travel details, accommodation, attractions and activities. State how it meets their needs, interests and motivations, preferences, time limit and budget.

M3 You must evaluate how components of your holiday minimise negative impacts and maximise positive impacts. Acknowledge any limitations.

PLTS

Through exploring issues from the perspective of your customer, you will be developing skills as an **independent enquirer**.

Functional skills

You will be practising your **Maths** skills when costing the holiday.

WorkSpace

Doug Garrett

Chief Executive – ReBlackpool

ReBlackpool is an urban regeneration company. The company was created to stimulate new investment regeneration and economic development in areas of economic decline.

Tell us something more about ReBlackpool and what it does

ReBlackpool is a private limited company funded by public and private investors. The Blackpool Resort Masterplan aims to transform Blackpool into a world-class visitor destination that will provide a sustainable year-round economy. ReBlackpool is delivering that plan, in terms of securing investment, promoting development and reporting on progress towards the masterplan. For example, we are using public funding to acquire Blackpool Tower, the Winter Gardens and the Golden Mile.

Public ownership will unlock investment to restore and refurbish them which will then be returned to private ownership and operation.

What is your role as Chief Executive?

I co-ordinate a team of about 25 people: planners, surveyors, fund raisers and a few marketing and administration staff. I am the key point of contact for our partners and am responsible for all high-level negotiation on projects. I sit on the Board of Directors and report to the Board on progress on key projects and how we are performing in terms of budget.

How did you get to your position?

My degree was in International Business and I always wanted to work in marketing. I worked for the railways marketing railcards then moved to an urban regeneration company, with responsibility for marketing but also business development. In each role I learnt as much as I could about what other people do.

Do you think your company has been successful in the regeneration of Blackpool?

Visitor numbers to Blackpool in 2009 increased by 20 per cent to 12 million. Several factors contributed to the increase: the recession encouraging a 'staycation', the poor exchange rate against the euro, and a major promotional campaign. Businesses with quality product, where investment had taken place, profited most from the increased business.

Think about it!

1 Find out more about ReBlackpool at reblackpool.com.

2 Find out where there are other areas of regeneration in the UK.

3 Check your understanding of terminology:

- Public guarantee
- Regional Development Agency
- Staycation

Just checking

1 What is meant by 'responsible tourism'?
2 What type of organisation is English Heritage?
3 How can a host community benefit culturally from tourism?
4 Give two examples of agents of tourism development in the private sector.
5 What is the government role in policy formulation for tourism?
6 Explain the role of Tourism Concern.
7 How does tourism development create jobs?
8 Explain 'leakage' and how it occurs.
9 What is meant by 'enclave tourism'?
10 Give examples of the negative social impact of tourism development.
11 How can leakage be avoided?
12 Give two objectives of agents of tourism development.
13 Give two examples of good practice of responsible tourism in specific destinations.

Assignment tips

- Remember to find out what is happening about tourism management in your home town.
- Collect information on responsible tourism wherever you travel – hotels and attractions often have leaflets and cards stating their policies.
- Here are some websites you might find useful for your research:

  www.globaleye.org.uk

  www.infoplease.com

  www.geographia.com

  www.responsibletravel.com

  www.thetravelfoundation.org

  www.toinitiative.org

  www.tourismconcern.org.uk

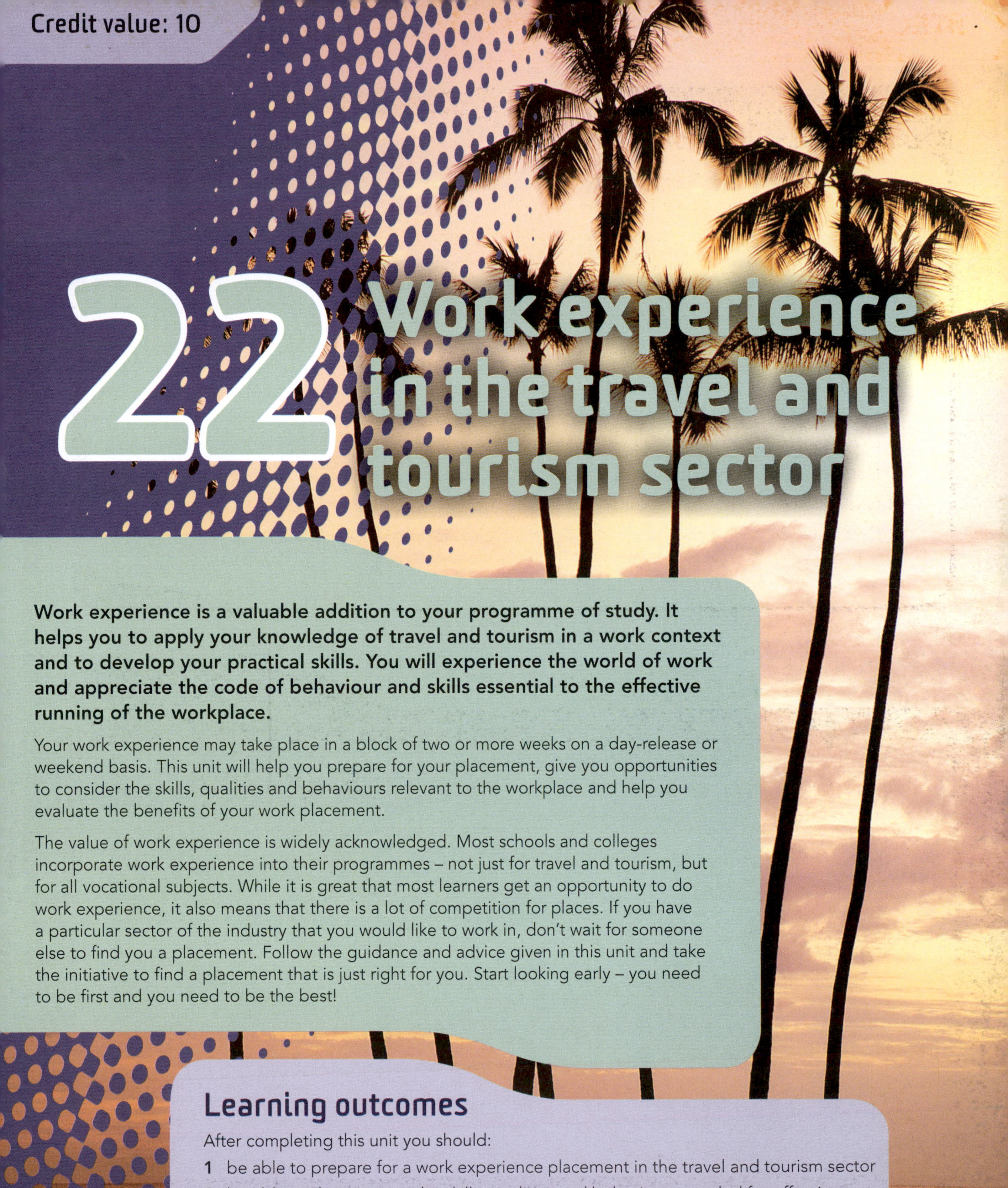

22 Work experience in the travel and tourism sector

Work experience is a valuable addition to your programme of study. It helps you to apply your knowledge of travel and tourism in a work context and to develop your practical skills. You will experience the world of work and appreciate the code of behaviour and skills essential to the effective running of the workplace.

Your work experience may take place in a block of two or more weeks on a day-release or weekend basis. This unit will help you prepare for your placement, give you opportunities to consider the skills, qualities and behaviours relevant to the workplace and help you evaluate the benefits of your work placement.

The value of work experience is widely acknowledged. Most schools and colleges incorporate work experience into their programmes – not just for travel and tourism, but for all vocational subjects. While it is great that most learners get an opportunity to do work experience, it also means that there is a lot of competition for places. If you have a particular sector of the industry that you would like to work in, don't wait for someone else to find you a placement. Follow the guidance and advice given in this unit and take the initiative to find a placement that is just right for you. Start looking early – you need to be first and you need to be the best!

Learning outcomes

After completing this unit you should:

1 be able to prepare for a work experience placement in the travel and tourism sector

2 be able to demonstrate the skills, qualities and behaviours needed for effective performance in the workplace

3 know the key features of the chosen work experience organisation

4 be able to evaluate own work experience placement.

Assessment and grading criteria

This table shows you what you must do in order to achieve a **pass**, **merit** or **distinction** grade, and where you can find activities in this book to help you.

To achieve a **pass** grade the evidence must show that you are able to:	To achieve a **merit** grade the evidence must show that, in addition to the pass criteria, you are able to:	To achieve a **distinction** grade the evidence must show that, in addition to the pass and merit criteria, you are able to:
P1 use resources and contacts to propose potential work experience placements in the travel and tourism sector, taking into account constraints **See Assessment activity 22.1, page 314**	**M1** explain how potential work experience placements could provide opportunities to meet personal, career and curriculum objectives **See Assessment activity 22.1, page 314**	
P2 prepare for work experience by completing relevant documentation and setting objectives for the placement **See Assessment activity 22.1, page 314**		
P3 demonstrate skills, qualities and behaviours during work experience and adherence to a code of conduct **See Assessment activity 22.2, page 318**	**M2** explain how skills, qualities and behaviours have developed during the work experience placement **See Assessment activity 22.2, page 318**	**D1** demonstrate personal effectiveness throughout the work experience process **See Assessment activity 22.2, page 318**
P4 describe key features of the work experience organisation, including own duties and responsibilities **See Assessment activity 22.2, page 318**		
P5 use supporting evidence to evaluate own performance on work experience and in meeting objectives **See Assessment activity 22.3, page 320**	**M3** assess the suitability of the designated role and its contribution to meeting objectives **See Assessment activity 22.3, page 320**	**D2** evaluate the overall success of the work placement, making justified recommendations for improvement **See Assessment activity 22.3, page 320**

How you will be assessed

This unit will be assessed by one or more internal assignments that will be designed and marked by your tutor. Your assignments will be subject to sampling internally and externally as part of Edexcel's quality assurance procedures. The assignments are designed to allow you to show your knowledge and understanding related to the unit. The unit outcomes indicate what you should know, understand or be able to do after completing the unit.

Sam, 17-year-old BTEC National learner

We were looking forward to work experience for ages. Two weeks off college and finding out what work was like. We spent ages talking about placements and where we wanted to go.

There are three travel agents in our town and although all would take learners, there was only room for one placement in each. I live about 20 minutes from the airport so I thought I would try there instead. There is a job centre at the airport, so I went to see them. I met a woman called Tracey, who seemed to look after recruitment. She explained that it was difficult to come for work experience because of all the security checks, but she did give me a contact name and number of a ground handling company to try.

I was nervous about phoning. The first time I called I got an answer machine, but I got through the second time. I managed to explain what I wanted and about my course. I remembered to give my name and say where I studied. The woman was very nice and invited me for an interview. I think I was lucky because she knew our college and had one of our old learners working for her.

My mum had to drop me off for the interview. I was dressed really smartly and I had looked on the internet to find out what ground handlers did. Mostly they look after check-in for airlines. I took my CV with me and gave it to her.

I was really pleased because she said I could come for two weeks. I loved it and learnt a lot. The bad part was having to start at 6 a.m. That was hard for my mum as well, because she had to drive me there.

Over to you!

1 Why is it important to provide a CV?

2 Practise phoning and asking whether work experience is available. Practise with a friend.

3 What would you wear for an interview?

1 Prepare for a work experience placement in the travel and tourism sector

Set off

Work placement

On your own, think about what you would like to get out of a work placement. Write down five key points that you would like to achieve. You will develop this later on, so just think quickly now and see what comes to mind.

Share your points with someone from your group and see if you are looking for similar or different things.

When you are ready, share with the larger group. Is everyone looking for the same thing? Are there some types of placements better suited to some learners than others?

1.1 Potential work placement organisations

Think about what kind of organisation you would like to work in. Here are just a few to consider:

- a travel agent
- a Tourist Information Centre (TIC)
- a tour company
- a tour operator
- a transport operator
- a hospitality provider.

All towns and cities have travel agents and hotels, but if you want to work for a tour operator you may have to travel. Your TIC will normally accept learners for placements, but there will be a lot of competition for places.

1.2 Contacts

A good place to start is by talking to your tutor or colleagues. They will be able to advise you on what you may enjoy and how best to gain useful experience. Here are some other useful contacts.

- **Coordinator** – many colleges and schools have a work experience coordinator whose role is to help you find a work placement. But the coordinator will have to find placements for many learners, so you might decide to find your own placement.
- **Family and friends** – use any contacts you can to find a work placement. Perhaps you have a family member or friend who works in travel and tourism?
- **Careers advisers** – they may be based in your college or school or in another centre, for example Connexions. They do not find work placements, but they will help you decide what type of placement will be suitable for you with your career goals in mind.

1.3 Other resources

- **Database** – your college or school should have a database of work placements previously used by travel and tourism learners. If a placement on the database appeals to you, notify your tutor and find out what the procedure is for making contact with the organisation. Often, colleges and schools prefer learners not to contact these organisations directly, to ensure they are not inundated with requests.
- **Newspapers** – look at job advertisements in the local newspaper to get ideas of organisations in your area which are suitable for work experience.
- **Job centres/websites** – if you are looking for a work placement in a specialist sector such as the airport sector, you will find that there is often a job

centre or website for recruitment. Examples include Manchester and Stansted airports. These centres will be advertising jobs, not placements, but will give you ideas on whom to contact.

1.4 Constraints

Once you have found a placement, you need to make sure you are fully prepared to start work. Spend some time finding out about the following issues.

Location of placement and transport access

Make sure you have the address of your organisation. Companies with their own websites often provide a location map which you can download. Find out the times of buses or trains before you start, to see how long the journey takes. It may take longer in the rush hour. Can you buy a weekly ticket to save money? Many learners do a practice run of their journey, so they do not have to worry about the journey on the first day.

Hours of work

If you had an interview your hours were probably explained to you. If not, telephone and ask. Find out also to whom you are responsible. It is embarrassing to arrive on the first day at the wrong time and not know who to ask for. Remember, you need to know your hours to fit in any other commitments and to arrange your travel.

Personal commitments

If you have personal commitments which affect your availability for work experience, you must inform your tutor and your employer and negoitate suitable hours. Acceptable commitments include an existing part-time job or family responsibilities. Do not expect employers to accommodate your social arrangements.

Accommodation

Most learners take up work placements locally. If yours is not in your own area, you will have to consider where you will stay. Occasionally learners find placements in resorts and are provided with accommodation, such as over-18s finding placements with Butlins. If you have family or friends to stay with elsewhere, think about taking up a placement in their area.

Equipment and clothing

Your employer will tell you if you need any special equipment or clothing. If a uniform must be worn, it will be provided. If you are unsure about what to wear, telephone and ask about the dress code. Do this in good time as you might have to buy some suitable clothes.

Always carry a pad and pen to write notes on what you are doing at work. You may have been given a log to complete as well. Consider taking an audio/video recorder to work or a camera. Tapes and photos will add interest to your project, but it is very important to ask permission before taking any pictures or recordings.

1.5 Documentation

Letter of enquiry or application

A letter of enquiry is a speculative letter, asking if there are any job opportunities. A letter of application relates to a specific job which has been advertised. You are most likely to be sending a letter of enquiry.

Make sure any letter you send:

- is addressed to the relevant person, for example the human resources manager or agency manager, by name if possible
- contains details of your course
- contains the dates you would like to go on work placement
- has a sentence or two on why you would like to have work experience in that organisation
- is word-processed in a business format
- has been checked by your tutor.

Travel and tourism organisations receive hundreds of requests for work experience. To increase your chances of success, try the following.

- Send out a lot of letters to different companies – some will not reply at all.
- Include a stamped addressed envelope to encourage a reply.
- Instead of a letter, send something different that gets you noticed – what about a press release stating you are available for placement, or a tape or CD about yourself?
- Visit the organisation personally, wearing suitable business clothes and take your CV.

Think about it

How many learners from your college or school are looking for work experience? How can you stand out from the rest?

Activity: Press release

38, St John's Street, Powertown, Lancs LA4 5DE
1 March 2005

PRESS RELEASE

Travel and tourism student seeks work placement!

An ideal opportunity for you to acquire the services of

Gemma Hudson

who is conscienctious, reliable an enthusiastic

AND ...

will cost you nothing!

Gemma is available for work placement from 17 May to 25 June 2010. The work placement is an important part of her BTEC National Travel and Tourism course at Trinity and All Saints College, Lancaster.

Further information about Gemma is attatched in her CV.

Interested?

Please contact Gemma on 0776 1234 56798, at the above address, or by e-mail at gemma_123@website.co.uk

1 Study the press release above. Produce a press release for yourself which you can send to prospective work placements.

2 Hold a discussion with your colleagues. What other ways can you think of to get your details noticed by employers?

CV and interview

Unit 6 explains how to produce a CV and prepare for an interview. It is highly likely that employers will ask to see your CV and they may invite you for an interview. You should keep an electronic copy of your CV and update it regularly so that it always available.

If you are invited for interview, prepare as you would if the interview was for a permanent job. Carry out research into the company, prepare questions for them and answers to their possible questions to you. Wear appropriate business clothes.

Write a list of what you should and should not do during an interview.

Letter of acceptance

Once you have been offered a work placement, whether by letter or verbally, write a letter of acceptance confirming the dates you will be attending the placement.

Activity: Letter of acceptance

Write a letter of acceptance for an offer of a placement at a hotel in your town.

1.6 Set objectives

What do you hope to achieve from your work experience? Objectives can fit into different categories. You should expect to develop personal skills, for example punctuality, and you will gain experience that should benefit your future career. In addition, think about what the placement will help you achieve in the curriculum areas of your programme.

Developing new skills

In the work environment you will have an opportunity to develop some, or all, of the following skills.

- **Customer care** – you will be dealing with members of the public, suppliers and colleagues and the customer care skills you develop will be of use whatever career you choose in the future.

- **Technical/practical skills** – you may learn to use specialist equipment and resources, for example reservation systems, other IT systems or you might be finding your way around directories.
- **Social/personal skills** – when you go to work you leave your personal problems at home. Develop a professional attitude showing respect and consideration for customers and colleagues alike.
- **Analytical/critical/problem-solving skills** – your work experience will present you with real challenges. Use your initiative to deal with any problems or incidents that occur. Bear in mind your limitations and refer issues to relevant managers if appropriate.
- **Prioritising tasks** – you will be given various tasks to do, sometimes from different members of staff. Learn how to judge which tasks are more important or urgent and do those first. If in doubt, ask.
- **Time-keeping** – punctuality shows your commitment to the placement. Remember to return punctually from breaks, as well as arriving on time for the start of work.
- **Self-motivation** – always ensure you have tasks to do. If necessary, ask for something to do or ask staff for an explanation and demonstration of what they are doing.
- **Action planning/research techniques** – you will have an assignment to complete on your placement. Use the resources available while at work, including people, to develop your planning and research skills.

Developing your career

Your work experience is the first step of your career – whether you eventually go into travel and tourism or not. Here are some of the benefits you can hope to gain from your placement.

- **Knowledge and experience** in an industry of the travel and tourism sector – this will help you decide whether your career lies there.
- **References** – if you perform well on your work placement, your employer should agree to provide a reference for future jobs.
- **Contacts** – you will start to build up a network of contacts who might help you in your future career.
- **A possible job** – employers often offer jobs (full- or part-time) to those people who perform well on work experience.
- **More for your CV** – you will build up experience, skills and possibly qualifications which can be included on your CV.

Activity: TIC placement

Study this example of Bijan's work placement at the local TIC. The centre puts all new staff through the 'Welcome Host' training programme. Bijan prepared some objectives before he went on his placement – these are shown in Table 22.1.

Bijan's objectives are useful as they remind him of the purpose of his work placement and give him a focus while he is there. They will also help him when he carries out his review of the work placement, as they provide a measure for his achievement.

Prepare your objectives for work placement under the headings used by Bijan in the example. Do not complete the comments sections at this stage. If you think you need more information about the placement to do this, discuss the types of activities you will be doing at work with your tutor and carry out some background research into the organisation.

Table 22.1 Work placement objectives

Objectives	Comments
Personal: • develop new skills with new colleagues • learn how to use accommodation reservation system • develop customer care skills • develop action-planning and problem-solving skills	
Career: • gain 'Welcome Host' qualification • gain useful contacts for the future • determine whether this sector is for me	
Curriculum: • collect evidence for completion of Work-based Experience unit • collect evidence for Working in Travel and Tourism, Customer Service, and Visitor Attractions units	

Supporting the curriculum

Make the most of your work placement by ensuring it fits in with the requirements of your course.

- Plan ahead to decide for which units you should be able to collect evidence.
- Collect evidence while you are at your placement.
- Ask if you can come back in the future if you need further evidence.

Assessment activity 22.1

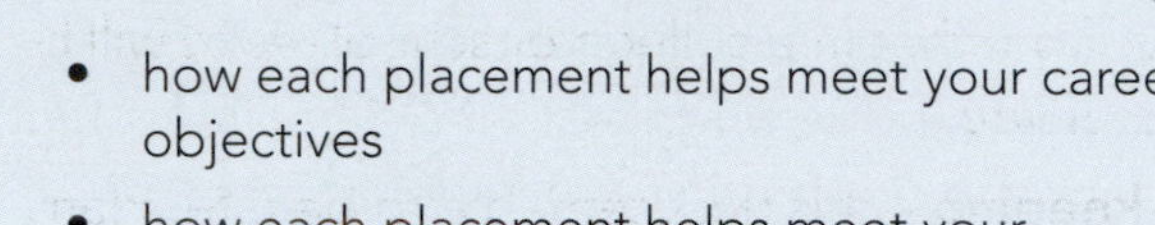

1 Find at least two potential work placements. Describe each placement in terms of the type of organisation, your potential roles and any constraints that may affect the choice of placement. P1

2 For one of your potential placements, complete the following:
   - a letter of enquiry or application
   - an up-to-date CV
   - an interview checklist
   - a letter or email of acceptance. P2

3 Set personal, career and curriculum objectives for the placement. P2

4 Explain why both placements are suitable for your work experience, considering the following:
   - how each placement helps meet personal objectives
   - how each placement helps meet your career objectives
   - how each placement helps meet your curriculum objectives.

You could present this information as a detailed, annotated table or as a report. M1

Grading tips

P1 Make sure you record all the sources you use to find potential placements to show you have used a wide variety.

P2 Make sure your objectives include personal, career and and curriculum objectives and that your documentation is correct.

M1 Explain clearly how your chosen placements could help you to meet your personal, career and curriculum objectives.

PLTS

By assessing yourself, identifying opportunities and setting goals, you will be developing skills as a **reflective learner**.

Functional skills

By writing letters and your CV, you will be practising your **English** skills in writing.

2 Demonstrate the skills, qualities and behaviours needed for effective performance in the workplace

2.1 Code of conduct

Skills are practical aspects of the job such as inputting data or communicating with customers. Qualities are personal characteristics such as initiative or sociability. Behaviours include politeness, punctuality and respect. These can be summarised in a code of conduct.

Those of you who have a part-time job will already understand that the world of work demands different behaviour from that in a college or school. A lot will be expected of you.

- **Time-keeping** – it is unacceptable to be late. Plan to arrive at least ten minutes before your starting time. Your employer will be asked to comment on your punctuality.
- **Attendance** – in a short placement, there is no reason why you should not attain full attendance. If exceptional circumstances occur, for example sickness, telephone your placement and your tutor at the earliest opportunity. Have contact details for work readily available. Make sure you are fit for work by avoiding late nights and drinking before, and during, the placement.
- **Demonstrating honesty and reliability** – of course you are honest and reliable and these are qualities you will demonstrate in the workplace. However, be aware that you will be working with people who do not know your qualities and behave in an open and honest way at all times.
- **Accepting authority and responding to instructions** – think about how you respond to authority. Are you able to accept that your immediate supervisor will tell you what to do? How do you respond to instructions? On work placement you should not question authority; you should graciously accept instructions and carry them out to the best of your ability. If you are not clear about what to do or need help, ask.
- **Accepting responsibility** – if you are asked to do something, however small, do it carefully and take responsibility for doing it properly. This does not mean that you can't ask for help when you need it.
- **Adhering to dress code** – you may be given a uniform to wear. If not, you will be given advice about what to wear. Even if it is not what you normally like to wear, respect the dress code and remember that the dress code is there to project a certain company image.
- **Being courteous and using appropriate language** – on your course you will study ethics in the workplace. Think about your attitudes to other people. Do you treat everyone with courtesy? Do you act and speak in a non-discriminatory manner? Set yourself high standards and adhere to them.
- **Adhering to rules and procedures** – consider your reactions to rules and procedures; most workplaces keep rules to a minimum, but there will necessarily be some as they are essential to health and safety and you must accept them.

2.2 Demonstration of skills

The skills you are hoping to develop were outlined in the section 1.4. Keep these in mind when you are at your placement. Each day, try to think of situations where you have demonstrated these skills and reflect on how you might have improved. Write notes in your log, including your reflections on your performance.

Skills you should think about include social, technical, problem-solving, action-planning, self-motivation and customer care, to name but a few.

2.3 Monitoring progress

Keep careful records. If possible, review your progress with the employer, or your tutor, as you go along. You may have been issued with a log book by your tutor. If so, complete it as instructed. Your tutor is likely to visit you on work placement and will talk to you, as well as ask for feedback from your employer. Your tutor will provide a review of your progress and all feedback will be used to write this.

3 Key features of the work experience organisation

While on work placement you will be expected to undertake research to produce a report about your work placement organisation.

3.1 Finding out about your organisation

Your placement may be day-release or an intensive block of work. Whatever the format, you should start your research immediately and put some time aside each day to work on it. If you leave it until the end of the placement, you will not be able to collect all the relevant information. This is a common problem – don't let it happen to you!

Make sure your employer and the staff at your work placement are aware of your assignment and then they will be prepared to help you. If there is not enough time during the working day to carry out your research, spend a short time each evening working on it and make a list of information you need to collect the following day.

How to find relevant information

Here are some ways to gather the information you need.

- **Interviews with staff** – most people are glad to talk about themselves. Take notes or make recordings of their responses (with their permission).
- **Resources** – make the most of the resources available at work, especially training manuals and information on policies and procedures.
- **Observation** – this is a very useful tool, particularly for looking at customer service. However, if you are observing the way staff operate, be discreet. Write notes later.
- **Keeping records** – you should keep notes on all aspects of your research as you work on it. Note any points that still need to be carried out. Keep copies of relevant documents for inclusion as appendices to your assignment.

What you need to find out

The following checklist is designed to help you. It includes examples of the kind of information you are expected to find out.

- **Description of organisation** – summarise what it does. For example, Tourism Concern is a registered charity which encourages sustainable tourism in destination countries, by working with communities and trying to find ways of reducing the social and environmental problems connected with tourism and increasing local benefits.
- **Sector** – here you indicate whether your organisation is in the public, private or voluntary sector. For example, Tourism Concern is in the voluntary sector.
- **Ownership** – who owns the organisation? Is it a public limited company, a sole trader or a partnership? For example, Thomson Holidays is a public limited company owned by shareholders.
- **Size** – you can indicate the size of the company by the number of employees, by the revenue of sales, or by its locations.
- **Organisation chart** – draw up an organisation chart of your work placement. Show key roles, line management and lines of communication. If the organisation is very large, just draw up a chart for your department. Add a description saying who does what and how they link with others.
- **Key activities** – what is the main function of the organisation? Is it responsible for marketing? Sales? Promotion? For example, a tourist information office seeks to promote tourism in the local area and provide information for visitor.
- **Products and services** – what does the organisation actually provide? For example, a travel agent:
  - books holidays, acting as intermediary between the customer and the tour operator
  - sells flights and other travel services
  - sells travel insurance
  - books excursions
  - sells currency
  - organises itineraries
  - gives travel advice.

  You can then detail specific products and services, for example listing the tour operators that the travel agent represents or the destinations it specialises in.

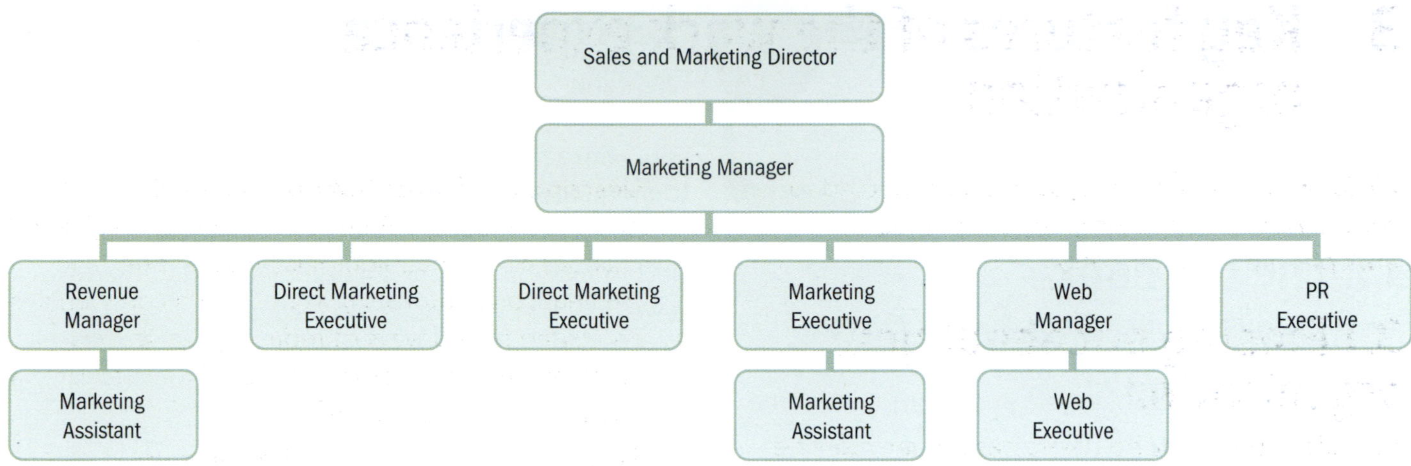

Figure 22.1: Organisation chart for a marketing department

- **Health and safety issues** – these include legislative and regulatory requirements, specific policies and procedures and security (see Unit 6: Preparation for Employment). When you arrive at your work placement you will be given induction training (essential for all new staff). It will introduce you to basic policies and procedures relating to your work environment, including basic health, safety and security requirements. Other relevant procedures will be explained to you. All health, safety and security requirements will be published in a manual or displayed in the workplace. Make sure you are familiar with all procedures.
- **Own role** – describe your own role while on work placement. What are your duties and responsibilities? Who do you report to and how do you link with others? Place yourself on the organisation chart.
- **Other staff roles** – you could find out about the roles of others in the organisation by interviewing them. Try to interview at least three people. Devise some questions to ask them. Find out their duties and responsibilites. Who do they report to? Find out about the progression opportunities within the company.

Case study: Bijan's log book

Tuesday 26 October 2010

Activities

First 4 hours of the day spent on the desk with Janine. Had to answer customer queries.

Given time in the afternoon to work on my project – used the intranet and accessed a lot of Regional Tourist Board information on structure and policy.

Skills developed

Customer care – learnt a lot from watching Janine and then dealing with customers myself.

Research

Found out a lot about the Regional Tourist Board.

IT

Used the intranet.

Problems and solutions

Had to help a German customer and I couldn't communicate at all! Managed to find a staff member who spoke some German.

Action points

- Acquaint myself with all the TIC leaflets and literature so I don't have to ask Janine for obvious things.
- Learn German?

1. How do you think the headings help Bijan?
2. What could Bijan do if he found he was writing 'made tea' or 'stamped brochures'?
3. Design your own log page.
4. Discuss your ideas with your group.

Activity: Questions

Plan the questions you need to ask at your placement to find out information on the key features of the organisation.

3.2 The log book

The first page of your log book should show your name, your employer's details, including contact names and telephone numbers and your tutor's name and telephone number.

Allocate a page for each day of your placement. It is important that the log is not merely a diary, but records the skills you are developing and any problem-solving you are involved in.

Page 317 shows an example of a log book for Bijan at the TIC.

3.3 Thinking ahead – evaluation

Once your work experience is at an end you will carry out an evaluation, but you need certain tools to help you. These should be used during the placement itself to monitor your activities and performance.

You may have been provided with recording documentation by your college or school. Otherwise, develop your own. You could include:

- a diary or log book
- attendance records
- a witness statement
- records of employer feedback
- an interview record sheet.
- a skills audit.

The docmentation needs to be linked to the objectives which have been set. Keep all the documentation in a portfolio alongside the materials (letters, CV, objectives chart) that you completed before the placement.

Assessment activity 22.2

1 Monitor your progress on work placement by keeping a daily log of activities undertaken. Make sure you include sections on the skills you develop and on how you adhered to an appropriate code of conduct. P3

2 Make sure your log has completed sections of:
- tutor review
- employer feedback.

These could take the form of signed observation sheets and signed witness testimony. P3

3 Collect information in preparation for completing a report on the key features of the organisation. Include all the factors listed on pages 316-317. You should also draw up an organisation chart. If the organisation is very large, just draw up the chart for the department you work in. P4

4 Demonstrate, in your log, how you have developed your skills, qualities and behaviour on placement. Relate this to tasks you have carried out and reported on in your log. M2 D1

Grading tips

P3 Ensure you provide evidence which confirms that you have displayed effective skills, qualities and behaviours when completing your work placement.

P4 Try to explain how different roles in the organisation are interlinked. Make sure you include a desciption of your own role and your reporting lines.

M2 Make sure you clearly relate the development of your own skills to tasks you reported on in your log.

D1 You need to demonstrate personal effectiveness in the workplace, but also in the preparation for the placement while undertaking all the other tasks for assessment. Personal effectiveness means producing accurate and professional looking documents when preparing for placement and behaving in a professional manner while on placement in order to give your centre a good reputation.

PLTS

You will demonstrate skills as a **self-manager** by organising yourself, showing personal responsibility, initiative, creativity and enteprise in your placement. You will collaborate effectively with others on the work placement, demonstrating skills as a **team worker** and you will be an **effective participator** by actively engaging in your placement in a responsible way.

Functional skills

By contributing to discussions on work placement, you will be practising your **English** skills in speaking and listening.

4 Evaluate your own work experience placement

4.1 Evaluation

How have you performed on work placement? Has it been successful?

You should consider:

- attendance and punctuality
- the new skills and knowledge you have gained
- how they can be used in the future
- behaviour in the workplace
- the objectives you fulfilled
- references
- possible career pathways and plans for future employment
- other opportunities for progression such as part time employment.

Supporting evidence

Before you complete your review, make sure you have the following information to hand:

- log book
- any interviews or witness statements
- employer feedback
- skills audit, for example a personal SWOT analysis (strengths, weaknesses, opportunities and threats)
- attendance and punctuality records.

Log book

See page 317.

Interviews

You might have carried out some interviews during your placement. Remember that interviews can be written, or recorded on audio or videotape. All types of records are valid.

Interviews might be useful to collect evidence for other units as well. Can you think of contacts in travel and tourism who you could interview? For which units would the information be useful?

Interviews or witness statements

These could be used to provide evidence of skills you have demonstrated, for example dealing with a customer. The witness must have observed you and will comment on your performance.

Employer feedback

Your employer will be asked to complete an evaluation sheet on your performance. It is often a series of tick boxes with space for brief comments. Your school or college will provide this and it will either be included in your log book or sent directly to the employer.

Skills audit

If you have kept detailed records during the placement, carrying out a skills audit will be straightforward.

The first stage could be a SWOT analysis (see page 320). Evaluate the strengths and weaknesses you demonstrated in your work placement. Identify any opportunities that arise from the experience. It is unlikely that you will find any threats, unless your experience was completely unsuccessful!

Activity: SWOT analysis

1 Copy and complete the following chart. Some examples have been entered for you.

Placement:		Dates:	
Strengths	**Weaknesses**	**Opportunities**	**Threats**
Full attendance	Struggled with the database	I was offered help with future assessments	

2 The next stage of the audit is to measure your achievements on work placement against the objectives you set yourself earlier. Return to the table you completed before your placement. Consider each of the objectives set and whether you met them. Complete the chart with your comments.

Assessment activity 22.3

1 Evaluate your performance on work placement in relation to the objectives you set in Assessment activity 22.1. P5
2 Assess how you, in your designated role at work placement, contributed to meeting your objectives. M3
3 Produce a critical evaluation of your work placement including an action plan with justified recommendations for improvement. Discuss what

Grading tips

P5 Make sure you evaluate based on your personal, career and curriculum objectives.

M3 You will need to make clear judgements. If there were shortcomings in the job role, make sure you discuss these if they impacted on your objectives.

D2 Make sure you clearly justify your recommendations.

PLTS

You will review your own progress and evaluate your experiences, informing future progress and demonstrating your skills as a **reflective learner**.

Functional skills

Ensuring your written work has accurate grammar, spelling and punctuation will help develop your skills in **English** – writing.

WorkSpace

Miley Williams

Work experience placement

Miley is a BTEC National learner and has a work experience placement at an independent travel agency in her town.

Miley, can you tell us about a typical day for you while on work placement?

I start at 9.00 a.m. The first thing is to put the kettle on. I am the most junior member of staff, but they all take turns to make the tea! Sometimes they make it for me. I begin tasks left for me by the manager – there's filing to do, checking the post and matching up details on our travel system. Today she showed me how to enter payments on the system too.

The manager spends some time sending out letters – she doesn't have to write them, she showed me how to call them up from the computer depending on what is needed. She asked me to do two by myself and I made sure she checked them afterwards.

From about 11.00 a.m. it gets busy with customers. I found out that we sell a lot of coach tickets as we are the only agent in town to sell them. Whenever customers come in and are looking at the brochures, one of us gets up to greet them and ask if we can help them. I was a bit shy at first, but now I am doing that easily. If they just want a brochure it's easy. I can do the tickets too, but if it is a proper booking I direct them to someone else, but I am allowed to sit and watch and listen.

A lot of customers make enquiries and I am learning to look up holidays for them on the Viewdata system. This is my favourite part of the job. It's lovely talking to customers and finding out where they want to go and why. Even if I have to sit with someone else at the moment and watch them do the searching.

I also have to sort out the brochures. I have also been shown how to make up files for each customer and record when they have booked and when the tickets were sent out, etc.

At about 4.30 p.m. the manager does the banking. I am not allowed to do this, but it is interesting to see what has to be done.

Think about it!

1. What kinds of tasks will you be able to do on work placement?
2. When there are things that you are not yet able to do, how can you make sure you still learn about them?
3. How will you show initiative on work placement?

Just checking

1 Name three potential work experience providers in your area.
2 How would an audio recorder and a camera be of use on placement?
3 What is the difference between a letter of enquiry and a letter of application?
4 What should you do if you are ill and cannot go to your placement?
5 Give two possible sources of information about a work experience organisation.
6 Where would you find out about health and safety regulations when you are on placement?
7 What is induction training?
8 Which documents will help you monitor your work experience placement?

Assignment tips

- Do not be too choosy about your placement – they are hard to find.
- Use all your contacts to help you find a place.
- Be prepared to work hard at any task, however menial.
- You should have a programme of activities for your placement. If not, ask politely for one.
- If for any reason you can't attend, let the employer and your tutor know promptly.
- Do not underestimate the importance of keeping a careful log.
- These websites will help you write your CV:
  - new.bbc.co.uk (go to Business, at the bottom of the page click on the drop-down menu for Life@ Work 'How to write your CV')
  - careersadvice.direct.gov.uk – go to Jobs and Careers

Credit value: 5

23 Residential study visit

This unit is one of the most exciting and challenging of the programme. Learners always enjoy it – not only for the visit itself, but also the organisation and preparation.

You are going to produce a proposal for a residential study visit, carry out a risk assessment for the visit and then participate in the visit.

By determining the aims and objectives of your visit, you will consider how it benefits you in terms of personal development, the research it allows you to do and the opportunities it presents to collect evidence for this and other units.

On your return, you will evaluate the visit and consider whether you met your original aims and objectives.

In this unit you will develop your organisational and teamwork skills, show your initiative and problem-solving skills.

Learning outcomes

After completing this unit you should:

1 be able to produce a suitable proposal for a residential study visit
2 know the reasons for and the process of risk assessment
3 be able to contribute to a successful residential study visit.

Assessment and grading criteria

The table shows what you must do in order to achieve a **pass**, **merit** or **distinction** grade and where you can find activities in this book to help you.

Assessment activity 23.1, page 336 meets all the criteria in this table.

To achieve a **pass** grade the evidence must show that you are able to:	To achieve a **merit** grade the evidence must show that, in addition to the pass criteria, you are able to:	To achieve a **distinction** grade the evidence must show that, in addition to the pass and merit criteria, you are able to:
P1 propose a study visit to meet the aims and objectives, taking into account constraints and considerations	**M1** explain how the proposal will meet the aims and objectives for the study visit, taking into account constraints and considerations	**D1** evaluate the success of the study visit through the achievement of the aims and objectives and the analysis of the feedback, making recommendations for future visits
P2 describe the reasons for and the process of risk assessment, completing a risk assessment for the proposed study visit	**M2** explain how hazards and risks identified in the risk assessment will be minimised	
P3 make a positive contribution during planning, prior to and whilst on the residential study visit	**M3** analyse own contribution and the results of the feedback to judge the success of the visit	
P4 prepare different methods of gathering feedback, evaluating the success of the residential study visit		

How you will be assessed

This unit will be assessed by one or more internal assignments that will be designed and marked by your tutor. Your assignments will be subject to sampling internally and externally as part of Edexcel's quality assurance procedures. The assignments are designed to allow you to show your knowledge and understanding related to the unit. The unit outcomes indicate what you should know, understand or be able to do after completing the unit.

Nathaniel, 20-year-old BTEC National learner

My group organised a residential study visit to Paris. I knew that I wanted to use the trip to collect information for my customer service assessment.

I made a list of the basics I would need to collect in Paris. I had done research on the internet too before I went. I chose three attractions from our itinerary that would help me with my customer service. I made a list of what I needed and took it with me.

Planning and making my list really helped me because it meant I didn't forget anything when I was there. I had a lot to do before the visit as I was in charge of collecting all the passport information, medical information and emergency numbers. I asked to see all the passports in advance to make sure everyone had one. They did, but one was Australian so I had to check if he could go to France without a visa. One girl was asthmatic so I had to check she had brought her inhaler when we left. I felt I had a lot of responsibility.

Once there, I was in charge of making sure everyone got to Versailles. First, I had to make sure they all got up on time. It took three attempts to get them all to breakfast. I really enjoyed it and I thought I learnt a lot about being responsible.

Over to you!

1 What kind of study visit would help you find evidence for other units?

2 How different is planning a residential trip to planning a day trip?

3 Will any of your group need visas to travel abroad?

1 Produce a suitable proposal for a residential study visit

Set off

Get organising!

Residential study visits are a feature of many educational programmes. For you, though, studying for a BTEC travel and tourism qualification, they are extra special. You not only get the chance to go away with your group and see one of the places you have been learning about, but you will also have the opportunity to organise the trip and find out for yourself how different transport systems compare, how to budget and how difficult it can be to accommodate the needs of a diverse group of people.

Think about day visits you have already been on as part of your course.

- Did you contribute to the organisation of those in any way?
- What were the objectives of the day visits?
- How useful were they?

1.1 Aims and objectives

Remember that your trip is a study visit and, although it should be enjoyable, it is not a holiday!

You can determine the aims and objectives before you know exactly where you are going – in fact your objectives will have an impact on the decision about where you go. If you want to do team-building activities, for example, you might choose an outward-bound centre. Once you know where you are going you can refine your objectives.

Start by discussing the aims and objectives as a group, but make sure you record them yourself as you will need them for your portfolio.

Show initiative from the start by setting some personal objectives for yourself. These could relate to being more independent or increasing responsibility for yourself and others. Some of your objectives will be educational as they will relate to what you are studying. You may also be able to use the visit to complete research for another unit.

The aim summarises the purpose of the trip. You have a chance to apply your marketing knowledge and write out the aim as a mission statement for the trip. The following example is the mission statement of a study trip to Amsterdam. You'll hear more about this and other trips as you work through this unit.

> Our mission is to organise a trip abroad that is educational and enjoyable. We want to achieve high standards of teamwork, initiative and assignment work.

Objectives are more specific and help you achieve your aim. Make sure all your objectives are SMART, that is: **S**pecific, **M**easurable, **A**chievable, **R**ealistic and **T**imed (see Unit 2 page 48).

Here are some ideas to consider when drawing up your objectives.

Educational

- The preparation for your study visit and the visit itself can be used to collect information and evidence for other units: for example, finding out about the features of different types of passenger transport.

Personal development

- Think about how the trip may help your personal development. There may be opportunities to be independent. Away from home possibly for the first time, you may be able to demonstrate qualities of initiative, teamwork or leadership.
- You will take responsibility for yourself and others by being responsible for part of the trip.

Interaction with others

- Use the opportunity to get to know your colleagues better and develop good working relationships.
- You may meet people from a different culture or country.

Outcome

- Consider whether the visit will aid your career development, perhaps by meeting people working in travel and tourism or by practising language skills.
- Determine the presentation of your work with your tutor – it could be a portfolio of work, a report or an oral presentation.

Case study: Study trip to Amsterdam

Here are the objectives determined by one group for their study trip. Remember that students can add their own group or personal objectives to the general list.

Objectives for a study trip to Amsterdam:

- to achieve excellent grades in this unit
- to enjoy our visit to Amsterdam
- to get practical experience of organising a trip
- to learn about a different culture
- to apply knowledge and skills from other units
- to work together successfully as a team
- to show initiative and work independently
- to gain wider key skills, especially improving own learning and working with others
- to ensure the visit is affordable.

Look carefully at this group's objectives. Decide whether each one is a SMART objective. Discuss this in your group.

What makes Amsterdam a suitable location for a study trip?

1.2 The proposal

Your proposal should be written and should include the following information:

- aims and objectives
- chosen destination and its location
- means and range of transport
- accommodation
- visits and excursions
- full itinerary, including arrival and departure points, times, distance and transport
- curriculum and development opportunities
- full costs.

Add to your proposal an account of how you have considered constraints, the features and benefits of the proposal and why you think your choice of destination and activities meet your aims and objectives.

1.3 Considerations

Where do you want to go?

Your residential study visit may take place in the UK or abroad. It may be located in an activity centre or in a holiday resort; you might visit a city or a beach.

When deciding on the destination, bear in mind the following:

- You can't please all of the people all of the time – you will have to compromise.
- Some students spend months arguing about where to go – then it's too late to organise the trip!
- Think carefully about booking using a package holiday company – it will affect how much work there is for you to do.
- If your tutor has decided on the destination, accept graciously and be positive about the choice – they know what they are doing!
- Be adventurous and approach new experiences positively.
- Accept that you will probably have to pay for the trip.

What type of study visit do you want?

You could include:

- visiting attractions
- investigating local tourist facilities
- looking at hotels and their operation
- taking part in sports and leisure activities
- finding out about the local culture.

For how long and where will you stay?

Your visit should last at least three days, but of course you can choose to go for longer.

You could stay at:

- a hotel
- a hostel
- student residences
- a campsite.

Hotels often offer good deals for groups of students, so don't assume you can't afford to stay in a hotel. Student residences will be available only outside term time.

You can use the following sources of information about accommodation:

- telephone reservations departments of large chains, e.g. Novotel
- internet sites of hotel chains
- specialist accommodation websites, e.g. Expedia (which has pictures) or Octopus
- destination guides (books or internet)
- local universities.

Activity: Costing your accommodation

Find out about different types of accommodation in Amsterdam. Cost each of them for a group of 15 students arriving on a Monday in April and leaving the following Thursday. Make sure you know what is included in the price and how many males and females are in the group.

How will you travel?

You will need to think about the following:

- What transport will you use – air, train, coach or sea?
- What is the cost of each route?
- How will everyone get to the departure point and How much will that cost?
- How will you get from the point of arrival to the destination?
- How will you travel within the destination?
- How easy or difficult will it be to book?
- Which route offers the best convenience and comfort?

You can use the following sources of information about travel:

- travel websites like Traveljungle or Travelsupermarket
- a travel agent
- enquiries office at the railway station
- coach companies
- airline websites.

Comparing potential destinations

To help you determine the suitability of the destination you should consider location, climate, safety and security. Some examples are shown in Table 22.1.

Table 22.1: Factors indicating the suitability of a destination

Location	Barcelona	Paris	London
Accommodation	Wide range of inexpensive accommodation – affordable for students	Some reasonable two-star hotels	Very expensive to stay in hotels
Climate	Mild climate in the spring	Less predictable than Barcelona	Who knows?
Access	Close to an airport	Several options for travel, air or Eurostar	Easy access by bus or train
Transport within destination			
Health, safety and security issues			
Seasonality			
Opportunities for learning			
Educational visits or talks			
Nightlife			

Think about it

Booking over the internet requires a credit card or debit card. There is an extra charge for using a credit card.

Activity: Comparing London and Berlin

1. Find out about Berlin and whether it is suitable for a three day visit for a group of 15. Draw up a table like the one above, comparing the suitability of the destination with that of London.
2. Find out what suitable activities could be included on the trip. At least some of the activities should have an educational benefit. You can add these activities to your table and compare with similar activities in London.
3. Prepare a three day itinerary of the activities showing all departure and arrival points and times.

What makes Berlin a popular destination for a city break?

1.3 Constraints

When researching destinations for your proposal you must consider constraints that will affect your choice.

Financial

Have you managed to get any funding for your trip or do you each have to pay for yourself? How much can you afford – what is your budget? What can you get for this budget in your chosen destination? What will you need to spend when you get to?

Legal

If the trip is abroad, each student will require a passport. Make sure they are applied for in good time – it can take a few weeks to process a passport. Some destinations, for example the Caribbean, require there to be at least six months left to run on a passport from arrival.

Check whether visas are needed, particularly if you have non-UK passport holders in your group. If you are responsible for passports, ask to see each student's passport before the trip and check it.

Remember to check on what you can and can't do in your chosen destinations – for example, in the USA you won't be able to drink unless you are 21.

Distance

Some potential destinations may be out of the question because they are too far away. They may cost too much and take too long to get to. It is best to decide on a location which will give you enough time to get there and enjoy a few days in the destination in the time you have allowed for your visit.

Risk

Is the destination safe? If there has been a natural disaster such as a flood, you may want to discount it from your options.

Activity: Costing your travel

Find three different routes to Amsterdam from your college or school. Cost each route for a group of 15 travelling from Monday to Thursday in April. For each route, point out any particular benefits or constraints.

What about your personal safety? Some destinations have a high crime rate – how safe would you and your possessions be? It may be that the destination is unsafe because it is politically unstable.

Activity: How safe?

You can find out about the safety of a destination by visiting the Foreign & Commonwealth Office website at www.fco.gov.uk. Find out what it says about travel to the following cities: Barcelona, Beirut and New York.

2 The reasons for and the process of risk assessment

2.1 Reasons for risk assessment

Part of your proposal should include a **risk assessment**. This will help you determine the suitability of your destination and it should increase the likelihood of success.

Carrying out a risk assessment is a legal requirement under the Health and Safety at Work Act 1974. Colleges and schools organising visits have a policy of completing risk assessments to determine whether a visit should go ahead. It is their responsibility to ensure the safety of all participants, staff, students and any others such as parents or drivers. If risks are identified then it may still be possible for a visit to go ahead as long as the risks are considered and minimised. Of course, it is impossible to eliminate all risk.

You should allocate roles and responsibilities for carrying out the risk assessment or elements of it and decide who is responsible for any contingency plans.

Key term

Risk assessment – the process of identifying what could go wrong, deciding which risks are important and planning how to deal with those risks.

2.2 Process of risk assessment

These are the steps to follow when carrying out the risk assessment.

- Identify the risks surrounding your project – these may relate to travel and transport, the destination itself, activities to be undertaken in study time or free time.
- Assess the likelihood of each problem occurring.
- Decide on action to be taken to reduce risks.
- Put in place systems to deal with the problems.
- Monitor the risks throughout the project.

The possible responses to risks are shown in Figure 22.1.

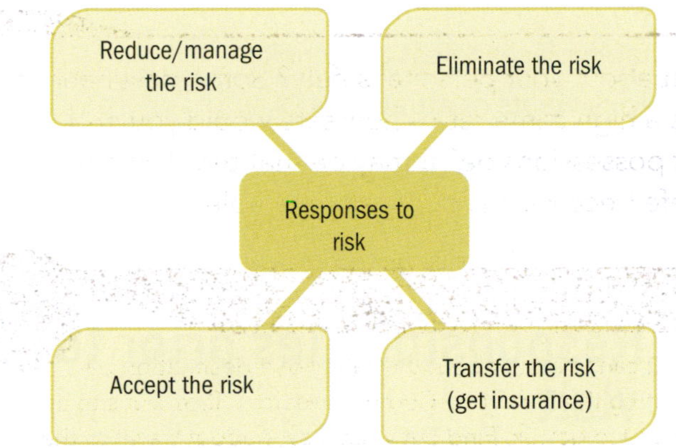

Figure 22.1: Responses to risk

Here are some **contingency plans** you can implement when planning and preparing your study visit to reduce risk.

- Write up a code of conduct that everyone agrees to follow.
- Prepare advice sheets on suitable clothing, climate expected, costs, etc.
- Hold a meeting to give verbal advice and discuss any potential issues.
- Use reputable travel companies.
- Ensure you have enough staff accompanying the visit.
- List the group's mobile numbers so that any lost member of the group has access to others.
- Record any necessary medical details.

Key term

Contingency plan – a plan made in advance to deal with anything that might go wrong.

Think of all the risks associated with organising and participating in a residential study visit. Here are some situations that might occur.

- Someone joins the trip without a passport.
- Someone arrives at Dover with a passport – but it is Australian and a visa is needed.
- Someone is taken ill on the first day.
- Two people crash on jet skis.
- A fight breaks out with a security guard.
- The group fails to meet at the check-in desk at the airport.
- A drunken party takes place in the hotel in spite of a no-alcohol rule.
- A bag is stolen from someone.
- A bad storm causes diversion of the plane to a different airport.
- A ferry strike means the whole group is stranded in Calais.

Activity: Risk assessment

Copy and complete the following risk assessment table. You can use the examples given, adding your own, or just use the form to take you through a risk assessment for your own trip.

Risk	How likely?	Response	Action/ contingency plan
Student joins trip without passport	Not very	Reduce risk	Check all passports prior to trip and issue reminders
Visas needed	Not very	Eliminate risk	Check passports and apply for visas in good time

3 Contribute to a successful residential study visit

3.1 Participation in the planning of the visit

Who does what?

Your participation is very important. This means not only going on the trip with a positive attitude, but fully participating in the organisation of and preparation for the visit.

You are likely to be assigned responsibility for a particular aspect of the study trip. This may be an individual responsibility or a small-group responsibility. Your responsibilities will include aspects of organisation and completing documentation.

Your tutor will make sure that each individual or group has an equal workload. However, be prepared to show initiative and help others where needed alongside your own tasks. Once you know your particular responsibilities you can set objectives for yourself or for your group, in addition to those set earlier.

The whole group will have meetings, perhaps weekly, to report on how they are progressing with their objectives and to pass on information to each other. Students may take it in turns to chair and minute those meetings.

The residential study visit can be successful only if each person completes the tasks set by the agreed deadlines. It is a useful exercise to determine all the deadlines as a group.

Regular meetings help with time management. If you have to report back to your group, it is difficult to confess that you haven't done anything!

Devising a code of conduct

Most schools and colleges issue a code of conduct for study visits which learners must sign. Why not produce your own code for your visit? Negotiate the terms and conditions with your tutor.

Producing study visit information

Produce an information sheet reminding participants of essential facts and what they need to bring with them. This should include:

- essential clothing items suitable for the climate at the destination
- comfortable walking shoes
- passports and other documents as appropriate
- currency information and suggested amount to allow for spending
- accommodation address and telephone numbers
- safety information
- suitable places to eat and drink
- special events or attractions.

Producing itineraries

Each learner must be issued with a copy of the itinerary including travel details, accommodation and activities.

3.2 Responsibilities prior to the visit

Even if you are not a member of the group responsible for administrative arrangements you must take responsibility for your own personal documentation. This will include:

- consents
- passport/visa
- medical information
- emergency contact details.

Medical information

Any learner with a medical condition should ensure the group leader is informed. This should also be declared for insurance purposes. Likely conditions are epilepsy, nut allergies or diabetes.

It is a good idea to take a basic medical kit along for minor mishaps. These are readily available and include plasters and bandages. If one of the group has a First Aid qualification, they might volunteer to take responsibility for managing information about medical needs.

Permissions

You must find out what documentation has to be completed in your school or college to organise a visit. Complete the documentation and ask your tutor to check and sign it. Expect the following as a minimum:

- school/college trip form – details of the trip, participants, staff, dates and costs
- parental consent form for under-18s
- risk assessment form
- list of participants and next of kin
- list of telephone numbers in case of emergency.

Remember to keep copies of all these documents for the group.

Insurance

If you are travelling within Europe, make sure each person has a valid European Health Insurance card. This entitles the holder to medical treatment within the EU. Ask to see the cards, which are available from the Post Office or can be acquired online at www.ehic.org.

You should also have a group travel insurance policy. Your school or college can arrange this for you through its own insurers – this will be the cheapest option. Otherwise, shop around with insurance companies.

3.3 Participation during the visit

Personal responsibility

You are responsible for your personal health, safety and security. This means respecting the code of conduct.

You agreed to a code of conduct before you left school or college, so remember that. It may have aspects of time management in it – you must consider your punctuality and reliability on your visit. Your tutor or group may set a curfew at night and will almost definitely require you to start work punctually in the morning. (Your tutor may not care whether you get up for breakfast!) You will also have set meeting points during the day and you will upset the whole group if you are not punctual.

The code of conduct may specify suitable clothing and what behaviour is allowed. For example, it is usual to agree that food and drink (especially alcohol) will not be taken into rooms.

Budgeting

You will have paid for your transport and accommodation prior to the visit. However, you will need spending money while away. You will have decided as a group how much money will be needed for food, travel within your destination and spending money. Try to allocate an amount to spend each day and do not be tempted to overspend. Don't carry all your money on you all the time. Think about safety and use a safe if you can.

Responsibility to others

Whenever you make contact with an organisation outside your college or school, you are representing your educational establishment, your course and ultimately yourself. Remember to:

- be polite
- greet the contact appropriately
- introduce yourself and your course/school/college.

Sometimes, unfortunately, you might have to deal with someone who does not have your high standards of customer service. Continue to be polite whatever the response. If you are meeting face-to-face:

- dress in a suitable manner
- speak and act courteously
- introduce yourself
- consider your personal hygiene
- use the host language if at all possible.

Activity: Introductions

You are arriving at your hotel in Paris as a group of 15. Practise greeting the receptionist and introducing your group, saying where you are from. Use French as much as possible – even if just for the greeting and to say thank you.

You also need to show consideration and courtesy to other members of your group, your tutors and your coach driver, if you have one. Remember to think about how your behaviour and attitude impacts on fellow passengers and other guests in your accommodation. People who are travelling on business or on holiday do not want to hear loud groups of young people on public transport. At night they will want to sleep rather than listen to you wandering from room to room and partying.

Being aware also means remembering your duty of care to your colleagues and looking out for their health, safety and security as well as your own.

Activity: Theft

Nick was a very responsible young man and he had been forewarned about the dangers of petty theft in Barcelona. In a bar with a large group of his schoolmates, he noticed that a young couple whom he did not know were hanging around the group and picking up a handbag left by the pool table. He stopped the couple from leaving and called out to his group to ask if they all had their bags. They said they did so he apologised to the couple for stopping them and they left the bar – with the bag. Then, a young girl appeared from the ladies room and realised her bag had been stolen!

Barcelona is notorious for this type of theft. Did Nick do the right thing? How could this situation have been avoided?

Cultural awareness

Be aware that different countries have different expectations and rules. For example, in most western European countries there are smoking bans in public places, or at least some restrictions.

Be aware that some areas of cities may be dangerous for tourists or where women in particular may feel unsafe. It is recommended that you always stay with another member of your group while on your visit.

Take the opportunity to converse in the local language and be appreciative of differences in religion, dress and food. Try new things and don't look for English food.

3.4 Evaluating the success of your visit

Success criteria

How do you decide if your residential study visit was a success? You may have had a wonderful time, but that does not necessarily mean you successfully completed this unit. You need to carry out an evaluation in which you consider the following questions:

- How suitable was the destination for your group and the activities you planned?
- Was the accommodation good value for money?
- Did all the travel arrangements work out efficiently?
- Did you manage to find your way around the destination?
- Did the destination have the facilities you needed, for example medical, currency exchange, shops?
- Was the visit the right length?
- Were your aims and objectives met?
- Did you all stay within your budget?
- Did you adhere to the group's code of conduct?
- Were your learning opportunities successful?
- Did you collect information as evidence for other units?

You have thought about success criteria as you have gone through the organisation of and participation in the study visit. You have set aims and objectives, both for your group and for yourself. You have made checklists of materials to research and collect for your assessments. You should keep a log of every task that you carry out, with records of telephone calls and copies of documents. You should also have made a log showing how you came up against problems and dealt with them. All of this information can be used in your evaluation.

Evaluation methods

While participating in the residential study visit you will gather evidence, so that you can succeed in this unit and possibly others.

You need to think about how you will evaluate the visit before you organise it, so that you collect the information you need throughout your planning and participation. The following ideas for evaluation take you through the full process of group and individual evaluation and will ensure you do the work thoroughly

Group evaluation

Consider carrying out a group evaluation half-way through the project. This is called a **formative evaluation** and it will help you tackle any problems which are apparent. At the end of the project it is called a **summative evaluation**.

Key terms

Formative evaluation – takes place while the activities are still happening.

Summative evaluation – takes place when the event is over .

The easiest way to do this is to carry out a **SWOT analysis** as a whole group. Repeat the SWOT analysis at the end of the project and keep records of both.

Key term

SWOT analysis – this means identifying **S**trengths, **W**eaknesses, **O**pportunities and **T**hreats.

The next stage of group evaluation is to meet as a group and decide whether you have met your objectives. List all the objectives and go through them, commenting on how successfully each was met.

Make notes and ensure you include recommendations for improvements in the future.

You can use the questions under 'Success criteria' on page 334 to help you and add extra questions if you think they are appropriate. Here are some examples.

- Were you able to work as a team?
- Did the weather affect the success of your visit?
- Were there any health, safety or security problems?
- What would you do differently next time?

Small-group evaluation

If you have worked in small groups your performance also needs to be evaluated. Peer evaluation can be carried out, where each group evaluates another group. Decide whether the group you are evaluating met their objectives by completing an evaluation form. Present the evaluation to the evaluated group, explaining what they think could be improved next time.

Your tutor will have been monitoring your progress during planning and during the residential study visit. They will have observed your contribution to meetings and how you interact with other team members. It is likely, too, that your tutor has accompanied you on the visit and has been able to see if you acted responsibly while away and carried out your tasks efficiently. Remember that your tutor will also be marking the unit assessment.

Activity: Evaluation

Design an evaluation form for a small group including:

- objectives and whether they were met
- comments on teamwork
- comments on time management
- comments on communication skills
- recommendations for improvement
- tutor evaluation.

Your tutor may decide to complete a witness statement giving evidence of your participation in the study visit.

Personal evaluation

You don't have to share your personal evaluation with the group, so be very honest with yourself.

Again, you or the group can design a form if you wish, but make sure you ask yourself the following questions.

- Did you achieve your personal objectives? List them and comment.
- How much did you contribute to the group objectives?
- Did you attend all the planning sessions?
- Did you meet deadlines?
- Have you improved your communication skills and how?
- Did you work well in a team?
- Did you work well independently?
- Did you show initiative?
- What would you do differently in the future?

Give examples of all your skills and successes.

Assessment activity 23.1

Produce a report on a residential study visit you have participated in. If you choose to produce a written report, ensure that you use the correct layout, appropriate headings and sub-headings. You may attach the itinerary and log as an appendix.

Your report should contain the following sections.

- Proposal for a study visit, including specific aims and objectives, full itinerary with details of transport, accommodation, day visits, entertainment and constraints and considerations. **P1**
- Explanation of how your choice of destination and itinerary allowed objectives to be met and how constraints and considerations were taken into account. **M1**
- Description of the reasons for and the process of risk assessment, and a risk assessment for the proposed study visit. The completed risk assessment must include at least six potential hazards; the controls put in place to reduce each risk must be clearly identified. Your evidence must include potential hazards relating to travel, to and from and within the destination, activities to be undertaken during the visit and hazards associated with free time. **P2**
- Explanation of how hazards identified in the risk assessment will be minimised. **M2**
- Log of participation in the study visit and in the planning process. **P3**
- Preparation of different methods of gathering feedback to evaluate the success of the visit. **P4**
- Analysis of own contribution to the success of the study visit, including results of feedback. **M3**
- Evaluation of the success of the study visit through achievement of objectives and analysis of feedback, with recommendations for future visits. **D1**

Make sure that you cover the full range, referring to the content and assessment guidance in the unit specification for detail required.

Grading tips

P2 Use the checklists in the text to help you, but make sure your risk assessment is specific to your group and your visit. Explaining how hazards will be minimised lends itself well to a table.

M2 If you choose to use a table to explain how hazards will be minimised, this must be very detailed.

P4 Make sure you are prepared to evaluate all the success criteria.

M3 Prepare for personal, peer and tutor evaluations so that you are able to give a thorough analysis of your own contribution to the success of the visit.

D1 Try to use all the evaluation methods suggested in the text to give a very thorough evaluation. Show that you understand what could have been improved upon and make appropriate recommendations.

PLTS

When you make recommendations for future visits you will identify improvements that will benefit others as well as yourself, developing your skills as an **effective participator**.

Functional skills

Using a range of writing styles when reporting on the project will help you to develop **English** writing skills.

WorkSpace

Emma Smith

Marketing manager

Why did you want to take on the role of marketing manager?

Our residential trip was to Marseille. As a group we had talked about the roles required to organise our visit and I was desperate to be in charge of marketing as that's what I want to do at university – tourism marketing. I was lucky because the tutor allocated marketing to me but with three others.

How did you go about marketing your residential trip?

We decided to work in pairs within our team of four. Joe and Ella were to design web pages for our college intranet and keep a photographic record of the trip. They also designed some posters to promote the trip in college.

Meanwhile, Ali and I had to get some publicity for our trip. We had no money for this! We started by finding out whom to contact at all the local papers. Then we designed a press release and sent it out to them all. There were only four papers to contact. We thought our work was done – but there were no replies.

When we had our next meeting our tutor asked "What happened when you phoned up to follow-up the press release?" We hadn't realised we would have to do that. We called again and had two positive responses.

Our next step was to organise our group for a photo shoot. Ali and I were interviewed by the papers so we planned what we had to say very carefully.

What did you do after the trip?

Ali and I wrote another press release and sent it to editors (we knew who they were now) along with a photo of the group in Marseille. Once again, it was published – on page 2 of the paper.

Think about it!

1 How would Ali and Emma evaluate their role?
2 What skills are important for this job?
3 What aspects of marketing does PR support?

Just checking

1 Explain what is meant by SMART objectives.
2 Give two possible objectives of a study trip.
3 Give two sources of information about accommodation.
4 How old do you have to be to drink alcohol in the USA?
5 How can you find out about how safe a country is?
6 What are the steps in a risk assessment?
7 What is a code of conduct?
8 What is a contingency plan?

Assignment tips

- Decide on the destination for your residential visit as early as possible so you can start planning.
- Think about which other units you can collect evidence for while on your trip.
- Be prepared to support others in their role as needed. This shows initiative – not all roles are as exacting as others and those with very challenging roles may need help.
- Review and evaluate regularly through planning – not just at the end of the project.
- Have contingency plans in place in case something goes wrong.
- Keep a log throughout planning and during the residential.
- The log should not just describe what you did but should analyse what went well, what went wrong and why. State how you solved problems and worked with others in your group.
- Hold regular meetings and be prepared to report on what you have done.

Glossary of key terms

A

Active listening – the process of demonstrating to a speaker both verbally and non-verbally that you are listening and that the information is being received. It is done by maintaining eye contact, nodding and expressing agreement in appropriate places.

Air passenger duty – a duty levied per passenger by the government. It is collected at the time of ticket purchase by the airline.

Airport code – every airport in the world has a unique three-letter code to identify it. You can find these codes at the Airline Codes website www.airlinecodes.co.uk.

Annual return – record of key company information which must be provided annually. Annual returns are filed at Companies House in London and are made publicly available.

Anticipated needs – those products or services that you think the customer might need; for example airport parking.

Audit – check on the accounts and accounting system of an organisation. An audit checks that the accounts show a true and fair view of the affairs of the company.

Auxillary sales – selling additional products and services that add value to the basic holiday or travel arrangements.

B

Balance of payments – one of the UK's key economic statistics. It measures the economic transactions between the UK and the rest of the world. It indicates the difference between spending on imports and exports.

Benefit – what the customer gains from a feature.

British Summer Time – daylight saving time in the UK. At 1:00 a.m. GMT on the last Sunday in March the clocks go forward by one hour and on the last Sunday in October they revert to GMT.

C

Cash flow – the assessment of money coming into a business and money going out at any given time.

Charter – these aircraft are usually contracted for a specific holiday season and run to a timetable set by the operator. For example, each major tour operator will need seats for its summer passengers flying to the Mediterranean. They fill every seat on the contracted aircraft and each seat forms part of the holiday package. The major tour operators own their own charter airlines, for example TUI owns Thomson airline.

Charter flights – flights that operate to holiday destinations and according to holiday demand. They do not operate every day to the same destination.

Classification data – the age, sex and occupation of the respondent. This is used to group respondents into categories.

Commission – a percentage of the value of the sale, paid by the supplier to the agent who made the sale.

Companies House – an executive agency of the Department of Trade and Industry (DTI) responsible for company registration in the UK. There are more than 2 million limited companies registered in the UK.

Competitive advantage – an advantage gained over competitors by giving better value to customers so that they choose your product and not the competitor's product.

Consolidated account – no longer a forecast, but an actual account of cash inflow and outflow for the year.

Contingency plan – a plan made in advance to deal with anything that might go wrong.

Contract out – when one business assigns a job to another business.

Co-operatives – organisations which are set up and run democratically by members. Any profi ts made are shared between the members.

Corporate image – the impression created and presented by a company; how a company is perceived.

Competitive advantage – an organisation strives to be better than (have an advantage over) its competitors. This could be through better pricing or a more attractive product. It could also be through a higher level of customer service.

Corporate social responsibility (CSR) – the way that companies manage their business to try and have a positive impact on society. (p.124)

Criminal Record Bureau (CRB) check – a process for gathering information about someone's criminal convictions and other cautions, reprimands and final warnings given by the police.

CSR (corporate social responsibility) – how an organisation manages its business activities to produce an overall positive impact on society. (p.271)

Culture – the shared traditions, beliefs and values of groups of people.

Customer loyalty – if customers receive consistently good service from an organisation they will want to use it again. They become loyal to that particular organisation because they can rely on its products and services.

D

Daylight-saving time (DST) – seasonal time changes to maximise daylight hours when people are at work.

Demographics – the study of the structure/make-up of the human population.

Deregulation – this occurs when a government decides to remove restrictions on the operation of a business to allow greater competition and hopefully greater efficiency and reduced prices for customers.

Dialogue – an easy, flowing conversation in which you are asking open and relevant questions will help you establish customers' needs while also building rapport.

Dividends – a share of profi ts made as a payment to shareholder.

Domestic visitors – people who are travelling in their own country for tourism purposes.

Dynamic packaging – industry jargon for tailor-making a package suited to the needs of a particular customer.

E

Economies of scale – these occur when a company is able to spread its costs over mass-produced goods or services. Savings can be achieved through discounts for bulk purchasing, rationalisation of administration systems and management and lower production costs.

Ecotourism – Ecotourism represents the ideal of minimising negative impacts and practising environmentally responsible tourism in relatively undisturbed natural areas.

E-meeting – another term for a web conference, that is, a meeting using web-based software, allowing people to communicate over the internet.

Enclave tourism – occurs when tourists spend the whole holiday in their hotel resort or when on a cruise ship all the activities and meals take place on board. In these circumstances, the local population does not benefit from the tourists being there.

Epidemic – an outbreak of a contagious disease that spreads rapidly and widely within an area.

European Union (EU) – the European Union is a partnership in which countries work closely together for the benefit of all their citizens. They work together on issues of common interest, where it is considered that collective action is more effective than individual state action.

Eurozone – the 16 countries that have adopted the euro as their common currency.

Executive director – usually a full-time employee of the company who also has management responsibilities.

F

Feature – a particular aspect of a product, for example location of hotel, excursions included, local pick-up etc.

Filter question – one that allows the respondent to omit certain questions which may not be applicable. For example, 'If you answer no to question 5, go to question 11'.

Flexible working – if employees can work the hours they want, they are better motivated to perform well.

Footfall – refers to the number of customers walking into retail premises.

Formative evaluation – takes place while the activities are still happening.

Franchise – buying the right to sell a company's products or services under a brand name.

G

Gateway airport – a major point of arrival or departure in a country, served by international scheduled services.

Green building – building methods that use energy efficient and non-polluting materials for construction.

Greenwich Mean Time (GMT) – a term used for world standard time. Each time zone to the east of Greenwich time zone is ahead of GMT, that is +1 hour, +2 hours, etc. Each time zone to the west is behind GMT, that is –1 hour, –2 hours, etc. Going eastwards you add hours to GMT and going westwards you subtract hours from GMT.

Gross Domestic Product (GDP) – a measure of the value of goods and services produced in an economy in a year. GDP indicates the wealth and economic development of a country. Countries with developed economies usually have high GDPs and countries with developing economies usually have low GDPs. (p.34)

H

Hub airport – an airport, usually major, that serves many outlying destinations and allows passengers to fly in and transfer to other flights. The outlying airports are known as 'spokes'.

I

IATA code – an International Air Transport Association (IATA) code is a unique three-letter code assigned to each airport, so there can be no confusion about which airport is which.
For example, Manchester airport in the UK has the code MAN and Manchester airport at Boston in New Hampshire USA is MNT.

Inbound visitors – people who visit a country which is not their country of residence for the purposes of tourism. If the visitor comes from France to the UK then they are outbound from France and inbound to the UK.

Internal customers – colleagues and other members of staff who work within the same organisation to provide products and services. External customers – people from outside the organisation who buy the products and services.

Itinerary – a detailed plan for a journey which is clear, chronological and accurate.

L

Leading questions – those which lead candidates to a specific answer rather than one they have considered themselves, for example: 'We really frown on lateness here. How is your punctuality?'

Leakage –the amount of money for supplies and services paid for outside a region: money that does not, therefore, benefit the local economy.

LEDW countries – countries in the less economically developed world.

Logo – a symbol used by an organisation (for example, the tick is the logo of Nike and the happy face the logo of TUI).

Long-haul – a flight of more than six hours.

Low-cost airlines – these have developed into major competitors to traditional scheduled airlines in recent years. They offer very few services, such as catering or allocated seats, but do offer low fares. The low fares are not available at peak times or to late bookers.

M

Market segmentation – identifying different groups of customers for a product. The members of each group will share similar characteristics.

Mark up – an additional price increase/cost.

MEDW countries – countries in the more economically developed world.

Mission statement – a concise statement about an organisation's purpose. Mission statements vary, but usually contain information about products, services, beliefs and values.

Multiplier effect (the) –the additional revenue, income or employment created in an area as a result of tourism expenditure.

N

National identity – the attachment people feel to their country of birth or residence through a set of shared behaviours and characteristics.

Niche marketing – catering for a small, specialist market.

Non-executive director – someone paid an annual fee to attend a number of board meetings and contribute to decision-making. They are invited onto the board because of their experience and skills.

Non-verbal communication (NVC) – communicating without saying anything. The most common type of NVC is body language – how we use our hands, facial expressions and gestures to convey our feelings.

P

Package holidays – holidays that include transport, transfer and accommodation with the following variations:

- **all-inclusive** – also includes all food and local drinks, and sports activities apart from motorised sports
- **full board** – includes breakfast, lunch and dinner
- **half board** – includes breakfast and lunch or dinner
- **bed and breakfast** – includes breakfast
- **accommodation only** – includes no food.

Pandemic – an epidemic of an infectious disease that spreads across a large region; for instance a continent, or even worldwide.

Performance-related pay – the better you perform or the more sales you make, the more money you are paid.

PEST analysis – an analysis that helps an organisation to take stock of the external factors affecting its business, identifying political, economic, social and technological factors. The PEST analysis helps with the SWOT analysis as it can point to opportunities and threats.

Private limited company – a company which is not listed on the London Stock Exchange and usually has limited liability.

Private sector – owned by shareholders or individuals rather than the state. They are commercial companies and usually aim to make a profit.

Privatisation – the government selling assets that were previously in the public sector to the private sector, to raise money.

Promotional plan – the detailed schedule of activities that are to be undertaken, where and when they are to be undertaken and the cost.

Public limited company (PLC) – a business that is owned by shareholders. Its shares are bought and sold on the London Stock Exchange. Avoid confusing this type of business with one which is 'in the public sector'. It is not the same thing. A business in the public sector is owned and usually financed and run by national or local government.

Public relations – the attempts made by an organisation to have a good image and maintain goodwill with the general public.

Public sector – public sector organisations are owned by the state and receive their funds from local or central government and usually aim to provide a service. Their policy will be directed by national or local government.

Q

Quango – an acronym which stands for Quasi Autonomous Non-Governmental Organisation, otherwise known as a non-departmental public body. Quangos are set up by government with government funding, but they work independently of government.

Quota – the number of people in different age or socio- economic groups to be questioned.

R

Rapport – positive relationship. You need to build a positive rapport with your client that is based on trust and confidence.

Respondent – the person who is answering the questions.

Responsible tourism – recognises the impacts of tourism on a destination and seeks to maximise the positive impacts and minimise the negative impacts.

Risk assessment – the process of identifying what could go wrong, deciding which risks are important and planning how to deal with those risks.

S

Scheduled – these airlines run to a regular timetable that is changed only for the winter and summer seasons. The flights depart even if not all the seats have been booked.

Scheduled flights – flights sold on a seat-only basis and run to a timetable, revised for winter and summer schedules

Schengen – Schengen is a small town in Luxembourg where, in 1985, five countries decided to remove border controls and checkpoints between their countries. This is known as the Schengen Agreement. There are now 25 Schengen countries. The removal of controls means that citizens can pass easily from one country to another to visit or even to work. This also has an impact on tourism: visitors can easily travel from one country to the next without being stopped, or having to show documents and answer questions about their movements.

Share capital – the money raised by selling shares in a business.

Short-haul – a flight of two to three hours.

Stated needs – needs the customer tells you about; for example 'I would like to book a single room for tomorrow night'.

Summative evaluation – takes place when the event is over .

Supplier – for a retail travel agent, a supplier can be a hotel, transport company, tour operator, insurance company, etc.

SWOT analysis – a means of measuring internal factors (Strengths and Weaknesses) and external factors (Opportunities and Threats) that infl uence the marketing and operation of a business. (p.126)

SWOT analysis – this means identifying Strengths, Weaknesses, Opportunities and Threats. (p.335)

T

Telephone conference – participants dial in to a pre-distributed telephone number and are all able to hear each other and speak. As some voices sound similar, it is good practice to state your name each time you contribute to the conference.

Topography – the shape and composition of the landscape, including mountains and valleys, and the pattern of rivers, roads and railways.

Tourism receiver – a country that tourists choose to visit. France is a major receiver.

Tourist arrivals – numbers of tourists visiting a country expressed in the numbers of visits.

Tourist receipts – the amount of money spent in a country by tourists.

Travel services – these include the goods and services consumed by travellers, such as accommodation, meals and transport (within the economy visited).

Tuc tuc – a motorised rickshaw or three-wheeled cart operated by a driver, commonly used in Asian countries and in some African countries.

U

UNESCO – The United Nations Educational, Scientific and Cultural Organisation seeks to encourage the identification, protection and preservation of cultural and natural heritage around the world considered to be of outstanding value to humanity.

Unstated needs – needs that will affect the customer's choice of product, but which they do not tell you about; for example, they do not say 'We went to Majorca last year and don't want to go there again'.

V

Voluntary sector – voluntary organisations are often charities or pressure groups. They do not always make a profit, but put funds into the company activities, for example, conservation.

W

Web conference – this takes place over the Internet and can incorporate sound and cameras or at its most basic, live messaging.

Web seminar – a tutor and delegates are online at the same time and delegates follow the resources online. The seminar can incorporate sound and cameras.

Index

T

U

V

W

Y